Television Fright Films
of the 1970s

Television Fright Films of the 1970s

DAVID DEAL

McFarland & Company, Inc., Publishers
Jefferson, North Carolina

The present work is a reprint of the illustrated casebound edition of Television Fright Films of the 1970s, *first published in 2007 by McFarland.*

LIBRARY OF CONGRESS CATALOGUING-IN-PUBLICATION DATA

Deal, David, 1958–
Television fright films of the 1970s / David Deal.
        p.   cm.
Includes bibliographical references and index.

ISBN 978-0-7864-9383-8 (softcover : acid free paper) ∞
ISBN 978-0-7864-5514-0 (ebook)

1. Horror films—United States—Catalogs.
2. Made-for-TV movies—United States—Catalogs.
3. Horror films—United States—History and criticism.
I. Title.
PN1995.9.H6D33 2014   791.43'6164—dc22   2007005129

BRITISH LIBRARY CATALOGUING DATA ARE AVAILABLE

© 2007 David Deal. All rights reserved

No part of this book may be reproduced or transmitted in any form or by any means, electronic or mechanical, including photocopying or recording, or by any information storage and retrieval system, without permission in writing from the publisher.

On the cover: Darren McGavin stars as
Carl Kolchak in *The Night Stalker,* 1972.

Printed in the United States of America

*McFarland & Company, Inc., Publishers
Box 611, Jefferson, North Carolina 28640
www.mcfarlandpub.com*

For my father

For my father

ACKNOWLEDGMENTS

The author would like to thank Larry Robertson for his technical assistance in completing the reviews, and Stephanie at Cinema Books for her skillful photo and illustration search. Thanks also to Julie Miller and Kris Parfett for their editing talents.

TABLE OF CONTENTS

Acknowledgments
vii

Preface
1

THE FILMS
5

*Appendix:
Telefright Chronology*
203

Bibliography
205

Index
207

PREFACE

Welcome to an exhaustive critical survey of the television fright films made in the 1970s. My initial exploration of these films revealed a lack of valid critical assessment, a gaping hole in the knowledge of and appreciation for an entire legacy of entertainment—the legacy of the "telefright." This volume hopes to right that wrong.

Part of the reason these films have been nearly forgotten is that very few of them have been given official home video releases. There are many fans who have only their memories—thirty-odd years old—of when these films were first aired or were shown in reruns. The bulk of the films reviewed here were found on the "gray market" (such as the Internet auction site, eBay), often copied from a rare late night showing, and sold without regard to copyright.

For those who came of age during the 1970s—myself included—viewing the films herein may trigger a nearly overwhelming nostalgia, the warm comfort of returned youth. To recognize every actor, every car, every type of technology, is to step into the manageable world of the past, escaping the sometimes strenuous, often unfathomable present. But, for every rediscovered cinematic gem, there are a handful of tedious, uninspired films which will try the viewer's patience.

The objective was to be as thorough and precise as possible, which meant including unlikable films and rejecting superior ones that, however competent, could not be construed to have frightful tones. This book is meant to point out the best of the telefright, but also to steer the reader away from wasting his precious time. Hopefully, this book will appeal not only to those who remember the films but to those on their own journey of discovery.

A Concise History of the Telefilm

By the mid–1960s, old movies were a popular staple of television programming. The studios, however, considered it "verboten" to release their newish movies to television, because they might entice audiences to stay away from the theaters. People could simply wait for the films to show up on the small screen.

In 1964, NBC began its "Project 120." It was the brainchild of producer Jennings Lang (the so-called father of the telefilm) and Universal's Lew Wasserman to make two-hour films for television. Their first effort was Don Siegel's remake of the 1946 film noir *The Killers*, but it was deemed too violent for television, and was diverted to theatrical release. The follow-up, *See How They Run* (October 7, 1964), with John Forsythe and Senta Berger, is generally accepted as the first telefilm. Project 120 would produce only one more telefilm, *The Hanged Man* (1964), with Robert Culp and Vera Miles.

Two years later, NBC was back with "World Premiere." The first film produced was *Fame Is the Name of the Game*, with Tony Franciosa and Jill St. John. It was a remake of the 1949 Alan Ladd movie *Chicago Deadline*, and spawned the TV series *The Name of the Game* in 1968. (CBS had earlier dipped their toes in the telefilm water with *Scalplock*, a pilot for the Dale Robertson western series *The Iron Horse*.) By the end of the 1966–67 season, World Premiere had presented a total of eight films.

The real explosion in telefilms, however, occurred in 1968 when Leonard Goldberg and Barry Diller came up with a revolutionary plan to make cheaper 90-minute movies for television, calling the showcase "ABC Movie of the Week." Suddenly, the telefilm, which had always been considered the ugly stepchild of film, was growing up. The form began tackling subject matter aimed more towards adults, and featured social issues that were meant to be taken seriously. Of course, the networks were constrained by FCC decency guidelines, which limited what the telefilm could contain and how the content could be portrayed. But movies made for television had come into their own.

The first supernatural thriller telefilm was *Fear No Evil*, March 3, 1969, with Louis Jourdan as psychic investigator David Sorell. Others broadcast prior to 1970 were *Night Gallery*, the pilot for the anthology series, and *Daughter of the Mind*, where Ray Milland is haunted by the specter of his dead daughter (which, alas, turned out to be an elaborate ruse).

The golden age of the telefilm, roughly 1968 to 1974, was a product of the same inspiration that took hold in theatrical features: the youth movement of the late 1960s. *Easy Rider* (1969) is usually considered the catalyst that led Hollywood to rethink its collective strategy, and permit the artist to dictate the direction of projects. This approach was short-lived, but it allowed an influx of creative and talented young people to the filmmaking ranks, resulting in some of the finest films and telefilms of that or any era.

Practical Considerations

Comparing telefilms to theatrical features may be an ego-stretching exercise for television executives, but for the viewer it will prove fruitless. Most of the telefilms discussed herein were shot, as theatrical features are, on 35mm film, but were made in a fraction of the time and on a fraction of the budget allowed features. And because of the smaller scale, television excelled at the character study rather than the special effects–filled epic. Therefore, the critical approach taken here is to compare telefilms to each other, ignoring, for the most part, their better-endowed theatrical brethren.

Star power is another measure of the difference between films and telefilms. Certainly, many movie stars appeared in telefilms, but far fewer television actors successfully made the leap to features. Television instead cultivated its own stars who guaranteed solid ratings. In a 1974 interview with *TV Guide*, producer Aaron Spelling put it this way: "Sure, we'd take Brando in the unlikely event he should offer himself. But he wouldn't get a 45 share of the audience. Liz Montgomery, on the other hand, would."

Talent behind the camera operated in much the same way. Many directors, such as Dan Curtis, John Llewellyn Moxey and E.W. Swackhamer, became telefilm experts over their careers. Of course, some now-famous directors got their starts in television before crossing over to theatrical features, Steven Spielberg being the highest-profile example. Other "big name" directors with telefilms to their credits here include John Badham, John Carpenter, Michael Crichton, Curtis Harrington, Wes Craven and Tobe Hooper. But these heavyweights did not create the bulk of the telefilms reviewed.

Overall, it is not quite fair to say that low expectations will serve the novice viewer well when approaching telefilms. But it is in one's best interest to take into consideration the scale, limitations and intent of the product, regardless of the pedigree, before passing critical judgment. There are many superior entertainment examples to be found in the humble telefilm, often created by little-known journeymen.

Defining "Fright Film"

With nearly 150 films reviewed in this book, it is safe to assume a liberal interpretation of the term "fright film" has been applied. Borderline entries such as *Betrayal* and *Death Once Removed* are considered on equal footing with outright horror films such as *Salem's Lot* and *Gargoyles*. And there are also "ringers," films that entice viewers with scary titles such as *Express to Terror* and *The Invasion of Carol Enders*, yet contain very little to be scared of, except, perhaps, in the quality department. The main criterion for inclusion is, naturally, an intent on the part of the filmmakers to frighten the viewer in some capacity, even if only in name.

In a more general sense, films were considered if they were made specifically for television, of course, and had their premiere on the American networks between January 1970 and December 1979, inclusive. The temporal guideline is arbitrary but handy.

Most telefilms were made to fit a 90-minute or two-hour timeslot, including commercials, making the films themselves run approximately 75 minutes or 100 minutes, respectively. The films had to be shown over a maximum of two nights, meaning that miniseries have been excluded. Series episodes that were edited together have been excluded from consideration, as have 90-minute or two-hour episodes of continuing series and two-hour series "specials."

Also excluded are most cop-centered crime thrillers, true-to-life stories, foreign productions, science fiction movies without fright elements, adventure films even with elements of peril, etc. There are exceptions to every rule, of course. For instance, the true-life story *The Legend of Lizzie Borden* is included because of the distance of the subject from the modern viewer, and the alien abduction movie *The UFO Incident* is included due to its questionable (yet convincing) authenticity. There are other examples (the British production *Count Dracula* being one) that skirt the exclusionary criteria, but the intent was always to be lenient and allow exceptions, especially if the quality of the film is superior.

Despite the relatively high number of films included, and my aim to write the definitive book on television fright films, there were some movies that were effectively out of reach. Readers are asked to forgive me if one of their favorites is not listed. Due to the limited availability of most of these films, the presentation quality of the video is neither considered nor noted.

Preface

Structure of the Book

The films are arranged alphabetically by the title used for the original airing. Each entry includes alternate titles if any, a plot synopsis, and critical commentary. This information is followed by a cast listing in credit order ("ao" denotes alphabetical billing and "oa" denotes "order of appearance" billing, when it was specified). There are also credits for director, teleplay, music, and production company, and details such as running time, air date and network. "Vehicles furnished by" credits are provided if they appeared in the film.

Memorable quotes or pertinent facts regarding the review copy of a film occasionally precede discussion of that film.

The appendix provides a chronology of the 1970s telefright phenomenon, listing the films in order of air date.

Among the illustrations in the book are several theatrical release posters. Some telefilms were indeed released for theatrical use overseas, occasionally with added footage to expand the running time. This was, naturally, an effort to capitalize on interests the networks had (and still have) in foreign markets. The posters printed in English were used in Great Britain or Australia. The foreign-language posters were printed for use in Turkey, Belgium, and other countries.

If more than one figure is given for a film's running time (e.g., "122/182 minutes"), the higher number represents an expanded version for theatrical release. If an expanded or theatrical release was used for the review appearing in this book, that fact is noted in the film's entry.

THE FILMS

All the Kind Strangers

AKA **Evil in the Swamp**

Photojournalist James Wheeler (Stacy Keach) is driving through Lebanon, Tennessee, on his way to California for a job when he spots a small boy carrying a large bag of groceries. Wheeler offers the boy a ride home and is subsequently led deep into the back country to an old house full of children of various ages. There is one adult in the kitchen, a redhead by the name of Caroline (Samantha Eggar) whom the kids call "Ma." Wheeler's suspicions are aroused when Caroline uses a free moment alone with him to scrawl the word "help" in the flour she's using to make bread. Wheeler then discovers his car has been disabled, making him a prisoner of this backwoods brood who trap adults in an effort to complete their family.

This would-be creepy Southern horror story offers very little in the way of chills or revelations, opting instead to wind down a brighter and, frankly, less satisfying path. The Tennessee locations are photogenic and Stacy Keach turns in a fine performance as Wheeler but the faux hillbilly antics will quickly wear thin on the viewer.

John Savage (*The Deer Hunter*) plays Peter, the eldest of the children seeking a traditional family unit. Five years previously their mother died in childbirth and their drunken father fell off the roof of the house to his death. Ever since, the children have been luring strangers into their fold, hoping they'll stick around and play house. When these unfortunates inevitably decline to stay, Peter kills them—unbeknownst to the rest of the clan. Instead of this being a moral lesson for the youngsters about not riding with strangers, it's one for the strangers not to pick up kids.

The children busy themselves by running the farm, singing hymns and feeding their vicious hounds chunks of meat. The eldest daughter, Martha (Arlene Farber, *I Drink Your Blood*), is a mute coming of age and she takes a shine to Wheeler. Martha flirts with him and lets her jealousy of Caroline get out of hand when she puts a rattlesnake in Caroline's bed. Notably, in a scene where Martha slinks out of the pond after cavorting with her siblings, she comes very close to exhibiting too much skin for 1970s network television.

When Wheeler's car mysteriously disappears, the kids take him across the pond in a leaky boat to show him what happened to it. His brand new $7000 car is lying in the deep end along with several other vehicles. It's an arresting, if not particularly well-executed, image. Watching Wheeler drive his new car through a wide creek on his way to the house for the first time provides one of the few amusing moments in the film. One would never have guessed that boat could float.

The rest of the film is made up of hackneyed dialogue and an annoying bluegrass score. One of Peter's younger brothers, John, is played by one-time heartthrob Robby Benson who is featured on the soundtrack singing a meaningful ditty. There is also an insipid musical interlude when Peter, deep in thought, wanders around the woods.

Wheeler tries to be clever a couple of times but his escape attempts fail. Finally, one night, the kids decide to vote on whether to keep Wheeler and Caroline around. It's supposed to be a moment of great tension but the viewer knows which way it is going to go. In the morning, Peter intends to kill the adults but the kids stand up against him and Wheeler miraculously convinces Peter to go with him into town and ask for help from the authorities.

Known primarily for his westerns, director Burt Kennedy had his best work behind him. Career highlights include the James Garner comedies *Support Your Local Sheriff!* and *Support Your Local Gunfighter*, the Raquel Welch vehicle *Hannie Caulder* and the amusing telefilm *Shootout in a One-Dog Town*. Surprisingly, among composer Ronald Frangipane's few credits is participation in the soundtrack for Alejandro Jodorowsky's bizarre cult film, *The Holy Mountain*.

Samantha Eggar, whose given name was Victoria Louise Samantha Marie Elizabeth Theresa Eggar, was born in London, the daughter of a British army brigadier and a Dutch-Portuguese mother. She hit the big time when she was named best actress at the Cannes Film Festival for *The Collector* but she is best known to genre fans for her appearances in the Italian horror film *The Dead Are Alive* and David Cronenberg's disturbing *The Brood*. She also hosted a segment of the notorious and short-lived speculative documentary series, *Unknown Powers*.

CAST: Stacy Keach, Samantha Eggar, John Savage, Robby Benson, Arlene Farber, Tim Parkison, Patti Parkison, Brent Campbell, and John Connell.

CREDITS: Director: Burt Kennedy; Teleplay: Clyde Ware; Music: Ronald Frangipane; Production: Cinemation Industries; Running Time: 73 minutes; Air Date: 11/12/74; Network: ABC

Are You in the House Alone?

This film is notorious not only for its subject matter, rape, but for its bad taste presentation and ambiguous political allegiances. The filmmakers can't make up their collective mind whether they are pursuing a right-wing agenda by bashing the liberal justice system or indicting the rich and powerful folks who abuse it. They seem to revel in the torment of the high school girl and play out the rape scene itself as a male fantasy rather than the despicable act of violation it is.

High school student Gail Osborne (Kathleen Beller) is found lying on the floor of her living room, battered and spent. She is taken to the hospital where the first words of the movie are spoken: "He raped me." The bulk of the film is told in flashback as Gail is tormented by notes left in her locker (one simply has the word "rape" scrawled across her photograph) and phone calls that put the poor girl in such a state of terror that she doesn't trust anyone. Gail vows to trap the rapist, who was freed on lack of evidence.

The flashbacks begin with a scene that clearly demonstrates the filmmakers' unabashed insincerity. Gail and her best friend Allison (Robin Mattson) strip down for a swim and by using a point-of-view camera set-up behind the bushes, director Walter Grauman allows the audience to identify with the stalker as he ogles the nubile teens.

Anyone believing that this film was in touch with the recreational activities of 1970s youth must have skipped the scene where Gail and her friends go out on a double date. After seeing a movie (*Three Days of the Condor*, a paranoid classic), the group goes to a malt shop, a type of hangout whose popularity had waned more than 20 years previous. This "innocent youth" theme co-opted from the 50s is furthered in another scene by the "doo wop" trio of boys seen at the high school complete with matching red satin jackets.

Any time Gail reaches out to someone for help, that person lets her down. Her counselor is pointedly portrayed as ineffectual, even incompetent. Her photography teacher is a leering, suggestive male who selects Gail to photograph herself in a "sexy" pose in front of the class. All the male students in the class drool over this with mouths agape.

Her friend Allison just wants Gail to forget about the notes, as does Gail's boyfriend Steve (Scott Colomby). Allison's boyfriend Phil (Dennis Quaid) is just a rich kid who cares about nothing but himself and his image with the other students.

Gail's parents are alternatively played as contented parents waxing romantic about their youth or raging monsters on the brink of divorce. Dad (Tony Bill) is a drinker who lost his job and mom (Blythe Danner, acting rings around everyone else) wants to self-actualize by selling real estate, at the expense of childrearing, of course.

The scene where Gail discovers that her dad is unemployed is unintentionally amusing. She travels to his office in San Francisco and the receptionist tells her that her dad got laid off over a month ago. The unbelieving Gail tells the receptionist that her dad leaves for work every morning just as he always has. The receptionist replies, "I guess a lot of the guys do that. They can't get used to breaking the routine." Gail finds her father in a bar, sitting by himself, pounding down the hard liquor. So much for being able to talk to Dad about her problems.

In one of her heart-to-hearts with her boyfriend, Gail admits that her ex-boyfriend left her because she led him on but wouldn't "put out." She then puts out for Steve, which makes her a slut in the filmmakers' eyes and deserving of what soon happens to her.

Gail does catch the rapist but the point here is not that justice is done. Instead, it is an opportunity to claim that "the system" is too easy on the criminal and that it is corrupt, due in no small part to the affluent whose power subverts the intention of the law. *Are You in the House Alone?* is an hour and a half of watching suspense drive a

Tony Bill and Blythe Danner in a publicity still for *Are You in the House Alone?* **(1978).**

young girl nearly out of her mind. The filmmakers place the audience in the minds of the lecherous and perverted, which feels like part of the problem and not part of a solution. By appealing to the lust of the viewer, the intentions of the filmmakers become muddled at best.

Kathleen Beller, who married musician Thomas Dolby, began her career in the soap opera *Search for Tomorrow* and in the 80s wound up as a regular on the nighttime soap *Dynasty*. Tony Bill was a successful producer by the time this film aired; he can also be seen in the 70s telefrights *Haunts of the Very Rich* and *The Initiation of Sarah*. The talented Blythe Danner, mother of Gwyneth Paltrow, also appears in the telefright *Dr. Cook's Garden*. Robin Mattson made a career of working in soap operas but early on she appeared in exploitation favorites *Bonnie's Kids*, *Candy Stripe Nurses* and *Phantom of the Paradise*. Scott Colomby will be familiar to fans of *Caddyshack* and the *Porky's* series of teen films. Dennis Quaid would make one more telefilm in the 1970s before the sleeper hit *Breaking Away* broke his career away from television.

Director Walter Grauman's best telefright of the decade was *Crowhaven Farm*. *Paper Man* is a quaint, less popular thriller he made shortly thereafter. Executive producer Charles Fries is considered the "godfather" of the television movie and his name is on the favorites *She Waits*, *Scream of the Wolf*, *The Strange and Deadly Occurrence*, *Night Terror* and many others in the 70s.

CAST: Kathleen Beller, Blythe Danner, Tony Bill, Robin Mattson, Tricia O'Neil, Dennis Quaid, Alan Fudge, Scott Colomby, Ellen Travolta, Randy Stumpf, Magda Harout, Sandra Sharp, Michael Bond, Lois Areno, Sandra Giles, Ted Gehring, Richard Molinare, David Leon, Art Kimbro, and Jayne Lyn Martin.

CREDITS: Director: Walter Grauman; Teleplay: Judith Parker, based on the novel by Richard Peck; Music: Charles Bernstein; Production: Charles Fries Productions; Running Time: 96 minutes; Air Date: 9/20/78; Network: CBS

Bad Ronald

Ronald Wilby (Scott Jacoby) is an outcast high school student who lives in an old house with his cloying mother. One day Ronald accidentally kills a young girl and, rather than face the risk of being separated, he and mom forge a hiding place for him in the house which is undetectable from the outside world. When his mom dies during an operation at the hospital, Ronald remains hidden in the house, retreating further and further into a fantasy world. Eventually a new family moves in and the now-demented Ronald decides to make his presence known—with disastrous results.

Bad Ronald is a serious study of mental deterioration—buoyed by solid direction and a good cast—that retains a cult following to this day. Director Buzz Kulik, who made the enormously popular telefilm *Brian's Song* a few years prior to this, maintains a creepy, claustrophobic atmosphere from the get-go. Most of the film is made up of interior shots and, with the Victorian house setting, the dark spaces and labyrinthine layout are perfect for exploring the cobwebs that cover and distort the brain of Ronald.

Emmy winner Scott Jacoby (*That Certain Summer*) keeps Ronald a low-key character and although the short running time denies the luxury of really detailing the crumbling mind of the young man, Jacoby ably communicates the mental breakdown. The faulty logic of a mind gone haywire could have easily been fleshed out for a two-hour time slot rather than the quick 90-minute slot for which the film was tailored.

Kim Hunter's experience (and Oscar-winning talent) gives the smaller role of Ronald's twisted mother a subtle depth and the two actors work well together. Hunter made her screen debut in Mark Robson's chiller *The Seventh Victim* and she won an Academy Award for her role as Stella in *A Streetcar Named Desire*. Shortly thereafter her name appeared in "Red Channels," an anti–Communist scare pamphlet, and she was subsequently blacklisted for several years although she was never a Communist. In 1968, the same year she appeared in the decidedly odd cult film *The Swimmer*, she took the role that genre fans most remember her for, as Dr. Zira in *Planet of the Apes*. She repeated the role in the sequels *Beneath the Planet of the Apes* and *Escape from the Planet of the Apes*. Hunter died of a heart attack in 2002.

One keeps waiting for a misstep on the part of the filmmakers but they are very careful with the material. Particularly affecting is Ronald's pursuit of the new family's youngest sister Babs (Cindy Fisher, in her debut) through the house and into the neighbor's house. Babs had immediately picked up on the unseen presence of the young man in the house and it was this sensitivity that drew Ronald to her. Luckily

Babs proves resourceful and it is she who is his ultimate undoing. *Bad Ronald* is a well-crafted piece of psychological terror worth the time and effort to locate.

Dabney Coleman and Pippa Scott are the parents in the family who move into the Wilby house and it is a treat to see the Eilbacher sisters, Cindy and Lisa, in their only film together as two of their daughters. Cindy had roles in the telefrights *Crowhaven Farm*, *Force of Evil* and *A Fire in the Sky* but Lisa stuck to more "respectable" material in the 70s.

CAST: Scott Jacoby, Pippa Scott, John Larch, Dabney Coleman, Kim Hunter, John Fiedler, Linda Watkins, Cindy Fisher, Cindy Eilbacher, Lisa Eilbacher, Ted Eccles, Roger Aaron Brown, Aneta Corsaut, Angela Hoffman, Karen Purcil, Shelley Spurlock, and Lesley Woods.

CREDITS: Director: Buzz Kulik; Teleplay: Andrew Peter Marin, based on a novel by John Holbrook Vance; Music: Fred Karlin; Production: Lorimar Productions; Running Time: 74 minutes; Air Date: 10/23/74; Network: ABC

The Bermuda Depths

AKA **It Came Up from the Depths**

Part Moby Dick, part fantastical romance, part allegorical mystery, this is a confounded, unclassifiable film. It is included here not only because it has its scary moments but because it is one of the most curiously original, if not entirely successful, of telefilms.

A disturbed young man, Magnus Dens (Leigh McCloskey), returns to his home in Bermuda where his scientist father had been killed in a mysterious accident years before. He meets up with an old friend, Eric, who is working with a scientist, Dr. Paulis (Burl Ives), exploring the species of undersea life in the Bermuda Triangle. We learn that Magnus has a connection in his past to a ghost that haunts the Triangle and soon the past and present will collide, sealing the fates of all involved.

Producers Rankin and Bass (Rankin wrote this story) are better known for their animated holiday specials but they did take a crack at a live-action project now and then. In fact, the director of *The Bermuda Depths*, Tom Kotani, also helmed the Rankin/Bass film *The Last Dinosaur*. Here, it is the model work that typifies the classic productions of the pair: a cliffside house, an historic wooden boat, a research vessel, a helicopter and, of course, a giant turtle.

The turtle is a key element to the story and a key weakness to the believability of the production. Magnus met a girl ghost when he was very young and the two of them found a turtle's egg. As the turtle grew, the boy and the ghost grew too, always appearing to Magnus the same age as he was. One day the ghost and the turtle disappeared into the sea and shortly thereafter Magnus's house was destroyed and his father was killed. The ghost turns out to be Jennie Haniver (Connie Sellecca, *Hotel*) and the story of her drowning is well-known around Bermuda. She was on a doomed ship and traded her soul to the Devil in order to survive, so she dwells, cursed, under the sea with the giant turtle.

Magnus's father was getting too close to discovering the turtle and so his experiments were put to an end. Dr. Paulis and Eric (Carl Weathers, Apollo Creed in the Rocky films) are continuing his work, studying the unusual growth of species in the deepest depths of the ocean, and Magnus's return triggers the re-appearance of the turtle. Eric becomes obsessed with the giant creature a la Moby Dick and suffers a fate similar to Captain Ahab's. Magnus, on the other hand, lives but suffers a crueler fate.

There are scary parts to this film — the destruction of the house, the shipwreck flashback and most of all the attacks on the research vessel — enough to qualify it as a fright film without too much of a stretch. The fantasy elements are admittedly romantic in nature but this is certainly not strictly a love story.

The Bermuda Depths is peopled almost completely with bad actors, another strike against believability. McCloskey is best

known to genre fans as the lead in Dario Argento's *Inferno* but he made a career in several television soaps. Sellecca plays Jennie the ghost but she doesn't have to do much except look beautiful, which she does very well. Former pro-footballer Weathers is way over the top and Ives only seems to be engaged every so often. With a better cast this could have been taken to another level.

There is a great title song, "Jennie," with lyrics by Jules Bass, that lends an otherworldly quality to the action and the Bermuda location photography is top-notch. Haunting at times, ridiculous at others, *The Bermuda Depths* is greater than the sum of its parts and is given a qualified recommendation for those with a romantic bent.

CAST: Leigh McCloskey, Carl Weathers, Connie Sellecca, Julie Woodson, Ruth Attaway, Burl Ives, Elise Frick, Nicholas Ingham, Kevin Petty, Nicole Marsh, George Richards, John Instone, Jonathan Ingham, Patricia Rego, Doris Riley, and Tracy Anne Sadler.

CREDITS: Director: Tom (Shusei) Kotani; Teleplay: William Overgard, from a story by Arthur Rankin, Jr.; Music: Maury Laws; Production: Rankin/Bass Productions; Running Time: 98 minutes; Air Date: 1/27/78; Network: ABC

Betrayal

Admittedly, this little film noir is mild in the terror department but the fears it depicts are very real nonetheless. First is the fear of being betrayed by people one trusts, a common enough theme in television movies of the time. Next is the fear of being trapped by circumstances and the choices one has made in the past. What's unusual about this film is that these fears are prevalent in both the criminal and victim. Lastly is the Hitchcockian fear of what to do with the body of the person you've just killed.

Gretchen Addison, aka Adele Murphy (Tisha Sterling), and her partner, Jay (Sam Groom), work as a team to extort rich old ladies. Their latest venture turns into a killing and the couple split up. She heads for the West Coast and he to Las Vegas. Adele then hooks up with Helen Mercer (Amanda Blake), a wealthy and lively older dame who solicited for a secretary but who's looking more for a companion. As Adele gets to know Helen, she begins to admire the lady's spark and independence and decides to change her ways. It's too late, of course. Jay has followed Adele and needs money. The two begin another scheme but things don't turn out the way they expect.

This low-key effort is directed by Gordon Hessler, best known for a string of spotty horror films in the late 60s and early 70s, and he plays it by the numbers here. The German-born, British-educated Hessler actually started his directorial career in American television on the *Alfred Hitchcock Presents* series before moving to features. He worked with AIP in England on several horror films, all of which were marked by troubled productions and mediocre results: *Scream and Scream Again*, *The Oblong Box*, *De Sade*, *Cry of the Banshee* and *Murders in the Rue Morgue*. Returning to the small screen in the mid-70s, Hessler had his name on several of the era's telefrights including *Scream Pretty Peggy*, *Skyway to Death* and *The Strange Possession of Mrs. Oliver*. In between, Hessler made the fantasy feature *The Golden Voyage of Sinbad* and the silly telefilm *KISS Meets the Phantom of the Park*. He worked his way back to features in the mid-80s, scoring a minor cult entry with *The Girl in a Swing* before effectively retiring, *Betrayal* does not take many chances but among its merits are strong female characters. Adele is the brains of the partnership with the sleazy Jay and Helen is known as "Deadeye" because she shot and killed her criminal handyman a few months back. Both characters have the wherewithal to deal with unusual situations—a talent that comes in particularly useful.

Amanda Blake was, of course, best

Theatrical release poster for *The Bermuda Depths* **(1978).**

known for playing Kitty Russell on the long-running *Gunsmoke* series for 18 years. Betrayal was her first telefilm after that series ended but she subsequently worked only rarely in the business before contracting AIDS from her last husband, a disease that contributed to her death in 1989.

Tisha Sterling, daughter of actors Ann Sothern and Robert Sterling, worked mainly in television but she did have roles in Bert I. Gordon's lamentable *Village of the Giants* and in Jonathan Demme's *Crazy Mama*. One of her last roles before retiring to Idaho was in *The Whales of August*, where she played Ann Sothern's character in flashbacks. Her telefrights include *Night Slaves* and *Snatched*.

Sam Groom, who now teaches acting in New York, played a couple of roles, coincidentally, on *Gunsmoke* before appearing in the telefrights *Beyond the Bermuda Triangle* and *Hanging by a Thread* where he plays his more-typical role of good guy. His genre credits are very few but include the acknowledged Canadian bomb *Deadly Eyes*, an adaptation of James Herbert's "The Rats." Composer Ernest Gold was nominated for several Academy Awards throughout his career and won an Oscar for his score for *Exodus*.

This film's minor amusements include Helen's array of atrocious fashions, the hideous décor of the interiors and the performance of an unnamed band at a party. The biggest disappointment is the contrived (and no doubt mandated) ending. Such things are to be expected but the viewer will feel let down anyway. Not interesting enough to merit a recommendation, *Betrayal* isn't completely a waste of time if one looks for the small pleasures, such as cameos by character actress Lucille Benson and B-queen Rene Bond.

CAST: Amanda Blake, Tisha Sterling, Dick Haymes, Sam Groom, Britt Leach, Edward Marshall, Ted Gehring, Dennis Gross, Eric Brotherson, Vernon Weddle, Rene Bond, and Lucille Benson.

CREDITS: Director: Gordon Hessler; Teleplay: James Miller, based on the novel *Only Couples Need Apply* by Doris Miles Disney; Music: Ernest Gold; Production: Metromedia Productions; Running Time: 74 minutes; Air Date: 12/3/74; Network: ABC

Beyond the Bermuda Triangle
AKA Beyond This Place There Be Dragons

It was inevitable that television would throw its hat into The Triangle. Whereas *The Bermuda Depths* was a ghostly fantasy less concerned with the well-known mysteries of the area and *Satan's Triangle* bizarrely ascribes the unexplained events to Satan himself, *Beyond the Bermuda Triangle* attempts to hang a human drama on a frail framework of disappearances.

After newlywed friends vanish in the Bermuda Triangle, millionaire Harry Ballinger (Fred MacMurray) begins investigating the legend surrounding the loss of lives off the coast of Florida. The newlyweds left behind a child, Wendy, who believes she can still hear the voice of her mother. When his fiancée also disappears while sailing there, Ballinger becomes convinced he has an opportunity to follow her.

Largely a waste of time and talent, *Beyond the Bermuda Triangle* is a slow and uneventful experience. The film seems long at 74 minutes and contains several stretches where nothing really happens. Writer Charles A. McDaniel trots out the familiar stories of boats and planes that have been lost over the years in the area. He saddles Ballinger with the theory that a "door" to an afterlife exists in the Triangle through which people are taken or can voluntarily enter. Needless to say, this theory is not one popularly subscribed to by aficionados of the phenomenon.

Ironically, Fred MacMurray, one of the most enduring of movie stars, is identified more often with his popular television series *My Three Sons* than with his many movie roles. It was his casting as Walter Neff in 1944's *Double Indemnity* that made him a star and his Disney comedies that hold the fondest memories for his film fans.

Supporting MacMurray here are familiar actors Sam Groom, as Jed the boat builder, and Donna Mills as Claudia, Jed's on-again off-again girlfriend. MacMurray's fiancée is played by Suzanne Reed who disappeared from screen acting altogether after an episode of *Barnaby Jones*.

Striking cutie Donna Mills has been a staple on television since the late 1960s when she became part of the original cast on the daytime drama *Love Is a Many Splendored Thing*. Her role as Abby on the long-running nighttime soap opera *Knots Landing* encompassed nearly the entire decade of the 80s; she received several Soap Opera Digest Awards for "Outstanding Villainess" while playing Abby but the Emmy has been an elusive prize for the still-active actor. Her career in the 70s includes many telefright films: *Haunts of the Very Rich*, *Look What's Happened to Rosemary's Baby*, *Smash-Up on Interstate 5*, *Fire!*, *Curse of the Black Widow* and *Hanging by a Thread*.

Dana Plato plays Wendy, the daughter of the newlywed wife. Convinced that her dead mother is calling, she takes off alone into the Everglades to find her. Why the child picked the Everglades to search is another unexplained mystery but as is typical of the film, nothing happens to her and she's quickly found. In real life the ill-fated child actor struck it big in the long-running *Diff'rent Strokes* series in the 80s but would die of a drug overdose in 1999 in what would eventually be determined a suicide.

Director William A. Graham has the distinction of directing an Elvis film (*Change of Habit*) and a film about Elvis a quarter of a century later (the telefilm *Elvis and the Colonel: The Untold Story*). He also made the unjustly forgotten telefilm gem *Thief* with Richard Crenna. Composer Harry Sukman's next two credits were for telefilms helmed by famous directors: *Someone's Watching Me* (John Carpenter) and *Salem's Lot* (Tobe Hooper); they were also his final scores. Filmed on location in Ft. Lauderdale, Florida, *Beyond the Bermuda Triangle* was a Playboy production. The company would fund another tepid fright telefilm, *The Death of Ocean View Park*, in 1979, capping an unremarkable run in the decade.

CAST: Fred MacMurray, Sam Groom, Donna Mills, Suzanne Reed, Dana Plato, Dan White, Ric O'Feldman, John Di Santi, Woody Woodbury, Joan Murphy, Frank Schuller, Clarence Thomas, Mickey Rooney, Jr., East Carlo, Herb Goldstein, Phil Philbin, Frank Logan, Jack Milavic, Jeff Gillen, Jim Swait, and Jack McCall.

CREDITS: Director: William A. Graham; Teleplay: Charles A. McDaniel; Music: Harry Sukman; Production: Playboy Productions; Running Time: 74 minutes; Air Date: 11/6/75; Network: NBC

Black Noon

Black Noon was television's first occult western. It is also notable for its high level of entertainment value and for the fact that it is one of the few telefilms where Satanic evil comes out on top. Disappointingly, it was never afforded an official release on home video.

Director Bernard L. Kowalski had helmed everything from grade Z pictures (*Night of the Blood Beast*, *Attack of the Giant Leeches*) to big-budget bombs (*Krakatoa, East of Java*) to cult favorites (*SSSSSSS*) prior to working almost exclusively in television through the mid-90s. His 70s telefrights include *Terror in the Sky*, *Women in Chains* and *The Woman Hunter*. Here, a fine cast, interesting imagery and a claustrophobic sense of impending doom help create one of the eras most enjoyably sinister entries.

Some time in the late 1800s, the Reverend John Keyes (Roy Thinnes) and his wife Lorna (Lynn Loring) find themselves stranded in the desert when their wagon breaks down. Just as things look bleakest, they are rescued by Caleb Hobbs (Ray Milland), his mute daughter Deliverance (Yvette Mimieux) and their work hand Joseph, who take them back to San Melas, a mining town on the brink of extinction. As time passes, the reverend flourishes in the town while his wife withers away, her health deteriorating daily. Keyes was on his way to take over a church in another town but the residents of San Melas would like him to stick around, so Deliverance is working a voodoo spell on Lorna to keep her bedridden until the townsfolks' evil plans can be set into motion.

This morality play about a man of God who falls prey to Evil begins with a burning church, its steeple consumed by the fires of Hell. The roaring flames cast their light on a beautiful, mysterious girl whom we later recognize as the witch, Deliverance. The image is a powerful and unmistakable one, setting the tone and cluing the viewer to the mighty forces at work.

The name of the town, San Melas, is eerily similar to the Spanish phrase "san males" which translates to "the evils." The folks in the town claim to be from New England and the architecture and their clothing all hearken back to "another time, another world," as Lorna describes it. Lorna can sense that something is wrong in the town but Keyes is blinded by his growing stature as healer and general bringer of good luck to the citizens of this literally godforsaken place.

The most curious and amusing scene is the "Darkness at Noon" sermon given by Keyes. Thinnes goes over the top as the evangelical preacher, bobbing and weaving and giving the strangest line readings in an effort to perhaps parody the theatricality of professional healers. It's a given that a handicapped boy (Buddy Foster) would be inspired enough by the performance to toss away his crutches and walk.

The acting career of Roy Thinnes began as a television hunk on the daytime drama *General Hospital* but he is best known to genre fans as architect David Vincent on the science fiction series *The Invaders*. It was on that show that Thinnes met Lynn Loring, whom he married in 1967. Besides their work on *Black Noon* they appeared together in the theatrical feature *Journey to the Far Side of the Sun* and another 70s telefright, *The Horror at 37,000 Feet*. The couple divorced in 1984. Thinnes has been a fixture on television for decades but for our purposes can also be seen in *The Norliss Tapes* and *Satan's School for Girls*.

Yvette Mimieux never looked more beautiful, her diaphanous gowns blowing in the breeze. She is best known for her roles in the science fiction films *The Time Machine* and *The Black Hole* and the exploitation entry *Jackson County Jail* but she is also something of a renaissance woman (dabbling in art, poetry, music and dance), not to mention an anthropologist and a very successful businessperson, particularly in the area of real estate. Her 70s telefrights include *Snowbeast*, *Devil Dog: The Hound of Hell* and *Disaster on the Coastliner*.

Ray Milland plays it low-key as the town's leader Hobbs but one can tell there's evil running under his façade of kindness. Milland, no stranger to genre fans, showed up in several telefrights during the decade including *The Dead Don't Die*, *Look What's Happened to Rosemary's Baby*, *Mayday at 40,000 Feet*, *Cruise Into Terror* and *The Darker Side of Terror*.

Rounding out the cast are cult favorite Gloria Grahame who has a small role as Lorna's nursemaid and a future teen heartthrob Leif Garrett in a cameo. The Bible-quoting Joseph is played by Hank Worden who was a fixture in westerns as far back as 1936. He had over 180 films to his credit but he never seemed to become an "actor," always maintaining a naïve charm and that odd line delivery to the end.

The biggest treat for genre fans is the great Henry Silva as the extortionist gunslinger Moon, who terrorizes the town for a share of the dwindling gold mine, showing up every so often looking for trouble. There is a good scene when Moon, in one of his ornery moods, tosses a gun on the ground and laughs as he dares someone to pick it up and use it. Moon intends to take Deliverance with him as this week's payment but as he turns to leave, Keyes picks up the weapon and shoots Moon in the back. Keyes has now committed the ultimate sin, sealing the fate of his soul.

The film also boasts visions and several

dream sequences, which are always a plus. These take place on foggy, black sets and contain imagery that, while none-too-cryptic, is still stylish and interestingly conceived. There is another remarkable sequence when the sickly Lorna gets out of bed and wanders outside, witnessing a weird ritual involving the town's kids, strange masks and a dead owl.

Lorna is at the center of the downright creepiest scene in the film. Near her earthly end and frantically trying to get through to her husband, Lorna pleads hysterically for the two of them to leave the town. Even though Lynn Loring as Lorna is immobile in bed at this point, the actor uses her eyes, and most exceptionally her voice, to create in her character a shattering desperation that cuts right to the viewer's bone. The last scene in the film is a neat twist that shouldn't be spoiled for those viewers who haven't yet seen this highly recommended gem.

George Duning, who did the music for the film, had been a world class composer with literally hundreds of films to his credit (including *Bell, Book and Candle*). Although the 70s were near the end of his productive years, Duning provided the soundtrack for *The Woman Hunter* and was music supervisor on *How Awful About Allan*, *The House That Would Not Die* and *Crowhaven Farm*.

CAST: Roy Thinnes, Yvette Mimieux, Ray Milland, (ao) Gloria Grahame, Lynn Loring, Henry Silva, Hank Worden. Also William Bryant, Stan Barrett, Joshua Bryant, Jennifer Bryant, Charles McCready, Leif Garrett, Dave Cass, Suzan Sheppard, Bobby Eilbacher, and Buddy Foster.

CREDITS: Director: Bernard L. Kowalski; Teleplay: Andrew J. Fenady; Music: George Duning; Production: Andrew J. Fenady Productions, Screen Gems Television; Running Time: 74 minutes; Air Date: 11/15/71; Network: CBS

The Brotherhood of the Bell

Many have considered the possibility that a secret organization is really running this country, one that can provide a man with anything that can be had with "money, privilege, and the best connections." Andrew Patterson (Glenn Ford) is a member of such a secret society—the 200-year-old Brotherhood of the Bell, which he joined in college. For 22 years, Patterson has been a successful professor at a prestigious institute, his family's economic path cleared of all obstacles by The Bell. When the brotherhood asks him to pay them back by blackmailing a friend and fellow professor, Patterson balks but goes through with it. After the suicide of his friend, the distraught Patterson decides to expose the organization, potentially destroying everything he has.

This is one of the very best television movies of the era, a paranoid thriller along the lines of John Frankenheimer's *Seconds*, which was clearly an influence. Director Paul Wendkos has his greatest telefilm success here. It's a first-rate production from the evocative cinematography of Robert B. Hauser to the eerie soundtrack by Jerry Goldsmith. Writer-producer David Karp sends the protagonist Patterson on a downward spiral, fighting an all-powerful conspiracy, and despite an "up" ending, the viewer can sense the futility of resisting The Bell.

The Brotherhood of the Bell, developed at a time of great social upheaval, makes it clear early on that it intends to side with those who would promote change. The first sequence, where a new initiate is brought into the fold, is presented with the dignity and solemnity of very old traditions. But something is odd. The wide-angle photography makes the scenes unreal and sinister, as if we're on the cusp of some unknown event. After the ceremony, when the new member confesses to Patterson that it seems weird to be part of the Establishment, Patterson says, "not part of, the Establishment."

Patterson has been unknowingly enjoying the fruits of belonging to the Bell, having never been asked in all that time to return any favors. His "senior" is Chad Harmon, played with great calm by Dean Jagger, who delivers the news to Patterson that The Bell has provided his every success. Patterson (and for that matter his father's business as well) has never competed for anything since joining the brotherhood. His entire world, including his marriage to his beautiful wife (Rosemary Forsyth), has been carefully crafted to provide for all of his needs. What a shock it is to Patterson to discover that all his life's successes have not been earned at all but were contrived from the very beginning—and that the bill has come due.

With this, the nightmare for Patterson begins, as the people he trusted suddenly turn against him, unbelieving and insincere, and he very quickly appears to be cracking up. The wildest scenes take place when Patterson goes on a television show to unmask the conspiracy. William Conrad delivers as the Jerry Springer–like television host Bart Harris who rides herd on a studio audience made up of his crazy followers. Patterson is humiliated in the sideshow atmosphere as various nutcases come forward to lay claim to knowledge of secret societies influencing our lives. Patterson has one last hope, the new initiate we saw at the beginning of the film, but it is unclear just how far he could get in his quest, even if the young man will help.

The fine performances of Dean Jagger and William Conrad have been mentioned but it is Glenn Ford who provides the determined center of the film. His no-nonsense persona is perfect for Patterson, who perseveres even at great risk. Will Geer, who was part of the conspiracy in *Seconds*, plays Patterson's father, a tough and competent ally to his son. Dabney Coleman has a supporting role here and cult favorite Robert Clarke (*The Man from Planet X*) has an unbilled cameo as a psychiatrist.

Paul Wendkos' first directorial effort was the revisionist film noir *The Burglar* with Dan Duryea. Aside from frothy theatrical fare, he worked mainly in television, directing many episodes of *The Invaders* and helming the first occult telefilm, 1969's *Fear No Evil*. His telefrights of the decade are a mixed bag and include the superior *Haunts of the Very Rich*, *The Strangers in 7A*, *Terror on the Beach*, the classic *The Legend of Lizzie Borden* and *Good Against Evil*.

One more note about the excellent soundtrack. Jerry Goldsmith was, of course, one of the best and most prolific composers in the industry and his work here is remarkable. The blend of classical and jazz is not only clever, its symbolism parallels the story. The classical element represents the mandate to reproduce exactly what the composer intended (as represented by The Bell) while jazz is about individuality and bringing to the music a piece of oneself (Patterson). The music of tradition and structure meets the music of rebellion and freedom. It is a brilliant blend and compliments the fine film for which it was written.

CAST: Glenn Ford, Rosemary Forsyth, Dean Jagger, Maurice Evans, Will Geer, William Smithers, Eduard Franz, Robert Pine, William Conrad, Scott Graham, Logan Field, Dabney Coleman, and James McEachin. Unbilled: Robert Clarke.

CREDITS: Director: Paul Wendkos; Teleplay: David Karp; Music: Jerry Goldsmith; Production: Cinema Center 100 Productions; Automobiles Furnished by Ford Motor Company; Running Time: 100 minutes; Air Date: 9/17/70; Network: CBS

The Cat Creature

"Beware the seal of Kah-ub-set, for he who dares to remove it will open the gates of Hell."

While cataloguing a private collection of Egyptian relics, Frank Lucas (Kent Smith) discovers a mummy wearing a golden cat's head amulet. When Lucas is out of the room, a thief steals the amulet and the mummy disappears. Lucas is then killed mysteriously and the investigating cop, Lt. Marco (Stuart Whitman), calls in an expert, Roger Edmonds (David Hedison), to help identify the missing amulet. Meanwhile the thief tries unsuccessfully to pawn the amulet at The Sorcerer's Shop, an occult supply house run by Hester Black (Gale Sondergaard). When Black's young salesgirl is killed in the same manner as Lucas, her replacement, Rena Carter (Meredith Baxter), is drawn into the investigation—and into the arms of Edmonds—as the murders continue.

Scripted by Robert Bloch, from a story by producers Douglas S. Cramer and Wilfred Lloyd Baumes (and Bloch himself), this is a fine example of the compact supernatural thrillers perfect for television. Bloch is, of course, most famous for writing the novel *Psycho*, and his name appears on other theatrical features such as the underappreciated *The Cabinet of Caligari*, the Joan Crawford shocker *Strait-Jacket* and the delirious *The Skull*, among others. But his only other telefright of the 70s was the lackluster *The Dead Don't Die*, which was, coincidentally, also helmed by Curtis Harrington.

Director Harrington, an inconsistent talent, had cut his teeth in the movies the previous decade on low-budget fare such as *Night Tide*, *Queen of Blood* and the overlooked gem *Games*. He would bounce back and forth between television and film for the rest of his career, with interesting, if not completely satisfying results. Aside from his other collaboration with Bloch mentioned above, his telefrights include *How Awful About Allan*, *Killer Bees* and *Devil Dog: The Hound of Hell*. Here he successfully recreates the moody thrillers of Val Lewton made in the 1940s, relying on creepy atmosphere and suspense.

A great deal of the entertainment in *The Cat Creature* is in the casting. Rugged leading man Stuart Whitman and *Voyage to the Bottom of the Sea* hero David Hedison carry the investigative angle of the story. Whitman's cinematic roots go back to uncredited appearances in the science fiction classics *When Worlds Collide* and *The Day the Earth Stood Still*. Equally popular in films and television for decades, Whitman was nominated for a Lead Actor Oscar for *The Mark* in 1961 and would hit it big on the small screen with *Cimarron Strip* later in the 60s. Genre fans know him from *Shock Treatment*, *Night of the Lepus*, *Crazy Mama*, *Eaten Alive* and as the Jim Jones cipher James Johnson in *Guyana: Cult of the Damned*. Whitman also made an excellent but little-known Italian cop thriller called *Blazing Magnums* and his other telefrights are *Revenge!* and *The Woman Hunter*. While Hedison gained enormous popularity with horror fans for *The Fly* back in '58 and would have a solid career since, this would be his only telefright of the 70s.

The supporters and cameos here add a dimension not usually present in TV horror films of the day. Gale Sondergaard is terrific as the occult shop's owner, Hester Black. The scene between Black and Edmonds, as she reads the tarot for him, is a well-written duel between his skepticism and her convincing beliefs. Sondergaard received the first Academy Award given for Best Supporting Actress in 1936 for *Anthony Adverse* and had memorable roles in *The Letter* and *The Spider Woman* among others before being blacklisted for refusing to testify in front of the House Un-American Activities Committee during the Red scare of the 1950s. Out of the business for 20 years, she returned to films in 1969 and this would be her only telefright of the coming decade.

Kent Smith (chosen, no doubt, for his famous roles in *Cat People* and *The Curse of the Cat People*) is the first victim, Lucas. His other telefrights include *How Awful About Allan*, *The Night Stalker* and *The Disappearance of Flight 412*. Ubiquitous character actor John Carradine plays the manager of a sleazy hotel and has roles of various sizes in the telefrights *Crowhaven Farm*, *The Night Strangler* and *Death at Love House*. Charlie Chan's "number one son" Keye Luke is the amulet thief in his only telefright appearance of the decade but most curious is Peter Lorre Jr. who appears as a dying pawnbroker. Lorre Jr. was really German-born Eugene Weingand, a notorious imposter who was once taken to court by Lorre for using his name. Lorre died before his case against Weingand was settled, allowing the impersonation to continue. Relative newcomer (but top-billed) Meredith Baxter was fresh off the *Bridget Loves Bernie* sitcom and would soon marry her co-star David Birney, modify her last name and become a fixture on television to this day.

Multiple Oscar- and Emmy-winning composer Leonard Rosenman (the former for *Barry Lyndon* and *Bound for Glory* and the latter for *Sybil* and *Friendly Fire*) provides the score here and would do so for the telefrights *The Phantom of Hollywood* and *The Possessed*.

Interesting oddball bits in *The Cat Creature* include the obvious lesbian customers at the shop, the hypnotic eyes of the avenging cat and a coroner who looks like a cadaver. There are some good eerie scenes such as the gathering of cats at Rena's house and the final cat death suffered by the mummy. All in all a very enjoyable ride, this tight little horror film is worth the time, especially for those with a fear of cats.

CAST: Meredith Baxter, David Hedison, Gale Sondergaard, (ao) John Carradine, Renne Jarrett, Keye Luke, Kent Smith, and Stuart Whitman. Also Peter Lorre Jr., John Abbott, Virgil Frye, and William Sims.

CREDITS: Director: Curtis Harrington; Teleplay: Robert Bloch, from a story by Douglas S. Cramer & Wilfred Lloyd Baumes and Robert Bloch; Music: Leonard Rosenman; Production: Douglas S. Cramer Company; Running Time: 72 minutes; Air Date: 12/11/73; Network: ABC

A Cold Night's Death

AKA Chill Factor

A Cold Night's Death is one of the leanest telefrights of the era. It is essentially a two-man show and the bulk of the action takes place on a single set. Regardless, it is a crackerjack production boasting a tight script, good acting and a feel for chilling, psychological isolation. In fact, celebrated writer Christopher Knopf (he adapted *20 Million Miles to Earth* as the second assignment of his career) was nominated for an Edgar Award for his achievement in creating a mystery that holds up after repeat viewings.

Scientists Robert Jones (Robert Culp) and Frank Enari (Eli Wallach) fly to the remote Tower Mountain Research Station to replace a colleague whose radio transmissions have stopped. They find the place trashed, the other scientist frozen at the radio. The monkeys used in the experiments have just barely survived the cold. The mystery deepens when the cause of death of the scientist is discovered *not* to be a heart attack as suspected. In fact, he simply froze to death when he should have easily been able to survive. Strange things begin to happen at the station, things that turn Robert and Frank against each other. Unless the pair can keep their heads and solve the mystery, they may end up dead too.

This is not a movie to watch in the wintertime. The production design is impeccable in convincing viewers that freezing to death is not out of the question. There is a scene late in the film where Jones is locked out of the station. His panic combined with clever sound design and frigid visuals leave no doubt that he has moments to live unless he can get inside. This telefilm stands up to bigger-budget productions such as *The Thing* (1982) when it comes to creating a life-threateningly cold environment.

Extremely well-rounded composer Gil Melle's electronic score reinforces a sense of remoteness and disorientation with the surroundings. Melle, also a painter and sculptor, wrote his first score for a theatrical release (*The Andromeda Strain*) but would work mainly in television throughout his career. His other big screen genre credits include *Embryo*, *The Sentinel* and *Blood Beach* and his telefrights of note are *The Victim*, *The President's Plane Is Missing*, *Trapped*, *Frankenstein: The True Story*, *Killdozer*, *The Missing Are Deadly* and *A Vacation in Hell*.

Robert Culp and Eli Wallach pull off their characters' strengths and weaknesses, their desires and denials, and make us believe the puzzling events. Culp would forever be known as Kelly Robinson in the enormously popular *I Spy* series but he has had a long career in film and television since. He even directed one theatrical feature, the criminally ignored modern film noir classic *Hickey & Boggs*. Usually better at light comedy, Culp nevertheless shines here in the demanding role of Jones. His other telefrights include the disaster film *Flood!* and the highly regarded *Spectre*. This would be the only telefright of the decade for the famous Eli Wallach.

It would not be fair to go too deeply into the plot because the fun is in sharing the discovery with the characters. Director Jerrold Freedman had worked on *Night Gallery* (and subsequently *The X-Files*) and has a flair for the offbeat material. Exterior filming took place at the Barcroft Station, part of the White Mountain Research Center in California. It is too bad that the film wasn't expanded to fit a two-hour slot instead of the usual 90 minutes. The extra time would have given it a little more breathing room and allowed for a richer experience. Make no mistake, however, *A Cold Night's Death* is a treat if it can be located.

CAST: Robert Culp, Eli Wallach, and Michael C. Gwynne.

CREDITS: Director: Jerrold Freedman; Teleplay: Christopher Knopf; Music: Gil Melle; Production: Spelling-Goldberg Productions; Running Time: 74 minutes; Air Date: 1/30/73; Network: ABC

Conspiracy of Terror

Satanic cults were a recurring subject of the telefilm. They often dressed their members in red robes and featured accoutrements such as goat's heads and flaming altars. *Conspiracy of Terror* has an easy, cheesy charm with its 70s suburban home development milieu, a corny husband-and-wife cop team and an obvious strain for credibility. It is second-rate in every way but will appeal to those who can value its inadequate assets.

A narrator welcomes us to the suburbs, a place we go to escape the tensions of the city, where all is peace and quiet. Husband-and-wife cops Jacob and Helen Horowitz (Michael Constantine and Barbara Rhoades) start their day like many of us do: they jump into their Fords and drive to work where they park next to each other. When a young boy comes into the station and makes a report about his lost dog, Jacob springs into action and discovers that the domestic animal population has all but disappeared in a neighborhood called Willow River Homes. Coincidentally, Jacob is assigned to another case in the same area: a realtor is found dead of a heart attack in a model home in the same development. But the realtor didn't die there, someone relocated him after he was dead. The two cases weave together as Jacob uncovers the cult of suburban Satanists that has been running rampant in this enclave of normalcy.

There is no doubt that this was a failed pilot for a series about those lovable Horowitzes. The film has a generally comic tone about it and sports subtitles that would have presumably introduced each week's episode, to wit: "Certain matters of religion and the deaths of persons unknown." Michael Constantine is a likable enough actor who will always be identified with the sitcom *Room 222* (for which he won an Emmy). He shows up in only one other telefright, *Death Cruise*. Barbara Rhoades, on the other hand, is an annoying actress and the two make an unlikely couple. The film spends some time detailing the familial tensions between the couple and Jacob's father (David Opatoshu) who doesn't like cops, guns or his son's Gentile wife. There would seem enough promising issues there to sustain a series but it was not to be.

By 1975 the networks had obviously mined out the occult possibilities. The plot here is trite and the filmmakers try desperately to bring some edginess to it by mentioning lurid details of previous unsolved cases in the housing development. The underlying themes about conformity throughout the film are interesting. For instance, several times the film makes use of statistical information designed to reduce the American individual to an "average" person. We are told about the average number of people in a home, the average number of cars they drive, the pets they have, and so on. When a young couple enters the model home for the development (and discovers the dead realtor) they are surprised to hear an automated greeting system that invites them to explore the house. They are told where to walk and where to look. Attempts to fight conformity—such as joining a Satanic cult, for instance—are dangerous to the common good. And one never can tell who could be a Satanist. In fact, the leader of the coven (Logan Ramsey) is the guy who raises an American flag in front of his house in the morning.

There is one small scene that stands out because it carries a tension that should have informed the entire film. It is a confrontation between a husband and wife about the consequences of their joining the cult. She has had second thoughts but he is now a true believer. The scene serves to give us some background but the actors, Roger Perry and Mariclare Costello, actually bring the scene to life and make one wish that level of creativity had been sustained throughout.

The climactic scene occurs when the happy couples pop down to the Black Mass like they were going to a backyard barbeque. They don their robes and pendants and make their solemn oaths to Satan. This is where the hesitant wife mentioned above decides to make a break for it. She knocks over a flaming pedestal, setting one of her neighbors on fire, and hides out amidst the safety of conformity—a house construction site. Just when things look darkest, when she's about to be pounced upon by the Satanists, the Horowitzes (a Jew and a Christian working together) arrive in time to round up the coven and make suburbia safe again from evil. The blatant moral of the story is that we should go to church and pray that Satanists don't invade our suburban neighborhoods.

The reliable director John Llewellyn Moxey (who began using his middle name at the suggestion of a numerologist) makes his mark only occasionally here, sticking to oft-used visuals even for the occult moments. Moxey's most famous genre picture was *The City of the Dead* aka *Horror Hotel*, and he would make *Psycho-Circus* before turning almost exclusively to television. His many telefrights include *The House That Would Not Die*, *A Taste of Evil*, *The Night Stalker*, *Home for the Holidays*, *The Strange and Deadly Occurrence*, *Where Have All the People Gone?*, *Nightmare in Badham County*, and *Smash-Up on Interstate 5*.

The composer on the film was Neal Hefti, famous for his theme for the *Batman* TV series. This would appear to be his only television horror film assignment of the 70s.

CAST: Michael Constantine, Barbara Rhoades, David Opatoshu, Roger Perry, Mariclare Costello, Normann Burton, Jed Allan, Arlene Martell, Logan Ramsey, Jon Lormer, Ken Sansom, Paul Smith, Stewart Moss, Bob Hastings, Shelley Morrison, Bruce Kirby, Judie Stein, Murray MacLeod, Eric Olson, Paul Bryar, John Finnegan, Ricky Powell, Ron Stokes, Beverly Bremers, Charles Cooper, and Dallas Mitchell.

CREDITS: Director: John Llewellyn Moxey; Teleplay: Howard Rodman, from the book by David Delman; Music: Neal Hefti; Production: Lorimar Productions; Running Time: 78 minutes; Air Date: 4/10/75; Network: NBC

Count Dracula

AKA Great Performances: Count Dracula

Count Dracula is quite simply the best television adaptation of Bram Stoker's *Dracula* ever attempted and it would certainly challenge most theatrical versions as well. It is stunningly realized with gorgeous photography and excellent performances, and filled with a powerful atmosphere of dread. It was made for the BBC in the United Kingdom (filming took place at Alnwick Castle) and was shown here in the States in three segments on *Great Performances* on PBS.

Rightly subtitled "a gothic romance," *Count Dracula* manages to maintain an earthiness and sensuality despite the confines of a television production. It was shot on video but it is a masterpiece of lighting technique that belies the sense of immediacy that often sabotages the format. The now-quaint video effects are surreal touches, pointedly applied, and have been made even more endearing by the passage of time instead of becoming distracting.

The production is rife with atmosphere that rarely feels forced, the sound design is as thoughtful as the visuals, and even the miniature work is clever. Note, when Dracula's carriage approaches to pick up Harker (Bosco Hogan), that the lamps look like eyes looming in the darkness. Or savor the flattened landscape when Lucy (Susan Penhaligon, *Patrick*) walks through the graveyard on a very gray day. The scene of the doomed ship that brings the dreaded Dracula to England as it lurches toward the rocks is a fine piece of work for the budget.

Louis Jourdan is excellent as the cosmopolitan bloodsucker, bringing an unusual, controlled grace to the role. He delivers famous lines such as "Listen to them, the children of the night, what music they make," with a smooth matter-of-factness that is remarkable. His Dracula is clearly a superior being in every sense not only to the other characters in the film, but also to the many actors who have essayed the role before and since.

Jourdan was born Louis Gendre in Marseille, France. After World War II, in which he was part of the French underground movement, Jourdan came to Hollywood to work for David O. Selznick in *The Paradine Case*, and made a memorable impression in *Letter from an Unknown Woman* with Joan Fontaine. He became the quintessential Continental lover in films such as *Three Coins in the Fountain* and his most famous film in America was, no doubt, *Gigi*, for which he was nominated for a Golden Globe. Jourdan starred in one of the premier ambience films of the spy genre, *To Commit a Murder*, before appearing in the first occult television film, 1969's *Fear No Evil*, as psychic investigator David Sorell. Its sequel, *Ritual of Evil*, is his only other telefright of the 70s. Genre fans will remember Jourdan as a villain in *Swamp Thing* and *Octopussy*.

Director Philip Saville had worked almost exclusively in television the two decades prior to this production and is still at it to this day. One wonders if the caliber of this picture was indicative of his work or a highlight. Either way, do not miss this superior example of a television film that breathes fresh life into an oft-told story.

CAST: Louis Jourdan, Frank Finlay, Susan Penhaligon, Judi Bowker, Mark Burns, Jack Shepherd, Bosco Hogan, Richard Barnes, Ann Queensberry, George Raistrick, George Malpas, Michael MacOwan, Susie Hickford, Belinda Meuldijk, Sue Vanner, Bruse Wightman, Izabella Telezynska, and O.T.

CREDITS: Director: Philip Saville; Teleplay: Gerald Savory, based on Bram Stoker's *Dracula*; Music: Kenyon Emrys-Roberts; Production: BBC; Running Time: 150 minutes; Air Date: 12/22/77 (UK); Network: PBS (US)

Crowhaven Farm

Crowhaven Farm is one of the touchstones of the television horror movie, lingering in the impressionable young minds of a certain generation. And it deserves to be remembered. The film boasts an excellent cast and a simple yet compelling story with a nice twist ending. It also manages to maintain a creepy atmosphere throughout, even though most of it takes place in the daytime. And its themes of inadequacy, sexual longing and betrayal are unusually adult in nature given the medium.

Maggie Porter (Hope Lange) and her husband Ben (Paul Burke) inherit Crowhaven Farm, a beautiful spread of land in Brampton, Massachusetts. Soon Maggie sees visions of Puritans, hears cries and laughter in the night and witnesses strange rituals and sacrifices. A neighbor loans Maggie books about the history of the township and the witchcraft that went on there in centuries past. Maggie begins to believe that she is a reincarnated witch and, stranger still, her previously barren marriage begins to bear fruit. The question becomes whether Maggie is truly a witch who has returned to this earth or if she is manifesting the seeds of her insanity.

Aside from the surface enjoyments of watching competent actors and second guessing the story, part of the fun of watching *Crowhaven Farm* is noting the details that make this well-rounded entertainment. A good deal of care and thought went into the production, particularly where the main characters are concerned. Ben's jealousy of other men is rooted in the childless union he has with Maggie. He obviously blames himself even though there is no physical explanation of why Maggie can't conceive. One neighbor, Kevin (Lloyd Bochner), is overly attentive to Maggie, putting her in defensive positions with Ben and further straining their marriage.

As it happens, a local orphan, ten-year-old Jennifer (Cindy Eilbacher), ends up living with the couple which creates yet another tension in the household. Jennifer obviously has feelings for Ben beyond her years, although he is too distracted to notice. Eilbacher, who was soon to be a familiar face on television, has an eerie beauty and sexual precociousness about her that makes her ideally suited for the role of interloper.

Maggie thinks of herself as the reincarnation of a certain Meg, who was born in 1666. She was killed because the locals believed her to be in league with the Devil since she suddenly became pregnant although she had been childless. The punishment was carried out by pressing her to death underneath a door by piling rocks on top of it. This is no doubt a metaphor for being oppressed in the extreme. Meg had survived the punishment by betraying a ten-year-old girl to the bloodthirsty mob as a witch. The events to follow should be allowed to unfold for first-time viewers without being revealed here.

Director Walter Grauman is at the top of his game and gorgeous Hope Lange gives a terrific performance as the tormented Maggie, who answers the questions of whether one can give away another person's soul and just what is received in the bargain.

Lange made her film debut in *Bus Stop* and was nominated for an Oscar for her supporting role in *Peyton Place*. She struck it big in television and is best remembered for the series *The Ghost and Mrs. Muir* for which she won two Emmys. She went into a long run on *The New Dick Van Dyke Show* before appearing in the genre favorite *Death Wish*. She was active throughout the 80s and 90s appearing in such diverse fare as *A Nightmare on Elm Street Part 2: Freddy's Revenge* and David Lynch's *Blue Velvet*. Her only other 70s telefright was *Fer de Lance*. Lange passed away in 2003 and was given a memorial tribute at the Academy Awards ceremony in 2004.

Paul Burke is a familiar face to television fans, appearing on the small screen from the mid–1950s through the 80s although many forget his role in the trash classic *Valley of the Dolls*. Burke also appeared in Ray Danton's *The Psychic Killer*. *Crowhaven Farm* would be his only telefright of the 70s. The ubiquitous character actor Lloyd Bochner shows up in *Satan's School for Girls* and as Cindy Eilbacher's father in *A Fire in the Sky*.

Crowhaven Farm is focused almost exclusively on the troubled couple and suffers mildly for it. Other characters aren't drawn as clearly as one would like and there is some confusion about motivations past and present. But it is still clearly worth the time to track this one down, especially given the cameo by genre specialist William Smith as a caring but vaguely sinister policeman.

CAST: Hope Lange, Paul Burke, Lloyd Bochner, John Carradine, Cyril Delevanti, Milton Selzer, Patricia Barry, Cindy Eilbacher, Woodrow Parfrey, June Dayton, Virgina Gregg, Louise Troy, Ross Elliott, Pitt Herbert, Dennis Cross, and William Smith.

CREDITS: Director: Walter Grauman; Teleplay: John McGreevey; Music: Robert Drasnin; Production: Aaron Spelling Productions; Automobiles furnished by Chrysler Corp.; Running Time: 74 minutes; Air Date: 11/24/70; Network: ABC

Cruise into Terror

AKA **Voyage into Evil**

"That there is a devil, there is no doubt, but is he trying to get in us or trying to get out?"

The phrase "so bad it's good" has been indiscriminately applied to many films, nearly to the point of meaninglessness, but it does fit this production: a jumbled hybrid of disaster and horror that pits an all-star cast of misfits against the son of Satan. For his first telefilm, *Quincy* series writer Michael Braverman devised an almost incomprehensible mishmash that is as enjoyable as it is terrible.

Eight Mexico-bound passengers are diverted by their overbooked cruise line to another ship, the "old battle wagon" *Obeah*. At the last minute they are joined by a ninth passenger bringing the total, including the four crew, to an unlucky thirteen. The *Obeah* shouldn't be sailing anywhere given the state of its equipment and its black cat mascot portends trouble on the high seas. Broken down in the middle of the Gulf of Mexico, the passengers bring aboard an Egyptian sarcophagus containing the offspring of Beelzebub, which they discovered during one of their pleasure dives. The presence of Evil brings out the worst in everyone and death soon stalks these unfortunates. Good may have a chance to defeat Evil but it is just as likely that the spawn of Satan will be given safe harbor, unleashing the apocalypse.

A terrific and, no doubt, handsomely paid cast helps to give some credibility to the outrageous events. Between problems, the level-headed Captain Andrews (Hugh O'Brian) sleeps with boozy divorcee Marilyn (Stella Stevens) and orders around a charming first mate, Simon (Dirk Benedict). The crackpot theorist Dr. Bakkun (Ray Milland), who dreamed up the possibility that ancient Egyptians traveled to Mexico and started the Mayan civilization, has his calculations questioned by mathematician Matt Lazarus (Frank Converse). Haunted by bad marriages are the greedy businessman Neal Barry (Christopher George) and his wife Sandra (George's real-life wife Lynda Day George), and self-important preacher Reverend Mather (John Forsythe) and his frustrated wife Lil (Lee Meriwether). A couple of young, single women, Judy (Jo Ann Harris, *The Beguiled*) and Debbie (Hilary Thompson), round out the list of passengers contending with fateful coincidences, leaps of logic and bouts of hysterics.

Several of the monikers in the film are rife with meaning. The ship *Obeah* is named after a form of folk magic and sorcery that is practiced in the West Indies. Reverend Mather shares his surname with Cotton Mather, the fanatic who instigated the Salem witch trials, and the mathematician Matt Lazarus is, of course, named after the Biblical character that Christ raised from the dead.

Shipboard scenes were filmed in the Channel Islands of California. The shark attack on snorkeling passengers reveals with embarrassing clarity certain practical and economic realities of the production. When Captain Andrews and Lazarus dive into the water to do battle with the blood-thirsty beasts, the scene is obviously filmed behind glass in a tank, drastically dampening our suspension of disbelief.

Dr. Bakkun's theory about the Egyptians can be proven if he can find a fabled tomb in Mexico. Convenience offers substantial assistance in providing context and plot movement. Lazarus and the Reverend Mather are well-versed not only in Bakkun's obscure theory but about ancient Egypt in general. Lazarus recalculates Bakkun's numbers and discovers that the ship is very close to the tomb. Mather provides the requisite dire warnings about the supposed curse on those who violate Egyptian tombs.

First mate Simon's job is primarily to give the captain bad news. It is he who regularly announces the ship's crises (beyond repair at various times are the engines, the radio, the electrical system and the fuel pump) and his appearances take on an unintentionally comical air as the messenger with undoubtedly dire news.

The reverend and his wife have some serious problems. Mather figures he's the one chosen by God to rid the world of this evil while his wife Lil rightly sees his tirades as pompous gestures. Mather is a dry alcoholic whose lack of amorous attention to his wife leaves her vulnerable to an unhealthy influence. When Lil visits the sarcophagus at night, it somehow convinces her to sleep with Lazarus. At her next encounter with Mather she tries to kill him while ranting in pseudo–Egyptian gibberish.

Christopher George, who does not look healthy here, has one good scene with Lynda Day about greed; he seethes as he delivers the line "No one has enough money!" There is plenty of philosophical meandering about the nature of good and evil in all of us but much of the dialog is obvious and inelegant: "I do read minds and yours looks like some pretty heavy reading." Director Bruce Kessler keeps the overall tone of the film fairly dark, however. It is played completely straight and is embroidered with Gerald Fried's soundtrack of spooky chanting *a la The Omen*. As such, *Cruise into Terror* comes recommended for its cheek *and* its cheese.

Top-billed Dirk Benedict is best known for his roles in two popular television series, *Battlestar Galactica* and *The A-Team*, and although he didn't make another telefright in the 70s, he will be remembered by genre fans as the metamorphosing David Blake in *SSSSSSS*. Frank Converse hit it big in television with the 1960s *N.Y.P.D.* series and has had a solid journeyman career since, but *Dr. Cook's Garden* would be his only other telefright. John Forsythe and Ray Milland were telefright regulars and Stella Stevens shows up in *The Night They Took Miss Beautiful* and *Express to Terror*. Christopher George, who passed away in 1983, was in one other telefright, appearing again with Lynda Day George in *Mayday at 40,000 Feet*. Hugh O'Brian can be seen in *Murder on Flight 502* but this would be the only telefright for Lee Meriwether and for 50s favorite Marshall Thompson, who has a small role here as Capt. Andy's boss.

CAST: (ao) Dirk Benedict, Frank Converse, John Forsythe, Christopher George, Lynda Day George, Jo Ann Harris, Lee Meriwether, Ray Milland, Roger E. Mosley, Hugh O'Brian, Stella Stevens, Hilary Thompson, Marshall Thompson, and Ruben Moreno.

CREDITS: Director: Bruce Kessler; Teleplay: Michael Braverman; Music: Gerald Fried; Production: Aaron Spelling Productions; Running Time: 100 minutes; Air Date: 2/3/78; Network: ABC

Cry Panic

David Ryder (John Forsythe) runs a man down with his car outside a small town. He goes to a nearby house where a lady offers him a drink while he calls the cops. When Ryder gets back to the scene, the body is gone. The sheriff, Ross Cabot (Earl Holliman), doesn't believe Ryder hit anyone but forces him to stay overnight in the town. After he goes out for dinner, Ryder returns to his room and discovers that it has been ransacked. Nothing is stolen, however, and Cabot now begins to insinuate that perhaps Ryder is mentally disturbed. The next day, Ryder's car doesn't run and when he and Cabot visit the house where Ryder used the phone, the lady there is now a different person. Ryder is either the victim of a conspiracy or he is losing his mind.

This is a thoroughly enjoyable, if unexceptional, example of a psychological terror film. A well-versed cast goes through the paces of a story designed to push the viewer's buttons. It plays on the urbanite's fear of being stranded in a small town, left to the mercies of the threatening locals. Additionally, to be the center of a Machiavellian plot that promises to engulf its victim is a fear worthy of a paranoid thriller. Thankfully, in this case the locals aren't bright enough to pull off any ambitious machinations. Ryder's perseverance, a quality universally desired, begins to unravel the hastily constructed ruse and things begin to go his way.

Forsythe plays Ryder with the natural confidence that made him not only a fixture in television but one of its most enduring and popular stars. Forsythe was the son of a Wall Street businessman who tried to discourage his son's interest in acting. Forsythe had barely embarked on a film career when World War II interrupted his progress. Following the war he went into television, where he would spend much of his effort aside from a few memorable turns in film such as the Robert Wise noir *The Captive City*, Jack Arnold's 3-D thriller *The Glass Web* and Alfred Hitchcock's *The Trouble with Harry*. The series *Bachelor Father* marked

John Forsythe in a publicity still for *Cry Panic* (1974).

Forsythe's first memorable television role. In the 1960s he did 30 episodes of *The John Forsythe Show* while appearing in films as diverse as *Kitten with a Whip*, *Madame X*, *In Cold Blood* and another Hitchcock, *Topaz*. In the 70s it was his uncredited voice that rounded up *Charlie's Angels* each week and practically the entire decade of the 80s was taken up with his role of Blake Carrington in *Dynasty*. Winding down a very special career, Forsythe was reportedly paid $5 million for his voice on the two *Charlie's Angels* films released in the new millennium. Forsythe's 70s telefrights include *Murder Once Removed*, *Terror on the 40th Floor* and *Cruise Into Terror*.

Amidst the tensions that are stacked up against Ryder, there are moments of humor. At one point Ryder is being intimidated by Cabot and he asks what crime he's being charged with. The reply is, "We're still working on it."

The film's other assets include one good shock moment (Ryder discovers the body of the man he hit) and a solid supporting cast. Genre fans know Earl Holliman from *Forbidden Planet* and his turn in the *Twilight Zone* episode, "Where Is Everybody?" but it was his long run with Angie Dickinson in the *Police Woman* series that made him a household name in the 70s. Not forgotten to aficionados of film noir, however, is his role as the hit man Mingo in the classic *The Big Combo*. Holliman's *Forbidden Planet* co-star, the famous Anne Francis, plays Julie, who deceives Ryder at the beginning of the film. Francis made only one other telefright during the decade, *The Haunts of the Very Rich*.

Ralph Meeker plays the most prominent conspirator, Chuck Braswell. Meeker's first significant film credit was in the Anthony Mann–James Stewart western *The Naked Spur* but, two years later, he would land the role that he will always be remembered for: Mike Hammer in Robert Aldrich's *Kiss Me Deadly*. Meeker's cocky persona was perfect as the volatile private eye who hit first and asked questions later, and it would serve the actor well in many character roles in the following decades. His telefrights include *The Night Stalker*, *You'll Never See Me Again* and *The Dead Don't Die*. Meeker's last film was the horror–science fiction thriller *Without Warning*, before he passed away in 1988.

Not surprisingly, there are liabilities to be considered here: unlikely coincidences, a very weak foundation beneath the house of cards writer Jack Sowards builds and actions by characters that don't ring true. But all in all, *Cry Panic* is recommended like comfort food: it is familiar fare, easily digested.

CAST: John Forsythe, Earl Holliman, Ralph Meeker, Norman Alden, Claudia McNeil, Anne Francis, Eddie Firestone, Harry Basch, Gene Tyburn, Jason Wingreen, Roy Applegate, Wesley Lau, Jason Ledger, and Pitt Herbert.

CREDITS: Director: James Goldstone; Teleplay: Jack B. Sowards; Music: Ken Lauber; Production: Spelling-Goldberg Productions; Vehicles furnished by Chrysler Corporation; Running Time: 74 minutes; Air Date: 2/6/74; Network: ABC

Curse of the Black Widow

AKA Love Trap

A friend of private eye Mark Higbie (Tony Franciosa) is murdered outside the bar where they had been hanging out. Higbie is drawn into a series of mysterious killings when a new client, Leigh Lockwood (Donna Mills), girlfriend of Higbie's dead buddy, asks him to find out more about the murder. Apparently there have been other victims of the same killer: all exhibited the tell-tale signs of death by spider—a very, very large spider. As Higbie investigates, the web of events begins to entangle Leigh and her fraternal twin sister Laura (Patty Duke Astin), one of whom was severely bitten by spiders when they were infants.

Director Dan Curtis, who passed away in 2006, is a famous name in television horror. As director and/or producer, his hits have been big, influential films and his misses have missed by a mile. *Curse of the Black Widow* falls somewhere in between. It has a good cast and an old-fashioned sense of fun about it but it also has a meandering feel and an alienating sense of forced legitimacy.

Curtis began his career with a hit, the long-running daytime horror saga *Dark Shadows*, in 1966. He would make its two spin-off theatrical releases *House of Dark Shadows* and *Night of Dark Shadows* before producing the phenomenally successful telefilm *The Night Stalker*. From that point forward, Curtis had carte blanche from the networks, and the 1970s were his most prolific years. He went to England and produced and/or directed several classical adaptations including *Dracula*, *Frankenstein*, *The Picture of Dorian Gray* and *The Turn of the Screw*. Curtis himself directed the *Night Stalker* sequel *The Night Strangler*, as well as *The Norliss Tapes*, *Scream of the Wolf* and the theatrical release *Burnt Offerings*. He then tackled the anthology format with *Trilogy of Terror* and *Dead of Night*. With *Express to Terror*, the pilot for the short-lived *Supertrain* series, Curtis's directorial horrors ceased until the revival of *Dark Shadows* and *Trilogy of Terror II* in the 90s. Curtis dabbled in non-genre fare as well, including film noir (*Shadow of Fear*, *Nightmare at 43 Hillcrest*), crime (*Melvin Purvis G-Man*, *The Kansas City Massacre*, *The Great Ice Rip-Off*) and wide-sweeping mini-series (*The Winds of War*, *War and Remembrance*). One other small supernatural film made in the 70s, *The Invasion of Carol Enders*, rounds out the work of one of the most influential names in television horror.

In *Curse of the Black Widow*, Tony Franciosa does a good job as the cocksure Higbie who seems particularly affected by the bizarre realizations he's forced to accept. Donna Mills is quite beautiful here but isn't given enough to do. Patty Duke Astin is fairly quiet until near the end and the rest of the big-name cast doesn't get much to chew on. Vic Morrow as the gruff cop Gully Conti is unusually low-key and even Sid Caesar has only a few lines (one of which, "You didn't come in here to eat an octopus," is clearly of his own choosing).

Higbie's secretary (Roz Kelly) goes by the name of "Flaps." In fact, many in the cast have nicknames: Rags, Flaps, Popeye, etc. This phony community of pals rings as false as the giant spider at the center of it all. There are also such diverse characters as an American Indian (Jeff Corey) well-versed in folklore, a gay morgue attendant and even a trio of hookers stationed across the street from Tower Records in downtown LA.

The film holds amusements both intentional and inadvertent. When a hairy tarantula surprises Higbie and Leigh, she scoops it up into a box, saying, "I'm sure it was much more frightened than you were." Higbie replies, "I doubt that." When cop Conti finally comes around to admitting the validity of the giant spider theory, he sarcastically remarks about calling a press conference announcing the threat of a big, black spider in LA: "I'll issue all my men giant cans of Raid and send them out after it."

On the inadvertent side, it is curious to note that Higbie spends twelve dollars on a two-foot model of a black widow spider just to see the hourglass on its stomach. Considering that this bit of "business" was solely foreshadowing, Curtis was clearly underestimating his audience. Also, notice when the Lockwoods' insane mother (June Lockhart) falls out of an upstairs window of their house. It would be difficult to mistake the heavy-set stuntman for a little old lady. And aficionados of 70s décor are well served by the interior design throughout this production.

Cinematically speaking, this is actually a well-photographed movie. Higbie's fall through the floor of an old house (unleashing a bevy of creepy crawlers) is nicely done, as is the shot of Olga (June Allyson) trapped in a web near the end of the film. The scenes shot from the point of view of the spider will evoke images of the fabled science fiction films of the 50s.

The level of "camp" is raised considerably when Patty Duke Astin takes on the disguise of her character's alter ego, Valerie Steffan. The black wig, German accent and gobs of red lipstick may not be enough to fool the viewer but it would seem to make her unrecognizable to her own sister.

The twist ending is predictable but without it the film would seem incomplete. *Curse of the Black Widow*'s most peculiar mystery is the reason for a picture of child actress Pamelyn Ferdin on the wall behind Flaps' desk. The reason for the in-joke may never be revealed but it won't detract from the enjoyment of watching this throwback to the B-movie conventions of the past.

CAST: Tony Franciosa, Donna Mills, Patty Duke Astin, June Lockhart, June Allyson, Max Gail, Jeff Corey, Roz Kelly, Sid Caesar, Vic Morrow, Michael DeLano, Robert Burton, Bryan O'Byrne, Tracy Curtis, Irene Forest, Bruce French, Mari Gorman, Elizabeth Grey, H.B. Haggerty, Crofton Hardester, Howard Honig, Rosanna Locke, and Robert Nadder.

CREDITS: Director: Dan Curtis; Teleplay: Robert Blees and Earl Wallace, based a story by Robert Blees; Music: Bob Cobert; Production: Dan Curtis Productions; Running Time: 97 minutes; Air Date: 9/16/77; Network: ABC

The Dark Secret of Harvest Home

Note: Reviewed is the 120-minute home video version of *The Dark Secret of Harvest Home*. The film was originally broadcast at 300 minutes.

Like all works of art, *The Dark Secret of Harvest Home* has its promoters as well as its detractors. The truncated home video version of this two-part adaptation of a popular novel, shorn of nearly two-thirds its original running time, still manages to be long and dull and the problems with it would not be overcome with the addition of more material. This old culture-clash chestnut is played for atmosphere rather than exploitation but the bulk of the film is lacking in both.

The Constantine family, Nick (David Ackroyd), his wife Beth (Joanna Miles) and their daughter Kate (Rosanna Arquette), cross an old New England covered bridge in their car one day and enter a nearly untouched world, one reminiscent of Amish society. Charmed by the quaint town of Cornwall Coome, the family picks up and leaves New York to join the idyllic community. Soon however, the layers of social custom are peeled away to reveal an unholy core and the family, who had been manipulated from the beginning, find themselves trapped by the isolated locals.

Thomas Tryon's novel *Harvest Home* was published in 1973 and in the five years it took to make it to the small screen, the main conceit of urbanites who find themselves in hostile, unfamiliar territory had been worn completely through. Add to this the pedestrian approach taken by director Leo Penn, who was so steeped in the economical television model by this time that he could crank out routine fare with his eyes closed. Toss in a largely competent but bland cast with inconsistent New England accents, a thoroughly forgettable score and horrors that even by the standard of 1970s television would be considered tame, and the result is one bloated and ultimately unsatisfying presentation.

Joanna Miles in *The Dark Secret of Harvest Home* (1978).

The Dark Secret of Harvest Home does have its assets, of course. Bette Davis doesn't even have to try to carry this film and her presence as Widow Fortune holds the entire production together. David Ackroyd (*Another World*) is underwhelming but Joanna Miles has more depth than many of her compatriot thespians.

The haunting dance scene of seduction in the cornfield is nicely realized and the small moments of horror seem more effective than the broad strokes that are supposed to deliver the "willies." Take for instance Nick's horrifying discovery of Jack Stump (Rene Auberjonois), his tongue cut out and his lips sewn shut, or the creepy atmosphere realized in the scene where an empty coffin is found in the cellar of the church.

The device that brings us into the Dark Secret is the mystery of one of the village girls who disappeared after supposedly rebelling against "the ways." This is not handled particularly well, however, culminating in a major plot revelation delivered by a doctor while eating a sandwich. "The ways" turn out to be only an extreme variation of paganism and Earth Mother worship in the manner of *The Wicker Man* which came out the same year as Tryon's novel.

Filming took place at Holden Arboretum in Kirkwood, Ohio, and the production's costumes and sound editing were deemed special enough to be nominated for Emmys. Director Penn, who suffered the ignominy of anti–Communist blacklisting in the 50s, is the father of actors Sean Penn and the late Chris Penn and the musician Michael Penn.

Those hoping to enjoy an early performance by cult favorite Rosanna Arquette will be disappointed. In the home video version she disappears after the opening sequences only to show up again an hour later in a village ritual in the role of an overtly sexual icon. One does wonder what changes she went though during her absence. The Internet Movie Database lists Bradford Dillman among the cast but he was not visible in the video version used for review.

CAST: Bette Davis, (ao) David Ackroyd, Rosanna Arquette, Rene Auberjonois, John Calvin, Norman Lloyd, Linda Marsh, Joanna Miles, Michael O'Keefe, Laurie Prange, Richard Venture. and the voice of Donald Pleasence. Lina Raymond, Tracey Gold, Michael Durrell, Dick Durock, Stephen Joyce, Steve Gustafson, Phoebe Alexander, Bill Balhatchet, Kathleen Howland, John Daheim, Martin Shakar, Grayce Grant, Earl Keyes, Paul S. Orgill, and Lori Street.

CREDITS: Director: Leo Penn; Teleplay: Charles E. Israel and Jack Guss, based upon the book *Harvest Home* by Thomas Tryon; Music: Paul Chihara; Production: Universal TV; Running Time: 120/300 minutes; Air Date: 11/23–24/78; Network: NBC

The Darker Side of Terror

Good scientist Paul Corwin (Robert Forster) is secretly cloned by his former teacher, bad scientist Professor Meredith (Ray Milland). Passed over for promotion, his work usurped by another scientist, the now-embittered Corwin decides to assist Meredith in accelerating the clone's growth. The experiment goes awry and the adult clone exhibits murderous tendencies that incriminate Corwin and force a symbolic showdown between the two selves.

With a title like *The Darker Side of Terror*, one could reasonably expect at least a somewhat scary experience. Instead, this is a borderline horror film given an overreaching, nonsensical title to lure an audience. And, contrary to some accounts, it is not television's first cloning movie. There was the previous *The Clone Master* (9/14/78), but it is not a fright film (nor is it particularly good science fiction). First place goes to *The Cloning of Clifford Swimmer* (11/1/74), part of ABC's *Wide World of Mystery* anthology series. *The Clone Master* fostered the classic misconception that a clone would retain the memories of the donor. *The Darker Side of Terror* doesn't make that mistake but indulges in the usual scientific mumbo-jumbo to gloss over the technical impossibilities and speed up the plot to provide timely, if not particularly exciting action.

The Darker Side of Terror feeds on the paranoia of the populace not only concerning the newly feasible technology of cloning, but also on the conservative fear of an unchecked scientific community and the possibility that advances in civilization will result in the reversion of our species to a more primitive state. Corwin actually states that people are afraid of science creating monsters on campuses across the country and that fellow scientist Meredith is going against God's will.

To its credit, the film attempts to explore the idea of what a clone would experience as it tries to relate to and integrate into the world, particularly its donor's world. Of course, the ultimate nightmare of this scenario is to have the clone sleep with the donor's wife and that is exactly what happens here. Up to this point in the film, the Margaret Corwin character (Adrienne Barbeau) had only been around to complain about not seeing her husband enough. Corwin's clone shows up, sweet talks her, and then they take off for a mini-holiday in San Francisco. When the clone has a violent confrontation with a couple of annoying skaters on the boardwalk, Margaret gets excited enough to suggest they go to a hotel immediately. The clone's bedside manner satisfies Margaret so either she couldn't tell the difference between the clone and her husband or else she preferred the clone. When Corwin learns of this, his only recourse is deadly revenge.

Moody photography is a considerable

asset to a production that includes plot clichés such as a *Columbo*-style cop and the clone's visit to a disco. The dependable Robert Forster does what he can with the material in his only telefright of the decade. Forster's first interesting film role was in George Cukor's trash classic *Justine* in 1969, the same year he appeared in a classic of another kind entirely, the breakthrough independent feature *Medium Cool*. From there he scored a couple of short-lived television series in the early 70s (*Banyon* and *Nakia*) but his career from that point on consisted largely of unexceptional television roles and low-budget exploitation features (Disney's high-profile flop *The Black Hole* not withstanding). Two of his better pictures in the 80s were cult favorites *Alligator* and *Vigilante*, but the A-list seemed to elude him. Finally, in 1997, Quentin Tarantino rescued Forster from B-movie oblivion and cast him with Pam Grier in *Jackie Brown*. The role reinvigorated the career of a fine actor who now seems to be getting the recognition he deserves.

The ubiquitous Ray Milland doesn't have a lot of screen time here and Adrienne Barbeau is the only other standout among the cast. Barbeau is most famous for the long-running series *Maude*, her roles in director-husband John Carpenter's horror films *The Fog* and *Escape from New York*, and for other 80s horrors such as *Swamp Thing* and *Creepshow*. She did, however, show up in two other telefrights in the 70s: *Someone's Watching Me* (where she met Carpenter) and *Red Alert*.

Director Gus Trikonis (*She's Dressed to Kill*) was a Broadway dancer-actor turned director. He made the enjoyable feature *The Evil* but he mostly stuck to highbrow fare such as *Supercock*, *Swinging Barmaids* and *Moonshine County Express*. The pair of writers on the production, Al Ramrus and John Herman Shaner, worked together on several features including *The Island of Dr. Moreau* and *Goin' South*. The words of Corwin to Prof. Meredith sum up nicely the overall sentiment concerning this scientific misfire: "Damn you, doctor, and everything you've done here!"

CAST: Robert Forster, Adrienne Barbeau, David Sheiner, John Lehne, Ray Milland, Denise DuBarry, Thomas Bellin, Heather Hobbs, Eddie Quillan, Raye Sheffield, Russell Shannon, Jim Nolan, Madeleine Shaner, John Shaner, Johnny Hock, and Tom Elliot.
CREDITS: Director: Gus Trikonis; Teleplay: Al Ramrus and John Herman Shaner; Music: Paul Chihara; Production: Bob Banner Associates and Shaner-Ramrus Productions; Running Time: 96 minutes; Air Date: 4/3/79; Network: CBS

The Dead Don't Die

Curtis Harrington and Robert Bloch's previous telefilm collaboration resulted in the fun and clever *The Cat Creature*. There, the team successfully updated the mood of the 40s Val Lewton films but here their attempt to recreate the Poverty Row horrors of the 30s falls a bit flat.

Don Drake's (George Hamilton) brother is sentenced to death for a murder he didn't commit. After his execution, Drake promises to find the real killer and clear his brother's name. Drake visits his brother's former boss, Jim Moss (Ray Milland), at the Loveland Ballroom to get details about the crime and meets the mysterious Vera LaValle (Linda Cristal). She claims Drake is in danger from a certain "Varek." When Drake thinks he sees his executed brother walking the streets, he is drawn into a dark world of the living dead.

The production, set in 1934 Chicago, is a deliberately dark visual affair. Shooting almost completely at night (the very few daytime scenes are gray days indeed), with very little overhead lighting even in the interior scenes, the filmmakers' aim was clearly to set a deadly serious and nightmarish mood. This bold tack (for a television movie) is understandable but actually works against the intention. The claustrophobia is palpable and without any leavening of humor, the viewer is smothered in gloomy atmosphere. The scenes in the ballroom during a dance marathon are a good symbolic example. With its subdued lighting and interminable organ music, it's no surprise that the dancers drop like flies.

Casting is another serious problem. Lead George Hamilton (*Love at First Bite*) is better with roles that require a light touch and Linda Cristal, who didn't need much of a career after the *High Chaparral* series funded her fortune, is so funereal in her approach that her beauty is the only light in her character. While Cristal didn't appear in any other telefrights in the decade, Hamilton shows up in *The Strange Possession of Mrs. Oliver*, *Killer on Board*, *Express to Terror* and *Death Car on the Freeway*.

Ray Milland doesn't convince as the villain of the piece, either. There are small roles for favorites such as Ralph Meeker as a disbelieving cop, Reggie Nalder as a zombie shopkeeper, and even a cameo for cult actress Yvette Vickers (*Attack of the Giant Leeches*) but overall there are not enough likable actors to pull in the viewer.

Nalder, who was born in Vienna, Austria, suffered facial burns as a young man but the circumstances surrounding his disfigurement remain shrouded in mystery. Nevertheless, it is his scarred face that made his career as a villain, most notably in Alfred Hitchcock's *The Man Who Knew Too Much* (1956 version). His genre credits are many including Dario Argento's *The Bird With the Crystal Plumage*, the notorious gore films *Mark of the Devil* and *Mark of the Devil II*, *Dracula's Dog* and the telefright *Salem's Lot* (as the vampire). Nalder passed away in 1991.

On the plus side, there is the most famous scene of Nalder rising from his coffin and chasing Drake down the aisle of the funeral home and the unexpected scene of Vera LaValle bursting into flames. Add to these a good dream sequence, with Drake stumbling around in a graveyard, and a couple of good zombie attacks, and you have a handful of satisfying moments. Many of the elements for a good horror movie are here but they don't coalesce into an effective whole, leaving the viewer with a depressing sense of wasted time.

CAST: George Hamilton, Linda Cristal, Joan Blondell, Ralph Meeker, James McEachin, Reggie Nalder, Ray Milland, Jerry Douglas, Milton Parsons, William O'Connell, Yvette Vickers, Brendon Dillon, Russ Grieves, and Bill Smillie.

CREDITS: Director: Curtis Harrington; Teleplay: Robert Bloch; Music: Robert Prince; Production: Douglas S. Cramer Company; Running Time: 90 minutes; Air Date: 1/14/75; Network: NBC

Dead of Night

Dead of Night is another unsold Dan Curtis pilot for a supernatural anthology series. His first, from 1975, was *Trilogy of Terror*; Curtis partnered with writer Richard Matheson on both attempts. As with all anthologies, this is a hit-and-miss affair. The good news here is that the stories get better as they go along, culminating, as with *Trilogy of Terror*, in a genuinely scary treat.

In "Second Chance," Frank (Ed Begley, Jr.) buys an old junk car (hit by a train decades ago) and restores it. When he takes it for a spin, Frank goes back in time to the night the car was wrecked. Frank's actions in the past create unexpected changes when he returns to the present.

This bit of saccharine is Richard Matheson's adaptation of a Jack Finney story. Its feel-good weightlessness leaves no impression and one has to wonder why they bothered except that it improves the chances of the other two stories. Ed Begley Jr., who takes the lead here, is the son of the Oscar-winning character actor Ed Begley. Ed Jr. is known as much for his multiple Emmy-nominated role on television's *St. Elsewhere* as for his staunch environmental views. Ubiquitous on television (and to a lesser extent in film) from the age of twenty, Begley Jr. had only one other role in a 70s telefright: a cameo in *Family Flight*. Story writer Jack Finney is most famous for writing "Invasion of the Body Snatchers" as a serial in *Collier's* magazine; it inspired several film adaptations.

In "No Such Thing As a Vampire," Dr. Gheria's wife Alexis (Anjanette Comer) appears to be suffering from the bites of a vampire. Gheria (Patrick Macnee) consults a young physician friend, Michael (Horst Buchholz), who discovers, in a horrible way, that things are not what they seem.

Short but well-played, this segment has the feel of a *Night Gallery* episode. Matheson adapts his own story here and has an excellent time playing on audience expectations. Viewers have grown accustomed to the vampire legend and will follow along until, put into the doctor's shoes, they discover as he does that karmic retribution is at hand. Patrick Macnee is utterly convincing as the nonplussed husband but neither Anjanette Comer nor Horst Buchholz have much of a chance to shine. It is nice to see Elisha Cook, who plays a key role as the butler who never questions his master. Compared to the previous segment, this slight story seems downright weighty.

Macnee (most famous for *The Avengers*) would not appear in any other of the decade's telefrights and Buchholz would show up only in one other: *Savage Bees*. Anjanette Comer, on the other hand, was a fixture on television during the 70s, making several telefright appearances including *Five Desperate Women*, *Terror on the 40th Floor* and *Death Stalk*.

In "Bobby," an unnamed woman (Joan Hackett) attempts an occult ritual to bring her drowned son Bobby (Lee H. Montgomery) back to life. This works all too well and the result forces her to face a terrible truth about her intentions.

Matheson's original teleplay is lean and frightening and drenched in an atmosphere of gothic dread. It's a dark and stormy night as the criminally underrated Joan Hackett starts drawing a pentagram on her living room floor, an occult effort to raise the dead. The ritual is short but very fruitful and her drowned son suddenly knocks on the front door. She accepts this strange turn of events rather easily which cues the viewer to her mental instability and creates an edgy reality. When Bobby starts asking probing questions, the general uneasiness begins to take shape. It isn't long before Joan realizes she's received more than she's asked for. A most chilling moment occurs when, in the midst of the chaos of frightful weather and events, the phone rings. The caller sounds like her absent husband but the conversation takes an unnerving turn. Lee H. Montgomery has a natural menace about him that Curtis exploits to great effect and Hackett proves her reliability and depth once again.

Hackett was a former fashion model who kick-started her acting career by winning an Obie for her performance in *Call Me By My Rightful Name* on Broadway in 1961. Her flair for both comedy and drama kept her busy in film and television for the next two decades. Leading roles in theatrical features included *Will Penny*, *Support Your Local Sheriff!* and *The Terminal Man*, and she was nominated for an Oscar for her supporting role in 1981's *Only When I Laugh*. Her 70s telefrights include *How Awful About Allan*, *Five Desperate Women*, *Reflections of Murder* and *The Possessed*. Hackett died of ovarian cancer in 1983 and the epitaph on her tombstone reflects her passion for napping: "Go Away—I'm Asleep."

Next to Robert Bloch, Richard Matheson is the most famous writer in television horror but plenty of feature films bear his name as well, most famously *The Incredible Shrinking Man*. Other genre film favorites include his works with Roger Corman (*House of Usher*, *Pit and the Pendulum*, *Tales of Terror*, *The Raven*), British classics (*Night of the Eagle* aka *Burn, Witch, Burn*, *The Devil Rides Out*), the films based on his novel "I Am Legend" (*The Last Man on Earth*, *The Omega Man*) and *The Legend of Hell House*. The romantic hit *Somewhere in Time* is also based on his work. Telefrights to his credit include *Duel*, *The Night Stalker*, *Dracula*, *The Night Strangler*, *Dying Room Only*, *Scream of the Wolf*, *The Stranger Within*, the aforementioned *Trilogy of Terror* and *The Strange Possession of Mrs. Oliver*.

CAST: "Second Chance": Ed Begley Jr., E.J. Andre, Ann Doran, Christine Hart, Orin Cannon, Jean LeVouvier, Dick McGarvin, and Karen Hurley. "No Such Thing as a Vampire": Patrick Macnee, Anjanette Comer, Elisha Cook, and Horst Buchholz. "Bobby": Joan Hackett and Lee H. Montgomery.

CREDITS: Director: Dan Curtis; Teleplay: "Second Chance": Richard Matheson, based on the story by Jack Finney; "No Such Thing as a Vampire": Richard Matheson, based on his story; "Bobby": Richard Matheson; Music: Robert Cobert; Production: Dan Curtis Productions; Running Time: 76 minutes; Air Date: 3/29/77; Network: NBC

The Deadly Dream

"My dreams are real."

Dr. Jim Hanley (Lloyd Bridges), a genetic researcher, is having frightening dreams involving a mysterious "tribunal" and its attempts to kill him. Evidence begins to suggest that these nightmares may have some basis in reality until finally Hanley discovers a much more disturbing truth.

This simple story deals with the question of where reality ends and dreams begin—and vice versa. Certainly there have been documented cases of disastrous premonitions in dreams that have come true in real life and even the benign experience of *déjà vu* would suggest there could be more to acts of the unconscious mind than mere mental exercise. But, of course, conclusive evidence is as fleeting as a dream itself.

The Deadly Dream is indeed a scary take on the question. In his dreams, Dr. Hanley is hounded by a mysterious organization, The Tribunal, to receive punishment for an unknown crime. This Kafkaesque situation is, naturally, unnerving and will strike a chord with anyone (which is to say, everyone) who has had such nightmares. When experiences in one world bleed over to the other, the comfort of waking into what was always assumed was reality, is considerably shaken.

Director Alf Kjellin, a Swedish actor with a long career in directing television shows, gets the most out of the material and the result is certainly one his finest hours. Many of the dream sequences take place in an abstract industrial setting, conjuring up a dreamscape that rings true. Interestingly, much of the "reality" of Jim Hanley is shot on the Universal back lot, an environment that is as artificial as it is recognizable to those who grew up watching television. This adds another—and unintended—level to the film which actually works to the story's benefit.

There are leaps in logic to move the plot along but considering that in dreams anything can happen, these are easily forgiven. Take, for instance, that Hanley can carry an object—first a camera, then a gun—with him into his dreams. This may temporarily challenge the viewer's suspension of disbelief but ultimately, given the point of the story, it makes some sense. Revealing almost anything but minor information about writer Barry Oringer's compelling story would succeed only in spoiling the fun for first-time viewers.

The Deadly Dream was the first "ABC Movie of the Weekend" and Kjellin is blessed with a stellar cast that is key to adding weight and involving the audience in this fast-moving, thought-provoking thriller. Lloyd Bridges is terrific as the scientist whose rock-hard beliefs in reality and tangible evidence are shaken to the point of no return. The rugged, athletic actor was born in California and had his first credited appearances in films in the early 40s after he signed a contract with Columbia. Seemingly doomed to B pictures, his roles improved when he started freelancing, including the lead in *Rocketship X-M* and a memorable supporting turn in *High Noon*. His television stardom was assured when he landed the role of Mike Nelson in the popular late-50s *Sea Hunt* series which even led to one season of *The Lloyd Bridges Show* in the mid-60s. The actor remained a favorite throughout the 70s and reinvented his career in 1980 by parodying his no-nonsense persona in the comedy *Airplane!* Bridges was nominated only twice for Emmys—30 years apart—and worked steadily until his death in 1998 of natural causes. His 70s telefrights include *Haunts of the Very Rich*, *Force of Evil* and *Disaster on the Coastliner*.

Janet Leigh plays Hanley's lovely wife

Laurel, Leif Erickson (*The High Chaparral*) plays his concerned boss Dr. Malcolm, and Carl Betz (*Judd for the Defense*) plays his friend Dr. Geary, all of whom have larger roles to play than Hanley suspects at first. The bad guys are top-notch too: Don Stroud as the threatening thug Kagan and Richard Jaeckel as the exasperatingly elusive Delgrave, roles the actors were born to play over and over again.

Composer Dave Grusin has been nominated for Oscars eight times (winning once for *The Milagro Beanfield War*) and for Grammys nine times (winning twice for *The Graduate* and *The Fabulous Baker Boys*). His only other score for a telefright in the decade was for *A Howling in the Woods*.

The conservative paranoia concerning scientific breakthroughs and tampering with nature is the backbone upon which the paranormal trappings are hung. These wailings of doom have been heard before but they are not the point of the film. *The Deadly Dream* manages to be cerebral and exciting in a way that few telefilms have even attempted since, making this a highly recommended effort.

CAST: Lloyd Bridges, Janet Leigh, Leif Erickson, Don Stroud, Richard Jaeckel, Carl Betz, Phillip Pine, and Herbert Nelson.

CREDITS: Director: Alf Kjellin; Teleplay: Barry Oringer; Music: Dave Grusin; Production: Universal TV; Running Time: 74 minutes; Air Date: 9/25/71; Network: ABC

Death at Love House

AKA The Shrine of Laura Love

Joel and Donna Gregory (Robert Wagner and Kate Jackson) move into Love House, the estate of Lorna Love, to research a book on the 1930s movie star. Love once had a romantic attachment to Joel's father who had painted a portrait of her that still hangs in the house. Gradually Joel becomes obsessed with Lorna, spending his days with drink and dream sequences. At the same time, Donna begins to realize that the danger they face from the dead Lorna is all too real when threats on her life begin to take shape.

This is a weak attempt to capture the gothic romantic atmosphere surrounding the mystery and decadence of old Hollywood. From murky production design to unmotivated acting and muddled period trappings, *Death at Love House* fails on nearly every count to involve the viewer in a story that had its possibilities. Director E.W. Swackhamer must have recognized early on that what looked good on paper was not going to translate to the small screen. There's a hangdog feel from the very beginning and the film never moves into a rhythm, dragging listlessly back and forth until it reaches its unsatisfying end. Swackhamer had similar luck in the 70s with *The Death of Ocean View Park* but much better results with *Death Sentence*, *Night Terror* and *Vampire*.

Location shooting inside and around Harold Lloyd's Greenacres Estate is a plus but one gets the feeling that the filmmakers didn't take advantage of the situation since most of the action could have taken place anywhere. The film does boast a decent cast, however. Robert Wagner and Kate Jackson make a good, likable team but they paint this one by the numbers and neither of their characters is particularly appealing. Jackson is beautiful in her undernourished way but her mousey quality comes to the fore too often. Wagner would not make another telefright in the decade but Jackson shows up in several including *Satan's School for Girls*, *Killer Bees* and *Death Cruise*.

More fun is to be had by catching the few big names found in smaller roles. There is John Carradine, who drives a monstrous car and gets to die early, Sylvia Sidney as the resident grumpy landlady and Dorothy Lamour, who is seen doing a coffee commercial (a bit of obvious irony). Joan Blondell plays a fan club president who is a complete twit, which should offend those who hold the Hollywood ideal in high esteem. Marianna Hill, who plays Lorna Love in flashbacks, was a character actress who may be familiar to genre fans for her appearances in *Black Zoo*, *Dead People* aka

Messiah of Evil, *The Baby*, *Schizoid* and *Blood Beach*.

Some of the attempts at depth are subtle, such as when the front door closes on Donna, as if she's not wanted, when the Gregorys first arrive at Love House. But most of the time, the viewer is hit over the head with clumsy bits of nonsensical spookiness, such as the glass shrine that entombs Lorna's embalmed body, or the stuffed black cat with the name Nosferatu. The worst of these offenses has to be the mysterious Father Eternal Fire who shows up in an old film of Lorna's funeral, decked out in a monk's robe covered in occult symbols, only to drop said cat on Lorna's coffin and make a dramatic exit. *Death at Love House* features boring dream sequences, more rain than LA's had in years, and even an Erich von Stroheim send-up but nothing will save this lackadaisical lollygagger.

The composer on the film, Laurence Rosenthal, was twice nominated for Oscars and won Emmys seven times. His telefright scores include *How Awful About Allan*, *The House That Would Not Die*, *Sweet, Sweet Rachel*, *The Devil's Daughter*, *Satan's School for Girls*, *Death Sentence* and *Murder on Flight 502*.

CAST: Robert Wagner, Kate Jackson, Sylvia Sidney, Mariana Hill, (ao) Joan Blondell, John Carradine, and Dorothy Lamour. Bill Macy, Joseph Bernard, John A. Zee, Robert Gibbons, Al Hansen, and Crofton Hardester.

CREDITS: Director: E.W. Swackhamer; Teleplay: Jim Barnett; Music: Laurence Rosenthal; Production: Spelling-Goldberg Productions; Automobiles Furnished by Ford Motor Co.; Running Time: 74 minutes; Air Date: 9/30/76; Network: ABC

Death Car on the Freeway

AKA Wheels of Death

The unseen driver of a van, dubbed "The Fiddler" because he listens to crazy fiddle music, attacks cars with lone female occupants on the Ventura Freeway. Up-and-coming ace TV reporter Janette Clausen (Shelley Hack) picks up on the story and connects the dots with previous similar accounts. When she puts herself in the driver's seat in order to trap the killer, he obliges by tracking her.

The underlying theme here is, of course, the empowerment (and subjugation) of women in a male-dominated society. Women's liberation issues were highly exploitable at the time and that is the angle taken here. However, the filmmakers, in order to examine the subject, must indulge in the very thing they claim to abhor: depicting women in situations of peril. This "Catch-22" can never really be overcome and one has to take it on faith that the filmmakers do indeed have the best intentions.

The terrorization of women in movies is an issue that still sparks debates on the debasement of women, artists' rights and responsibilities and the influence of media on the impressionable psyche. Writer William Wood brings these and other interesting subjects to the fore but director Hal Needham just wanted to make a car stunt movie. Needham made other car movies such as *Smokey and the Bandit*, *Cannonball Run*, et al. but he has many more credits as a stunt coordinator. He also acts and has a small part here as a driving instructor who gives Clausen tips on defensive driving.

Another subject brought up is the automobile as double-edged sword. The car is a tool that has empowered women by providing them with the mobility that helps them compete in the marketplace. But it can also be used as a weapon against women, the whole point of the film. Automobile advertising is generally directed towards men, appealing to factors of primal instinct and masculinity. So it's interesting that the Clausen character drives a sporty Datsun 240-Z, a car that was probably more typically purchased by men.

There are plenty of images suggesting women in power. Besides the female newscasters of the television world, there are nurses and even one woman working with a table saw. George Hamilton plays Clausen's estranged husband who seems to have his own struggles with powerful women. Casting is all over the map but notables include a clueless (male) cop (Peter Graves), Frank Gorshin as Clausen's boss, Barbara Rush as Clausen's rival newsperson, Dinah Shore and future *Dallas* star Morgan Brittany as victims and cult favorite Sid Haig as a motorhead.

This is a movie for fans of 70s cars. Just ignore the weighty subjects and enjoy the good car stunts, waiting for that spectacular final crash that is second only to *Duel's* truck going over a cliff for visual (and metaphoric) impact.

CAST: Shelley Hack, (ao) Frank Gorshin, Peter Graves, Harriet Nelson, Barbara Rush, Dinah Shore, Abe Vigoda, and Alfie Wise. Also George Hamilton, Robert F. Lyons, Tara Buckman, Morgan Brittany, Nancy Stephens, Gloria Stroock, Hal Needham, Jim Negele, Sid Haig, Buddy H. Farmer, Hank Brandt, Marguerite DeLain, Roger Aaron Brown, and Jack Collins.

CREDITS: Director: Hal Needham; Teleplay: William Wood; Music: Richard Markowitz; Production: The Shpetner Company; Running Time: 91 minutes; Air Date: 9/25/79; Network: CBS

Death Cruise

Three couples win a free Caribbean cruise but not one of them can remember entering any sort of contest. Shortly after leaving port, these passengers begin dying off, one by one, until there is but one single panicky might-be victim left as the ship reaches its destination. It is up to the ship's doctor to figure out the mystery of this near-perfect crime before the murderer can escape for good.

Death Cruise is light and airy with no horrific overtones to the plot. The underlying crime is cleverly conceived, however, and

Kate Jackson and Edward Albert prior to their departure in *Death Cruise* (1974).

the murderer is particularly ruthless in that the victims are not deserving of their fate. There is a bit of gallows humor but basically this is a network-friendly body count movie.

All three couples have their marital problems, of course (the better to fill up the running time), but all are relatively sympathetic characters.

For the record, there are the Carters, Jerry and Sylvia (Richard Long and Polly Bergen). He's a notorious cheat, or so Sylvia insists. Next are the Radneys, James and Mary Francis (Edward Albert and Kate Jackson). She wants a baby and he doesn't. Lastly, we have the Masons, David and Elizabeth (Tom Bosley and Celeste Holm), trying to renew their long marriage now that their kids have moved out. She's having a hard time accepting the "loss." Michael Constantine plays the amateur detective, Dr. Burke, and Cesare Danova plays the captain.

Director Ralph Senensky injects very little energy into the production but there is occasional—and tasteful—dark humor. (After his wife is killed, Mason says, "They're keeping her in the refrigerator.") The crime must be allowed to unfold and details of the skillful plotting will be withheld here. The murderer is easy to spot and the killings are rather ordinary but the reason for the slaughter of these people and the twist ending are well worth the wait.

Along the way, the viewer is urged to note some of the unfortunate choices in fashion and interior design. The costume designers obviously found challenge in their work because the clothes all seem ill-fitting or just plain ugly. The same can be said for the thrift store look to the furnishings. This must be the smallest and tackiest ship in the fleet—on the inside. The exterior shots were filmed on the *Queen Mary* when it was docked in Long Beach.

Death Cruise is Richard Long's last film appearance. The popular television actor would be dead of multiple hearts attacks at the age of 46, less than two months after its network premiere. Long entered films directly out of high school, scoring a contract with Universal. What followed were juvenile supporting roles (he was one of Ma and Pa Kettle's kids) and eventual leads in B pictures. Genre fans remember him from *Cult of the Cobra* and *House on Haunted Hill* prior to his almost-exclusive move to television. He was a semi-regular on *Maverick* and *77 Sunset Strip* before he became a star on the long-running series *The Big Valley*. Following that, he had a short run in the popular *Nanny and the Professor* series. In 1957, Long married 50s scream queen and *Playboy* Playmate Mara Corday, who remained his wife until his untimely death.

Kate Jackson and Edward Albert also played a couple in *Killer Bees*, broadcast earlier this same year. One of this film's most memorable scene scenes involves a black-gloved Jackson shooting skeet off the prow of the ship. Her command of the weapon combined with her pixie-like beauty will leave a lingering image. Polly Bergen shows up in *Murder on Flight 502* but neither Tom Bosley nor Celeste Holm would make another telefright in the decade. Michael Constantine has the lead in his only other genre telefilm of the 70s, the Satan cult thriller *Conspiracy of Terror*.

CAST: Richard Long, Polly Bergen, Edward Albert, Kate Jackson, Celeste Holm, Tom Bosley, Michael Constantine, Cesare Danova, Amzie Strickland, Alain Patrick, Maurice Sherbanee, West Gale, and Mark De Vries.

CREDITS: Director: Ralph Senensky; Teleplay: Jack B. Sowards; Music: Pete Rugolo; Production: Spelling-Goldberg Productions; Running Time: 74 minutes; Air Date: 10/30/74; Network: ABC

Death Moon

Workaholic Jason Palmer (Robert Foxworth) is troubled by dreams of strange rituals. When his doctor prescribes a vacation, Jason takes off for Kauai, where his great grandfather was a missionary. It turns out Jason has been cursed for his ancestor's attempts to suppress the pagan worship of the wolf god so he turns into a werewolf on the full moon.

DOLUNAY / DEATH MOON

ROBERT FOXWORTH • JOE PENNY • FRANCE NUYEN

Onu bu adaya getiren nedir?
Tuhaf şeytan güçler mi?
Esrarengiz hisler mi?
Filmi seyrederken korkmaya
hazırlıklı olun.

Rüya gibi bir ormanda, titreyen ateşler, düşündürücü güçlere sahip putperestlerin dinsel törenlerini yöneten büyücü Tapula, kurt suratlı Tiki esrarengiz bir ortam içindedirler. Bir grup 19. yüzyıl misyoneri, putperestlerin dinsel törenleri içine dalarlar. Tapula lanetler okurken baltasıyla Tiki'ye vurur... "Korku sevenlerin filmi."
SÜRESİ 89 Dakika

EMI

154
Gerilim
Altyazı
Dublaj

 **ART & VİDEO**
OLGUNER GÖRÜNTÜ SİSTEMLERİ
SAN. ve TİC. A.Ş.

Bu film Umut Sanat Ürünleri tarafından OLGUNER GÖRÜNTÜ SİSTEMLERİ San. ve Tic. A.Ş. için ithal edilmiştir.

Nispetiye Cad. No: 7/2 Levent/İstanbul
Telefon: (1) 164 72 34-164 72 35

Death Moon is your basic postcard from the Hawaiian islands, a vacation for all involved. The production is, by and large, exceedingly dull, enlivened only by incidentals. The viewer can take solace in the bold, bad 70s fashions and décor or the presence of familiar faces in supporting roles: Charles Haid (*Hill Street Blues*) as a room thief, Joe Penny (*Bloody Birthday*) as the hotel's head of security and France Nuyen as an ageless witch.

Robert Foxworth's werewolf makeup isn't bad but his transformation scenes are jittery, distracting affairs. His love interest is Barbara Trentham, who has the austere beauty of Barbara Carrera, and the couple spends most of their time driving around the island in a Volkswagen Thing. Trentham had a short acting career (including roles in *The Possession of Joel Delaney* and *Rollerball*) before leaving the profession to marry John Cleese, a marriage that lasted nine years.

Foxworth came late to film acting (his first credit came when he was nearly 30) but his talents have been in demand, primarily in television, for decades. He was Elizabeth Montgomery's partner for over 20 years until her death in 1995. His genre credits include *Damian: Omen II*, *Prophecy* and the science fiction telefilm *The Questor Tapes*. His 70s telefrights include *The Devil's Daughter*, Dan Curtis's *Frankenstein* and *It Happened at Lakewood Manor*.

Eurasian (Vietnamese and French) actress France Nuyen was born in France and had a tremendous success on Broadway in 1958 opposite William Holden in *The World of Suzie Wong*. Her first film credit, *South Pacific*, was in the same year and she worked with Holden again in *Satan Never Sleeps*. She was in the little-remembered science fiction feature *Dimension 5* before working on the *I Spy* series where she met and married Robert Culp, a stormy marriage which lasted only three years. Her genre credits include *Battle for the Planet of the Apes* and the Sergio Corbucci spaghetti western, *Shoot First ... Ask Questions Later*. Her only other telefright is *Horror at 37,000 Feet*.

Composer Paul Chihara's first film credit was *Death Race 2000*. He is now highly regarded for his original classical works but in the 70s he contributed scores for *The Dark Secret of Harvest Home*, *A Fire in the Sky* and *The Darker Side of Terror*.

Director Bruce Kessler (*Simon, King of the Witches*) made the delirious *Cruise Into Terror* which was broadcast earlier the same year. Whereas *Cruise Into Terror* was recommended for being outrageous, there is very little here to interest the average viewer. As Michael Weldon put it in the *Psychotronic Encyclopedia of Film*: "*Death Moon* is the best werewolf movie of April '78."

CAST: Robert Foxworth, Joe Penny, Barbara Trentham, Dolph Sweet, Charles Haid, Debralee Scott, France Nuyen, Carole Kai, Branscombe Richmond, Joan Freeman, Albert Harris, Lydia Lei Kayahara, Mitch Mitchell, Don Pomes, Terry Takada, Carol Avery, Robert Witthans, and Donna White.

CREDITS: Director: Bruce Kessler; Teleplay by George Schenck, story by Jay Benson & George Schenck; Music: Paul Chihara; Production: Roger Gimbel Productions; Running Time: 92 minutes; Air Date: 5/31/78; Network: CBS

The Death of Ocean View Park

Sheila Brady (Diana Canova) is having premonitions of a disaster at a local amusement park run by Sam Jackson (Mike Connors). It seems that Sheila is tuning into a mysterious force out to destroy the park which will result in its spectacular demise.

The genesis of this film has its own curious story. The soon-to-be-demolished Ocean View Park in Norfolk, Virginia, was specifically purchased by Playboy Enterprises to shoot a movie around the destruction of the aged amusement park. The result is what one would expect: a plot (thin enough to be jotted down on a cocktail napkin) that drags on and on in overstuffed "disaster movie" fashion until the destruc-

Turkish theatrical release poster for *Death Moon* (1978).

tion that everyone has been waiting for wrecks havoc across the screen.

Yes, this is a horror movie but only technically. The unexplained phenomenon that attacks the park remains unexplained throughout, although it is dismissed as "an act of God." The trouble starts with an oddball hurricane (real footage), then takes over the rides in the middle of the night, causes power outages, creates a sinkhole in the beach and finally results in explosions that bring down the features of the park entirely.

Mike Connors breezes through his role as Sam Jackson. Of Armenian descent, Connors was born Krikor Ohanian in Fresno, California, and in his early film roles in the 1950s he used the name "Touch" Connors, a holdover nickname from his college basketball days. Among his early films were the Joan Crawford vehicle *Sudden Fear* and several Roger Corman pictures including *Swamp Women*, *Five Guns West*, *Day the World Ended* and *The Oklahoma Woman*. Connors was also in fare as diverse as *The Ten Commandments*, the rock 'n' roll exploitation number *Shake, Rattle and Rock!* and Edward L. Cahn's *Voodoo Woman*. At the same time, he was mining television, even scoring his own series before decade's end with *Tightrope* for one season. In the 60s, Connors hit it big on the small screen after appearing in *Harlow* with Carroll Baker and giving an excellent turn as a secret agent in *Kiss the Girls and Make Them Die*. It was the private detective show *Mannix* that made Connors a household name, however. The series ran for eight years and Connors was nominated for Emmys four years running (he was nominated six times for Golden Globes, winning once). Connors has worked steadily since, even producing and starring in the slasher film *Too Scared to Scream* in 1985, but to a generation, he will always be Joe Mannix.

Jackson co-owns the park with the ambitious and somewhat careless Tom Flood (Martin Landau). Diana Canova is best known for her role on the sitcom *Soap*. Jackson's love interest, Paula Williams, is played by Caroline McWilliams.

The bulk of the film is full of cardboard relationships, lame attempts at comedy, topical references to Jerry Brown, the Bee Gees, et al. and wide-eyed extras looking at the camera. There is a visit to a disco and to the Edgar Cayce Foundation for a primer on psychic powers. One truly amusing sequence has co-owner Tom Flood taking a solo ride on the roller coaster to prove it's safe although Martin Landau does not appear to be enjoying the experience.

In the last ten minutes or so, the movie delivers and the extraordinary explosions are a sight indeed. In fact, some of the stunts look as if safety might not have been the special effects crew's top priority. But everybody except Flood—who takes a mighty fall off the Ferris wheel—appears to escape serious injury.

Director E.W. Swackhamer handles the various unconvincing plot elements in journeyman fashion. The cast is largely undistinguished, with Connors and Landau carrying the bulk of the film on their capable shoulders. *The Death of Ocean View Park* may hold some interest to viewers who lived in the vicinity at the time but with only ten good minutes it is difficult to recommend.

CAST: Mike Connors, Diana Canova, Perry Lang, Caroline McWilliams, James Stephens, Mare Winningham, Martin Landau, Mel Stewart, Aarika Wells, Janina Mathews, Mark Armstrong, Linda Brooks, Sean Butterfield, Richard De Angelis, Will Decker, Tom Donnelly, Gerald Gough, Leon Greenberg, Jon Jackson, Marty McGraw, Richard Rhodes, Gerry Rowe, Lorrie Snyder, Red Wiggins, Annie Oringer, Paul Tomayko, Kathryn King, Tony Pellerin, Jay Lockamy, Jeana Tomasino, and Jill Leatherbury.

CREDITS: Director: E.W. Swackhamer; Teleplay: John Furia and Barry Oringer; Music: Fred Werner; Production: Playboy Productions Inc.; Running Time: 100 minutes; Air Date: 10/19/79; Network: ABC

Death Sentence

AKA Murder One

Don Davies (Laurence Luckinbill) murders his mistress, Marilyn, after she threatens to expose their affair to his wife, Susan (Cloris Leachman). Much to her delight, unhappy housewife Susan is chosen for jury duty at the murder trial where Marilyn's drunkard husband John (Nick Nolte) is the accused. Susan slowly begins to suspect her own husband of the crime, based on material evidence presented, which not only poses moral and ethical questions for her. Soon she realizes she should fear for her life.

Only marginally a terror film, *Death Sentence* qualifies based on the first person fright of Susan as the terrible truth is revealed and, most importantly, the maniacal performance of Laurence Luckinbill when husband Don's façade of congeniality finally breaks down.

The bulk of *Death Sentence* is typical of the courtroom drama, a subgenre of the crime movie that would not usually be classified as a fright film. However, as the suspicion of her husband's guilt builds, the atmosphere surrounding Susan and her troubled psyche creates a sense of terror more commonly associated with the horror film. And the grand finale, with all the cards on the table, is full-fledged psycho-horror.

Casting is a plus here with the two major roles filled by capable actors Leachman and Luckinbill. Solid support is supplied by familiar actors William Schallert and Alan Oppenheimer as the dueling lawyers. This is an early, unexceptional role for Nick Nolte as the accused husband and fans looking for a meaty performance from the actor are bound to be disappointed.

E.W. Swackhamer was hit-and-miss with these thrillers but here he succeeds at building suspense; note how the weather continues to get worse throughout the film as Susan's world crumbles. Another interesting point is how Susan, liberated by her newfound responsibilities as a juror and finally beginning to feel fulfilled as a person, is punished with the one-in-a-billion occurrence that her own husband—a part of herself, as it were—is guilty of the very crime she must contemplate.

These weighty issues and the toll they take on Susan are communicated with great skill by the gifted Cloris Leachman. She is more commonly known for her comic roles, particularly as the flighty Phyllis Lindstrom in the *Mary Tyler Moore Show* and *Rhoda* and the spin-off series *Phyllis*. Her associations with Mel Brooks (*Young Frankenstein*, *High Anxiety*, etc.) have cemented that reputation further. But many forget that she won a much-deserved Oscar for her portrayal of desperate housewife Ruth Popper in *The Last Picture Show*. Leachman was born in Des Moines, Iowa, and was a runner-up in the 1946 Miss America pageant (as Miss Chicago). Her first credited roles were in television and she would go on to be the only actress to win five Emmys in five different categories. Her other film roles of interest here include a small but pivotal turn in *Kiss Me Deadly* and the lead in Jonathan Demme's drive-in classic *Crazy Mama*. Leachman has worked non-stop in film and television for decades including the 70s telefrights *Haunts of the Very Rich* and *Dying Room Only*. Two of her children show up in this production: Morgan and Dinah Englund.

CAST: Cloris Leachman, Laurence Luckinbill, Nick Nolte, Alan Oppenheimer, William Schallert, Yvonne Wilder, Herb Voland, Hope Summers, Peter Hobbs, Doreen Lang, Murray MacLeod, Bing Russell, Meg Wyllie, Lew Brown, C.J. Hincks, Vernon Weddle, Robert Cleaves, Jack Collins, Dick Winslow, Pat Patterson, Morgan Englund, and Dinah Englund.

CREDITS: Director: E.W. Swackhamer; Teleplay: John Neufeld, from the novel *After the Trial* by Eric Roman; Music: Laurence Rosenthal; Production: Spelling-Goldberg Productions; Vehicles Furnished by Ford Motor Co.; Running Time: 71 minutes; Air Date: 10/2/74; Network: ABC

Death Stalk

Two couples, Jack and Pat Trahey (Vince Edwards and Anjanette Comer) and Hugh and Cathy Webster (Robert Webber and Carol Lynley), have their whitewater river-rafting trip interrupted by four escaped cons. The criminals tie up the men and abduct the women for their flight to freedom down the river. Jack and Hugh must escape their bonds, track the fleeing cons and rescue their wives.

Death Stalk may be a run-of-the-mill crime story but it boasts a great cast that make their characters believable; consequently, the terror elements seem that much more real. Vince Edwards had been a champion swimmer but appendicitis forced a career change that led to acting and directing. He was in Stanley Kubrick's *The Killing* and the little-known but interesting hit man movie *Murder by Contract*. He hit it big in television in the early 60s as the brooding doctor on *Ben Casey*, and at the height of his popularity recorded several albums of songs. He worked steadily for the next three decades and passed away in 1996. *Sole Survivor* is his only other telefright of the 70s as an actor but he also directed *Maneater*.

The famous model-turned-actress Carol Lynley is no stranger to film and television buffs, having begun her long career in the mid–50s. A few of her more interesting films are *Shock Treatment*, the excellent spy picture *Danger Route* and, of course, *The Poseidon Adventure*. Her telefrights include *The Night Stalker*, *The Elevator* and *Flood!*

Robert Webber often played heels and villains during his 40-year career. He had supporting roles in many memorable Hollywood productions such as *12 Angry Men*, *The Sandpiper*, *The Dirty Dozen*, etc., and worked with his friend, director Blake Edwards, in *Revenge of the Pink Panther*, *10* and *S.O.B.* But occasionally he played the lead and some of these are interesting pictures indeed. He is excellent as the amnesiac in Hammer Films' *Hysteria* and in two of Franco Prosperi's angst-ridden crime films, *Professional Killer* and *Every Man Is My Enemy*. Webber had a recurring role in the popular *Moonlighting* series before passing in 1989.

British director Robert Day worked with Boris Karloff in *The Haunted Strangler* and *Corridors of Blood* and had a hand in the *Danger Man* and *The Avengers* TV series. Day also made the underrated *First Man Into Space* and the Ursula Andress vehicle *She* and his telefrights include *Ritual of Evil* and *The Initiation of Sarah*. His experience with suspense combined with the blessing of having actors who knew what they were doing make this a compelling slice of scary adventure.

Vic Morrow is excellent as the smart, tough Brunner, the leader of the cons. Neville Brand has a good time with his role as the ugly, horny Shepherd and Norman Fell fits the bill as the scrawny, mean Cody. This was a couple of years before Fell's career-defining role as Mr. Roper on the *Three's Company* series but snickers in the audience will die down fast. Larry Wilcox (*CHiPs*) plays the young, semi-innocent boy, a character here strictly for contrast.

The victims of these desperate characters are interesting in their own right as well as they find the means to survive in this difficult situation. Jack and Hugh are partners in a law firm (Hugh is the boss) so office politics play out as the two men chase after their women. Unexpected strengths and weaknesses come to the fore when circumstances force action. The same can be said for the wives, Pat and Cathy. Neither is in a perfect marriage, naturally, so each can rationalize their actions as necessity as they deal with the men they call "animals." Pat has a telling line to Cathy as she suggests that they sleep with their captors in order to escape alive: "Oh, just close your eyes and you'll think it's one of the lushes from your country club."

The end holds no surprises but during the journey the characters twist and turn like the river they traverse and the outdoor locations are an unusual and exciting setting for the human drama. Plus, it is clear the actors did a lot of their own rafting (not all, of course), which adds to the depth of this recommended film.

CAST: Vince Edwards, Carol Lynley, Anjanette Comer, Vic Morrow, Neville Brand, Norman Fell, Robert Webber, and Larry Wilcox.

CREDITS: Director: Robert Day; Teleplay: Stephen Kandel, John W. Bloch, based upon the novel by Thomas Chastain; Music: Pete Rugolo; Production: Wolper Pictures; Running Time: 73 minutes; Air Date: 1/21/75; Network: NBC

The Devil and Miss Sarah

Notorious outlaw Rankin (Gene Barry) rides with a small band of renegades who consider him the Devil. When Rankin is captured by a posse, his renegades attack but the wounded marshal manages to hand Rankin off to farmer Gil Turner (James Drury) and his clairvoyant wife Sarah (Janice Rule) before expiring. Turner tries to get Rankin to civilization for jailing but Rankin, who has a telepathic influence over Sarah, has other ideas.

The few critical assessments of this film have been unduly harsh, considering it slow going and noncommittal. On the other hand, viewers with reasonable expectations should find it a well-acted, low-key western with an added spice of the supernatural. *The Devil and Miss Sarah* is by no means perfect, of course, but it has enough going for it to rate a recommendation.

Gene Barry gives an excellent performance as Rankin, who uses his psychic abilities for evil. Recognizing Sarah's second sight, he exploits her weak nature, having fun with his power over her. Sarah proves to have very little will of her own as Rankin mentally bosses her around. Janice Rule certainly was beautiful but her performance as Sarah is one-note and even her complete domination by Rankin near the end is unconvincing. James Drury is likable and solid but his depiction of the obstinate, simple-minded Gil leaves us no one to really identify with, one of the film's failings.

Drury is known primarily for his westerns on film and television, most famously *The Virginian*, but he did have a role in the science fiction classic *Forbidden Planet*. Rule was somewhat of a rebel early in her career but she worked steadily in film and television until her passing in 2003. Some of her roles were in genre or cult films such as *Bell, Book and Candle*, *The Ambushers*, *The Swimmer* and Robert Altman's *3 Women*.

Janice Rule succumbs to Gene Barry's will in *The Devil and Miss Sarah* **(1971).**

Gene Barry may not be remembered for his take on Rankin but his performance is a cut above his usual smarmy, chauvinistic characters. Barry was born Eugene Klaas in New York City and was considered a violin virtuoso in his youth. His third film role was in the classic *The War of the Worlds* but it was television that would be his primary acting outlet. His most famous series were *Bat Masterson*, *Burke's Law* and *The Name of the Game*, dapper characters all. Steven Spielberg would call upon Barry for a cameo in his 2005 *War of the Worlds* remake.

The supporting cast is also a plus. The great Charles McGraw as the wounded and dying sheriff is terrific but he doesn't last long. Fourth-billed is Slim Pickens, who has one good scene and then, unfortunately, is killed off. Much more time is given to cult figure Logan Ramsey as the annoying, self-centered businessman Holmes who accompanies the Turners. He too is coerced by Rankin to subvert Turner's authority, not that he needed much of a push.

The few plot holes and editing problems in *The Devil and Miss Sarah* don't amount to too much distraction. The dialogue may not evoke the Old West too often but it can be entertaining, such as when Rankin spouts the line, "You gentlemen have an abundance of patience. I'll have to remember to carve something appropriate on your grave markers."

Director Michael Caffey worked with James Drury on *The Virginian* as his very first assignment and would continue exclusively in television in the coming decades. He wouldn't make any other telefrights in the 70s but he did work on the *Kolchak: The Night Stalker* series. Caffey is, by the way, the father of Charlotte Caffey, one of the musicians in the 1980s pop group The Go-Go's. Composer David Rose was nominated for Oscars for his scores for *The Princess and the Pirate* and *Wonder Man* and he wrote the famous song "The Stripper." If the viewer doesn't expect Satan to appear or Hell's Gate to swallow anyone up, the Utah-filmed *The Devil and Miss Sarah* will prove to be solid western entertainment that offers a bit more than the usual oater.

CAST: Gene Barry, Janice Rule, James Drury, Slim Pickens, Charles McGraw, Donald Moffat, and Logan Ramsey.

CREDITS: Director: Michael Caffey; Teleplay: Calvin Clements; Music: David Rose; Production: Universal Television; Running Time: 74 minutes; Air Date: 12/4/71; Network: ABC

Devil Dog the Hound of Hell

It's Halloween, 1978. America cozies up to the TV for *Devil Dog the Hound of Hell*. With a title like that, one should be forgiven for expecting the film to be a campfest. The material certainly could have been treated as such but director Curtis Harrington and his good cast play it completely straight, which accounts for the general success of the picture.

A group of Satanists buys a top breeding German Shepherd and performs a ritual calling for the dog to bear the puppies of Satan. Later, Mike and Betty Barry (Richard Crenna and Yvette Mimieux) discover their own dog has been killed by a car. Their kids, Charlie and Bonnie (Ike Eisenman and Kim Richards), end up getting a puppy from a passing vegetable vendor (one of the Satanists) and as the dog Lucky grows, the corruption of the family becomes evident. Mike, however, seems to be largely unaffected and begins to put the pieces together, finally consulting supernatural forces in the hopes of defeating The Beast.

As mentioned, the good cast goes a long way toward making this admittedly far-fetched story seem believable. The ever-dependable Richard Crenna gives his Mike depth and is a center of dogged rationality. The generally undervalued journeyman actor was born in Los Angeles and began appearing in film and television in the early 1950s. His big break came with the long-running *The Real McCoys* series in 1957 and from then on, his reliable talent for both comedy and drama kept him busy for more than four decades. Some of his more interesting theatrical features are *Wait Until Dark*, the cult film *Red Sky at Morning*, Jean-Pierre Melville's crime story *Un flic*, the spaghetti western character piece *The Man Called Noon*, the horror favorite *The Evil* and the lesser genre pictures *Death Ship* and *Leviathan*. Two of his best non-genre telefilms are the existential *Thief* and the comedy western *Shootout in a One-Dog Town*. It is also worth watching *A Fire in the Sky* for yet another excellent performance from this much-beloved actor who passed away in 2003.

Gorgeous Yvette Mimieux is equally credible as Betty, who turns from a loving "everymom" into a cynical bitch who is capable of some very unladylike behavior. The first we see of a change in Betty is a naughty night-time swim in the neighbor's pool but she soon turns to acts of betrayal that are downright wicked.

One of the things that works here is that the corruption of the family is a subtle affair. There's no wildly divergent behavior by any member, only small, logical changes that add up to evil. The recognizable young actors, Eisenman and Richards, may be a bit too sweet in the beginning but both have the talent to keep Charlie and Bonnie's metamorphosis from becoming clichéd or hammy. The kids' descent is a long slope that starts with "normal" unhealthy acts such as lying, cheating and stealing and ends up with secret midnight rituals. Ike and Kim worked together several times, most memorably as siblings in the Disney favorites *Escape to Witch Mountain* and *Return from Witch Mountain*. Kim also had a bit part in the Dan Curtis production *The Picture of Dorian Gray* and Ike shows up in *Terror Out of the Sky*.

The few moments of humor are intentional. When Mike goes to his doctor to seek some sort of help, the unbelieving medico suggests, "Two weeks in Hawaii alone with Betty would do you both a world of good [pause] and I'm going to give you this prescription, some tranquilizers." When Mike reaches further for help, visiting an occult shop, the owner, upon viewing a picture the kids drew, says, "Pity it isn't a one-eyed devil, a one-eyed devil's not your brightest." (The lead-up to this scene seems to be missing. It isn't shown what precipitated Mike's visit to this shop but the gap must have been a conscious editing decision.)

Mike ends up in Ecuador to consult a shaman (Victor Jory). The viewer has to go with the idea that Mike could just up and fly to South America but these scenes add credibility to the character and the story. There's a nice industrial setting for the final showdown between Mike and the devil dog and the special effects, while minimal, are convincing enough. There are some creepy moments (Mike checking his daughter's reflection while she sleeps) and some hideous interior décor, and the ending is satisfying, so for some spooky entertainment that is better than its title, check this one out.

The Satanists are led by the statuesque actress Martine Beswick, best known to horror film fans for her role in *Dr. Jekyll and Sister Hyde*. But she was also the first actress to appear in three James Bond films: *Dr. No* (she danced in the credit sequence), *From Russia With Love* and *Thunderball*. After duking it out with Raquel Welch in *One Million Years B.C.*, Beswick went on to another loincloth epic, *Slave Girls* aka *Prehistoric Women*. Among her other credits are Oliver Stone's first feature, *Seizure* and Joe Dante's cult hit *Piranha*.

Stephen and Elinor Karpf, the writers of this film, also collaborated on *Terror in the Sky* and *Gargoyles*. Composer Artie Kane's theatrical release credits include the genre pictures *The Bat People*, *Eyes of Laura Mars* and *Waterworld*.

CAST: Richard Crenna, Yvette Mimieux, Kim Richards, Ike Eisenman, Lou Frizzel, Ken Kercheval, Martine Beswick, R.G. Armstrong, Tina Menard, Gertrude Flynn, Bill Zuckert, Jerry Fogel, Lois Ursone, Frederick Franklin, Bob Navarro, Jack Carol, James Reynolds, and Victor Jory.

CREDITS: Director: Curtis Harrington; Teleplay: Stephen and Elinor Karpf; Music: Artie Kane; Production: Zeitman-Landers-Roberts Productions; Running Time: 95 minutes; Air Date: 10/31/78; Network: CBS

The Devil's Daughter

When her mother dies, Diane Shaw (Belinda Montgomery) must come to terms with the fact that she is the spawn of Satan. It seems she's the conflicted offspring of an unholy union between her mother—who had since found religion—and the Evil One himself. Pursued by Devil worshippers led by Lilith Malone (Shelley Winters), Diane's future looks bleak until she meets Steve Stone (Robert Foxworth), whose marriage proposal portends happiness.

The Devil's Daughter is generally dismissed as an inferior rip-off of the genre classic *Rosemary's Baby*, a comparison that may be superficially appropriate but is also unfair. It is the rare case indeed that a telefilm could achieve the artistic heights of its much more well-endowed kin, the theatrical release. That aside, while no gem in the rough, this is still an entertaining and fast-moving film with enough to offer on its own to merit a viewing.

A good cast, some intentional yet subtle humor, a few visual flourishes and a downbeat ending all assist the predictable material to nearly become a formidable dark comedy. Nearly. Director Jeannot Szwarc worked quite a bit on Rod Serling's *Night Gallery* and this feels like an extended *NG* episode. In fact, the hilariously obvious painting of Satan that adorns Lilith's living room could have been directly pulled from that series. Szwarc began his career in television but did venture into film, somewhat successfully, with *Bug*, *Jaws 2* and the romantic hit *Somewhere in Time*, among others.

The movie is peopled with recognizable actors, and half the fun of the film is spotting them. The supporters include Diane Ladd as Diane's mom, Ian Wolfe as a kindly priest, Jonathan Frid (*Dark Shadows*) as Lilith's "chauffeur-companion," Abe Vigoda (*Barney Miller*) as an expert in ancient dances, Robert Cornthwaite (forever remembered as the fanatical scientist in 1951's *The Thing from Another World*) as a not-so-kindly priest and last but not least Joseph Cotten in the role of a lifetime.

Aside from the painting of Satan, other humorous touches include the Poole sisters (Thelma Carpenter and Lucille Benson), an odd pair of twins—one black and one white—who dress alike and have opposite-colored cats. There is also much purple prose ("You are promised in marriage to the Prince, the Demon of Endor") from Satanists standing around in living rooms—the same cult who posed in their robes for a picture, all smiles from happier days, that ends up in Lilith's scrapbook.

We are let down by an ill-defined central character, however. At one point, Diane spaces out and mentally forces a young boy to walk out into traffic, nearly getting him run down by a car. She saves him, of course. This is the only instance we see of her evil side but since she's the daughter of Satan, one would expect her to show a little more chutzpah in the evil department. The characters are constantly mentioning Diane's dreams but these are never shown, which is a disappointment. Then there is the old "horses disturbed by her presence" routine and the required romantic cutaways that slow things down.

There's a good scene at the "ancient dance" party where Diane instinctively knows the steps and another when she cleverly (she thinks) uses her standing in the cult to threaten the leaders. It's always refreshing when there is not a happy ending but overall enough luster is lacking to prevent this from being more than a minor diversion.

Writer Collin Higgins' credits include the cult film *Harold and Maude* and the comedies *Silver Streak*, *Foul Play* and *Nine to Five*.

CAST: Shelley Winters, Belinda J. Montgomery, Robert Foxworth, Jonathan Frid, Martha Scott, Joseph Cotten, Barbara Sammeth, Diane Lad(d), Lucille Benson, Thelma Carpenter, Abe Vigoda, Ian Wolfe, Robert Cornthwaite, Rozelle Gayle, Jr., Nick Bolin, Lillian Bronson, Sharon Barr, Jock Livingston, Grace Lenard, Gail Bonney, and Mark Thomas.

CREDITS: Director: Jeannot Szwarc; Teleplay: Colin Higgins; Music: Laurence Rosenthal;

Production: Paramount Television; Running Time: 72 minutes; Air Date: 1/9/73; Network: ABC

The Disappearance of Flight 412

Air Force flight 412, on a routine test mission, encounters three UFOs. When two fighters deployed to engage the UFOs disappear from the radar screens, 412 is mysteriously rerouted to an abandoned base. Col. Pete Moore (Glenn Ford), in charge of 412 but given the runaround about its location, begins a crusade to find his men and aircraft. Meanwhile, the men are in the hands of Special Intelligence being "reprogrammed" to doubt the existence of the UFOs they encountered.

In 1974 the UFO craze was going strong. Speculative documentaries covering paranormal phenomenon—everything from Bigfoot and the Loch Ness Monster to the Bermuda Triangle, Kirlian photography and UFOs—were commonplace in theaters and on television screens. A part of all this conjecture was, of course, paranoia. Conspiracy theories about governmental cover-ups, particularly concerning unidentified flying objects and the havoc they supposedly wreak, were a major component of the genre.

This film takes a UFO encounter by the military as the starting point in detailing the systematic breakdown of the "facts" their trained men reported. One thread has Col. Moore and Maj. Mike Dunning (Bradford Dillman) tracking down their men, determined to unravel the deliberately deceptive web drawn by their own superiors. The other

Guy Stockwell (left) and Glenn Ford in *The Disappearance of Flight 412* (1974).

thread follows the interrogation of the men by the SID (led by Guy Stockwell), as they are mentally broken to doubt the accuracy of what happened.

Looking at it 30-plus years later, *The Disappearance of Flight 412* seems like standard procedure, everything you would expect from the military in that situation. Col. Moore's crusade to find answers and change behaviors is futile and hopelessly naïve, and the resistance put up by the men (led by David Soul), likewise. This is part of the point of the film, of course, while the rest trades in the feelings of paranoia some civilians have about the military, which still holds true today. All in all, this is a very matter-of-fact presentation in keeping with the subject matter. It has a good cast and a bit of atmosphere but there is probably very little of interest to viewers except as a curio of the times.

Although lesser known than his younger brother Dean, Guy Stockwell had a long career in film and television. One of his first roles was in the teen exploitation number *The Beat Generation* in 1959. Over the years Stockwell worked solidly, appearing in adventure and war films, many of the baby boomers' favorite television shows and such diverse fare as Larry Cohen's *It's Alive* and perhaps most surprisingly, Alejandro Jodorowsky's art house hit *Santa sangre*. Later in life, Stockwell became a respected acting teacher before passing in 2002. Director Judd Taylor also made the superior telefright *Revenge!* Co-writer George Simpson is better known as a sound editor on mainstream Hollywood movies.

CAST: Glenn Ford, Bradford Dillman, David Soul, Robert F. Lyons, Guy Stockwell, Greg Mullavey, Stanley Clay, Jonathan Lippe, Jack Ging, Ken Kercheval, Edward Winter, Simon Scott, Kent Smith, Cynthia Hayward, Jesse Vint, Morris Buchanan, James Storm, and Brent Davis.

CREDITS: Director: Judd Taylor; Teleplay: George Simpson and Neal R. Burger; Music: Morton Stevens; Production: Cine Films, Inc.; Running Time: 73 minutes; Air Date: 10/1/74; Network: NBC

Disaster on the Coastliner

Disgruntled Trans Allied Railroad employee Jim Waterman (Paul L. Smith)—whose family was killed in a suspicious train wreck years ago—arranges for a computer failure that puts a southbound train carrying the vice-president's wife on a collision course with a northbound train carrying various other fascinating characters. All Waterman wants is for the truth of the railroad's negligence in the wreck that killed his family to come out but that might not be so easy: time is running out quickly.

Despite the claim of the title, *Disaster on the Coastliner* is a terror film, specifically a *terrorism* film. The fantasy that a computer-controlled railroad could succumb to sabotage to the point that trains could be made to collide is eclipsed by the very real terror of human vengeance, this time brought on by corporate corruption. People distrust Big Business, and for good reason. It has become more and more difficult for the individual to penetrate the corporate monolith and rash behavior can seem like the only recourse.

Comparatively speaking, this "group peril" film is not all that bad. It is not overburdened with too many star turns and it does take an interesting chance or two. The location work in Connecticut adds authenticity and the finale sports some decent stunt work and not-too-shabby special effects. But, like its kin, it depends on the improbable to propel the plot and features the usual righteous and happy ending.

The film begins with a refreshing bit of business, however. Lloyd Bridges plays Al Mitchell, a hard-ass Secret Service agent assigned to hang out in the railroad control room to make sure the vice-president's wife has a safe journey. He immediately butts heads with supervisor Roy Snyder (E.G. Marshall), the "egghead" in charge of the all-powerful computer. The situation is played for light humor, a nice change from the usual dour confrontations of men on a mission. In fact, the point of *Airplane*-style parody is nearly reached when Mitchell threatens to shoot the computer once things start going awry. Naturally, the men cultivate a mutual respect over the course of events but it's still a pleasant riff on the serious characters the actors usually played at that time.

Smarmy William Shatner is Stuart Peters, a con man who becomes a hero. He entangles Paula Harvey (Yvette Mimieux) in his efforts to avoid arrest on the train and since she's having marital problems with husband Matt (Robert Fuller), she falls for another lying, cheating man, but this time he really has a heart of gold. Peters ends up saving the day in the end by getting his stunt double to do some train-riding antics just in the nick of time.

Villain Waterman went to extremes to get his point across, endangering hundreds of people in his quest for the truth, but a man whose family has been killed has nothing left to lose. For some reason, Waterman has a little kitten that he gives to a group of youngsters at the train station, which seems quite a stretch just to give this terrorist character some dimension.

Pat Hingle is the conductor of the southbound train who is much too dense to recognize the many signs of potential doom. Raymond Burr plays the railway's sensible board chairman, Estes Hill, but very little is made of the vice-president's wife who is only in a couple of shots. Her presence in the film is merely to add tension but it seems likely the terror would have been just as real without her.

Director Richard Sarafian had made the cult film *Vanishing Point* a few years prior to this but there is not much here to distinguish his touch. Composer Gerald Fried worked with Stanley Kubrick several times including *Killer's Kiss*, *The Killing* and *Paths of Glory* and was nominated for an Oscar for *Birds Do It, Bees Do It*. As well as providing music for many classic television shows, Fried's theatrical genre credits include *The Vampire* (the 1957 John Beal version), *The Return of Dracula*, *I Bury the Living* and *The Cabinet of Caligari*. His other 70s telefrights were *The Spell* and *Cruise into Terror*.

As mentioned earlier, the stunts in *Disaster on the Coastliner* are adequate and the miniature train wreck at the end is passable (except for the "Amtrak" on the side of the train that was supposed to be part of the fictional railroad!). But most is forgiven and thanks to a few unusual touches this is an acceptable distraction.

CAST: Lloyd Bridges, Raymond Burr, Robert Fuller, Pat Hingle, E.G. Marshall, Yvette Mimieux, William Shatner, Paul L. Smith, Arthur Malet, Harry Caesar, Jacque Lynn Colton, Lane Smith, Sandy McPeak, Virginia Kiser, Rockne Tarkington, Michael Pataki, Peter Jason, Peter MacLean, Jerry Ayres, Julie Mannix, Steve Jerro, Ron Prince, Dago Dimster, Carole Hemingway, Carl Gordon, Eric Poppick, Jason Ronard, Herbert Bress, Tony Matranga, and Norman Alexander Gibbs.

CREDITS: Director: Richard Sarafian; Teleplay: David Ambrose; Music: Gerald Fried; Production: Moonlight Productions and Filmways Pictures; Running Time: 92 minutes; Air Date: 10/29/79; Network: ABC

Dr. Cook's Garden

Simple country doctor Leonard Cook (Bing Crosby) tends his small town Vermont patients as if they were plants in his private garden. When Jim Tennyson (Frank Converse) returns home from medical school to hang up his shingle, he discovers that Cook has been discreetly "weeding out" patients whose time he has deemed has come, including one patient very close to Jim.

The character of a kindly doctor as serial killer makes its first, but not last, appearance in a television movie (see *Murder Once Removed*) here. One of the last icons of blind trust, the family doctor has always been seen as somehow above the human frailties that produce the social aberrant. Of course, that's not the case but it's a stroke of cynical brilliance to depict doctors not only as human but as murderers.

Ira Levin's (*Rosemary's Baby*) play is transplanted, if you will, to the outdoors in this pleasant production that successfully captures the idyllic qualities of small town life. There is a lot of picturesque scenery in *Dr. Cook's Garden*, which was shot on location in Woodstock, Vermont, and designed specifically to appeal. Audiences are expected not to question the supposedly despicable acts of Dr. Cook because the result is unequivocally positive.

Dr. Cook was an ideal role for the much-beloved Bing Crosby who, for many, evokes an innocent charm. He gives a good performance and Cook's arguments for killing people are really rather convincing, especially when posed against those of the weaker character of the young upstart Jim. Frank Converse doesn't cut it as the correct yet self-righteous Jim, who seems unnaturally determined to dig up the worst dirt possible upon his return home. It is doubtful that much of the audience can really identify with him even though he is technically in the right. The ever-lovely Blythe Danner and likable stalwart Barnard Hughes fare better as locals who look up to the old doc.

Coincidentally, Robert Jackson Drasnin, who composed the score, also contributed the soundtrack for that other killer doctor telefilm *Murder Once Removed*. Drasnin's first film credit is for *Teenage Devil Dolls* and his work in the 60s includes scores for the cult classic *Ride in the Whirlwind* and Bert I. Gordon's *Picture Mommy Dead*. Another cult credit of his is the low-budget shocker *The Candy Snatchers*. His other 70s telefrights are *Crowhaven Farm* and *A Taste of Evil*.

Director Ted Post is most famous for working with Clint Eastwood (*Hang'em High* and *Magnum Force*), but also made *Beneath the Planet of the Apes* and *The Harrad Experiment*. His telefrights include the interesting *Night Slaves* and *Five Desperate Women*. Post's competent work here combined with a (mostly) good cast makes for a satisfying viewing experience in a folksy-yet-subversive way. There is even a nice bit of irony at the end to sweeten the pot.

CAST: Bing Crosby, Frank Converse, Blythe Danner, Bethel Leslie, Barnard Hughes, Carol Morley, Staats Cotsworth, Jordan Reed, Abby Lewis, Fred Burrell, Thomas Barbour, and Helen Stenborg.

CREDITS: Director: Ted Post; Teleplay: Art Wallace, based upon a play by Ira Levin; Music: Robert Jackson Drasnin; Production: Paramount Television; Vehicles Furnished by General Motors Corporation; Running Time: 74 minutes; Air Date: 1/19/71; Network: ABC

Don't Be Afraid of the Dark

Don't Be Afraid of the Dark is—along with *Duel* and *Salem's Lot*—one of the most often-remembered telefilms of the era. It left quite an impression on a generation that still gets chills down its collective spine when the film is mentioned. This cult favorite delivers the spooks all right, thanks in large part to sensitive direction, clever special effects and a good cast.

Alex and Sally Farnham (Jim Hutton and Kim Darby) inherit an old Victorian house that harbors a terrible secret. To her horror, Sally discovers that she has been chosen by the little creatures living there as a sacrifice. She must convince Alex of the danger and overcome the supernatural beings that torment her.

This slight story was perfect for the 90-minute time slot given most network movies. There's very little room for fluff and things must happen quickly to get the audience hooked. Expert director John Newland had created the late-50s series *One Step Beyond* which dealt with real-life experiences with the supernatural. Working steadily through the 60s and 70s, his flair for fright extended to series work on Boris Karloff's *Thriller* and Rod Serling's *Night Gallery*.

Here, Newland creates a spooky atmosphere largely through the overlooked art of lighting. *Don't Be Afraid of the Dark* is lit like a horror movie—pools of light glow amidst shrouds of darkness and mysterious shadows abound. Even a darkened party scene is justified as reticence to reveal the house remodeling underway. The truth is fear of the dark is universal, especially when prune-faced goblins tug at our bedclothes.

The three little gnome-like creatures with shrunken faces are among the very best (and best-remembered) monsters of the era. The motif of darkness works in favor of the special effects too, of course. Good looks at the little horrors are few and that allows the viewer's imaginations to work towards the success of the film. The oversize props used are clever and simple and kept in the shadows. Whether climbing up big stairs or wielding giant straight razors, these little monsters fit into our world very convincingly.

Kim Darby, looking rather dowdy here, does a good job of going through the paces. Her Sally trips into a surreal world of gloom and, although she never really gets a grip on things, she still shows some resolve. Jim Hutton, as her ever-disbelieving husband Alex (a role originally assigned to George Hamilton), is fine in the thankless part and William Demarest (*My Three Sons*) gives solid support as the cranky handyman Mr. Harris who knows more than he lets on.

It is Sally's friend Joan (Barbara Anderson) who surprises the most, however. She is the first to pick up on Sally's sexual frustration and marital stress as the possible cause of all the commotion. Joan's admittance that she shares some of the same problems as Sally opens up an empathy between the two, which explains why Joan ultimately believes Sally's wild tales. Anderson is probably best known for her Emmy-winning role as Eve Whitfield on the *Ironside* series and she shows up in several fright films from the 70s including *SST—Death Flight*.

Writer Nigel McKeand was a sometime

Kim Darby believes gnomes are out to get her in *Don't Be Afraid of the Dark* **(1973).**

actor and did double duty on the film as a demonic voice. Prolific composer Billy Goldenberg is adept at both classical and pop music and has been in demand, providing music for film and television since the mid–60s. His telefright scores include superior work on *Ritual of Evil*, *Duel*, *Terror on the Beach*, *Reflections of Murder*, *The Legend of Lizzie Borden*, *The UFO Incident* and *One of My Wives Is Missing*.

A classic of the era and the genre, *Don't Be Afraid of the Dark* is a must-see for anyone who fears the things that beckon in the dark, that peer from hiding places in the shadows or that whisper in the night,

Dracula

"It's your spirit we want, your spirit we need."

CAST: Kim Darby, Jim Hutton, Barbara Anderson, William Demarest, Pedro Armendariz Jr., Lesley Woods, Robert Cleaves, Sterling Swanson, J.H. Lawrence, William Sylvester, Don Mallon, Celia Kaye, Elizabeth St. Clair, Monica Henreid, Robert Priest, and Ted Swanson. Creatures played by Felix Silla, Tamara DeTreaux, and Patty Maloney.

CREDITS: Director: John Newland; Teleplay: Nigel McKeand; Music: Billy Goldenberg; Production: Lorimar Productions; Automobiles Furnished by Chrysler Corporation; Running Time: 74 minutes; Air Date: 10/10/73; Network: ABC

Dracula

AKA **Bram Stoker's Dracula**

In *Dracula*, director Dan Curtis collaborates once again with writer Richard Matheson. Curtis shot several movies on location in England around this time (see *The Picture of Dorian Gray*, *The Turn of the Screw*) which were aired on American networks. None of these are particularly engaging films, for various reasons, but *Dracula* still splits Curtis's fans due mainly to the casting of Jack Palance in the lead role.

What ultimately makes or breaks a Dracula film is ... Dracula. It is the author's opinion that Jack Palance was miscast as the mighty bloodsucker. But any opinion on this boils down to what one expects of a Dracula. Those who prefer an erudite, cosmopolitan and sophisticated Dracula will find very little of these qualities conveyed by Palance. He looks like a thug in a cape, his underplayed line readings (and occasional accent) are mumbled and his presence in the character seems practically nil. Curtis defended his choice, naturally, but the film proves an unimpressive exercise rather than an inspired interpretation.

The faithfulness of any writer's adaptation of Bram Stoker's famous novel has little or no bearing on the success of a Dracula film, so the usual nitpicking in that regard can be dispensed with. Familiarity with the basic story is a given by now and this version follows the expected course: Dracula comes to England for the food, one of the few tourists to do so.

Overall, the film looks quite nice, although the advantage of the authentic locations is sometimes thwarted by uninspired lighting of the interiors. The supporting cast has few standouts, indeed. Nigel Davenport is adequate as a larger, more vigorous Dr. Van Helsing and Fiona Lewis makes a mighty fetching Lucy. Simon Ward (*Frankenstein Must be Destroyed*), however, is a bland little Arthur Holmwood and one could use the same adjective to describe Penelope Horner as Mina.

Composer Robert Cobert worked extensively with Dan Curtis throughout his career and, in fact, his credits mirror Curtis's with only minor variations. The DVD release of *Dracula* features interviews with Curtis and Palance. For an excellent television Dracula, the Louis Jourdan version *Count Dracula* is recommended.

CAST: Jack Palance, Simon Ward, Nigel Davenport, Pamela Brown, Fiona Lewis, Penelope Horner, Murray Brown, Virginia Wetherall, Barbara Lindley, Sarah Douglas, George Pravda, Hanna Maria Pravda, Reg Lye, Fred Stone, Roy Spencer, John Challis, Nigel Gregory, John Pennington, Martin Read, and Gita Denise.

CREDITS: Director: Dan Curtis; Teleplay: Richard Matheson, based on the book by Bram Stoker; Music: Robert Cobert; Production: Dan Curtis Productions; Running Time: 100 minutes; Air Date: 2/8/74; Network: CBS

Duel

Duel is one of the best and most famous television movies of the golden age. Much has been written about the film, and director Steven Spielberg has, of course, gone on to become a household name. Spielberg followed

Theatrical release poster for *Dracula* (1974).

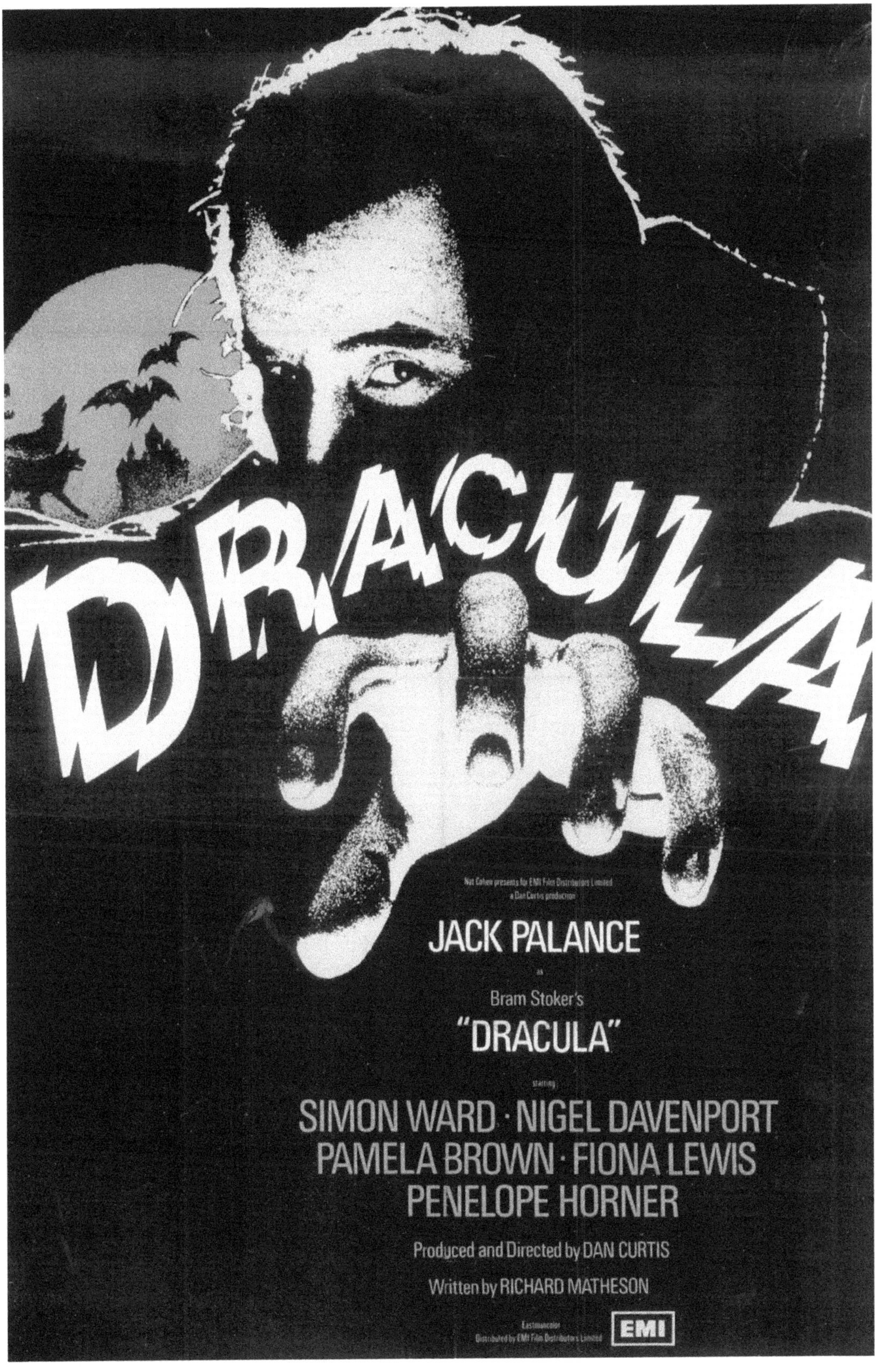

this up the next year with another TV fright film, *Something Evil*, but after *Jaws*, which came out a mere three years later, he would never be able to make a lean film like this again. Surprisingly, the man who has been credited for ushering in the blockbuster (and blamed for the demise of the small Hollywood movie) takes the bare bones of a story and turns it into a classic of terror and suspense.

Everyman David Mann (Dennis Weaver) is driving his Plymouth Valiant (a symbolic steed) across the California desert for a business meeting. Feeling emasculated lately—a fight with his wife about another man's inappropriate attentions—Mann finds himself menaced to a life-threatening point for no reason by an unknown assailant in an old semi-truck. Mann must eventually validate his masculinity by dueling to the death with his faceless tormentor.

The situation strikes a chord with our car-happy culture: in the automobile we have immeasurable freedom of mobility, an empowering sense of who we are and who we'd like to be, and a formidable aphrodisiac at our disposal. Suddenly, we are inexplicably attacked in our precious mini-world by someone or something unknown—something powerful enough, wily enough, to kill us. All drivers have been in minor situations in their cars—accidents, near-accidents, and just moments of inattentiveness—that put our lives somewhere near the line, if not actually on it. The first phrase that comes to mind nowadays is "road rage." *Duel*, however, is more a symbolic battle, not just a little bad blood between commuters.

Duel is a riveting expression of Kafkaesque horror. The vast loneliness of the desert, the deadly seriousness of the situation, and the inability to muster any help combine to make a deep and fearful impression. Richard Matheson's simple story gives Spielberg the chance to concentrate on the mechanics of suspense; the ebb and flow of events is masterfully handled. Dennis Weaver as Mann narrates his thoughts during the ordeal, providing a shape to his (and the viewer's) feelings of self-doubt, anger and futile speculation. The climactic battle culminates in an awesome crash that has left a generation breathless. The film still holds up beautifully today.

In between the life-and-death suspense, there is a fun supporting cast and memorable dialogue to enjoy. Charles Seel is the old guy who asks Mann if he has whiplash, Lucille Benson is the Snakerama lady, Eddie Firestone is the café owner ("Through the door, on the right, down the hall, turn left, second door"), Lou Frizzell is the bus driver ("If I had to vote on who's crazy around here, it'd be you") and Shirley O'Hara is the café waitress.

Weaver, who passed away in 2006, was much beloved by the television-watching public over a career that spanned five decades. Born in Joplin, Missouri, he was a college track star and a Navy pilot. Supporting roles in films gave way to major stardom on television with his character Chester Goode on *Gunsmoke*, a role he played for nine years. His most memorable part in film during that period was as the decidedly odd motel night manager in Orson Welles' *Touch of Evil*. Weaver had other successful television series including *Gentle Ben* and the popular *McCloud*, and remained working and in the public eye until he died. While he did not venture into genre cinema often (*What's the Matter with Helen?*) he did make one other telefright in the 70s, *Terror on the Beach*.

Spielberg gives a fascinating talk about the making of *Duel* on the Universal DVD which is worth the time. The version used for this review contains more material than was originally televised, which was inserted for the Japanese market where *Duel* was released theatrically.

CAST: Dennis Weaver, Jacqueline Scott, Eddie Firestone, Lou Frizzell, Gene Dynarski, Lucille Benson, Tim Herbert, Charles Seel, Shirley O'Hara, Alexander Lockwood, Amy Douglass, Dick Whittington, Carey Loftin, and Dale Van Sickel.

CREDITS: Director: Steven Spielberg; Teleplay: Richard Matheson; Music: Billy Golden-

Theatrical release poster for *Duel* (1971).

The most bizarre murder weapon ever used!

The killer's weapon a 40 ton truck! The victim's only defense a startling trap!

"DUEL"

Starring
DENNIS WEAVER Screenplay by RICHARD MATHESON · Based on his published story
Directed by STEVEN SPIELBERG · Produced by GEORGE ECKSTEIN · A UNIVERSAL PICTURE · TECHNICOLOR®
Distributed by Cinema International Corporation

berg; Production: Universal TV; Running Time: 90 minutes; Air Date: 11/13/71; Network: ABC

Dying Room Only

While driving across the desert, Bob and Jean Mitchell (Dabney Coleman and Cloris Leachman) stop at a lonely roadside café and motel. While Jean is in the restroom, Bob disappears. Jean must then deal with the uncooperative locals who deny seeing her husband leave. Things turn from bad to worse when suddenly Jean's car is driven away, leaving her stranded. Jean manages to contact the sheriff but the lack of any kind of proof of a crime means she must take it upon herself to find her husband.

Richard Matheson's teleplay, from his short story, strikes familiar chords of fear: stuck in the middle of a lonely, unforgiving desert with ill-tempered locals and an unbelieving authority figure. The situation, though light on plot, does make for some tense scenes as Jean struggles against what seem to be impossible odds.

What really helps the film is the good cast. Cloris Leachman shines as Jean, who holds herself together as she comes up against barriers that would make a weaker person simply give up. It's good to see strong female characters overcome adversity, a central theme of television movies from the era.

Ross Martin and Ned Beatty play the rednecks at the café, put upon by the "moron city folk." Martin will, of course, forever be Artemus Gordon of *The Wild, Wild West*, but here he gets to be in a bad mood the entire time and plays it to the hilt. Martin shows up again in another telefright, *Skyway to Death*, before his death of a heart attack in 1981. Beatty plays the ultimate hick. A consummate actor, Beatty could play parts like this with one arm tied behind his back. Late in the game he gets off a good line to Jean: "The only thing I'm gonna regret, lady, is that I'll only have ten minutes alone with you before I kill you."

Not given much to do, Dabney Coleman creates a memorable character who spouts lines such as "These two men happen to be jerks and this ... is a dump." Dana Elcar is the well-meaning but powerless sheriff. At least he wasn't in on the conspiracy too.

This story of frustration has the feel of dream logic at first as Jean's world suddenly turns into a series of unexplainable roadblocks, but a completely satisfying wrap-up is what this film lacks. The ending won't be spoiled here but it is enough to say that it is somewhat disappointing. Low expectations will go a long way towards making this mildly scary film an enjoyable viewing experience.

Director Philip Leacock keeps the tension taut, especially during the first half. Leacock was nominated twice for prizes at the Cannes Film Festival: once for the Grand Prize of the Festival for *The Kidnappers* and once for the Golden Palm for *High Tide at Noon*. In the 60s, Leacock settled primarily into television, working on the popular shows of the day. His telefrights in the 70s include *When Michael Calls* and *Killer on Board*.

Composer Charles Fox was twice nominated for Oscars (*The Other Side of the Mountain*, *Foul Play*) and won two Emmys, both for *Love American Style*. Among his many credits are *Barbarella*, *The Green Slime*, *The Drowning Pool* (the song "Killing Me Softly with His Song"), *Bug* and the telefrights *Women in Chains* and *The Stranger Within*.

CAST: Cloris Leachman, Ross Martin, Ned Beatty, Dana Elcar, Louise Latham, Dabney Coleman, and Ron Feinberg.

CREDITS: Director: Philip Leacock; Teleplay: Richard Matheson, based on his short story; Music: Charles Fox; Production: Lorimar Film Entertainment; Automobiles Furnished by Chevrolet Motor Division; Running Time: 71 minutes; Air Date: 9/18/73; Network: ABC

The Elevator

Thieves Pete Howarth (Don Stroud) and Eddie Holcomb (James Farantino) rob an investment company in a high-rise building. While making their getaway, they become separated when Pete won't fit in the elevator that Eddie boards with the money. When mechanical failure disables the elevator, Eddie's claustrophobia threatens the survival of his fellow passengers. Meanwhile, Pete and Eddie's girlfriend Irene (Carol Lynley) make their way back into the building—which has been closed for a holiday weekend—in order to retrieve the money.

The term "disaster movie" may loom a bit large in describing the scale of events in *The Elevator*. There is definitely group peril but the crime elements that surround the basic premise add much-needed dimension to a confining plot. The film plays on several everyday fears: shoddy construction practices, amoral business decisions and the everyday criminality in our midst—not to mention being trapped in an elevator!

Despite expectations to the contrary, *The Elevator* is a fairly tense exercise with occasional outbursts of cold-hearted violence. Director Jerry Jameson does a good job of creating action in the tight space and has a solid, if not particularly star-filled cast to put through the wringer. Jameson began his work in television in the late 1960s directing episodes of the various popular series of the day before becoming a telefilm specialist beginning in the mid-70s. His ventures into theatrical features have not been universally applauded (*The Bat People, Airport '77, Raise the Titanic*) but some of his few telefrights are capable: *Hurricane* and *A Fire in the Sky* are a cut above although *Terror on the 40th Floor* seems tired.

The cross-section of humanity in *The Elevator* includes lonely old lady Amanda (Myrna Loy), frustrated building manager Marvin (Roddy McDowall), stubborn teen Robert (Barry Livingston) and his mom (Jean Allison). Dr. Reynolds (Craig Stevens) and his wife Edith (Teresa Wright) are also trapped with the doc's secretary-lover Wendy (Arlene Golonka).

Lies (and the lying liars who tell them) seem to be the main theme here. From the construction workers who must have lied about the safety and readiness of the elevators to the lies of the building managers about the advantages and facilities of the property (Roddy has an amusing moment of confession about the building being made of lies). Amanda lies about her reasons to view a penthouse suite while the doctor is lying to his wife by having an affair. Even the boy feels lied to by his mother about his inheritance.

As far as the criminal element goes, James Farentino as Eddie does a pretty good job of panicking as does his girlfriend Carol Lynley. But the real winner here is ruthless killer Pete. Don Stroud, ever the bad guy, plays Pete with a callousness rarely seen on the tube at the time and has the honor of being the center of the most terrifying scene in the film: After Pete and Irene rescue Eddie from the elevator shaft, Eddie reveals that the folks in the elevator saw the gun and money. Pete grabs a blowtorch (the building is still under construction) and proceeds to burn through the elevator cable while the helpless group watches him through the trap door in the ceiling. It's a shocker and Stroud wins the award for most cold-blooded killer on television that year.

Stroud has played unrepentant villains most of his career. He was born in Hawaii, growing up on the beaches to become the fourth-ranked surfer in the world. When tapped to be Troy Donahue's stunt double in the series *Hawaiian Eye*, Stroud caught the acting bug and moved to Hollywood, working at the famed Whisky A Go-Go nightclub. His first role was as a sheepherder in the Doris Day vehicle *The Ballad of Josie* in 1967 and he would go on to menace the hero in film and television for the next 30 years. Among his many credits are the underrated Curtis Harrington thriller *Games*, *Bloody Mama*, *Murph the Surf* (as Murph), *Death Weekend* aka *The House by the Lake* and *The Amityville Horror*. Stroud has a Black Belt in Karate and, in 1973, posed nude for *Playgirl* magazine. At the end of the millennium he returned to Hawaii where he now resides. His other telefrights include *Deadly Dream* and *Express to Terror*.

As expected, *The Elevator* comes to a righteous conclusion. Pete gets his just deserts, shot down in the parking garage, spilling the money in true film noir style. Eddie and Irene are caught and the rest of the folks escape death. Viewers still in doubt are advised that they could do worse than watch this fast-moving bit of entertainment.

It may surprise some to learn that this nail-biter was co-written by Dave Ketchum, better known for his comedic work as Agent 13 in the *Get Smart* series where he was forever stuffed into odd spaces on his assignments. Ketchum may also be recognized as "Murph" in a series of commercials for Union 76 gas stations that aired in the 70s and 80s. Composer John Cacavas contributed the score for this and other telefrights, namely *She Cried Murder* and *SST—Death Flight*. Among his theatrical genre credits are *Horror Express*, *The Satanic Rites of Dracula* and *Mortuary*.

CAST: James Farentino, Roddy McDowall, Craig Stevens, Don Stroud, Teresa Wright, Myrna Loy, Carol Lynley, Arlene Golonka, Barry Livingston, Jean Allison, Paul Sorensen, Ed Deemer, Will J. White, Jack Griffin, and Jason Wingreen.

CREDITS: Director: Jerry Jameson; Teleplay: Bruce Shelly & David Ketchum; Music: John Cacavas; Production: Universal TV; Running Time: 79 minutes; Air Date: 2/9/74; Network: ABC

Express to Terror

If one was looking for the nadir of Dan Curtis's 1970s output, look no further. *Express to Terror* is the home video release title of the pilot for Curtis's short-lived *Supertrain* series, about a state-of-the-art cross-country express train and the unfortunates caught riding it. Apparently the idea was to make a *Love Boat* on wheels and, based on the result, it is understandable why it didn't catch on.

It is the inaugural run of Supertrain, a nuclear-powered, high-tech train traveling from New York to Los Angeles. Among the mindless disco-revelers aboard is Mike Post (Steve Lawrence) who is making the trip to pay off his substantial gambling debts in LA. Post begins fearing for his life when several unexplained accidents lead him to believe the mob is out for his blood. With the help of his drunkard friend Rick Prince (Don Meredith) and his newfound love, air-head Cindy (Char Fontane), Mike manages to accomplish very little of interest.

Lawrence seems simply befuddled here and Meredith as his besotted friend is just simple. Cindy, the love interest, is menaced by Don Stroud as her criminal boyfriend. Smaller roles and cameos are supplied by Keenan Wynn, Vicki Lawrence, George Hamilton, Stella Stevens, Fred "Hammer" Williamson and Robert Alda. Most, if not all of this cast are utterly wasted and working well beneath their capabilities.

With its disco theme, utter lack of suspense or frightful events and what seems to be drug-addled plotting, *Express to Terror* is a prime example of the worst entertainment excesses of the era's television offerings. It is mind-numbingly terrible, an embarrassment on all levels; the pilot and the series have been deservedly forgotten. Its scary title and pedigree were the reasons the film has been included and as a warning in case a Curtis fan was tempted to make the big mistake of watching this entertainment crime.

The astute may notice that famous voice artist Paul Frees is the (uncredited) engineer of the train.

CAST: Steve Lawrence, Char Fontane, Don Stroud, Keenan Wynn, Deborah Benson, Ron Masak, Don Meredith, Vicki Lawrence, George Hamilton, Stella Stevens, Fred Williamson, Edward Andrews, Patrick Collins, Harrison Page, Robert Alda, Nita Talbot, Aarika Wells, William Nuckols, Michael Delano, Charlie Brill, John Karlen, Frank R. Christi, H.M. Wynant, Anthony Palmer, Howard Honig, Allen Williams, Parley Baer, Sid Conrad, Robert Karnes, Cameron Young, Sylvester Words, Orin Cannon, Chuck Mitchell, and Bert Conway. Uncredited: Paul Frees

CREDITS: Director: Dan Curtis; Teleplay: Earl W. Wallace, from a story by Donald E. Westlake & Earl W. Wallace; Music: Bob

Cobert; Production: Dan Curtis Productions; Running Time: 95 minutes; Air Date: 2/7/79; Network: NBC

The Eyes of Charles Sand

As the sole surviving son of his family, wealthy stock broker Charles Sand (Peter Haskell) inherits a special gift called "The Sight," a unique type of extra sensory perception. After witnessing several bizarre visions, Sand becomes embroiled in a murder mystery, and harnesses his gift to ferret out the culprits in a family plot.

First shown on leap day 1972, *The Eyes of Charles Sand* was obviously intended as a series pilot but it didn't get picked up, making this the one and only tale of the reluctant psychic investigator. Since this is a murder mystery it would be unfair to reveal too much of the plot, but in a nutshell, Sand is stalked by Emily Parkhurst (Sharon Farrell) who claims that her brother has been killed by her elder sister Katherine (Barbara Rush) and Katherine's husband Jeffrey (Bradford Dillman). The family's explanation that Emily is suffering from degenerating mental health is then called into question by Sand.

The film opens with a genuinely frightening dream sequence. On a dark set a coffin lies surrounded by a circle of lit candelabras. Off to the side stands Charles Sand, his eyes illuminated by spotlight. He walks to the casket and opens it to reveal an old man. Suddenly, the man opens his eyes—which are solid white orbs—and sits up, pointing accusingly at Sand, who then wakes up in a start. The phone rings and it is Sand's aunt Alexandra (Joan Bennett, *Suspiria*) who tells him that her husband, Sand's uncle, has just died. Sand's life has just changed and, although he is reluctant to accept the gift, there's no denying that it will impact him in ways he cannot conceive of or change.

Dripping with gothic atmosphere and supported by several creepy set pieces and a couple of good shocks, *The Eyes of Charles Sand* would seem to have a lot going for it. But this is simply a common plot trussed up with supernatural bows. Director Reza S. Badiyi is more concerned with visuals than with reining in the actors. This is evident in the unbridled performances, particularly that of Sharon Farrell, whose Emily quickly becomes an annoying parody of insanity. The film takes a chaotic turn about an hour in when the *real* crazy person in the family

Bradford Dillman and Barbara Rush plot to seize an inheritance in *The Eyes of Charles Sand* **(1972).**

goes off the deep end, raging through the old, dark house with a large knife. All in all *The Eyes of Charles Sand* is an amusing watch that had potential but its weaknesses outweigh its strengths.

Peter Haskell gives a comparatively low-key performance as the burdened Sand. His career has been concentrated largely in television since the mid–60s (landing the short-lived *Bracken's World* series in 1969) with only the occasional foray into film (he has appeared in two of the *Child's Play* horror franchise films, for instance). He can also be seen in *The Phantom of Hollywood* and *The Night They Took Miss Beautiful*. Sharon Farrell was a fixture on television in the 60s and 70s and although she didn't appear in any other 70s telefrights, she has a few interesting film credits including *It's Alive*, *The Premonition*, the cult hit *The Stunt Man* and *Night of the Comet*.

Barbara Rush will be familiar to fans of 1950s science fiction for her roles in *When Worlds Collide* and *It Came from Outer Space*. Beginning in the 60s, she has worked primarily and steadily in television including stints on the daytime serials *Peyton Place* and *All My Children*. Her other telefrights are *Moon of the Wolf* and *Death Car on the Freeway*.

Solid, Yale-educated journeyman Bradford Dillman began his acting career with a bang when he won a Theater World Award for his role in *Long Day's Journey into Night* on Broadway in 1956. He bested that when he moved into film, taking the top acting prize at Cannes for *Compulsion* in 1959. What followed has been a long career in supporting and lead roles, villains and heroes, in both film and television. His genre credits include *Monstrosity* aka *The Atomic Brain* (as narrator only), *Escape from the Planet of the Apes*, *The Resurrection of Zachary Wheeler*, *Bug*, *The Swarm* and *Piranha* and the telefrights *Five Desperate Women*, *Revenge!*, *Moon of the Wolf*, *Last Bride of Salem* and *The Disappearance of Flight 412*. In 1997, Dillman published an amusing and recommended collection of anecdotes entitled *Are You Anybody?: An Actor's Life*.

Adam West (*Batman*) has a small part as Sand's psychiatrist friend Paul Scott and there's an even smaller part for famous cowboy Donald "Red" Barry as Scott's horse trainer. Writer Henry Farrell penned the novels that inspired the films *What Ever Happened to Baby Jane?*, *Hush ... Hush, Sweet Charlotte* and the telefright *How Awful About Allan*. He also wrote the screenplay for *What's the Matter With Helen?* and the teleplay for *The House That Would Not Die*. There is no music credit on *The Eyes of Charles Sand* but apparently Henry Mancini sued (and won) over the unauthorized use of his music for *Wait Until Dark*.

CAST: Peter Haskell, Barbara Rush, Sharon Farrell, Bradford Dillman, Adam West, Joan Bennett, Ivor Francis, Gary Clarke, Owen Bush, Donald Barry, and Larry Levine.

CREDITS: Director: Reza S. Badiyi; Teleplay: Henry Farrell and Stanford Whitmore, from a story by Henry Farrell; Music: Henry Mancini (uncredited); Production: Warner Bros. Television; Running Time: 74 minutes; Air Date: 2/29/72; Network: ABC

Family Flight

David Carlyle (Kristoffer Tabori) returns to his parents' house after 18 months away just as they are about to fly in their small plane from San Diego to Guaymas, Mexico with a family friend—and David's ex-girlfriend—Carol Rutledge (Janet Margolin). During the flight the weather turns bad and, with the radio knocked out of commission by lightning and the compass not working, they are forced to land in the middle of the Baja desert. The plane is only slightly damaged so they decide to build a runway and attempt to fly out but more obstacles lie ahead for the family.

This survival story features Rod Taylor and Dina Merrill as the parents, Jason and Florence Carlyle. For the most part, *Family Flight* takes a logical, realistic approach to the perilous events it portrays until the final reel, when it takes a detour into the land of extreme coincidences. Four-time Emmy-winning director Marvin Chomsky (*Evel*

Knievel) pays particular attention to detail and coaxes good and even sometimes affecting performances from his cast.

As far as family drama goes, David is haunted by the death of Carol's brother who fell out of a dune buggy David was driving. The event zapped David's self-confidence which is why he disappeared for a year and a half. For her part, Carol has come to terms with the grief and helps David in that regard. Dad Jason is an ex–Navy pilot with notions of manhood that may be old-fashioned but which help the family survive under the unusual and trying circumstances. Mom Florence is an alcoholic driven to drink by the loss of her sense of self under the smothering pressure of being Jason's wife, not to mention the trauma of not knowing where her son was all those months.

None of these family problems are treated sensationally, however, and the realistic interpersonal relationships make us care that the family holds together when worse comes to worse. Take for instance the confrontation between father and son near the end of the film. The night before the planned takeoff on the desert runway that has taken four days to build, David falls asleep with the plane's radio on, which wears the battery down to nothing. Unable to start the plane, Jason strikes out in anger at his son. Instead of a fistfight, the boy merely breaks down and cries, an unusual and truthful reaction.

Realism also wins out in scenes such as Florence's withdrawal when her vodka runs out, the capturing of water in the desert by using a plastic sheet and a cup, and in having to eat raw snake (cooking it would suck the moisture out of the meat).

Conversely, the final scenes stretch credibility to the maximum. Jason is injured when turning the prop by hand to get the plane started so David flies them out. This large victory is undermined when David flies in the wrong direction and takes the plane 80 miles out to sea. As luck would have it, an aircraft carrier spots the plane and the finale has David, running out of gas, attempting to land the plane on the ship. The family's luck holds out even in this far-fetched scenario, although the viewer's suspension of disbelief may fly out the window.

The desert scenes were filmed in Lucerne Valley, California, and the aircraft carrier that saves the day is the USS *Ranger*, CVA-61, out of San Diego. The impressive flying sequences, and there are several, are credited to one-legged stunt pilot Frank Tallman who died in a plane crash in 1978. Ed Begley, Jr. has a cameo as a hitchhiker David picks up on his way to the most unusual and stressful vacation of his life.

Writer Guerdon Trueblood was somewhat of a telefright specialist in the 1970s with credits for *Sole Survivor*, *The Savage Bees*, *SST—Death Flight*, *It Happened at Lakewood Manor*, *Tarantulas: The Deadly Cargo* and *Terror Out of the Sky*. He also wrote the story for *Jaws 3-D* (for which he was nominated for a Razzie Award for Worst Screenplay), acted in the subtle horror film *Meatcleaver Massacre* and directed the interesting cult crime film *The Candy Snatchers*. Oscar-nominated composer (for *The Color Purple*) Fred Steiner wrote music for many *Twilight Zone* and *Star Trek* episodes and the telefright *Night Terror*.

CAST: Rod Taylor, Dina Merrill, Kristoffer Tabori, Janet Margolin, Gene Nelson, Richard Roat, Paul Kent, James Sikking, Bill Zuckert, Ed Begley, Jr., and Arnold Turner.

CREDITS: Director: Marvin Chomsky; Teleplay: Guerdon Trueblood; Music: Fred Steiner; Production: Universal TV; Running Time: 74 minutes; Air Date: 10/25/72; Network: ABC

Fer de Lance

AKA **Death Dive; Operation Serpent**

While the Navy submarine *Fer de Lance* is docked somewhere in South America to pick up a team of SeaLab scientists, a sailor buys a basket full of poisonous baby snakes and brings it back aboard the sub. The snakes escape and begin biting the crew. Then, sickened crew members at the helm cause the sub to become lodged in the ocean floor. Chief Officer Russ Bogan (David Janssen) must get his sub untangled while battling the deadly serpents.

Amazingly enough, this disaster-horror hybrid has quite the pedigree: It was written by the famed Leslie Stevens, creator of the landmark television series *The Outer Limits*, who somehow convinced *OL* alumni composer Dominic Frontiere (who did the music here as well) to executive produce. The genesis of the story idea is in question. It could have been alcohol-induced inspiration or perhaps a desperate move to avoid paying taxes. Single jeopardy for the submarine crew apparently wasn't enough to get the project off the ground, hence the combined threat that ups the proverbial ante.

Stevens sold his first play when he was 15. His career in film and television, as writer-producer-director, took off in the mid–1950s, and throughout the next two decades he was involved, in one way or another, with several of the more successful television series of the era. His most potent contribution to television was, of course, *The Outer Limits* in the early 60s. Stevens' most interesting project in the film world was *Incubus*, an occult "magic realism" story he wrote and directed, which starred a pre–*Star Trek* William Shatner. What makes the film unique to American cinema was the decision to have the dialogue spoken in Esperanto, the "international language" developed in the late 19th century. The only copy of the film known to exist was located recently in a French archive and released to DVD.

Unfortunately, in the case of *Fer de Lance*, journeyman television director Russell Mayberry is unable to make a silk purse out of the sow's ear that Stevens handed him. A couple of "name" cast members (Janssen and Hope Lange as SeaLab doctor Arlene Wedell) cannot eclipse the ridiculous premise. There are also lackadaisical performances, unimaginative visuals and silly plot contrivances (the unhinged crew member who starts shooting at the snakes, for instance). To top it off, for some reason the film was padded out for a two-hour time slot. The drama and excitement of handling two disasters was obviously more than could be squeezed into a 90-minute slot.

The only remarkable thing about *Fer de Lance* is, unfortunately, the story idea. There is really nothing here—aside from Janssen's frequent requests for brandy—that will amuse or entertain the viewer.

Nebraska-born Janssen was one of the most popular television stars of the 60s and 70s. His low-key, even angst-ridden demeanor struck a chord with the public and kept the actor very busy until his death of a heart attack in 1980. The early 50s were, for Janssen, a time of forgettable B pictures (*Cult of the Cobra* being the only genre exception) but he hit it big on television with the *Richard Diamond, Private Detective* series at the end of the decade. In the mid–60s his star went even higher when he landed his most memorable role as Dr. Richard Kimble in *The Fugitive*, the final episode of which was watched by more people than any other program in the then-history of television. His other popular, if not as long-running, series were *O'Hara, U.S. Treasury* and *Harry O* and his telefrights include *Moon of the Wolf* and *Mayday at 40,000 Feet*.

The supporting cast consists of relatively minor players and untalented unknowns. Frank Bonner (*WKRP in Cincinnati*) plays Compton, the thoughtless snake buyer and other recognizable actors are Ivan Dixon (*Hogan's Heroes*) and Jason Evers (*The Brain That Wouldn't Die*). Dominic Frontiere contributed scores to the telefrights *Revenge!* and *Haunts of the Very Rich*. *Fer de Lance* was released to theaters in Britain under the title *Death Dive*.

CAST: David Janssen, Hope Lange, Ivan Dixon, Jason Evers, Charles Knox Robinson, George Pan, Robert Ito, Ben Piazza, William Mims, Shizuko Hoshi, Frank Bonner, Richard Le Pore, Sandra Ego, Felipe Turich, Alain Patrick, Robert Burr, Richard Guthrie, Phillip Montgomery, Elvenn Harvard, and Bill Catching.

CREDITS: Director: Russell Mayberry; Teleplay: Leslie Stevens; Music: Dominic Frontiere;

Production: Leslie Stevens Productions; Running Time: 98 minutes; Air Date: 10/18/74; Network: CBS

Fire!

Fire! is another Irwin Allen–produced disaster movie, following closely on his previous year's *Flood!* (also directed by Earl Bellamy). It comes late in the 70s cycle of television disasters but Allen would try one more before the decade was out, the cable-car knuckle-biter *Hanging by a Thread*. An edited version of *Fire!* and *Flood!* would later be paired together by NBC as television's first disaster double-bill.

Larry Durant (Neville Brand), a prisoner on work detail in the forest, starts a fire as a means of escape. His plan is foiled but the fire, which was thought to be extinguished, rekindles into a full-blown raging inferno endangering not only the forest but also the nearby community.

Ernest Borgnine is Sam Brisbane, a lumber mill owner lusting after Martha Wagner (Vera Miles) who runs a nearby lodge. Alex and Peggy Wilson (Alex Cord [*The Dead are Alive*] and Patty Duke Astin) are practically-divorced doctors brought back together by the adversity. Donna Mills is Harriett Malone, a teacher who loses one of her kids near the fire and spends much of the film on the couch at the lodge, and Lloyd Nolan is the old doctor. Walt Fleming (Ty Hardin) runs a prison farm that houses convicts Durant and Frank (the soon-to-be-famous Erik Estrada, *CHiPs*).

Ty Hardin's off-screen life is more in-

The romance between Vera Miles and Ernest Borgnine is jeopardized in *Fire!* (1977).

teresting than the films he's made. He was born in New York City and was raised in Texas. His break in films came with a contract with Paramount who put him in B pictures in the 1950s such as Jack Arnold's *The Space Children* and the classic *I Married a Monster from Outer Space*. When Clint Walker threatened to walk out on his popular television series *Cheyenne*, Warner Bros. stepped in and hired Hardin as a bargaining chip, giving him the role of Bronco Layne. When Walker reconciled with the studio, Hardin continued in a series of his own called *Bronco* which ran for four years. After a few movie roles (*Wall of Noise*, *Palm Springs Weekend*), Hardin moved to Europe in the mid-60s and starred in several interesting films such as Sergio Corbucci's violent spy flick *Moving Target* and the Joan Crawford British shocker *Berserk!* When his cinematic capital ran out in the early 70s, Ty turned to entrepreneurship which resulted in his bust for selling hashish in Spain in 1974. Back in the US, about the time of this film, Ty had turned to evangelical religion and radical politics, leading a group of "freedom fighters" called the Arizona Patriots who preached anti–Semitism and tax evasion. The organization was raided by the FBI in 1986 and Ty managed to escape prosecution. While he did make a few forgettable films in the 90s, Hardin is effectively retired from show business.

Fire! is a by-the-numbers disaster film, predictable even to the point of the type of parody that fueled the theatrical comedy *Airplane!* just a couple of years later. Most of the cast appears to be simply marking time, keeping their faces in front of a public that was probably not watching anyway. Borgnine is the only one who's even trying but the Oscar winner can't help it, he always gives 110 percent.

Vera Miles lent her considerable talents to the telefrights *A Howling in the Woods*, *The Strange and Deadly Occurrence* and *Smash-Up on Interstate 5* and Patty Duke Astin shows up in *She Waits*, *Curse of the Black Widow*, *Killer on Board* and *Hanging by a Thread*.

Just about any time a helicopter made an appearance in television in the 1970s or 80s, it was piloted by James W. Gavin. Besides handling the flying chores, Gavin often took on stunts, second unit photography, aerial coordination and even acting (as he did here) on many productions, too often with no credit. He is the founder of the Motion Picture Pilots Association and also worked extensively in the film world (*Vanishing Point*, *Hickey & Boggs*, *Blue Thunder*, and *Firefox*, to name just a very few). His telefrights include *Flood!*, *Disaster on the Coastliner*, *The President's Plane Is Missing*, *Fer de Lance*, *Hanging by a Thread* and *The Stranger*, among others. Gavin's passing in 2005 was not related to any aerial accident.

Fire! was filmed in Yamhill, Oregon, a picturesque location that adds some interest to the tired proceedings. But for a television disaster fix, *Flood!* or *Hurricane* offer more entertainment value than this burned-out example.

CAST: Ernest Borgnine, Vera Miles, Patty Duke Astin, Alex Cord, Donna Mills, Lloyd Nolan, Neville Brand, Ty Hardin, Gene Evans, Erik Estrada, Michelle Stacy, Patrick Culliton, and James W. Gavin.

CREDITS: Director: Earl Bellamy; Teleplay: Norman Katkov and Arthur Weiss, from a story by Norman Katkov; Music: Richard LaSalle; Production: Irwin Allen Productions; Running Time: 98 minutes; Air Date: 5/8/77; Network: NBC

A Fire in the Sky

Astronomers Jason Voight (Richard Crenna) and Jennifer Dreiser (Joanna Miles) try to warn Phoenix, Arizona, of the impending impact of a comet while the government and the local media wrestle with creating a useless panic and the people's right to know. In the biggest "I told you so" of the century, Phoenix is demolished.

A Fire in the Sky was billed as television's biggest special effects extravaganza up to that time. Press releases claimed the use of a record 5,700 extras and that the miniature work in the destruction scenes was the most extensive ever. The three-hour television event was later nominated for two Emmys for Film Sound Editing and Creative Technical Crafts. Nearly 30 years later, the filmmakers' technical accomplishments are the weakest aspect of this disaster movie, long surpassed by the capabilities of the computer in generating images of believable devastation. Fortunately for the 21st-century viewer, *A Fire in the Sky* is still one of the best examples of its ilk in the areas of writing and acting.

Richard Crenna, in his bearded phase, is the unorthodox scientist, Voight, who, when the president calls, says, "Take his number, tell him I'll call him back." When the news breaks, Voight is commanded by the president (Andrew Duggan) to work with fellow scientist and good-looker Jennifer Dreiser (Joanna Miles), who had discovered the comet. The relationship is cantankerous at first but it soon warms to resemble love. Crenna and Miles have a good chemistry together as they fight to be allowed to warn the population of impending doom.

Crenna's descriptions of the holocaust—the explosion will disintegrate every building within 100 miles, it will be followed by an earthquake and hurricane-force winds that will blow the rubble around (and it gets more descriptive once he is allowed on television)—are convincing and terrifying. Incensed by the soft-pedaling news conference given by the Arizona governor ("I've heard weather reports more frightening than that"), Voight visits the governor (Nicolas Coster) and his family at their home to convince him of the seriousness of the situation. When the governor's little girl asks what a comet is, Voight goes over the line, explaining, "A comet is a mindless chunk of rock and ice and this one's going to hurt your mother and your father and all of your friends."

The governor and his slimy advisor Mac (Kip Niven) are trying to keep a lid on the looming disaster for the usual reasons of preventing panic and needless expense. The local media are represented by acquiescent newspaper publisher David Allan (David Dukes) and his wife, defiant television station owner Sharon Allan (Elizabeth Ashley). The married couple were each given a media outlet by her daddy to run as they see fit and Sharon wants to break the story while David goes along with the governor. Sharon and David have more of an understanding than a marriage and in fact, Sharon used David's lover, journalist Carol (Maggie Wellman, out of her acting league), to get the scoop about the comet out of David. Although threatened with loss of her FCC license, Sharon eventually puts Voight on the air which causes the panic but also saves many lives. The much-overlooked Ashley gives a standout performance, one of the best in the film.

The military believes it can destroy the comet while it is still in space traveling at 40 kilometers per second. A Titan rocket is launched and, in a television event of its own, misses the target, twice. When this happens, the 1.25 million population all try to leave Phoenix at the same time.

Side stories include that of Stan Webster (ex-footballer Merlin Olsen), who takes a group of kids camping in the desert prior to the comet news breaking. The survival-oriented trip means no radio so the group is ignorant of what's happening. Eventually, they figure it out and dig holes in the ground to survive. Later when the National Guard picks them up, Stan asks about going back to Phoenix and the soldier remarks, "There ain't no such place any more."

Also, poor cowboy Tom Reardon (a young Michael Biehn) wants to marry wealthy Paula Gilliam (Cindy Eilbacher) but he has to get the idea past Paula's uptight dad Paul (Lloyd Bochner), who, by the name he gave his daughter, wishes he had had a son. Bochner is terrific as the constantly antagonized Paul who bursts with dialogue gems such as "This land was never meant for anything but Indians and snakes." His best scene is the dinner where Tom announces his intention to marry Paula. Paul is livid, explaining that Paula will not be marrying the "redneck aborigine" but attending Radcliff where "she'll meet people who breed horses, not bounce all over them." Bochner's reading of his final line to Tom is priceless: "The crepes *a la* Lorraine are excellent; I recommend you try them." Needless to say, Paula stays behind to be with her redneck aborigine instead of fleeing with her parents.

The devastation of Phoenix comes well after the two-hour mark (without commercials) but the sequence now looks very cheap and unconvincing, which is no reflection on the talent of the artists who created it. The style is reminiscent of similar scenes of destruction found in genre offerings from the early 60s sword-and-sandal epics or science fiction movies. Reportedly the sequence lasted four minutes in the film's original airing but was chopped to two minutes thereafter. In the copy used for this review, a TNT cable showing, the destruction lasted about two minutes, fifteen seconds.

The newspaper named in the film is *The Phoenix Sun Times*, a now-defunct local paper, not the major outlet the movie suggests, and the television station used is KTAR, the actual NBC affiliate in Phoenix. Those familiar with the Phoenix of the 1970s will recognize the few local landmarks that existed for the filmmakers to "destroy" in downtown at the time, the Civic Plaza and the Hyatt-Regency Hotel among them. Another kind of Phoenix landmark, local actor Pat MacMahon, has a small role as the TV news director. MacMahon is much-beloved for his clever characters on the long-running local kid show, *Wallace and Ladmo*.

CAST: Richard Crenna, Elizabeth Ashley, David Dukes, Joanna Miles, (ao) Lloyd Bochner, William Bogert, Nicolas Coster, Diana Douglas, Andrew Duggan, Marj Dusay, Cindy Eilbacher, John Larch, Kip Niven, Jenny O'Hara, Merlin Olsen, and Maggie Wellman. Also Michael Biehn, Bill Williams, Al White, George Petrie, Elta Blake, Roy Gainter, Pat MacMahon, Cecelia Allen, Dino Bachelor, Hank Hendrick, Bill Heywood, Burke Rhind, Brad Zinn, and Bud Conlon. CREDITS: Director: Jerry Jameson; Teleplay: Dennis Nemec and Michael Blankfort, from a story by Paul Gallico; Music: Paul Chihara; Production: Columbia Pictures Television; Running Time: 150 minutes; Air Date: 11/26/78; Network: NBC

Five Desperate Women

An escapee from a mental hospital kills an employee of an isolated island resort and takes his place. Five women book the island for their reunion and when one of them is killed, they realize they are in mortal danger from a homicidal maniac. But it is unclear whether it is the boat captain, Jim Meeker (Bradford Dillman), or the caretaker, Michael Wylie (Robert Conrad), who threatens them.

Five Desperate Women sports one of the finer ensemble casts of the era's genre films. Julie Sommars (*Matlock*) is Mary Grace, who seeks to escape a cloying relationship with her invalid mother. Denise Nicholas (*Room 222*) is Joy, a promising intellectual who has resorted to prostitution. Joan Hackett is Dorian, a pathological liar due mainly to her inferiority complex. Anjanette Comer is Lucy, a whiny alcoholic, and Stefanie Powers is Gloria, beautiful but frigid.

Powers was born in Hollywood and, seemingly, born to stardom. She had a contract with Columbia at the tender age of 15 and her popularity, particularly in television, has hardly abated since the early 1960s. Although associated with fluff such as *Tammy Tell Me True* and *Palm Springs Weekend* early in her career, genre fans prefer her roles in Blake Edwards' *Experiment in Terror* and the Hammer film *Fanatic* aka *Die! Die! My Darling!* during the same period. As April Dancer in *The Girl from U.N.C.L.E.*, Powers' celebrity in television was assured, even though that series was short-lived. In the 70s, between television assignments, she was back with Hammer Films for *Crescendo* and then made the little-known *Invisible Strangler* before landing her most popular series *Hart to Hart* with Robert Wagner. Powers' telefrights include *Sweet, Sweet Rachel*, *Paper Man* and *Skyway to Death*.

Unfortunately, the women are pigeonholed caricatures and the capable actors aren't given much of a chance to shine. Given that all of these ladies are attractive yet seriously flawed, it's a shame time does not allow the opportunity to get under their skin a bit more before the terrorizing begins. This also means there is no one to really identify with or for the women to play off of since none of them are very well adjusted or defined.

The male contingent is interesting but stuck in the same boat. The filmmakers do a good job of keeping us in suspense as to the identity of the maniac and both Robert Conrad and Bradford Dillman are actors who have a disingenuous quality so that casting works well. But since both actors have to be suspicious for the bulk of the film, we're not allowed into their characters either.

Director Ted Post had a better feel for the folksiness of *Dr. Cook's Garden* than he seems to have for a group of neurotics; perhaps with a longer running time he could have made a more satisfying whole. The first hour of the film is promising as the suspense is built up but the last act is an unconvincing letdown. There is enough of merit in *Five Desperate Women* to recommend a watch for fans of the actors as long as the viewer doesn't expect a classic.

Co-writer Marc Norman would go on to win an Oscar for *Shakespeare in Love* and his partner on this film, Walter Black, wrote for several animated cartoon shows in the 1960s including *The Jetsons*, *The Flintstones*, *Jonny Quest* and *Space Ghost*. Composer Paul Glass scored many episodes of *Night Gallery*, the telefright *Sole Survivor* and the Hammer film *To the Devil a Daughter*.

CAST: (ao) Anjanette Comer, Bradford Dillman, Joan Hackett, Denise Nicholas, Stefanie Powers, and Julie Sommars. Also Robert Conrad, Connie Sawyer, and Beatrice Manley.

CREDITS: Director: Ted Post; Teleplay: Marc Norman and Walter Black, from a story by Larry Gordon; Music: Paul Glass; Production: Aaron Spelling Productions; Running Time: 74 minutes; Air Date: 9/28/71; Network: ABC

Flood!

One step above director Earl Bellamy's other elemental disaster film *Fire!*, *Flood!* tells the tale of greed trumping logic, resulting in the "I told you so" catastrophe guaranteed by the title. This time the officials of the resort town of Brownsville, Oregon don't want to relieve the bulging dam because it would spoil the fishing and therefore the economy.

Paul Blake (Martin Milner) is the Chicken Little of the movie, warning deaf ears of impending doom. He's sweet on Mary Cutler (Barbara Hershey) whose father John (Richard Basehart) is the town mayor and Paul's major adversary. Top-billed Robert Culp is Steve Brannigan, rogue helicopter pilot-turned-hero, and Cameron Mitchell is Sam Adams who is in charge of the dam. Sam's pregnant wife Abbie (Carol Lynley) has picked a bad time to go into labor and gets stuck in her house with the water rising. Mayor John's young son Andy (Eric Olson) manages to get himself trapped right where an explosion is planned to stem the flow of water.

The usual human drama precedes the pandemonium, which manifests itself as a combination of some fairly impressive miniature work, stock footage and cheapskate, stage-bound water tank action. There are bit parts for Roddy McDowall as a not-very-convincing fisherman, future teen heartthrob Leif Garrett (see also *Black Noon*) and Gloria Stuart, who graced the early horror films *The Old Dark House* and *The Invisible Man* and, of course, the phenomenon known as *Titanic*.

Martin Milner tends to be overlooked for his work in telefilms but he generally gives good performances, as he does here and in *Runaway!*, *Hurricane* and *SST—Death Flight*. Richard Basehart plays the villain as he does in *Sole Survivor* and *Maneater* and Roddy McDowall shows up in *Terror in the Sky*, *A Taste of Evil* and *The Elevator*.

Cameron Mitchell has risen to the status of icon to genre film fans. Born in Dallastown, Pennsylvania, this minister's son entered the film world after WWII, gaining notice for his support in *Death of a Salesman* in 1951. Just prior to that was his role in *Flight to Mars*, his first science fiction credit.

Mitchell excelled in action, adventure and western pictures, achieving mainstream television stardom as Buck in the long-running *High Chaparral* series. But it is his genre roles that may prove to outlive his conventional acting career. In the 50s, the old-fashioned horror potboiler *Gorilla at Large* was his only other genre credit, but the 60s offered the opportunity for Mitchell to work with the great Mario Bava in *Last of the Vikings*, *Erik the Conqueror*, the classic giallo *Blood and Black Lace* and *Knives of the Avenger*. Mitchell finished off the 60s with *Man Eater of Hydra* and the classic of another sort, *Nightmare in Wax*. Although working steadily in television in the 70s, Mitchell managed roles in the infamous *The Toolbox Murders*, *The Demon*, and others. He was still going strong in the 80s with the feverish *Cataclysm*, *Silent Scream*, *Without Warning*, and many more. All four of Mitchell's film credits in the 90s were genre-related. Mitchell succumbed to lung cancer in 1994.

Composer Richard LaSalle's genre credits include *The Day Mars Invaded Earth*, *Diary of a Madman*, *Twice-Told Tales*, *The Time Travelers*, and many more. He also scored the companion telefilm *Fire!* and *Hanging by a Thread*.

CAST: Robert Culp. Martin Milner, Barbara Hershey, (ao) Richard Basehart, Carol Lynley, Roddy McDowall, Cameron Mitchell, Eric Olson, Teresa Wright, Francine York. Also Whit Bissell, Leif Garrett, Ann Doran, Elizabeth Rogers, James Griffith, Edna Helton, Gloria Stuart, and Jack Collins.

CREDITS: Director: Earl Bellamy; Teleplay: Don Ingalls; Music: Richard LaSalle; Production: Irwin Allen Productions; Running Time: 99 minutes; Air Date: 11/24/76; Network: NBC

Force of Evil

AKA Tales of the Unexpected

There are some questions about this film that remain unanswered. The title sequence states *Quinn Martin's Tales of the Unexpected* and "Tonight's episode: 'Force of Evil.'" The date the film aired has not been determined but it is assumed it was shown on NBC, the network that carried the series. It is narrated by William Conrad, who was also credited as such on the series, implying that "Force of Evil" was the pilot episode for *Tales of the Unexpected*, which ran for eight episodes in 1977. One thing is not in question: this is a superior example of a fright film made for television.

Dr. Yale Carrington (Lloyd Bridges) is visited by Teddy Jakes (William Watson), a former employee who was convicted and sentenced to prison for the rape and murder of a young girl. Jakes had approached Carrington at the time of the crime and asked for an alibi but Carrington had refused. Now Jakes is back and has revenge on his mind. After Jakes terrorizes the Carrington clan and Yale's brother Floyd (John Anderson), the local sheriff, is unable to offer help within a legal framework, Carrington decides to kill Jakes. Once the deed is done, the Carringtons relax, but that was not really the end of Jakes.

The central theme here is the feeling of helplessness that arises when The Law cannot help the law-abiding folks who need it. But of course, law-abiding folks taking The Law into their own hands is not the answer either as Dr. Carrington discovers. Comparisons to *Cape Fear* are unavoidable, especially since the plots are very similar, right down to the mother and daughter being trapped on a boat with the psychopath.

Bridges is excellent as the concerned family man driven to murder. Pat Crowley is his wife Maggie, who stands by her man even to the point of helping to dispose of Jakes' body. Eve Plumb (*The Brady Bunch*) is daughter Cindy, who seems rather dense and way too cheerful to be real. And son John is played by William Kirby Cullen, who volunteers several of his college football buddies to beat up Jakes (they fail miserably).

But William Watson in the role of Jakes is where things break down a bit. Sure he's not a very attractive fellow and he's certainly an unappealing type but he's only vaguely threatening. There is no undercurrent of menace, no seething hatred of what Carrington stands for that seems to drive Jakes. The shoes of Robert Mitchum (or for that matter Robert De Niro) are awfully big to fill but it would be safe to venture that other "bad guy" television actors of the time (think Don Stroud) would have wrung more out of the role.

There is an additional layer of horror to the proceedings in that Jakes worked in the crematorium of the hospital, disposing of the amputated parts of patients, and amputation is a theme maintained throughout the film. When we first meet Carrington he has just performed an amputation on an accident victim. A friend of the family, mistaken for Cindy, is run over by a boat driven by Jakes while she is waterskiing and has to have her leg amputated. Speaking of Cindy, she has a dream that features Jakes throwing body parts into a furnace (a nod to premonitions since at the point in the film when she has the dream she has no knowledge of Jakes or what his old job was). The amputation theme is echoed even in the dialogue when Maggie says that Jakes is "managing to tear us apart, piece by piece."

Today, of course, Jakes would not get away with his stalking as laws have been passed to prevent that sort of terrorizing but one must bear in mind the timeframe. Director Richard Lang keeps the tension taut and uses visual flourishes to maintain a sense of the unreal. The desert community setting lends an air of isolation for the characters and there is even a disturbing twist ending for this very competent thriller.

Writer Robert Malcolm Young's credits include *The Crawling Hand* and *Escape to Witch Mountain* and the telefright *The Ghost of Flight 401*. He also wrote and directed the curious, claustrophobic 1962 thriller *Trauma*. Composer David Shire (ex-husband of actress Talia Shire) wrote the scores for the cult films *Drive, He Said* and *Steelyard Blues*, Francis Ford Coppola's *The Conversation*, *The Taking of Pelham One Two Three*, *All the President's Men* and *Norma Rae* (for which he won an Oscar for Best Original Song). His telefrights include *Isn't It Shocking* and *Killer Bees*.

CAST: Lloyd Bridges, Pat Crowley, Eve Plumb, William Watson, John Anderson, William Kirby Cullen, Jerry Ayres, Cynthia Eilbacher, Steve Itkin, and Stephen Coit.
CREDITS: Director: Richard Lang; Teleplay: Robert Malcolm Young; Music: David Shire; Production: Quinn Martin Productions; Automobiles Furnished by Ford Motor Company; Running Time: 100 minutes; Air Date: 1977; Network: NBC

Frankenstein

Note: The film under review is the 126-minute home video incarnation, not the original 180-minute (with commercials) broadcast version.

It can be somewhat hampering for reviewers when it comes to critical evaluations of Frankenstein films. The much-beloved Universal Studios cycle of Frankenstein films that kicked off in the 1930s have become icons of horror. Admittedly, it is difficult to top director James Whale, mad doctor Colin Clive, and above all, Boris Karloff as the Monster. One might ask what more could be said. Britain's Hammer Films breathed new life into the story (and spin-offs) with the use of color and gore effects beginning in the late 1950s. Hammer focused their series on Peter Cushing as Dr. Frankenstein but apart from relishing Cushing's performances, the degenerating sequels hold little lasting appeal. All other cinematic versions of Mary Shelley's story seem to be generally pointless rehashes.

Dan Curtis's production is not an exception. Shown over two nights as part of ABC's late night *Wide World of Mystery* series, this is one of several adaptations of literary classics produced (and sometimes directed) by Curtis. These occasionally benefited from interesting location work but all suffered from budgetary constraints such as being shot on video, the immediacy of which gives everything the throwaway look of a soap opera. This production in particular plays cheap and claustrophobic, hardly the riveting horror tale–socially significant

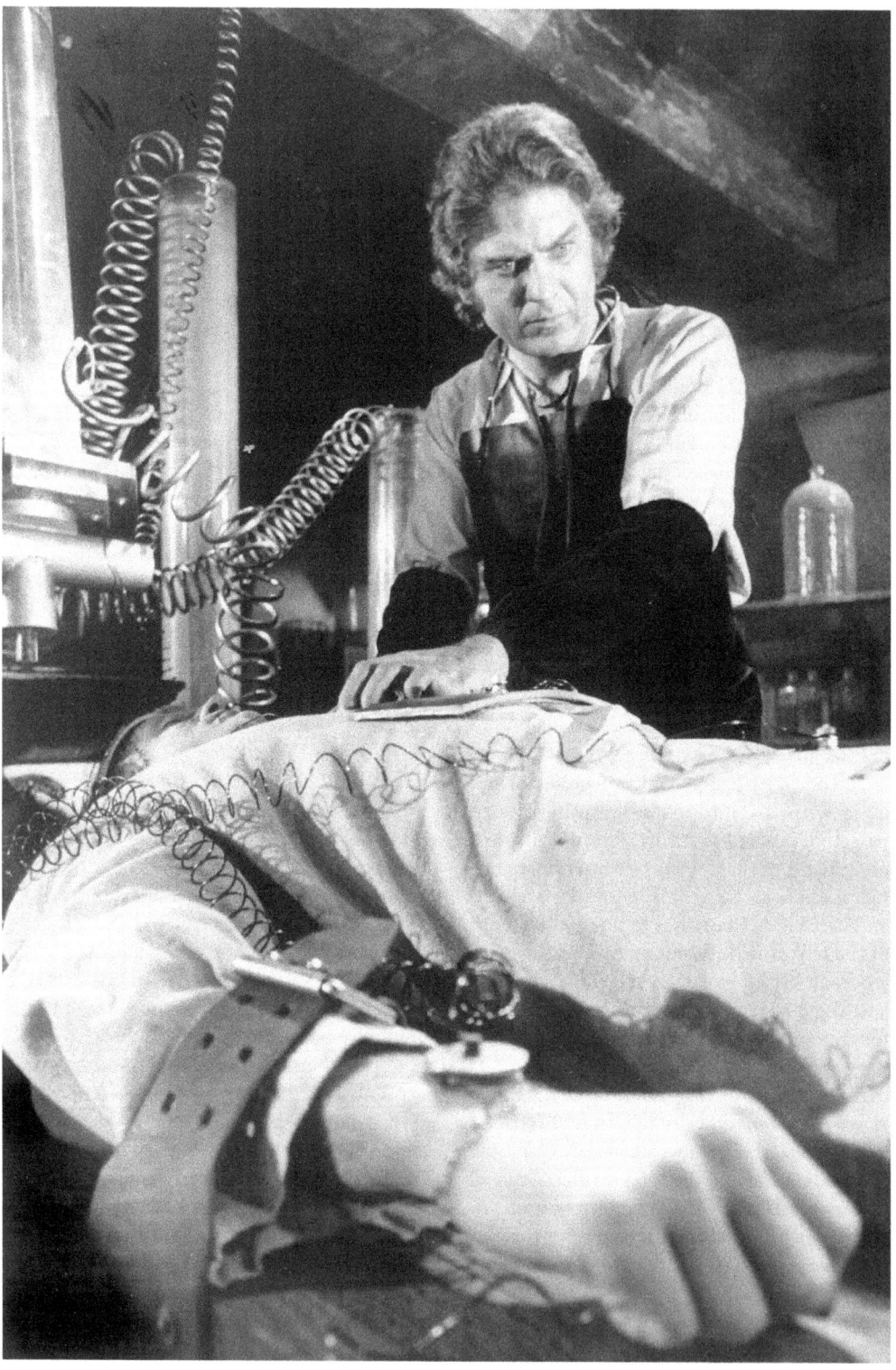

Bo Svenson (on table) and Robert Foxworth in *Frankenstein* (1973).

commentary the story was when first published. Curiously, part one of *Frankenstein* was shown the same night (and on the same network) as another Dan Curtis production, *The Night Strangler*, the highly anticipated sequel to his *The Night Stalker*.

Director Glenn Jordan's reverential approach to the material results in a staid and calcified product devoid of suspense or emotional pull. The line readings given by the cast make it seem as if everyone is saying something Very Important all of the time. Jordan fared somewhat better directing Curtis's production of *The Picture of Dorian Gray*, which aired three months later, and with *One of My Wives Is Missing*.

Robert Foxworth, who rarely exhibited much depth as an actor, doesn't break from his usual performances here: his dinner theater Frankenstein is hardly convincing as a man driven by curiosity, intellect and madness. Susan Strasberg comes across best as Frankenstein's long-suffering fiancée but her screen time is limited, of course. No doubt Bo Svenson got the part of the Monster because of his physical size but his tormented creature is as paper-thin as the rest of the production. A young Willie Aames (*Eight Is Enough*) plays Frankenstein's young brother and cult figure John Karlen has a small part as Frankenstein's short-lived assistant Otto, who is accidentally hugged to death by the Monster.

Karlen's acting career started in the late 50s but he hit the relative big time and began a long term relationship with Dan Curtis with the *Dark Shadows* series. He was in both theatrical features *House of Dark Shadows* and *Night of Dark Shadows* and continued to pop up in Curtis productions over the years (*The Invasion of Carol Enders*, *The Picture of Dorian Gray*, *Trilogy of Terror* and several non-genre entries). His most famous television credit is as Harvey Lacey on the long-running *Cagney & Lacey* series for which he won an Emmy in 1986. Karlen holds a special place in the hearts of genre fans, however, for his role as the doomed honeymooner in the classic vampire tale *Daughters of Darkness*.

This version of Frankenstein, which should be considered for completists only, was duly forgotten by the time yet another (and superior) version aired the following November, *Frankenstein: The True Story*.

CAST: Robert Foxworth, Susan Strasberg, Heidi Vaughn, Bo Svenson, John Karlen, Philip Bourneuf, Robert Gentry, Jon Lormer, William Hansen, and Brian Avery.

CREDITS: Director: Glenn Jordan; Teleplay: Sam Hall (adaptation by Sam Hall and Dan Curtis, from the novel by Mary Shelley); Music: Robert Cobert; Production: Dan Curtis Productions; Running Time: 126/180 minutes; Air Date: 1/16–17/73, Network: ABC

Frankenstein: The True Story

Note: The film under review is the 122-minute home video incarnation, not the original 182-minute broadcast version.

The reader is advised to peruse the review of Dan Curtis's production of *Frankenstein* for an overview of a few of the cinematic adaptations of Mary Shelley's famous story.

Shorn of a good portion of an hour for home video (the broadcast version ran over two nights in two-hour timeslots with commercials), this adaptation of the oft-told story benefits from a star-studded cast, lush production values and a generally irreverent attitude. Though it may not be director Jack Smight's finest hour (*Harper* would probably take that honor), this is certainly one of the finest television versions. Smight also helmed *The Illustrated Man*, *Airport 1975* and *Midway* and the telefright *The Screaming Woman*.

Leonard Whiting (Romeo in Franco Zeffirelli's *Romeo and Juliet*) is good in the role of the monster maker and Michael Sarrazin is certainly adequate as the product of Frankenstein's tampering with the laws of nature. James Mason is very interesting indeed as the opportunistic Dr. Polidori, the insane fop who dogs Frankenstein. Jane Seymour, who had just made a star-making splash in *Live and Let Die* that summer,

plays the bride of the Monster and is at the heart of the film's most notorious scene. There is even a small part for Tom Baker (*Doctor Who*) as a ship's captain.

David McCallum is great as Dr. Clerval ("My name will be a household word!"), whose precipitous meeting with Frankenstein kicks off the nasty goings-on. McCallum has suffered the curse of television celebrity since he became a teen idol in the role of Illya Kuryakin in *The Man from U.N.C.L.E.* in the mid–60s. Despite decades of exceptional work he has never escaped identification with the phenomenally popular series, another example of that double-edged fate of fame. Born into a musical family in Glasgow, Scotland, McCallum sidestepped a career in music for one of acting in the late 50s. He made minor splashes in *Billy Budd* and *The Great Escape* and in two episodes of *The Outer Limits* before landing his role of a lifetime, Illya, for which he was nominated for two Emmys. McCallum was again nominated for the Hallmark Hall of Fame telefilm *Teacher, Teacher*, starred in the highly-regarded *Hauser's Memory*, and landed a short-running series, *The Invisible Man*. His genre credits include *Dogs*, *The Watcher in the Woods*, *The Haunting of Morella* and the telefright *She Waits*.

The filmmakers' decision to push the limits of what was acceptable on American television at the time, by throwing in a bit of grue (the way Hammer did in the late 50s), helps keep this production lively. All in all, *Frankenstein: The True Story* is a memorable take on a story that still speaks to each new generation, whether that generation reaches back to the classic versions of Universal or Hammer, or falls under the spell of a contemporary monster for a few chills and a lesson on morality.

CAST: James Mason, Leonard Whiting, David McCallum, Jane Seymour, Nicola Pagett, Michael Sarrazin, Michael Wilding, Clarissa Kaye, Agnes Moorehead, Margaret Leighton, Ralph Richardson, John Gielgud, Tom Baker, Dallas Adams, Julian Barnes, and Arnold Diamond.

CREDITS: Director: Jack Smight; Teleplay: Christopher Isherwood & Don Bachardy, from the novel by Mary Shelley; Music: Gil Melle; Production: Universal TV; Running Time: 122/182 minutes; Air Date: 11/30–12/1/73; Network: NBC

Gargoyles

Dr. Mercer Boley (Cornel Wilde), who is working on a book about demonology, and his daughter Diana (Jennifer Salt) stumble upon the skeleton of a gargoyle while driving through New Mexico. When a group of newly hatched gargoyles attempts to retrieve the skull in Dr. Boley's possession, one of them is killed. The monsters return for their dead and kidnap Diana so she can teach them about mankind in their quest to destroy us. Dr. Boley then rounds up a makeshift posse to retrieve her.

Gargoyles is an old-fashioned spook show in the manner of films made 20 years prior: light on characterization and heavy on the monsters. It is also one of the finest television movies of the era and it still holds up today because it is fun and scary entertainment for all but the youngest members of the family.

The film opens with a montage of demon pictures and the like, over which is heard narration about Satan's fall from grace and the persistence in our culture of his minions, the gargoyles. The voice is that of Vic Perrin, who will be familiar to viewers of the classic *Outer Limits* show. Perrin also dubbed the voice of the main gargoyle played by Bernie Casey, albeit electronically altered for a creepy effect.

While the film is a bit plot-heavy, director Bill Norton, in only his second effort at the helm, keeps things moving at a lightning pace. The shoddy parts go by quickly enough for the viewer to forget them and the spooky moments hang in the memory long after the end credits.

It also helps that the film was shot on lo-

Spanish-language theatrical release poster for *Frankenstein: The True Story* (1973).

cation in and around Carlsbad Caverns in the desert of New Mexico, lending that air of authenticity lacking in many of the films made for the small screen. The cave interiors, especially the egg chamber, are reminiscent of the sets from the original *Star Trek* series: the colorful lighting and clever camera set-ups give the impression of a much larger space.

The gargoyle costumes and makeup—by craftsmen Stan Winston and Milt Rice—are duly famous, having won an Emmy Award for their quality and diversity. It is said that no two gargoyles are alike and after several viewings it seems that could very well be true. These monsters often move in slow motion, a nice stylish touch more common now than at the time. The flying shots are somewhat stilted and unconvincing but, as mentioned, the sense of fun overwhelms any serious deficiencies.

Yes, there are other moments that might let down a lesser film. The dirt bikers that help Dr. Boley search for his kidnapped daughter seem rather silly today, as does the clichéd redneck sheriff who hounds them. The head gargoyle who fondles and nuzzles Diana is a bit much but this serves to make his mate jealous, a plot contrivance essential to Dr. Boley's survival.

The positive elements far outweigh the silliness in any case. The chills arise when the search party finds a driverless truck going around in circles, the inside covered with blood. Shortly thereafter they find poor Mrs. Parks (Grayson Hall) hanging upside down from a telephone pole. That's when a couple of the bikers call it quits. The gargoyle attack on the search party is quite exciting since it occurs in the dark and the search party is clearly outnumbered.

The cast is adequate with a few standouts. Cornel Wilde is a likable and capable hero and Scott Glenn (*The Right Stuff*), who makes the ultimate sacrifice, maintains a devil-may-care attitude to the end. Grayson Hall (*Dark Shadows*) as the imbibing Mrs. Parks makes her small part memorable as does Woody Chambliss (*The Devil's Rain*) as Uncle Willy, who discovered the nasty-looking skeleton in the first place.

Finally, there's a smart ending that provides for dignity on both sides of this little war, a rarity in America's winner-takes-all society. Ultimately, *Gargoyles* is an intelligent, creative and fast-moving monster romp worth a look.

CAST: Cornel Wilde, Jennifer Salt, Grayson Hall, Bernie Casey, Scott Glenn, William Stevens, John Gruber, Woody Chambliss, Jim Connell, Tim Burns, Mickey Alzola, Greg Walker, and Rock Walker.

CREDITS: Director: B.W.L. (Bill) Norton; Teleplay: Stephen and Elinor Karpf; Music: Robert Prince; Production: Tomorrow Entertainment Inc.; Running Time: 74 minutes; Air Date: 11/21/72; Network: CBS

The Ghost of Flight 401

On December 29, 1972, an Eastern Airlines L-1011, flight 401, crashed in the Everglades killing many of the passengers and crew. Salvaged parts from the airplane were used as replacements in other L-1011s and, subsequently, crews on those planes claimed to see a ghost of a crew member killed on flight 401.

The Ghost of Flight 401 concentrates on the allegedly true sightings by various crew members of the ghost of Don Cimoli (Ernest Borgnine), the navigator who died in the hospital following the crash. Our window into the inner workings of Eastern Airlines is through the character of Jordan Evanhower (Gary Lockwood), a crew union representative of the company. Eastern's first reaction was to delete flight logs that mention sightings of ghosts and to require employees who claimed to see them to visit psychiatrists for a little reorientation.

The film is competently made by director Steven Hilliard Stern (*The Devil and Max Devlin*) and features a good cast. Watch for up-and-comer Kim Basinger as a flight attendant and Russell Johnson (*Gilligan's Island*) and Howard Hesseman (*WKRP in Cincinnati*) as the pilot and copilot, respectively, of the doomed flight. An uncredited Paul Frees does the opening and closing narration and provides various voices along the way, including the overdubbing of the priest at Cimoli's funeral.

When Cimoli's voice is finally caught on tape using a flight recorder, a group of his fellow crew members consult mediums (Eugene Roche and Alan Oppenheimer) in an attempt to exorcise Cimoli's ghost. The mediums provide the crew (and the viewer) with a primer about what supposedly causes apparitions of the recent dead, the capper on the various philosophical discussions about the fear of death, etc., that are peppered throughout the film.

Eastern apparently acquiesced and removed the salvaged parts from other planes and the sightings ceased. For one interested in the subject this is a reverent telling of a real-life supernatural mystery. The film is based on the controversial book by John G. Fuller, who also dramatized the experiences of Barney and Betty Hill in *The Interrupted Journey*, which was made into the telefilm *The UFO Incident*. Composer David Raksin's credits include *The Undying Monster*, the haunting theme from 1944's *Laura*, *What's the Matter with Helen?* and the classic film noirs *Force of Evil* and *The Big Combo*. Another telefilm made about flight 401, *Crash*, dealt strictly with the tragedy itself.

CAST: Ernest Borgnine, Gary Lockwood, Tina Chen, Kim Basinger, Tom Clancy, Howard Hesseman, Russell Johnson, Robert F. Lyons, Allan Miller, Alan Oppenheimer, Carol Rossen, Eugene Roche, Luis Avalos, Ted Hartley, Byron Morrow, John Quade, Beverly Todd, Angela Clarke, Gordon Connell, Kerrie Cullen, Margie Gordon, Deborah K. Harmon, Anna Mathias, Mark L. Taylor, Lynn Wood, Missy Francis, and Meeno Peluce. Uncredited: Paul Frees

CREDITS: Director: Steven Hilliard Stern; Teleplay: Robert Malcolm Young, based on the book by John G. Fuller; Music: David Raksin; Production: Paramount Television; Running Time: 94 minutes; Air Date: 2/18/78; Network: ABC

Good Against Evil

New York, 1955. A woman who had been seduced by the leader of a Satanic cult, a certain Mr. Rimmin (Richard Lynch), gives birth to a baby girl and then is mysteriously killed. The child is watched over by the cult as she grows to maturity. It is now 1977 and the girl is a 22-year-old fashion designer in San Francisco. She is Jessica Gordon (Elyssa Davalos) and she is about to meet Vietnam vet and freelance writer Andy Stewart (Dack Rambo) and fall in love. This doesn't sit well with Mr. Rimmin, however, who has plans for Jessica to bear the child of the demon Astaroth.

The opening sequence of the film—the nightmarish birth of Jessica and her mother's subsequent death—is handled with aplomb. The dark hospital milieu and the frantic cries of the mother as she tries to prevent the birth create a claustrophobic atmosphere worthy of any horror film of the era, made-for-television or not. Unfortunately, the rest of the picture pales in comparison.

Once Jessica "meets cute" with Andy—he smashes his van into her brand new Capri—too much time is taken up with their flowering romance and not enough is spent with the evil doings of Rimmin and his followers. However, there are occasional Satanic warning signs along the way that point to disaster. First, Jessica receives a strange fortune from a street performer that reads, "In the second millennium, the child of the child shall inherit the Earth and havoc shall reign." Then there is a horse incident, a common harbinger of Satanic evil, at least in the movies.

When Jessica and Andy make plans with a priest to be married, all hell breaks loose. The priest senses evil and is killed for meddling, his church desecrated for good measure. Rimmin then spirits Jessica away to New Orleans while planning to have Andy diverted by an old flame (Kim Cattrall), whose child Rimmin somehow causes to be possessed. Enter the exorcist, Father Kemschler (played by Dan O'Herlihy like a drunken Max von Sydow), who solves that problem. The new friendship forged by this ordeal sends Andy and Kemschler off together to search for Jessica.

Good Against Evil was designed as a pilot for a buddy series about Satanic evil.

Needless to say, the series wasn't picked up. Weak as it is, the film has a surprisingly solid pedigree. It was directed by veteran Paul Wendkos and was written by Hammer Films alumnus Jimmy Sangster. Sangster's writing career took off with the massive hits *The Curse of Frankenstein* and *Horror of Dracula*. He went on to pen primarily horrors (*The Revenge of Frankenstein*, *The Mummy*, *The Brides of Dracula*, etc.) and psychological thrillers (*Taste of Fear*, *Paranoiac*, *Hysteria*, etc.) for the company. In the 70s, Sangster came to work in American television, writing the telefrights *A Taste of Evil* and *Scream, Pretty Peggy*. Among his directorial credits are *The Horror of Frankenstein* and *Lust for a Vampire*. Additionally, Argentinean-born world-class composer Lalo Schifrin (*Mannix*, *Mission Impossible*) contributes his only telefright score of the decade here, but it is well below his best work.

On the acting front, *Good Against Evil* has only one winner. The leads are vacuous and O'Herlihy chews the scenery mercilessly but Richard Lynch, as the immortal slave of Satan, Rimmin, takes the honors with a low-key performance that oozes evil. Lynch accomplished a similar feat in the telefright *Vampire*.

On the plus side: Note the scene where Rimmin, upset about Jessica's amorous leanings, meets with her boss Agnes (Erica Yohn), whose assignment it was to discourage the young lovers. Rimmin sits calmly, saying nothing, while Agnes pleads for her life. Suddenly the room is filled with a hoard of cats who swarm over Agnes, causing her death. The San Francisco locations add some much-needed appeal as well.

Good Against Evil's few ups are more than matched by the downs, however. The worst of these occurs with the schizophrenic split the film takes when the retread plot of *The Exorcist* becomes apparent. The rule of the day seems to be a combination of silly dialogue exchanges (Andy: "Father, we're not living in the dark ages"; Kemschler: "You can prove that?") and absurd action (Astaroth, through the possessed child, tries to smother Kemschler with a pillow).

Astaroth, by the way, is one of the seven princes of Hell who visited the famous Faust. It is said that he can be summoned on Wednesday and that he emits a powerful, fetid odor, a trait he has in common with this film.

CAST: Dack Rambo, Elyssa Davalos, Richard Lynch, Dan O'Herlihy, John Harkins, Jenny O'Hara, Leila Goldoni, Peggy McCay, Peter Brandon, Kim Cattrall, Natasha Ryan, Richard Sanders, Lillian Adams, Erica Yohn, and Richard Stahl.

CREDITS: Director: Paul Wendkos; Teleplay: Jimmy Sangster; Music: Lalo Schifrin; Production: Frankel-Bolen Productions; Running Time: 85 minutes; Air Date: 5/22/77; Network: ABC

Hanging by a Thread

A group of friends, known as the Uptown Club, decide to take a tramway to the top of a mountain for a barbeque. At the last minute, one of their members, Paul Craig (Sam Groom), who had been hiding out under police protection so he can testify against his boss, joins the group for the outing. On the way up, lightning hits the car, fusing its wheels to the cable and stranding the group 7,500 feet above the ground between towers. Darkness descends and rescue attempts are hampered by the storm. Meanwhile, two hit men after Craig are steadily making their way up the mountain as the group reminisces about the events that brought them there.

Passengers on the Palm Springs Aerial Tramway are threatened for the last time during the 1970s (see also *Skyway to Death*) in this Irwin Allen production. Shown over two nights—each a two-hour slot—*Hanging by a Thread* is another bloated example of the genre by "disaster master" Allen (*Fire!*, *Flood!*). At over three hours, sans commercials, this is an endurance test for even the most rabid fan of the telefright. The cast is adequate but none of them have what one might call "marquee value" and the story is padded out with no less than a dozen flashbacks as the group awaits rescue.

Bert Convy is the rich alcoholic Alan Durant who owns the tramway. He's engaged to Ellen Craig (Donna Mills) who has a son by her ex-husband, Paul, the fellow who is the target of the hit men. Craig is hunted for turning state's evidence on his boss, the mob-fronted military contractor Lawton (Cameron Mitchell). Half of the flashbacks detail the Craigs' crumbling marriage (something they have in common with every other couple here), Paul's move to work for Lawton, and his lengthy protection at a safe house with cop Mitchell (Roger Perry). When Paul confronts Lawton with details about his company defrauding the government, Lawton threatens him by saying, "Dead men don't whistle." Paul contacts Mitchell and they hole up waiting for Lawton's trial. At one point Mitchell had to kill a murderous phony postman who was after Paul, so why he lets Paul go on the outing when Paul's life is clearly in danger, is anyone's guess.

The Uptown Club's other members are Jim and Sue Grainger (Burr DeBenning and Patty Duke Astin) and Eddie and Anita Minton (Oliver Clark and Joyce Bulifant). Each have their own troubles and their own stories to tell. Flashbacks reveal that Jim and Sue don't like each other (Sue claims, "It's important to find something to bicker about in a marriage") and that ruthless, greedy Eddie sent his own brother to prison for "irregularities" in their business. Ex-footballer Jim has the worst luck of the group when he accidentally sets a fire in the car and suffers severe burns. Patty Duke Astin's real-life (at the time) husband, John Astin, was in the earlier cable car disaster telefilm *Skyway to Death* so apparently it was her turn.

Wealthy Alan Durant has his own flashbacks covering his parents' problems (mom was a tramp) that eventually caused Alan's drinking problem. We also learn that Alan's father (Peter Donat) gave Alan the tramway for a birthday present; in fact, he bought the boy the whole mountain. Alan's ranch is the setting for the final flashback which reveals the group's big secret: they killed a man. Well, they didn't exactly kill him but they certainly caused his death by putting him on a horse when he was drunk and he was killed when he fell off. This little *faux pas* was covered up by Alan's father, who justified it by saying, "Calling the police won't bring him back."

Paul Craig is the hero who frees up the cable car after the mechanic flown in to help falls to his death while trying to walk the cable from the tower to the car. Paul also applies the handbrake on the top of the car so it doesn't crash into the building at the base of the mountain, the same ending used in *Skyway to Death*. Mitchell had eliminated the hit men who came for Paul so the Craigs can reconcile and go back into hiding together.

Paul Fix (the sheriff in the western series *The Rifleman*) is the mob boss who has Lawton around his little finger and Ted Gehring is the chief engineer at the base who has his hands full. Admittedly, being trapped in a cable car is scarier at night but this film did nothing for the reputation of disaster telefilms.

Director Georg Fenady helmed *Terror in the Wax Museum* and *Arnold*. Writer Adrian Spies (pronounced "spees") adapted a Curt Siodmak novel for the highly regarded science fiction thriller *Hauser's Memory*.

CAST: Sam Groom, (ao) Patty Duke Astin, Joyce Bulifant, Oliver Clark, Bert Convy, Burr DeBenning, Peter Donat, Paul Fix, Deanna Lund, Donna Mills, Cameron Mitchell, Roger Perry, and Michael Sharrett. Also Ted Gehring, Steven Marlo, Elizabeth Rogers, Lonny Chapman, Brendon Boone, Jacquelyn Hyde, Doug Llewelyn, Randy Gray, Bill Harlow, and James Gavin.

CREDITS: Director: Georg Fenady; Teleplay: Adrian Spies; Music: Richard LaSalle; Production: Irwin Allen Productions; Running Time: 185 minutes; Air Date: 5/8–9/79; Network: NBC

Haunts of the Very Rich

A disparate group of travelers find themselves on a fabulous first class flight to the Portals of Eden, the location of which is unknown to all. The passengers include Dave Woodrough (Lloyd Bridges), a would-be ladies man stuck in a bad marriage, Ellen Blunt (Cloris Leachman), a rather plain spinster, Albert Hunsicker (Ed Asner), a cantankerous businessman, Annette Larier (Anne Francis), a stressed housewife, Lyle and Laurie (Tony Bill and Donna Mills), a newlywed couple, and the Reverend John Fellows (Robert Reed), a man of God who has lost his faith.

Shortly after they arrive in paradise, they are greeted by their host Seacrist (Moses Gunn). Each is afforded the room of their dreams in the palatial hotel—all except Hunsicker, who's given the equivalent of a cheap motel room ("I could be in Schenectady, for crying out loud!"). What seems at first to be heaven quickly deteriorates into their own private hell, as a powerful storm leaves the guests without electricity, much fresh water or food, air conditioning, etc. It soon begins to dawn on them that perhaps there is more going on than just a simple vacation as they search for an explanation for their predicament.

The first point of reference for the modern viewer of this type of film would be *The Twilight Zone*. But this story actually has roots—however unacknowledged—going back to a play by Sutton Vane. The play, called *Outward Bound*, first saw the light of celluloid under that very name in 1930, and was remade as *Between Two Worlds* in 1944. Curiously enough, credit for the writing of this version is given to William Wood from a story by T.K. Brown.

Technicalities aside, *Haunts of the Very Rich* can be counted as one of the very best telefilms of the era. It sports a dynamite cast, superior writing and top talent behind the camera. Director Paul Wendkos is in top form here and he is working with the likes of composer Dominic Frontiere (*The Outer Limits*) and art director Eugene Lourie. The Russian-born Lourie had a long and distinguished career as an art director, production designer, set decorator and even as a director. He will be recognized by genre fans for his work on films such as *The Beast From 20,000 Fathoms*, *The Giant Behemoth*, *Gorgo* and *Crack in the World*, among others.

The cast is a fine ensemble indeed. The much-beloved Lloyd Bridges is excellent as Woodrough, the shackled husband yearning to be free. Only his wardrobe suffers a greater humiliation, with its loud jackets and pink pants. Upon his arrival, Woodrough gets the swinging bachelor pad room complete with round bed and hi-tech sound system. Cloris Leachman shines as Ellen, the wallflower given the chance to bloom, and Ed Asner has the skill to make even the gruff Hunsicker sympathetic. Anne Francis is given the somewhat thankless role as the self-pitying housewife Annette, but she handles the role easily. Tony Bill and Donna Mills, as the bickering newlyweds, have only that one note to play. Moses Gunn gives his Seacrist an exasperating calm.

Interestingly, the most agonizing moment is provided by Robert Reed, never considered a heavyweight acting talent. He is far from the suburban sitcom of *The Brady Bunch* with his character of Fellows, who is straining to find meaning in his life. Fellows was drawn to this vacation for the opportunity to observe an indigenous native tribe and to join them in ceremonies that might provide a beacon for this lost man of God. Fellows disappears from the action while on his private expedition, but his return lends an unexpected glimmer of gravity. He describes the Indians as "an undersized and incredibly dirty tribe who bury their defective young alive. I participated in their peyote ceremony. From that point on, the whole experience was unspeakable." There is more to the scene and it is perhaps the actor's finest work. Reed can also be seen in *Snatched*, *Nightmare in Badham County* and *SST—Death Flight*.

The exteriors for the film were shot in a gauzy fashion at Villa Vizcaya on Biscayne Bay in Miami. The estate is now open for tourism and could be considered an interesting pilgrimage for fans. Hopefully the experience would be better than what the characters here undergo. As Hunsicker says, "This isn't just another day at Happy Acres."

CAST: Lloyd Bridges, Cloris Leachman, Edward Asner, Anne Francis, Tony Bill, Donna Mills, Robert Reed, Moses Gunn, Phyllis Hill, Michael Lembeck, Susan Foster, Beverly Gill, and Todd Martin.

CREDITS: Director: Paul Wendkos; Teleplay: William Wood, based on a story by T.K. Brown; Music: Dominic Frontiere; Production: ABC Circle Films; Running Time: 75 minutes; Air Date: 9/20/72; Network: ABC

Home for the Holidays

AKA Deadly Desires

It was a dark and stormy night. And day. And night. It is hard to tell exactly, since time seems elastic in this country house terror film. Whether this phenomenon is a stylistic choice of the filmmakers or merely a technical shortcoming is up to interpretation.

Four sisters, estranged from their tyrant father, are beckoned back home for Christmas. Dad (Walter Brennan) suspects his new wife Elizabeth (Julie Harris) of slowly poisoning him since her first husband had succumbed to a toxic toddy. Elizabeth was cleared of guilt in the death but all concerned have their doubts. When the daughters begin to die at the hands of a mysterious killer, suspicion solidifies.

Home for the Holidays must be considered one of the less distinguished writing credits of Joseph Stefano. Stefano is best known for two of his many accomplishments: producing and sometimes writing for TV's *The Outer Limits* and for writing the screenplay for *Psycho*. However he spent the 1970s churning out only a few scripts for telefilms, including *Revenge!* and *Snowbeast*. (Memorable lines are rare here, but one, spoken by the father about his wife, comes to mind: "That woman has ears that can hear sunshine.")

The cast, however ill-used, is a fine ensemble. The daughters are Eleanor Parker as Alex, the eldest, Jessica Walter as Frederica, the pill-popping alcoholic, Jill Haworth (*Tower of Evil*) as Joanne, the pragmatist, and Sally Field as Christine, the wide-eyed innocent.

Notice the four names are all masculine—Alex, Freddy, Jo, and Chris—and that the last has the name of divinity, Christine. No doubt the naming convention is meant to imply that the father had always wanted sons and was therefore unforgiving of his progeny, which caused the break in family ties. Such subtleties are admirable but unnecessary since the film does not aspire to be a work of art.

The directorial talents of John Llewellyn Moxey seem to be missing in action. There is very little visual flair or suspense, where a touch of either would have gone a long way. The faults of the script will be apparent to those with experience in mystery. In other words, there are no surprises here. The killer is obvious since most of the small cast is killed off and the denouement contains the usual moral certainty.

Jessica Walter has been nominated for Emmys four times, winning once in 1975 for *Amy Prentiss*. Walter was born in Brooklyn and earned kudos for her theater work before venturing into film and television in the early 60s, including a three-year run in the soap opera *Love of Life*. A fixture on television since, she nevertheless made a big genre splash in Clint Eastwood's *Play Misty for Me*. In the 80s, she was on the long-running *Trapper John, M.D.* series and had a recurring role on the *Three's Company* sequel series *Three's a Crowd*. The 90s saw her in a recurring role in *Coach* and the new millennium brought Walter another popular series hit with *Arrested Development*. Her telefrights of concern are *Women in Chains*, *Hurricane*, *Vampire* and *She's Dressed to Kill*.

Composer George Tipton did the score for the cult animated feature *The Point* and Terrence Malick's *Badlands*, and he was nominated for an Oscar for his additional score for *Phantom of the Paradise*.

CAST: Sally Field, Jill Haworth, Julie Harris, Eleanor Parker, Jessica Walter, Walter Brennan, John Fink, and Med Flory.

CREDITS: Director: John Llewellyn Moxey; Teleplay: Joseph Stefano; Music: George Tipton;

Production: Spelling-Goldberg Productions; Running Time: 75 minutes; Vehicles Furnished by Chrysler, General Motors; Air Date: 11/28/72; Network: ABC

Horror at 37,000 Feet

Horror at 37,000 Feet is either a meditation on the inherent savagery of the human race, on the primal fears and ancient behaviors that tether us to the past, no matter how far we advance with our technology, or just a silly horror movie.

Architect Alan O'Neill (Roy Thinnes) uproots the remains of a cursed abbey from his wife's familial estate in England, with the intent of flying them to America and using them in their home. It is the night of the summer solstice and a full moon glows bright over Heathrow Airport. With the abbey in the cargo hold, ten passengers board the red-eye flight, and it isn't long before the spirits of those long-dead break free and threaten to destroy the plane. What the spirits want and how they will be satisfied occupies the little time remaining for those on the fateful flight.

Horror at 37,000 Feet is the only credit for V.X. Appleton whose story formed the basis for the film. It was Emmy-wining director David Lowell Rich's first supernatural film for television but he would go on to make the cult favorite *Satan's School for Girls*, *Runaway!* and another flight fright film, *SST—Death Flight*. As if he couldn't get enough, Rich closed out the 70s with the feature *The Concorde: Airport '79*. Rich also made the Three Stooges vehicle *Have Rocket, Will Travel*, *Madame X* with Lana Turner and *Eye of the Cat*.

Readers may find similarities between this and *Cruise Into Terror* which would air five years later on a rival network. In that film, the passengers of a boat are threatened with none other than the son of Satan. Here it is merely the spirits of ancient druids howling for a sacrifice that the cast must outwit.

The ensemble of this horror-disaster hybrid must have collectively asked themselves what they were doing in a film as outlandish as this. Jane Merrow (*Hands of the Ripper*) plays architect O'Neill's wife, Sheila. Among the others are millionaire businessman Glen Farlee (Buddy Ebsen); a Mrs. Pinder (Tammy Grimes), who seems very knowledgeable about the druid spirits; a man of God, Paul Klovalik (William Shatner), who's lost his faith; his wife Manya (Lyn Loring); a model (France Nuyen); a doctor (Paul Winfield); a cowboy (Will Hutchins) fresh from making a spaghetti western in Italy; and a little girl (Mia Bendixsen) flying alone. Captain Ermie Slade (Chuck Connors), Jim Hawley (Russell Johnson) and Frank Drisocll (H.M. Wynant) are in the cockpit.

Things start to go wrong as soon as the flight leaves London, and soon the plane is being mysteriously held in place, suspended in midair. The mysterious entity smashes out of its container in the cargo hold and freezes Mrs. Pinder's dog Damon to death. The cold then makes its way into the cabin, and when Slade and Hawley investigate, Hawley is quick-frozen. The evil power rips up the floor of the plane and an ugly brown goop bubbles up. That is about the extent of the malevolent manifestations, as if the evil were so unspeakable the viewer should never be allowed to see it.

Sheila O'Neill, whose family built the abbey, passes out and speaks Latin, which prompts Mrs. Pinder to explain a bit about what's going on. It seems the abbey was built on a sacred grove of the druids who had performed human sacrifices. Every hundred years at the solstice, the spirits of the ancient druids come back demanding a sacrifice. Mrs. Pinder opines that Sheila is the sacrifice they want.

The panicked passengers then jump to wild conclusions, much to the entertainment of the viewer. They decide to attach Sheila's fingernail clippings and strands of her hair to the little girl's doll, and offer that to the spirits as a substitute sacrifice for Sheila. As Glen Farlee so eloquently puts it: "Maybe she's right. What other explanation could there be? Everything's gone crazy!" The plan doesn't work so the group decides to light a fire on the plane to keep the evil spirits away, but soon the fire burns out and all looks hopeless.

The real star of the show is the cynical Reverend Klovalik. William Shatner, as Klovalik, drinks heavily and spouts wizened axioms such as "The closer to heaven, the more discordant," and generally demeans his fellow passengers and their foolishness. His change of heart and proposed solution near the end of the film are wholly expected and would be missed if they didn't happen.

Fans of the comedy *Airplane!* may find humor in a line spoken by the lantern-jawed captain, Ernie Slade. Earlier he had been frostbitten by the cold and was given painkillers by the doctor. When the effects of these seem to be wearing off, he is offered more of the pills. He responds, "Might as well. No use saving them."

For a nonsensical good time, *Horror at 37,000 Feet* offers up plenty in the way of entertainment. Forget the sometimes overwrought attempts at gravity (lines such as "If there are devils, there must also be gods.") and enjoy the level of silliness long ago abandoned by network television.

CAST: (ao) Chuck Connors, Buddy Ebsen, Tammy Grimes, Lyn Loring, Jane Merrow, France Nuyen, William Shatner, Roy Thinnes, Paul Winfield. Also Will Hutchins, Darleen Carr, Brenda Benet, Russell Johnson, H.M. Wynant, Mia Bendixsen, Gerald Saunderson Peters, Robert Donner, Peter Ashton, and Veronica Anderson.

CREDITS: Director: David Lowell Rich; Teleplay: Ron Austin and Jim Buchanan, from the story by V.X. Appleton; Music: Morton Stevens; Production: Trident Television Associates; Running Time: 71 minutes; Air Date: 2/13/73; Network: CBS

The House That Would Not Die

Ruth Bennett (Barbara Stanwyck), an executive secretary at the Department of Agriculture, is on leave to take possession of a house in Amish country she inherited from her aunt Hattie. Ruth drags along her niece Sara (Katherine Wynn) to live with her, and both love the old house for about a week. Then the haunting begins. Ruth hears voices and Sara seems strangely affected by the old place as does neighbor Pat McDougal (Richard Egan), a professor who knows about "witchcraft, black magic, [and] spiritism." Smart young student Stan (Michael Anderson, Jr.), who favors Sara, is the first to catch on to the supernatural events: Pat and Sara are being possessed by the ghosts of tenants from long ago.

This romantic ghost story moves at a good clip and contains the necessarily low-budget (yet effective) bits of business that provide a modicum of atmosphere. Director John Llewellyn Moxey's experience helps to guide this so-so entry so the viewer is less apt to notice the cramped sets and general dearth of locations.

The House That Would Not Die features poltergeist-type activities, a dream sequence, two séances, psychotic behavior, creepy attics and cellars and a grisly dénouement. However, the film lacks a certain weight that would draw the viewer into the proceedings. Things happen so fast—not only the spooky stuff but the discovery of important information—that one doesn't have time to get much into the characters.

The séances are amusing if not particularly eventful. There is a lot of wind as meaningful glances go around the table and finally the medium calls it quits, advising Ruth and company to flee the house. It is interesting that all involved put up little resistance to the idea of ghostly possession, buying into the unusual happenings without blinking an eye.

Barbara Stanwyck (in her telefilm debut) and Richard Egan help hold things together but the juvenile leads, Katherine Winn and Michael Anderson, Jr., are eclipsed when in the same room with those old pros. This passable but ultimately forgettable ditty will provide enough entertainment on the journey to discovering the cause of all the ghostly fuss.

The House That Would Not Die was based on the novel *Ammie, Come Home* by Barbara Michaels, who acted in several episodes of *Burke's Law* in the early 1960s. Katherine (Kitty) Winn would soon take the top acting prize at Cannes for her role opposite Al Pacino in *Panic in Needle Park*. She also appeared in *The Exorcist* and *The Exorcist II: The Heretic* before saying goodbye to the acting business. Michael Anderson, Jr., the son of director Michael Anderson (*Logan's Run*), had a longer career than Winn but other than appearing in a couple of his father's movies (*Logan's Run* included) his work is largely devoid of genre interest.

CAST: Barbara Stanwyck, Richard Egan, Michael Anderson, Jr., Katherine Winn, Doreen Lang, and Mabel Albertson.

CREDITS: Director: John Llewellyn Moxey; Teleplay: Henry Farrell, based on the novel *Ammie, Come Home* by Barbara Michaels; Music: Laurence Rosenthal; Production: Aaron Spelling Productions; Automobiles Furnished by Chrysler Corporation; Running time: 74 minutes; Air Date: 10/27/70; Network: ABC

How Awful About Allan

Allan (Anthony Perkins) is a disturbed man who developed a psychosomatic blindness following the accidental house fire that killed his father and damaged his sister's face. Some time after the tragedy, Allan's sight has partially recovered, and he returns home to live with his sister in the hopes of coming to terms with the event and regaining his sight. But someone is bent on tormenting the poor fellow and finally tries to kill him.

Director Curtis Harrington's moody production *How Awful About Allan* strikes a somber tone and maintains it with blurry POV shots that describe Allan's visual impairment, odd dream sequences, a melancholy score by Laurence Rosenthal, serious rainstorms and fine acting by all involved.

Perkins was forever typecast as a weirdo after *Psycho* and the role of Allan is no exception. Julie Harris, as Allan's sister Katherine, wears a small protective covering on her cheek to shield her scarred face. But her sunken demeanor betrays her own psychological injury at the loss of her father. In one of Allan's dreams—which are brought on by medication—it is hinted that Allan suspects a vaguely improper relationship between father and daughter. This being network television fare, one is required to read between the lines to discern this, however.

Harris was nominated for a Best Actress Oscar for 1952's *The Member of the Wedding*, a role she recreated from Broadway, and she has been nominated 11 times for Emmys, winning three. She is also the most nominated performer in Tony history for her stage work: ten nominations and five awards. Harris was born in Grosse Point Park, Michigan, and was almost immediately recognized for her talent upon her Broadway debut in 1945. Her most famous role in the 50s was opposite James Dean in *East of Eden*, but it was in the following decade when she played the role that cemented her genre credentials: that of the fragile Eleanor in Robert Wise's *The Haunting*. Other interesting credits include *Harper*, *Reflections in a Golden Eye* and Sam Raimi's *Crimewave*. Harris can also be seen in the telefright *Home for the Holidays*.

Joan Hackett plays Olive, the next door neighbor who was apparently close enough to Allan to inspire rumors of marriage. She is forever coming in the back door and scaring the heck out of Allan, but she is genuinely concerned about her former lover. Olive makes a big mistake early in the film and drags Allan out of the house for a ride in the car. When she leaves him for a moment to return some books to the library, Allan's tormentor takes the opportunity to frighten him enough to take off with Olive's car. This unintentionally amusing scene breaks the mood as Allan bounces off curbs, nearly colliding with cars until he runs into a light pole about a block away.

Certain questions do arise. Why is Allan so afraid of his ex-girlfriend Olive? What was Allan like before the accident? He mentions at one point about "getting back to his music" (he listens to classical music), but there isn't much of a clue as to Allan's life before. Why do the local authorities let Katherine just board up the burned room on the second floor? It would certainly be considered unsafe. What is the point of the twist ending? It seems tacked on for no good reason.

Red herrings must abound in a story like this. There is a mysterious student roomer with a scratchy voice who comes and goes at all hours. And the absent fiancé of Allan's sister, who shows up late in the game driving a cab, has a similar whisper he claims is due to a cold.

The best scene is Allan's dream of exploring the burned-out room where his father died. The sequence doesn't last long but it is photographed with great care: the light plays off the black charcoal of the burned wood, creating angular shapes and dark recesses, a vacuous, frightening space of familial guilt. It looks very much like a picture of Allan's tortured mind and is the visual highlight of this above-average gothic thriller.

Julie Harris and Anthony Perkins in *How Awful About Allan* (1970).

CAST: Anthony Perkins, Julie Harris, Joan Hackett, Kent Smith, Robert H. Harris, Molly Dodd, Billy Bowles, Trent Dolan, William Erwin, Jeannette Howe, and Kenneth Lawrence.

CREDITS: Director: Curtis Harrington; Teleplay: Henry Farrell, based on his novel; Music: Laurence Rosenthal; Production: Aaron Spelling Productions; Automobiles Furnished by Chrysler Corporation; Runtime: 73 minutes; Air Date: 9/22/70; Network: ABC

A Howling in the Woods

Fans of television's *I Dream of Jeannie* will no doubt want to track down this re-teaming of its stars Barbara Eden and Larry Hagman. The gothic mystery *A Howling in the Woods*, based on the novel by Velda Johnston, tells the sordid tale of a sad love affair that ignites a small town's misguided revenge.

Snappily dressed Liza Staines Crocker (Eden) returns to her childhood home in Stainesville, Nevada, to seek a quick divorce from her husband Eddie (Hagman). The Staines were the wealthy family in the now-failing mining town, but Liza's encounters with the citizens belie the community's claim to be "The Friendliest Town in Nevada." Once at the family's lodge, Liza joins her stepmother Rose (Vera Miles) and Rose's son Justin (John Rubinstein), but her father has already left for Mexico and is incommunicado. Liza hears the story of a local child's unsolved murder but her quest for answers meets with resistance at every turn.

Larry Hagman and Barbara Eden are involved in a small town mystery in *A Howling in the Woods* (1971).

There is a mystery tearing this small town apart, and the baleful howling in the woods could be part of the answer.

Although competently directed and cast, *A Howling in the Woods* seems stretched to its limits to accommodate a two-hour timeslot. The sordid elements of the story—which will not be completely revealed here—do little to spice up what is ultimately a tepid experience. And the happy ending not only feels tacked on but smacks of a betrayal of character.

Daniel Petrie was no stranger to the director's chair by this point. He worked mainly in television (his TV credits go back to the 1940s) and he made the critically acclaimed theatrical feature *A Raisin in the Sun* in 1961. He would go on to make the famous Sally Field vehicle *Sybil* and the telefright entry, *Moon of the Wolf*. Here he hits all the required notes: graveyard scenes, violent thunderstorms, and finally a spooky basement where the mystery is revealed.

Eden certainly looks the part of a fish out of water. She parades about in a series of fashionable outfits and drives a big Mercury around the two-bit town. Her Liza has a certain amount of determination, but also must make the mistakes that will further the plot. Hagman's role of Eddie is one of lesser time—he shows up halfway through to convince Liza to return to him—and lesser weight. Eddie isn't really integral to the plot, and even his active stance near the end merely gets in the way.

Vera Miles was in her prime around this time. Ever beautiful and talented enough to give depth to a transparent character, Miles makes us feel sorry for the weakness displayed by Rose. John Rubinstein, on the other hand, never comes across as anything other than the bad influence he played countless times. Even the most naïve of viewers won't believe his smarmy "concerned act" for a minute.

Rubinstein is the son of the famous concert pianist Arthur Rubenstein, so it isn't surprising that John would have a second career in music. As a composer, Rubenstein's credits include the Robert Redford vehicles *The Candidate* and *Jeremiah Johnson*, the television series *Family* in which he starred, and Monte Hellman's *If China 9, Liberty 37*. His acting career began in the late 60s, and he has appeared regularly in film and television for more than three decades including the lead in the psychedelic western *Zachariah* (for which he also did the music) and the horror entry *The Car*. His other tele-frights are *Something Evil* and *She's Dressed to Kill*.

A Howling in the Woods is lucky to have several solid, recognizable character actors in the cast. The ever dependable George Murdock and Ford Rainey play their parts as troublemaker and conflicted sheriff, respectively, with ease. Cult favorite Ruta Lee, who gave support in many television shows of the 60s and 70s, has a small part, as does little Lisa Gerritsen who played Bess Lindstrom on the long-running *Mary Tyler Moore Show*. Tyne Daly, who plays the murdered girl's mother, would go onto fame and fortune as half of the popular *Cagney & Lacey* cop series.

Location shooting in Lake Tahoe gives some unusual flavor to this adequate production. The cast is the draw rather than the story, so those looking for favorite faces will find more entertainment than those looking for a compelling mystery.

CAST: Barbara Eden, Larry Hagman, John Rubinstein, Vera Miles, Tyne Daly, Ruta Lee, George Murdock, Ford Rainey, Bill Vint, Karl Swenson, and Lisa Gerritsen.

CREDITS: Director: Daniel Petrie; Teleplay: Richard De Roy, based upon the novel by Velda Johnston; Music: Dave Grusin; Production: Universal TV; Running Time: 94 minutes; Air Date: 11/5/71; Network: NBC

Hurricane

AKA **Hurricane Hunters**

Hurricane follows the meandering path of tropical storm Hilda as it gains strength and earns the designation of hurricane, before making landfall in Mississippi. The dates used, August 17 and 18, are the same dates that the real hurricane Hilda hit the gulf coast in 1964, although the characters are fictitious, and events are dramatized and updated to the present day of 1974.

Wise old scientist Dr. McCutcheon (Will Geer) and his new assistant, Lee Jackson (Michael Learned), track the storm from the National Hurricane Warning Service in Coral Gables, Florida. The conflict here (and there isn't much of one) is that McCutcheon tends to rely on his instincts, while Jackson favors the strict scientific method of predicting the behavior of weather phenomena. Both actors were in the midst of the long-running *The Waltons* when this was filmed, and their chemistry together translates well from the Depression-era milieu of the series to modern times.

Martin Milner, who was just beginning his run of disaster telefilms, here plays Air Force pilot Hymie Stoddard, who is in charge of a crew that flies into the eyes of hurricanes to drop sensors. When they reach the eye of Hilda they notice a boat stuck in the calm, and are given the duty of rescuing the hapless couple Paul and Louise Damon (Larry Hagman and Jessica Walter). Barry Livingston plays their worried son stuck at home.

Others in the cast include Barry Sullivan as Stoddard's dad and Frank Sutton as Bert Pearson, a fellow too stubborn to evacuate his home. Sutton, who will always be known as Sgt. Carter on the *Gomer Pyle* series, does a good turn here as the cocky Pearson who'd rather hunker down and throw a hurricane party than take the storm seriously. The resulting irony of his actions are of the "I told you so" variety, but Sutton's skill in creating a whole character with little screen time courts feelings of empathy with the

Will Geer and Michael Learned (best known for her role as Olivia Walton on *The Waltons*) chart the path of deadly weather in *Hurricane* (1974).

viewer, overshadowing the character's snide superiority. *Hurricane* would be Sutton's last movie. He died of a heart attack at the age of 50 shortly after filming completed.

Hurricane is one of the era's few TV disaster films that manages to create some emotional resonance with its characters. The combination of a script that tries hard to play it real, and good actors given the same chance, makes it a higher quality experience. The actual footage of hurricanes and the resulting devastation is impressive, and gives a sense of experiencing events first hand. The special effects on display when the Damons are stuck in the eye of the hurricane on their boat are admittedly weak, but they do provoke an eerie feeling.

Oddly, the fate of Stoddard and his crew as they make their way back from the eye is mishandled. We are with them as their plane starts exhibiting problems but the lack of resolution leaves the viewer feeling a bit cheated. Blame for this, however slight, must fall on the shoulders of experienced director Jerry Jameson. *Hurricane* might not blow anyone away but the cool breeze of competence is refreshing.

Watch for the soon to be famous Patrick Duffy (*Dallas*) in a small role as Pearson's nervous neighbor. Writer Jack Turley wrote the telefright *Terror on the 40th Floor* and Bert I. Gordon's *The Empire of the Ants*. Composer Vic Mizzy also worked on *Terror on the 40th Floor*, but is most famous for his theme for *The Addams Family*.

CAST: Larry Hagman, Martin Milner, Jessica Walter, Barry Sullivan, Michael Learned, Frank Sutton, Will Geer, Lonny Chapman, Ayn Ruymen, Barry Livingston, Jim Antonio, Jr., Ric Carrott, Jack Colvin, Alan Landers, Charles Lampkin, Maggie Malooly, Read Morgan, Jessica Rains, Paul Tully, Patrick Duffy, Sam Edwards, Carl Mikal Franklin, Jerry Hardin, James Jeter, Thomas Leopold, Ken Menard, Stephen Rogers, and Tracy Savage.

CREDITS: Director: Jerry Jameson; Teleplay: Jack Turley, from the novel by William C. Andersen; Music: Vic Mizzy; Production: Montagne Productions; Running Time: 75 minutes; Air Date: 9/10/74; Network: ABC

The Initiation of Sarah

Carrie goes to college. *The Initiation of Sarah* is a pitiable attempt to cash in on the Stephen King–Brian De Palma 1976 blockbuster, shameless in its imitation and inept in its half-hearted stretch to innovate.

Telekinetic Sarah Goodwin (Kay Lenz) leaves for Waltham College with her sister Patty (Morgan Brittany). Sarah is the outcast wallflower adopted into the Goodwin family under mysterious circumstances. She ends up at the loser sorority while Patty, the pretty, favored daughter, is picked by the premier sorority, headed by first-class bitch Jennifer Lawrence (Morgan Fairchild). The rivalry between the two organizations goes back many years and involves the death of a pledge, again under mysterious circumstances. Housemother Erica Hunter (Shelley Winters) was somehow involved in the scandal and continues to hold a grudge. Mrs. Hunter seizes the rare opportunity and tries to harness the undisciplined power of Sarah to take revenge.

Lenz gives a good performance as the put-upon Sarah, whose powers are showcased in mild manifestations such as cracking nearby mirrors and dunking Jennifer Lawrence in a fountain. Lenz appeared on television for the first time at the tender age of eight weeks, and has hardly been absent from the medium since. Her breakthrough role would have been as the troubled free spirit in *Breezy* in 1973, if the film had not been ignored by the public (she was nominated for a Golden Globe, however). As it was, the telefilm *Lisa, Bright and Dark* secured her a solid fan base and a lifetime of work. Her marriage to teen idol David Cassidy in 1977 garnered much publicity, and their union lasted six years. She had a hit feature with *White Line Fever* and would go on to another horror entry, *House*. Other notable roles include that of a policewoman in the revealing thriller *Stripped to Kill*, and providing the voice for superhero American Maid in the cult cartoon series *The Tick*. Lenz has been nominated several times for Emmys, winning one in 1988. Unfortunately, she made no other telefrights in the 70s.

The oft-scorned Shelley Winters does better in the early scenes where her low-key performance gives the film its only, and fleeting, depth. Towards the end of the film, however, her stumbling, unconvincing theatrics betray a distinct lack of direction. Amongst the other players, Morgan Fairchild plays it mean and superficial as usual, the temperament that would suit her well in the coming years on nighttime soaps. Robert Hays, who would soon hit it big with *Airplane!*, has a minor role devised merely to set up the humiliation scene stolen from *Carrie*. Morgan Brittany suffices in the role of Sarah's conflicted sister, Patty. But *The Initiation of Sarah*'s main claim to fame is the casting of a clutch of actors with familial ties to more famous talents including Kathryn Crosby, Tisa Farrow, Elizabeth Stack, Talia Balsam, Deborah Ryan, Nora Heflin and even Debi Fries, the daughter-in-law of executive producer Charles W. Fries.

Director Robert Day was capable of better things, but here seems content with the pedestrian staging of ridiculously contrived situations. Contributing to an unsatisfying experience are the vague, half-developed plot points concerning the past. These are important dropped balls that would have explained the characters' motivations. For instance, what happened those many years ago when Mrs. Hunter was involved in a pledge's suicide? And why is it intimated that Mrs. Hunter may be Sarah's real mother? These elements go unexplained and unresolved, leaving the viewer adrift in a pond of copycat moments and sketchy purposes.

CAST: Kay Lenz, Tony Bill, Kathryn Crosby, Morgan Fairchild, Morgan Brittany,

Robert Hays, Shelley Winters, Tisa Farrow, Elizabeth Stack, Deborah Ryan, Nora Heflin, Talia Balsam, Michael Talbott, Jennifer Gay, Susan Duvall, Albert Owens, and Debi Fries.

Crew: Director: Robert Day; Teleplay: Don Ingalls, Carol Saraceno & Kenette Gfeller; Music: Johnny Harris; Production: Stonehenge Productions; Running Time: 97 minutes; Air Date: 2/6/78; Network: ABC

The Invasion of Carol Enders

Producer-director Dan Curtis had his hand in several intimate productions in the early 1970s, which were shot on videotape in Canada. *The Invasion of Carol Enders* is one of these. All of said movies skirt the definition of fright film but *The Invasion of Carol Enders'* supernatural element combined with Curtis's involvement qualify it for inclusion here.

Carol Enders (Meredith Baxter) and her fiancé Adam Reston (Christopher Connelly) are attacked while spooning in lover's lane, and Carol is seriously injured when she attempts to escape. Meanwhile, Diana Bernard (Sally Kemp), the wife of a doctor, is fatally injured in an automobile accident. Both patients are sent to the same hospital, and Carol makes a miraculous recovery just as Diana dies. Upon awakening, Carol claims in very convincing terms to be Diana. When the police determine that Diana was murdered, Carol/Diana leaves the hospital to find the killer.

This mild-mannered story of possession will not appeal to those with a fancy for the macabre. It plays more like a soap opera mystery that happens to have a kernel of the supernatural driving the action. The story, by Merwin Gerard, whose credits include the telefilms *The Screaming Woman*, *The Victim* and *She Cried Murder*, was adapted by Gene Raser Kearney. Kearney wrote several *Night Gallery* episodes and the cult favorites *Games* and *Night of the Lepus*.

Meredith Baxter was in the midst of her breakthrough television series *Bridget Loves Bernie* when *The Invasion of Carol Enders* aired. She also appeared in the rat horror film *Ben* in 1972 and Curtis Harrington's telefilm *The Cat Creature* the next year, but her most famous roles were in the long-running series' *Family* and *Family Ties* in the 80s.

Peyton Place alumnus Connelly and familiar character actor Charles Aidman handle the flummoxed husband roles with ease. Connelly's Adam Reston even helps the police in their investigation, playing an important part in solving the mystery. Curtis favorite John Karlen plays Diana's ex-husband, the number one suspect in her death. Most surprising is the small part for Tony Russel as the Bernards' attorney. Russel is most famous in genre circles for his European output in the 1960s, including Antonio Margheriti's *Wild, Wild Planet* and *War of the Planets* and the Eurospy adventures *Secret of the Sphinx* and *Target Goldseven*. In a little known (but unmistakably damaging) career blunder in the early 60s, Russel turned down the lead in Sergio Leone's vastly influential western *A Fistful of Dollars*, which doubtless precipitated his only modest (but appreciated) output.

Dan Curtis has an executive producer credit on this film, and an uncredited nod for direction because several snippets of footage—including Diana's car crash—are taken from *The Norliss Tapes*, which aired the previous year. Director Burt Brinkerhoff was an actor, mainly on television in the 50s and 60s, and this was his first film at the helm. He would go on to make the horror film *Dogs*, and yet another television adaptation of *Frankenstein* in 1987.

Spooky atmosphere is decidedly lacking in the production aside from an occasional remark, such as a doctor's reminiscence of an experience in India where the air was "thick with the spirits of the dead, it was like incense." Dating the action to the early 70s is a scene involving the technological innovation known as a photocopier. But those interested enough to track down this film won't be nitpicking.

CAST: Meredith Baxter, Christopher Connelly, George DiCenzo, John Karlen, Charles

Aidman, Sally Kemp, Cris Nelson, Phil Pine, Tony Russel, and Patricia Hindy.

CREDITS: Director: Burt Brinkerhoff; Teleplay: Gene Raser Kearney, from a story by Kearney and Merwin Gerard; Music: Robert Cobert; Production: Dan Curtis Productions; Running Time: 68 minutes; Air Date: 3/8/74; ABC

Isn't It Shocking?

Despite the flippant title, *Isn't It Shocking?* is a body count movie with a creepy killer who uses a unique method of murder. Revenge, however misplaced, is the motive in this subtle yet winning film that deserves to be remembered.

The elderly in the small, sleepy town of Mount Angel, Massachusetts, are dying of heart attacks at an alarming rate. Police Chief Dan Barnes (Alan Alda) seems at a loss to explain what seem like natural deaths. When one of his officers, Jesse Chapin (Lloyd Nolan), is found dead, Barnes, with the help of his secretary Blanche (Louise Lasser), puts together a pattern but the motive and the identity of the killer is still out of reach.

Director John Badham works with a clever script and a good cast to forge a surprisingly engaging mystery. The British-born Badham had worked on several television series including Rod Serling's *Night Gallery* before this, his first telefright. The next year would see his superior *Diabolique* telefilm remake *Reflections of Murder* air before he hit the big time with *Saturday Night Fever* in 1977. Badham would continue to make popular films (*Dracula*, *Blue Thunder*, *WarGames*, etc.) throughout the 80s and 90s,

(Left to right) Alan Alda, Louise Lasser and Ruth Gordon in *Isn't It Shocking?* **(1973).**

until his return at century's end to the medium that had originally fostered his talent.

As mentioned, casting is a plus. Alan Alda gives an excellent, low-key performance as Chief Barnes, and his chemistry with Louise Lasser seems genuine. Alda had just begun his long-running series *M*A*S*H* the previous year. Lasser would soon begin the short-run series that she would forever be identified with, *Mary Hartman, Mary Hartman*.

These two receive top support from Lloyd Nolan, Liam Dunn (*Blazing Saddles*), Ruth Gordon and Will Geer. Patricia Quinn, who plays Barnes' lover, began her career only a few years earlier by playing the fabled Alice in Arthur Penn's cult favorite, *Alice's Restaurant*.

Edmond O'Brien plays the sweets-crazed killer who has a seriously warped sense of self-worth. O'Brien won the Academy Award for Best Supporting Actor for 1954's *The Barefoot Contessa*, and he was nominated in the same category ten years later for *Seven Days in May*. He was born in New York and, at one point, was a neighbor to Harry Houdini. In the 1940s, O'Brien hit his stride in films noir such as *The Killers*, *The Web* and *White Heat*, culminating in his most famous noir role as the doomed Frank Bigelow in 1950s *D.O.A.* Other interesting roles for the character actor include Ida Lupino's *The Hitch-Hiker*, Jack Webb's *Pete Kelly's Blues*, the 1956 *1984* (as Winston Smith), *Fantastic Voyage*, the excellent *To Commit a Murder* and *The Wild Bunch*. O'Brien continued to work into the 70s (*Dream No Evil*, *They Only Kill Their Masters*), but this would be his only telefright in the decade before his death of Alzheimer's disease in 1985.

The key to the success of *Isn't It Shocking?* is the intelligent script by Lane Slate, for which he won an Edgar Allan Poe Award. The characters of the small town (shot in Mount Angel, Oregon) are drawn with a light touch and an eye for everyday realism. The murders—there are six of them—are not taken lightly, and there are two that are particularly affecting since the viewer is allowed to come to know and like the characters.

The few moments of action, such as the car chase in the cornfield, are deftly handled, and David Shire's sprightly soundtrack is appropriately respectful when required by events. *Isn't It Shocking?* shows the talent and skill that would springboard John Badham to fame, and is recommended as a little gem in the rough.

CAST: Alan Alda, Louise Lasser, Edmond O'Brien, Lloyd Nolan, Will Geer, Ruth Gordon, Dorothy Tristan, Pat Quinn, Liam Dunn, Michael Powell, and Jacqueline Allan.

CREDITS: Director: John Badham; Teleplay: Lane Slate; Music: David Shire; Production: ABC Circle Films; Running Time: 74 minutes; Vehicles provided by Chrysler Corporation; Air Date: 10/2/73; Network: ABC

It Happened at Lakewood Manor

AKA **Panic at Lakewood Manor; Ants!**

Workers at a hotel construction site next to the Lakewood Manor resort uncover a particularly savage strain of ants. When ant attacks cause a fatal accident involving two of his workers, site manager Mike Carr (Robert Foxworth) investigates, and unknowingly unleashes the horde, thereby threatening the resort next door. Eventually, Mike and several others become trapped in the resort by the ever-advancing ants, and options for rescue become increasingly elusive.

Mike is engaged to Valerie Adams (Lynda Day George), who runs the resort owned by her mother Ethel (Myrna Loy). Mike also has a pal who gets involved in the action, Vince (Bernie Casey). The resort is the target of greedy developers Tony Fleming (Gerald Gordon, *General Hospital*) and Gloria Henderson (Suzanne Somers) as the future site of a casino hotel. Hunky handyman Richard Cyril (Barry Van Dyke, son of Dick) is hit on by backpacker Linda Howard (Karen Lamm), thereby creating a love interest. Lamm appeared in the telefright *The Night They Took Miss Beautiful* and the weak horror entry *The Unseen*, but she is more famous for her celebrity marriages to Robert Lamm of the rock group Chicago, and twice to Dennis Wilson of The Beach Boys. Peggy (Anita Gillette) and Lionel White (familiar character actor Steve Franken) are inspectors from the board of health investigating the accident.

This hybrid of the by-now familiar disaster film and the trendy eco-horror cycle was filmed in Vancouver, B.C. It is hilariously inept in every department: conception, scripting, direction, acting, photography, editing, etc. But it does manage never to be boring, and is unintentionally funny quite often. Director Robert Sheerer got nowhere with his acting career in the 1940s, and began helming television shows in the 60s. His few features include the Disney romp *The World's Greatest Athlete* and *How to Beat the High Co$t of Living*, but his work in television would eventually result in four Emmy nominations. This would be his only venture into telefright territory.

After the requisite ant attacks (a little boy, a kitchen worker, etc.), *It Happened at Lakewood Manor* settles into the various rescue efforts afforded the trapped players. The helicopter rescue of wheelchair-bound Ethel is particularly eventful. They manage to get Ethel out of the upstairs window and into the chopper, but when it lands it blows the ants all over the place, covering the crowd that has gathered. The extras then do the ant dance and get sprayed with water hoses like it was spring break. Amidst all this chaos, the fire chief (Brian Dennehy) decides to light the gasoline-filled trench that has been dug around the resort. The insanity continues as hunky Richard falls out of a hotel window, and has to make a death-defying six-foot leap onto a bulldozer.

When inspector Peggy takes in a sample of the ants for testing, the scientist she consults immediately launches into the standard chemical-poison-mutation theory that fully explains everything. What is amazing here is how the scene lacks any subtlety whatsoever. The scientist even has at his fingertips a video of ants eating other bugs, to point out the "possibilities." He shows up later for more exposition about ants, claiming they have stickers on their little legs so they can't be wiped off.

As expected, the special effects are below par. The fake ants spread around to bulk up the numbers of the real ants are completely unconvincing. Large chunks of this mobile army don't ever move. The superimposed shadows that are supposed to pass for armies of marauders are equally unpersuasive.

The cast members' mouths are endlessly full of inane dialogue. At the time, Suzanne Somers was on the cusp of her career-defining role as the bimbo Chrissy in the sophisticated sitcom *Three's Company*. Her character says things such as "Haven't you ever heard of the Eleventh Commandment: Thou shalt not live in plastic?" and (pointing to her head) "Look beyond all the bumps and you may see that there's a head up here." The latter line gets this response from her lover: "I may not see it, baby, but I sure do hear it."

Top-billed Foxworth plays it macho as Mike, all beard and bravado, but he calms down in one of the premier silly scenes in the film. Mike, his fiancée Valerie and developer Fleming are the last to be stuck in the resort. As the dreaded ants are coming into the room, the scientist tells them by phone that if they don't move or breathe on the ants, and allow the ants to crawl all over them, they won't be bitten. Mike cuts some wallpaper off the wall and makes tubes for each of them to breathe through. The image of these three covered in ants, listening to Mike's calming yoga voice, is a special moment. Soon, Fleming can't stand it and tries to jump into the pool from the window. He misses. The pair left are rescued by contamination-suited firemen in an amusing continuation of the delirious proceedings.

In the end, the know-it-all scientist says not to fret about the ants that were spread all over. "They'll lose their force," he says knowledgeably. If this movie is a joke, it is cleverly conceived, though poorly executed. If it is serious, then it is shameless in its inferiority. And a hell of a lot of fun for it.

CAST: Robert Foxworth, Lynda Day George, Gerald Gordon, Bernie Casey, Barry Van Dyke, Karen Lamm, Myrna Loy, Anita Gillette, Steve Franken, Brian Dennehy, Suzanne Somers, Moose Drier, Barbara Brownell, Bruce French, Stacy Keach Sr., Rene Enriquez, Vincent Cobb, and Jim Storm.

CREDITS: Director: Robert Scheerer; Teleplay: Guerdon Trueblood; Composer: Ken Richmond; Production: Alan Landsburg Productions; Running time: 100 minutes; Air Date: 12/2/77; Network: ABC

Killdozer

Lloyd Kelly (Clint Walker) is running a short crew, clearing a base camp for Warburton drilling teams on a small island 200 miles off the coast of Africa. When a bulldozer comes in contact with a long-buried meteor, a malevolent alien force is transferred to the machine, which then goes on a destructive, murderous rampage.

Famed science fiction author Theodore Sturgeon wrote the novella that inspired *Killdozer*. It is debatable, of course, how much of Sturgeon's eloquence is retained in the telefilm, but since he worked on the screenplay, cries of sabotage hold less weight. The resulting film does maintain a sense of humor about itself—a quality that greatly enhances the experience—and slices of Sturgeon's wicked satire are still intact. For instance, it is clearly intended that notorious government contractor Halliburton is being skewered as the Warburton Company, "WarCo" for short.

Jerry London (*Shogun*), whose résumé looks like the life of television itself, began his directorial career in the late 1960s, on series such as *Hogan's Heroes* (which he helped produce) and *The Bob Newhart Show*. *Killdozer* would be his first telefilm credit, and the only one of the 1970s that would qualify as a fright film. His talent is apparent: the pace is kept swift, the better to glide over the script's logic holes.

The small cast is blessed with several strong performers. Clint Walker is top-notch as the dry alcoholic Kelly, who is trying to salvage the job and his career. The 6' 6" Norman Eugene "Clint" Walker was born a twin in Illinois, and worked as a deputy sheriff, carnival roustabout and an oil prospector, among other odd jobs, before becoming an actor. Walker became an instant star in 1955 with the long-running *Cheyenne* series, which practically ushered in the television western phenomenon. The muscular leading man had success in film as well, with roles in *The Night of the Grizzly*, *The Dirty Dozen*, *Sam Whiskey* and *Deadly Harvest*,

Clint Walker must outwit an alien force in *Killdozer* (1974).

among others. Walker also shows up in two more telefrights: he gives an excellent performance in Dan Curtis's *Scream of the Wolf* and lends much-needed support in the lesser *Snowbeast*.

Rounding out the *Killdozer* cast are Carl Betz as Dennis Holvig, Neville Brand as mechanic Chub Foster, villainous character actor James Wainwright, James A. Watson, Jr., and Robert Urich, who has a small part here as victim number one, would go on to stardom in the crime series *Vega$*.

This cat-and-mouse story, where explanations for the fantastical events are neither given nor required, succeeds despite its shortcomings. Gil Melle's computer-based score tries to invoke the otherworldly, but it only distracts from the action. The Indian Dunes location is a dead giveaway that the production stuck close to Southern California. Although held up as a poster child for the ridiculousness of the television fright film, *Killdozer* is a surprisingly entertaining, well-acted distraction that holds up after multiple viewings.

CAST: Clint Walker, Carl Betz, Neville Brand, James Wainwright, Robert Urich, and James A. Watson, Jr.

CREDITS: Director: Jerry London; Teleplay: Theodore Sturgeon and Ed MacKillop' adapted by Herbert F. Solow, based on the novella by Theodore Sturgeon; Music: Gil Melle; Production: Universal TV; Running Time: 69 minutes; Air Date: 2/2/74; Network: ABC

Killer Bees

Edward van Bohlen (Edward Albert) returns to his ancestral home at the urging of his pregnant fiancée Victoria Wells (Kate Jackson). The town of van Bohlen sprung up around the family's vineyard, which is now run by Edward's grandmother, "Madame" (Gloria Swanson), who has a strange rapport with the bees that sweeten the wine. Edward, the black sheep of the family, has been shunned for leaving the family business to attend law school, and the unannounced presence of Victoria causes discord amongst the clan. Meanwhile, bee attacks against outsiders are on the rise.

One of the better bee movies of the era, *Killer Bees* is a low-key rumination on matriarchal society, the social form of the bees themselves. "Madame" runs the van Bohlen family with an iron hand, and both the family's business and the town surrounding the vineyard, have prospered. The honey provides the van Bohlen wine with a unique sweetness, and the bees, who seem to have a telepathic relationship with "Madame," protect the vineyards and the family from outside interference.

The family believes that Edward and Victoria represent a threat to the status quo, a disruption to the finely oiled machine that has provided it wealth and power over the years. But it isn't the presence of the couple that threatens the family, it is the emotional response the family shows them that is the real danger.

The disdain with which "Madame" treats Victoria is echoed by the entire family towards the couple. Edward's father Rudolf (Craig Stevens) is cold to his son, as are Edward's brothers Helmut (Roger Davis) and Mathias (Don McGovern). Edward had been expecting this treatment. Before meeting the family, Victoria claims they are just people, after all. But Edward responds with, "No, they're van Bohlens."

The bees however, attracted to and protective of the family, do not share their emotions. The family's emulation of the bee society—protecting and serving the queen—is flawed in a human way. The bees understand that the ultimate good of the hive is what drives them, and events transpire that prove them right. The hive/family does survive, but only because they are forced to take a larger view of their sheltered life.

Gloria Swanson, in her telefilm debut and next-to-last film overall, seems to relish the old world character she's given here. Her German accent and dramatic flourishes are both thick. The actors around her are easily overshadowed, and the respect shown her "Madame" seems to draw from a genuine source.

Killer Bees

Gloria Swanson has a strange rapport with the bees in *Killer Bees* (1974).

Curtis Harrington, whose telefrights of the period are usually a cut above, seems fully engaged here. There is no temptation to pull out the stops, and those wishing to see mass bee attacks and grand destruction will be disappointed. The focus is on the character of the family—not necessarily individual characters—and Harrington approaches the film as a symphony rather than a collection of smaller, more intimate pieces.

As is typical of a Harrington picture, the minor parts are filled with familiar faces if not familiar names, talented character actors who bring that extra something to their roles, no matter how small. Two of these to watch out for are Jack Perkins, as a frustrated salesman who becomes the first victim of the bees, and Liam Dunn, as the resigned café owner. Also note the first film appearance of John Getz, as a gas station attendant. Getz would later come to prominence thanks to the Coen brothers' *Blood Simple* and David Cronenberg's *The Fly*.

The film was shot at Oakville Vineyards in Napa Valley, and the van Bohlen ancestral home is reportedly now owned by Francis Ford Coppola. On a technical trivia note, the now famous director Joel Schumacher (*The Lost Boys*) had his first, and thus far only, "Production Design" credit on this film. Writers Joyce and John William Corrington worked together on *The Omega Man*, Martin Scorsese's *Boxcar Bertha* and *Battle for the Planet of the Apes*.

CAST: Edward Albert, Kate Jackson, Roger Davis, Don McGovern, Gloria Swanson, Craig Stevens, John S. Ragin, Liam Dunn, Donald Gentry, Robert L. Balzer, Jack Perkins, Daniel Woodworth, John Getz, and Heather Ann Bostain.

CREDITS: Director: Curtis Harrington; Teleplay: Joyce Corrington and John William Corrington; Music: David Shire; Production: Robert Stigwood Organization; Running Time: 74 minutes; Air Date: 2/26/74; Network: ABC

Killer on Board

By the end of 1977, the networks had had more than their share of disaster films, intentional or not. *Killer on Board* is a film as tired as the genre. It features lame jokes, inane situations, cardboard characters, and even ugly, ill-fitting costumes. The cast of all-stars goes through the motions to make a film that is now truly and duly forgotten.

A viral disease sweeps through a cruise ship just departed from the Philippines. Once we get to know them, the crew and passengers begin to drop like flies. Diverted from Honolulu to San Francisco, the ship is quarantined, which triggers a standoff between the remaining healthy passengers and the crew.

Philip Leacock directs the expected conflicts and personal dramas by the numbers. This was undoubtedly a paid vacation for all concerned, and the result is predictably lazy.

Of the ensemble cast, no single performance stands out. The film tends to pass before the eyes without any particular highs or lows. Claude Akins is the ornery captain deferred from a freighter with his doctor friend, Murray Hamilton. Hamilton, who looks genuinely ill here, has one good acting moment on his death bed. Frank Converse, a theatrically trained actor, seems miserable in his role as another doctor at odds with Hamilton.

Jane Seymour, whose character is hit upon continuously by the male cast, was in the midst of her burgeoning stardom at this time, and is one of the few rays of light visible. William Daniels plays his usual cantankerous complainer, and George Hamilton, who never had the opportunity to play in any of the better fright telefilms of the era, has only a few scenes before his character mercifully dies.

Mourning widow Patty Duke Astin continues her put-upon roles by being thrown down a flight of stairs in front of her son. John Roper has the only moment of true terror here as the junkie musician who, suffering from withdrawal, imagines he sees a boat coming alongside and jumps overboard. The moment he realizes his error, and watches the cruise ship sail away, is worthy of nightmares.

One line, spoken by Converse concerning experience, will ring true to the viewer: "Some men have a thousand of them while others have the same one a thousand times." While it may not be the one-thousandth disaster film, *Killer on Board* may very well feel like it.

Writer Sandor Stern was born in Canada, and is the brother of director Steven Hilliard Stern (*The Ghost of Flight 401*). His writing credits include *The Amityville Horror* and the interesting thriller *Pin...*, which he also directed. His telefright credits include *The Strange and Deadly Occurrence*, *Where Have All the People Gone?* and *Red*

Susan Howard and George Hamilton in a publicity still for *Killer on Board* (1977).

Alert. Prolific composer Earle Hagen is most famous for writing the theme for the *I Spy* series.

"Filmed on location in Hawaii, on the Pacific Ocean, in San Francisco and at Burbank Studios."

CAST: (ao) Claude Akins; Patty Duke Astin, Len Birman, Frank Converse, William Daniels, George Hamilton, Murray Hamilton, Susan Howard, Jeff Lynas, Jane Seymour, and Beatrice Straight. Also Michael Lerner, Thalmus Rasulala, John Roper, Bonnie Bartlett, Joshua Bryant, John Durren, Edward Callardo, Rafael Campos, Fritzi Burr, Trudy Desmond, Jay Varela, John Dewey-Carter, Patrick McNamara, Norman J. Andrews, Rudy Challenger, Jim Storm, Fred Lerner, Robert S. Busch, Kandy Berley, Lee F. Stetson, Gene Massey, Howard Curtis, Johnnie Walker, Jr., Wallace W. Landford, Dane A. Taylor, Donald R. Smith, Joseph W. Vida, Natt Christian, David Hinton, and Rene Paulo.

CREDITS: Director: Philip Leacock; Teleplay: Sandor Stern; Music: Earle Hagen; Production: Lorimar Productions; Running Time: 98 minutes; Air Date: 10/10/77; Network: NBC

Last Bride of Salem

Artist Matt Clifton (Bradford Dillman), his wife Jennifer (Lois Nettleton) and their little girl Kelly (Joni Bick) rent a house in the small town of Salem Village, where Matt can work in peace and quiet. The Cliftons are told about the town's history of witchcraft, and about a certain Prosper Morgan who vowed to put an end to the local witches. Soon, Matt seems possessed with painting a nearby house where, it is reputed, the witches held their Black Masses. Kelly, too, is taken with dark moods and makes friends with a mysterious man in the woods. Mom Jennifer consults the local preacher, who forms a theory that the Cliftons' ancestry ties in with the town's past, and which may mean the family is in serious danger.

Last Bride of Salem, originally shown on the *The ABC Afternoon Playbreak*, was deemed popular enough to later merit a showing in prime time. This surprisingly effective, gothic tale of the occult was shot on video, probably in Canada, and earned star Bradford Dillman a Daytime Emmy.

Though it was Dillman who walked away with the award, Nettleton gives the tour de force performance, as the mother desperate to save her family from the powers of darkness. Nettleton was Miss Chicago of 1948 and made her Broadway acting debut in 1949, but it would be television, beginning in the early 50s, where most of her major work would be accomplished. The actress was ubiquitous in the medium from the 60s on, where she had memorable turns in *The Twilight Zone*, *Route 66* and many other popular shows. Her feature film output includes *Dirty Dingus Magee*, Arthur Hiller's *The Man in the Glass Booth*, Wes Craven's *Deadly Blessing*, the kitsch classic *Butterfly* and *The Best Little Whorehouse in Texas*. Her other 70s telefrights include *Terror in the Sky* and *Women in Chains*.

Signs of the unusual are present right from the outset. *Last Bride of Salem* begins with Kelly's nightmare of a Black Mass, even before the family has moved to Salem Village. When the family arrives, Kelly recognizes the nearby house as the one in her dream. And the caretaker of the Cliftons' house draws the symbol of an upside down cross on their back door soon after the family moves in.

The legend of Salem Village is told by the local doctor, who is described (in jest) by the preacher as "our only doctor, so try very hard to stay well." Back in 1691, witchcraft was rampant in the town, with trials and burnings at the stake a common occurrence. One local, Prosper Morgan, who lived in the house the Cliftons have rented, set out to find the witches. He didn't have to look far because they were in a grove of trees behind the creepy house across the way, the house that Kelly saw in her dream. Morgan set fire to the grove, killing all but one witch, who made a pact with the devil to live long enough to wipe out the Morgan clan. This witch was crafty, always leaving one Morgan alive to carry on the name, thereby assuring his immortality. The Morgan murders always take place on the vernal equinox, March 21, a date soon approaching.

It would be unfair to first-time viewers to reveal the entire mystery that involves the Cliftons, but it has something to do with Matt's ancestry, and therefore his daughter. Both come under the spell of the coven, but the full intent of the witches is not revealed until the final minutes. Matt's paintings of the suspect house (he does several) culminate in a close-up of the front. This painting is somehow used to transport Matt and Kelly into the house from his studio. The strange scene has the two walking toward the painting before Jennifer discovers they have disappeared.

The forces of good are represented by Jennifer, of course, who fights for her family, but also the local preacher, Hiram Fletcher (Murray Westgate), and the caretaker's mute son, Thomas Whately (Robert Hawkins). It is Fletcher who does his homework and solves part of the mystery; however, the witches paralyze the preacher before he can act. The mute Whately tries to warn Jennifer but she doesn't understand what he is telling her. We learn that Whately's tongue was cut out by his own father, a bargain that kept the witches from killing the boy.

The name "Abihu" figures prominently in the film. The preacher invokes the name in a sermon as one who defied God, and brought death from the heavens (Leviticus Ch. 10). Kelly also calls her mysterious friend by that name; that man turns out to be the leader of the witches.

The end of the film contains the required twist that suggests Evil lives on despite our best efforts. Whenever someone says, "The nightmare is over," it is a safe bet they are wrong. An unbilled, and quite young, John Candy can be spotted in the church congregation, and at the Black Masses as one of the witches.

Director Tom Donovan worked on many daytime dramas, including *General Hospital* and *Love Is a Many Splendored Thing*, both of which he produced. Writer Rita Lakin penned the telefright *Women in Chains*.

CAST: Lois Nettleton, Bradford Dillman, Paul Harding, Joni Bick, Murray Westgate, Susan Rubes, James Douglas, Patricia Hamilton, Robert Hawkins, Ed McNamara, Rex Hagon, and Moya Fenwick. Not billed: John Candy.

CREDITS: Director: Tom Donovan; Teleplay: Rita Lakin, based on a story by Ken Johnson, Justin Edgerton, and Rita Lakin; Music Supervisor: Sybil Weinberger; Production: R.L. Square; Running Time: 73 minutes; Air Date: 5/8/74; Network: ABC

The Legend of Lizzie Borden

"The story you are about to see is based largely on fact. It is considered one of the most infamous and bizarre murder cases of the past century."

Fall River, Massachusetts, August 4, 1892. The bodies of Andrew and Abby Borden are discovered in their home, the victims of a brutal axe murder. Daughter Lizzie (Elizabeth Montgomery) is found to be "probably guilty" at the coroner's inquest, and she is remanded to jail. A trial ensues the following June and she is found not guilty.

The Legend of Lizzie Borden is a classic telefilm. And for good reason. The impeccable production has a sense of the eerie about it, as if the filmmakers fell under the spell of the frightening and folkloric story they were telling. Director Paul Wendkos seems particularly inspired, and the result garnered a Golden Globe nomination for Best Motion Picture Made for TV and an Edgar Allan Poe Award for writer William Bast (*The Valley of Gwangi*). Composer Billy Goldenberg concocts a harpsichord score that invokes thoughts of a disturbing nursery rhyme, perhaps inspired by the famous "Lizzie Borden took an axe …" poem.

Wendkos's leading lady, the incomparable Elizabeth Montgomery, was nominated for an Emmy for her performance as the decidedly odd Lizzie Borden. The beautiful, talented and much-beloved Montgomery was the darling of American television. Daughter of the actor Robert Montgomery, she made her television debut on the *Robert Montgomery Presents* show. In fact, Elizabeth worked on many of the live television shows of the 50s, such as *Kraft Television Theater* and *Studio One*. Her film roles included *Johnny Cool* but she came into her own, of course, as Samantha Stevens in the Bewitched series, which ran from 1964 to 1972. Her appearances on television following *Bewitched* were reduced, but specifically designed to break away from the image of Samantha that the public loved so much. The telefright *The Victim* was her first role after the series, and she would go on to purposefully different characters in telefilms such as *Mrs. Sundance*, *A Case of Rape*, *Act of Violence*, etc. Although she could never fully escape her role of the sprightly witch, Montgomery's abilities led to nine Emmy nominations before her death of cancer in 1995.

The Legend of Lizzie Borden begins with the discovery of the crime; the details of the Borden family life—and the conjectured murder—unfold in flashback throughout the subsequent trial. The sense of the unreal is immediately apparent when the first time we see Lizzie she is standing at the door, as if in a daze, after the bodies are discovered. The character of Lizzie is portrayed as a complicated mixture of childlike naiveté and clever calculation, as in a scene that takes place the night after the crime. In the wee hours, Lizzie sneaks down the stairs to the parlor where the bodies of her parents are lying. She raises the blood-soaked sheet covering her father and gives him a gentle kiss, oblivious to the horrible tableau around her.

Subtitles break the film into sections. "The Accusation" covers the coroner's inquest where, contradicting the testimony of the maid, the Borden family is revealed as seriously dysfunctional. The wealthy Andrew Borden was a notorious skinflint, forcing the family to subsist on spoiled mutton broth of late, and both parents are shown to be unpleasant all around.

"The Ordeal" shows Lizzie awaiting trial in jail, where more personality quirks are unveiled. On one hand she seems obsessed with picking out the most flattering, expensive clothes for the trial, and on the other reveals the hurt at being described as "the sphinx of coldness." It is also in this section where the filmmakers' allusion to the necrophilia of Lizzie's mortician father is none too subtle.

"The Trial," which began on June 5, 1893, covers the first few days of testimony, with protesters outside the courthouse carry signs proclaiming Lizzie's innocence. Here, we learn that Lizzie had been given morphine shots on a regular

Elizabeth Montgomery in a publicity still for *The Legend of Lizzie Borden* (1975).

basis for nearly a year, the time it took the case to come to trial.

"The Betrayal" brings to light that Lizzie burned the dress she was wearing the day of the murder, and "The Trump Card" relates how the prosecution was unable to prove that an axe found on the Borden premises was used in the murder.

"The Verdict" is where we finally see the filmmakers' idea of how Lizzie committed the crime. The jury foreman's answer hangs in mid-air while we watch Lizzie meticulously go about slaughtering first her stepmother, and then her father, with only a moment of comprehension of the horrible deed. The fact that she was found not guilty is blamed more on the inadequate prosecution than on the idea she was actually innocent.

Thankfully, the filmmakers realized that an all-star cast would have detracted from the impact of this finely tuned production, so instead all of the supporting roles were given to dependable and familiar character actors. Katherine Helmond (*Soap*) plays Lizzie's sister, and Fritz Weaver her father. Hayden Rorke (*I Dream of Jeannie*) has a cameo as a journalist, and John Zaremba (*The Time Tunnel*) plays a judge. The prosecuting attorney and defense attorney are played by Ed Flanders (*Salem's Lot*) and Don Porter (*The Norliss Tapes*), respectively.

In closing we are told that Lizzie moved away, living the life of a wealthy spinster until she died in 1927, at the age of 66. The public still has a macabre fascination with this curious and horrendous unsolved murder, similar to that of the undying mystery of Jack the Ripper. This compelling, imaginative film is perhaps the best and most accomplished version to date. Highly recommended.

CAST: Elizabeth Montgomery, (ao) Fionnuala Flanagan, Ed Flanders, Katherine Helmond, Don Porter, and Fritz Weaver. Also (ao) Bonnie Bartlett, John Beal, Helen Craig, Alan Hewitt, Gail Kobe, Hayden Rorke, Amzie Strickland, Robert Symonds, and Iggie Wolfington. Also John Zaremba, J. Edward McKinley, Norman Stuart, Jon Lormer, Lynn Wood, Olan Soule, Judson Morgan, John Alvin, Patricia Wilson, Tracie Savage, Gloria Stuart, and Joan Crosby.

CREDITS: Director: Paul Wendkos; Teleplay: William Bast; Music: Billy Goldenberg; Production: George LeMaire Productions; Running Time: 92 minutes; Air Date: 2/10/75; Network: ABC

Look What's Happened to Rosemary's Baby

AKA **Rosemary's Baby II**

"He has his father's eyes."

Eight-year-old Adrian (Stephen McHattie), the young spawn of Satan, is spirited away by his mother, Rosemary (Patty Duke Astin). The cult that arranged the blasphemous birth, led by Roman and Minnie Castevet (Ray Milland and Ruth Gordon), soon recover the child with the help of prostitute Marjean Dorn (Tina Louise), who raises the child as his aunt. Come Adrian's twenty-first birthday, the decision must be made whether he is worthy of the role he was chosen for, or if he must be used to further the plot and then be killed.

Aired two days before Halloween, 1976, this ill-conceived and grossly mishandled sequel to the smash hit *Rosemary's Baby* is sure to disappoint even the most forgiving genre fan. What could have been an interesting, even provocative meditation on the duality of our nature is instead a disjointed collection of shallow scenes filled with half-baked ideas.

Among Sam O'Steen's half dozen lackluster directorial credits is *Queen of the Stardust Ballroom*, for which he received an Emmy nomination and was given the Directors Guild of America Award. Interestingly, Arkansas-born O'Steen, who died in 2000, had a sterling career as an editor, working on some of the finest films of the late 60s and early 70s, including *Cool Hand Luke, Carnal Knowledge, The Graduate, Chinatown*—and *Rosemary's Baby*. What events led to his participation in *Look What's Hap-*

pened to Rosemary's Baby and caused the near-absolute failure of the project, are not known.

The inherent evil of the adolescent Adrian is demonstrated by his finding and crushing a black Easter egg, by his bedroom decorations of devil puppets, swastikas and baby dolls hung upside down, and by the burn on his chest caused by his mother's cross necklace. The 20-year-old Adrian is played by Stephen McHattie, who was almost 30 at the time, a discrepancy that is readily apparent. McHattie's breakthrough role was that of James Dean, in the telefilm of that name which aired earlier that same year. He is still working in film and television, amassing more than one hundred credits to date. McHattie tries to bring some life to the conflicted character of Adrian/Andrew but ultimately, the confusion of identity—and of the production itself—weighs down the performance.

The film is broken into segments or "books," the first being "The Book of Rosemary," in which mother and child try to escape their fate. Patty Duke Astin as Rosemary unleashes her thespian gifts in a desperate attempt to bring gravity to the situation, but without any character establishment, her histrionics are for naught. This section does contain perhaps the most memorable scene in the film, however. After meeting hooker Marjean, Rosemary is duped into getting on a bus without Adrian. The doors close, the bus leaves, and Rosemary discovers to her horror that no one is driving. She has just boarded the express to Hell.

In "The Book of Adrian," we find the grown version to be a rascal who drives a black Triumph TR7 too fast. He lives in a den of iniquity called Marjean's Castle Casino with his "aunt." This section is where the prominently billed Broderick Crawford has his two lines of dialogue, and where we meet Adrian's friend Peter Simon (David Huffman). The heavy-handed allegory that is Peter Simon flunked out of divinity school, wears bright colors—in contrast to Adrian's basic black—and dies at the hands of the cult in a Christ-like pose. The casino features a generic rock band with the mime-painted Adrian as the "vocalist" who doesn't have to sing because his presence alone on stage manages to corrupt all the local teens.

It is during this rock bliss that Roman Castevet, present for Adrian's twenty-first birthday, utters the excellent line, "There must be more joy in hell over the corruption of one innocent than all the chanting of the ungodly." Ray Milland as Roman gives the film's best performance. Unfortunately, the lines he's given to say are rarely as compelling and colorful as that one. Ruth Gordon reprises her role as Minnie Castevet from *Rosemary's Baby*, but she seems justly uninspired, and the usually eccentric Gordon personality is muted here. George Maharis as Adrian's father shows up occasionally, but does not influence much of the action.

As mentioned, the birthday is a significant one for Adrian and the cult. When he is not deemed evil enough to be Satan's son, a poorly defined cataclysm takes place, and next we see Adrian awaking from a coma in "The Book of Andrew." He now wants to be called by his given name, Andrew, and coerces his doctor Ellen (Donna Mills) to help him escape and embark on a vague mission.

The surprises of the final act will not catch most viewers off guard, but the film's most amusingly iconic image occurs late, when Ellen is seducing Andrew. A vision is visited upon the young man and he sees Ellen as a giant bird attacking him. The sight of Mills covered in black feathers, like the Big Bird of Satan Street, is reward enough for those with the constitution to bear with this unfortunate entertainment.

Surely one of the era's most unsuccessful fright telefilms, *Look What's Happened to Rosemary's Baby* should be avoided by all, except those with a fascination for derailed attempts at filmmaking.

CAST: Stephen McHattie, (ao) Patty Duke Astin, Broderick Crawford, Ruth Gordon, Lloyd Haynes, David Huffman, Tina Louise, George Maharis, Ray Milland, and Donna Mills. Also Beverly Sanders, Brian Richards, Buck Young,

Philip Boyer, D.J. Sullivan, Andy Stone, and Calvin Rose.

CREDITS: Director: Sam O'Steen; Teleplay: Anthony Wilson, based upon *Rosemary's Baby* by Ira Levin; Music: Charles Bernstein; Production: The Culzean Corporation; Running Time: 92 minutes; Air Date: 10/29/76; Network: ABC

Maneater

Two couples on holiday are stranded overnight at a roadside attraction when their motor home breaks down. The tourist trap is run by ex–circus animal trainer, Brenner the Great (Richard Basehart), and features two man-eating tigers. The next day, their vehicle repaired, the couples visit a remote camping spot recommended by Brenner, and discover to their horror that Brenner has plans to hunt them with his tigers.

Maneater is a simple tale swiftly told, lean and to the point. The Brenner the Great back story is summed up in a couple of sentences: he was accused of being unable to handle his own cats after they killed someone, and was fired from the circus to end up running a dying tourist attraction. Basehart, dressed in a safari outfit, plays Brenner with just the right amount of insane glee, without competing with the tigers over chewed scenery.

Vince Edwards directs his first telefilm here, and his flair for economical storytelling is readily apparent. Edwards also co-wrote this modern riff on *The Most Dangerous Game*, throwing tigers into the mix to spice up the old chestnut about hunting humans.

Brenner just wants to awaken the instinct for survival in the two couples, in order to provide himself with satisfying sport, an amusement, we discover, that he has tried before. Nick and Gloria Baron (Ben Gazzara and Sheree North) and their young friends Shep and Polly (Kip Niven and Laurette Spang, also paired as a couple in *Runaway!*) don't seem up to the challenge at first. They are repeatedly foiled in their early plans by Brenner, and resort to simply running in an effort to make it to a nearby ranger station. This is what Brenner wants, of course, and the tigers, denied their normal diet, begin their relentless chase.

Gazzara centers the character of Nick with a calming confidence. Gazzara was born in New York, and made big splashes in his first two films, *The Strange One* and *Anatomy of a Murder*. The 1960s saw his cinematic capital fall off, but he hit it big on television with the series *Run for Your Life*, as the doomed lawyer, Paul Bryan. In the 70s, Gazzara worked several times with his good friend, cult director John Cassavetes, as in *Husbands* and *The Killing of a Chinese Bookie*, and he starred in the highly regarded *Saint Jack*. At the same time he was in the telefrights *When Michael Calls* and *Pursuit*. At the end of the 80s, Gazzara's career was renewed with roles in the popular *Road House*, and, finally, with high-profile parts in David Mamet's *The Spanish Prisoner*, the Coen brothers' *The Big Lebowski* and *The Thomas Crown Affair*, among others. He continues the streak in the new millennium, finally winning an Emmy for the 2002 telefilm *Hysterical Blindness*.

In order for the story of *Maneater* to work, one of the hunted must have some knowledge of the behavior of tigers and/or survival skills. Luckily, Nick has both. He knows, for instance, that tigers won't jump into a hole, so he persuades the injured Shep to wait in a dry well with Polly, while he and Gloria continue on for help. This tactic would normally have cost the young couple their lives, but, for some reason, Brenner spares them. Apparently the situation wasn't sporting enough for him.

The highlight of this big cat-and-mouse game is watching the tigers as they pursue the hapless victims. The fact that most of the action takes place at night doesn't work in the viewer's favor, but the two beautiful animals have their share of photogenic moments. One sequence, in which the tigers swim through a swamp while Nick and Gloria hide under the water using the old breathe-through-the-reed trick, is particularly effective.

The ending, which turns on a wildly

convenient circumstance, seems rushed, no doubt because of the short running time. Although denied a grand finale, Brenner still manages to fit in a short soliloquy, taking a Zen attitude about his folly. *Maneater* is a competent, enjoyable little thriller marred only by its necessitated brevity.

CAST: Ben Gazzara, Sheree North, Kip Niven, Laurette Spang, Richard Basehart, Claire Brennan, Stewart Raffill, Lou Ferragher, and Jerry Fitzpatrick.

CREDITS: Director: Vince Edwards; Teleplay: Vince Edwards & Marcus Demian; Music: George Romanis; Production: Universal TV; Running Time: 69 minutes; Air Date: 12/8/73; Network: ABC

Mayday at 40,000 Feet!

Transcon Airways flight 602 from Los Angeles, bound for Chicago and New York, picks up a mad dog prisoner with a police escort in Salt Lake City. When the cop suffers a heart attack, the prisoner takes his gun and shoots a passenger and the pilot, who happened to be at the rear of the plane. His stray bullets also take out the hydraulic systems. The prisoner is subdued, but the inexperienced co-pilot must attempt to land the plane without automated control.

David Janssen, as pilot Pete Douglas, stars in another double jeopardy disaster film (see *Fer de Lance*), this time an airplane thriller based on Austin Ferguson's novel *Jet Stream*. With Douglas removed from the action early, his co-pilot Stan Burkhart (Christopher George) and his engineer Mike Fuller (Don Meredith) get to play the heroes.

The human drama includes Douglas's wife Kitty (Jane Powell), who is undergoing exploratory surgery for breast cancer while he's flying home. Burkhart's old flame, Susan Mackenzie (Maggie Blye, *The Entity*), to whom he's just proposed, is wounded by the prisoner, Greco (Marjoe Gortner). Fuller is simply a wolf in cowboy hat, who shows unexpected composure throughout the ordeal, winning the heart of flight attendant Cathy Armello (Lynda Day George).

Broderick Crawford plays Marshal Riese, the cop with heart trouble. Ray Milland plays cranky Dr. Joseph Mannheim, who was just nailed with a malpractice suit in LA, and calls the flight attendants "waitresses." Harry (Hari) Rhodes is military man Belson, who is called the N-word by Greco, and Shani Wallace (Wallis) is another flight attendant, Terry Dunlap.

The issue of landing the plane *sans* hydraulics doesn't seem to be the showstopper for Burkhart and Fuller that it was for the crew of *SST—Death Flight*. There was some concern, played up by officials for drama's sake, that Burkhart would not be able to steer the plane once it had landed. But, aside from a minor braking problem that saw the plane overshooting the waiting emergency teams, the disaster was much ado about nothing.

This unexceptional drama was directed by Emmy winner Robert Butler (*Night of the Juggler*), who worked on just about every television show available in the 1960s. Butler was also a Disney regular, making the Kurt Russell vehicles *The Computer Wore Tennis Shoes*, *The Barefoot Executive* and *Now You See Him, Now You Don't*. Producer-writer Andrew J. Fenady, brother of director Georg, wore at least one of those hats for the telefrights *Black Noon*, *The Woman Hunter* and *The Stranger*, and the features *Terror in the Wax Museum* and *Arnold*. Composer Richard Markowitz did the music for the fantasy *The Magic Sword*, the cult western *The Shooting*, and the telefrights *The Stranger*, *Panic on the 5:22* and *Death Car on the Freeway*.

CAST: David Janssen, Don Meredith, Christopher George, Ray Milland, Lynda Day George, Maggie Blye, Marjoe Gortner, Broderick Crawford, Tom Drake, Christopher Norris, Hari Rhodes, Warren Vanders, Shani Wallis, Jane Powell, William Bryant, John Pickard, Steven Marlo, Jim Chandler, Phillip Mansour, Al Molinaro, Kathleen Bracken, Bill Catching, Norland Benson, Philip Baker Hall, Bert Williams, Buck Young, Bill Harlow, Alan Foster, and Gary McLarty.

Theatrical poster showing Australian alternate title for *Mayday at 40,000 Feet!* (1976).

CREDITS: Director: Robert Butler; Teleplay: Austin Ferguson, Dick Nelson, Andrew J. Fenady, from a novel by Austin Ferguson (*Jet Stream*); Music: Richard Markowitz; Production: A.J. Fenady Associates; Running Time: 88 minutes; Air Date: 11/12/76; Network: CBS

The Missing Are Deadly

Writers Katharyn and Michael Michaelian gathered the clichés, and director Don McDougall put a somnambulistic, second-tier cast through the paces, to spawn a forgettable slice of 70s disaster hokum. The human drama falls flat, the tension is slack, and the main preoccupation of the characters appears to be marking time.

Dr. Margolin (Ed Nelson) has been resting on his laurels, running the Margolin Institute in the eight years since his scientific breakthrough. Meanwhile, Dr. Durov (Leonard Nimoy) has been conducting unauthorized experiments at the institute with a deadly disease called Mombassa fever. Dr. Margolin's troubled genius son Jeff (Gary Morgan) sneaks into a secured area and steals a mouse infected with the disease, taking it with him camping with his brother David (George O'Hanlon, Jr.) and David's girlfriend Michelle (Kathleen Quinlan). When the theft is discovered, it's a race against time to find the kids and discover a combating serum to avoid an epidemic.

One indicator of the quality of this production is the subtitles that inform the viewer of the temporal borders of the action. The first one is "Tuesday July 28," while the second and final subtitle is "September 3 8:00 am." The inconsistent format and pointless use of these markers are a telling sign that afterthought was a key factor in slapping the film together.

Mombassa fever, we are told, has a 75 percent fatality rate and yet, after all is said and done, only one person dies during the course of the film, and that death is explained away as a heart attack ("The disease seems to pick a weak spot and attack there").

For something so deadly and contagious, it is simply amazing that more lives weren't lost. After all, Dr. Margolin was earlier tossing out frightful descriptions of a pandemic, where 120 million people could perish in a three-month period.

Ed Nelson's natural nervousness serves him well as the stressed-out Margolin. Nelson was born in New Orleans, and early in his career became a regular in the quickie productions of Roger Corman, securing a place in the hearts of genre film buffs. His roles at this time include *Swamp Women*, *Attack of the Crab Monsters*, *Invasion of the Saucer Men*, *Night of the Blood Beast*, *The Brain Eaters* and *A Bucket of Blood*. Beginning in the 60s, Nelson became a fixture on television, and a hot item as Dr. Michael Rossi on *Peyton Place*. He would work solidly through the 90s, and shows up in the telefrights *The Screaming Woman* and *Runaway!*

Gary Morgan, who now has more credits as a stunt man than as an actor, had parts in *Fuzz*, the sexploitation number *The Student Teachers* (where his character is named Joe Dante) and *Logan's Run*. Interestingly, O'Hanlon, Jr. and Quinlan were cast as brother and sister in the previous year's telefright *Where Have All the People Gone?* O'Hanlon, Jr.'s father was the original voice of George Jetson. Quinlan's most famous film of this era was probably *I Never Promised You a Rose Garden*, but she would go on to roles in such diverse fare as the cult film *Nightmare in Blood*, Oliver Stone's *The Doors* and the 2006 remake of *The Hills Have Eyes*.

Frankly, the fact that *The Missing Are Deadly* has effectively gone missing has saved many viewers from overexposure to boredom. Attempts to identify and quarantine any entertainment value have proven fruitless.

CAST: Ed Nelson, Leonard Nimoy, George O'Hanlon, Jr., Gary Morgan, Marjorie Lord, Kathleen Quinlan, Jose Ferrer, Armand Alzamora, John Milford, Irene Tedrow, Bill Smillie, Louis James Oliver, Paul Sorensen, Keith Walker, Abraham Alvarez, Joe Alfosa, Lois Walden, Marla Gibbs, Drew Michaels,

Squire Fridell, Jennifer Lee, Tom McFadden, Eddie and Lo Russo.

CREDITS: Director: Don McDougall; Teleplay: Katharyn & Michael Michaelian; Music: Gil Melle; Production: Lawrence Gordon Productions; Vehicles Furnished by The Ford Motor Company; Running Time: 72 minutes; Air Date: 1/8/75; ABC

Moon of the Wolf

A grisly killing in the swamp kicks off an investigation by Sheriff Aaron Whitaker (David Janssen). Following the bizarre deaths of his deputy and a prisoner (the iron bars of the jail were torn from the wall), Whitaker begins to believe there's a werewolf stalking the good citizens of Marsh Island, Louisiana.

Moon of the Wolf has a lot going for it: a rock-solid cast, the experienced direction of Daniel Petrie (*Sybil*), location shooting in Louisiana, and a story featuring a real monster of the old-fashioned variety. Things begin promisingly enough when the first actor on screen is old favorite Royal Dano, with a shotgun in his hands, as he discovers the first victim. When world-weary David Janssen enters the scene soon thereafter, the viewer may feel assured of superior entertainment.

Unfortunately, *Moon of the Wolf* does not live up to expectations. This slow-moving drama seems to take forever to unfold, as the folks of the small Louisiana town introduce themselves. The identity of the werewolf is telegraphed in advance by the casting of the shifty Bradford Dillman as Andrew Rodanthe, a member of the socialite founding family who should be above suspicion. Barbara Rush plays his sister Louise, newly returned to the area, who confesses to having had a crush on Sheriff Whitaker years ago.

The film is heavy on the human drama of the community, and it is a full 40 minutes before the next killings by the monster. Admittedly, this attack scene is a highlight, with the unseen killer tearing apart the jail to get at the brother (Geoffrey Lewis) of the first victim. The sheriff seems nonplussed throughout the running time, spending more time trying to encourage a romance with Louise than in trying to solve the murders.

The filmmakers also take liberties with the traditional werewolf folklore, which may rile horror aficionados. Supposedly, burning sulfur will repel the werewolf, and the "Lycanthropia Veritum" from which Andrew suffers is inherited and can be controlled with a mysterious medication. Until, that is, the sufferer eventually becomes immune to the drugs, and cannot control his nightly urges. Also, there is an old man who can see the pentagram on the werewolf's next victim, a talent that had, up until this point, been reserved for the werewolf himself. In a final act of blasphemy, a werewolf can be killed with bullets blessed by a priest.

The werewolf makeup used here is fashioned more after Henry Hull's in *WereWolf of London* than Lon Chaney's in *The Wolf Man*. Dillman's face is left relatively hairless, but the addition of a little black nose was an ill-advised choice that reduces the horrific impact of the monster. All told, *Moon of the Wolf* is a misfire still worthy of some consideration.

Rail-thin character actor Royal Dano, who added colorful support to film and television productions since 1950, may be best remembered by some as the voodoo-tormented husband in the *Night Gallery* episode entitled "I'll Never Leave You—Ever." Dano was born in New York, and began his career in B-pictures at Universal. What followed was solid work in films of all types, including many westerns, until his death of a heart attack in 1994. Early in his career Dano established himself in the westerns of Anthony Mann (*Bend of the River*, *The Far Country*, etc.) but his talent was equally in demand for prestige pictures such as *Moby Dick*, *The Trouble With Harry*, *7 Faces of Dr. Lao* and *The Right Stuff*. His genre credits include *Dead People* aka *Messiah of Evil*, *Big Bad Mama*, *Killer Clowns from Outer Space* and *The Dark Half*, his last film. Throughout the years, Dano was cast several times as Abraham Lincoln, and it is his voice that is still used for the Lincoln audio-animatronic figures at Disneyland and Disneyworld.

CAST: David Janssen, Barbara Rush, Bradford Dillman, John Beradino, Geoffrey Lewis, Royal Dano, John Chandler, Claudia McNeil, Paul R. DeVille, Dan Priest, Robert Phillips, Serena Sande, George Sawaya, Dick Crockett, Sonny Klein, Emory Hollier, and Teddy Airhart, Jr.

CREDITS: Director: Daniel Petrie; Teleplay: Alvin Sapinsley, based on the novel by Leslie H. Whitten; Music: Bernardo Segall; Production: Filmways Pictures; Running Time: 74 minutes; Air Date: 9/26/72; ABC

Murder on Flight 502

Airline security chief Robert Davenport (George Maharis) receives a note saying there will be murders committed on flight 502, already on its way from New York to London. The culprit is determined to be in the first class section, greatly narrowing down the suspects. Davenport works with pilot Captain Larkin (Robert Stack) and a policeman who happens to be on board, Detective Myerson (Hugh O'Brian), to determine the identity of the psychopath. In the meantime, the killings begin.

Murder on Flight 502 is another star-studded journey on yet another Airplane of Amazing Coincidences. This sloppy mystery features a villain with vague motivations, characters who speak in clichés, and contrived drama based on long-shot twists of fate. The tiresome trip is only somewhat redeemed by a violent conclusion, which boasts a little gunplay and a human torch. Reaching the payoff ending, however, is an endurance test that requires much patience and forgiveness on the part of the viewer.

Robert Stack (left) and Hugh O'Brian must stop a killer in *Murder on Flight 52* **(1975).**

The humdrum passenger list includes has-been rock star Jack Marshall (Sonny Bono), who is seated next to one of his biggest fans, Marilyn Stonehurst (Elizabeth Stack, daughter of Robert). Hard-drinking mystery writer Mona Briarly (Polly Bergen) sits next to suave thief Paul Barons (Fernando Lamas). Ray and Claire Garwood (Dane Clark and Laraine Day) sit together. Dr. Kenyon Walker (Ralph Bellamy) has an unknowing connection with Otto Gruenwaldt (Theodore Bikel). Oldsters Ida Goldman (Molly Picon) and Charlie Parkins (Walter Pidgeon) talk of times past. Punk prankster Millard Kensington (Danny Bonaduce, *The Partridge Family*) stays out of the way, and flight attendants Karen White (Farrah Fawcett-Majors) and Vera Franklin (Brooke Adams) deliver the drinks.

Gruenwaldt blames Dr. Kenyon for his wife's death because Kenyon couldn't pull himself away from a party in time to attend her. The Garwoods blame their daughter's death on rocker Marshall because she died of a drug overdose at Marshall's house. The chances for both grudge matches to be on one flight, both unintended, must be astronomical. These soap opera elements are what help stretch this thinly plotted, who's-going-to-do-it mystery to fill a two-hour time slot.

When Gruenwaldt has a heart attack during the flight, who should shepherd him through but Dr. Kenyon? The two make up in the end, and plan a chess match. As for the other conflict, Marshall takes his fan Marilyn up to the bar to play some guitar in an excruciating but (mercifully) short scene. This is when Ray Garwood takes the opportunity to attack Marshall with a steak knife. After that fight, the two make amends because Marshall lies to Garwood, telling him what a swell gal his junkie daughter really was.

But the real point of the film is the murder plot by parties unknown. Since it is a mystery who the killer is and who he (or she) is going to kill, it would be unfair to reveal much more here. It is safe to say, however, that the murderer is not the priest who wears fingernail polish. This little character eccentricity is never explained, but it is the tip-off that this priest is not really a priest. The killer is made known 15 minutes before the end, as he (or she) struggles to articulate the muddled revenge motive that got him (or her) this far.

Television has often been accused of being out of touch with the real world, and this film would lend some credence to that claim. Sometimes it is the small things, such as flight attendant Karen, who is on her last run because she's looking forward to a house with a white picket fence and a couple of kids. She says she's been liberated long enough. Or when rocker Marshall is lent credibility because he is soon to be cast in a spaghetti western—a genre that had been out of vogue for years by that time. Or it could be the blatant pandering to celebrity by having Bono's character utter the phrase "The beat goes on." The telefilm in general has plenty to offer but this subpar entertainment by George McCowan (*Frogs*) does the industry's reputation no good.

CAST: (ao) Ralph Bellamy, Polly Bergen, Theodore Bikel, Sonny Bono, Dane Clark, Laraine Day, Fernando Lamas, George Maharis, Farrah Fawcett-Majors, Hugh O'Brian, Molly Picon, Walter Pidgeon, and Robert Stack. Also Brooke Adams, Danny Bonaduce, Vincent Baggetta, Rosemarie Stack, Elizabeth Stack, Steve Franken, Philip Sterlino, Pepper Martin, Yolanda Galardo, Bob Hackman, Don Hanmer, Glorie Haufman, Byron Morrow, George Petrie, and Dave Shelley.

CREDITS: Director: George McCowan; Teleplay: David P. Harmon; Music: Laurence Rosenthal; Production: Spelling-Goldberg Productions; Running Time: 97 minutes; Air Date: 11/21/75; ABC

Murder Once Removed

AKA The Obsessive Doctor

Dr. Ron Wellesley (John Forsythe) is wooing Lisa (Barbara Bain), the wife of prominent businessman Frank Manning (Richard Kiley). Manning has his suspicions about the couple, and discovers that Wellesley has a shady past—he was implicated, and cleared, in a double murder. Manning confronts Wellesley in an attempt to dissuade the doctor from killing him. Wellesley, however, moves forward with his plans to do away with Manning, and have Lisa for himself.

This small-town film noir holds a certain pleasure despite the coincidences required to move the plot forward. The leading cast is first-rate, and the finite scope of the action works in favor of the story for a change. Charles Dubin, who rarely ventured outside of television and was one of the primary directors involved in *M*A*S*H*, directs with a sure hand, compacting time with a finely oiled efficiency.

Wellesley is another murderous doctor, but unlike Bing Crosby's practitioner in *Dr. Cook's Garden*, his motivations are sinister indeed. We learn about Wellesley's past in a little tour-de-force of exposition. Manning confronts Wellesley while they are playing golf, and the juxtaposition of the courtly formalities of the game and the incendiary conversation works wonderfully. It is during this scene that Manning tosses out the excellent tagline: "I'm hoping to persuade you not to kill me."

At first, Wellesley seems perfectly rational although somewhat daring when it comes to his relations with women. He has a small practice with a friendly nurse (Reta Shaw), and he's kind enough to treat returning Vietnam veteran Fred Kramer's (Wendell Burton, *The Sterile Cuckoo*) drug addiction with discretion. The light behind his eyes brightens, however, when musing about occasionally being on the "winning side" as a doctor—the side of Death—because it's ultimately a losing battle prolonging life.

Since this is not a mystery story, it won't spoil the reader's enjoyment to reveal that Wellesley does indeed murder Manning. It is fascinating in a macabre sense to watch

(Left to right) Barbara Bain, Richard Kiley and John Forsythe observe the social niceties in *Murder Once Removed* (1971).

the quick-thinking Wellesley devise his plan, commit the deed, and then try to tie up the loose ends as they unravel. John Forsythe, an actor with a confident persona, is perfect to play the doctor who falls apart little by little until his final psychotic breakdown.

Richard Kiley and Barbara Bain are fine as the Mannings. Reliable Joseph Campanella plays the cop who is suspicious of how neatly the case closes up, and who eventually determines the guilty party. Recommended for viewers wanting comfortable, competent entertainment. The ending will catch most by surprise, as the final twist on a twist is revealed in the last few seconds.

Formidable character actress Reta Shaw, who plays the nurse here, will be recognized by television fans as Hope Lange's housekeeper in the *Ghost and Mrs. Muir* series. She also lent high-profile support in the Disney pictures *Mary Poppins* and *Escape to Witch Mountain*. Often playing meddlers and busybodies, Shaw's acting career began relatively late: she made her television debut in her 40s. She worked in A-pictures (*Picnic*) and lowbrow comedies (*The Ghost and Mr. Chicken*) with equal ease, but television was her main venue. This would be her only telefright. She passed away in 1982 of natural causes.

CAST: John Forsythe, Richard Kiley, Reta Shaw, Wendell Burton, Joseph Campanella, and Barbara Bain.
CREDITS: Director: Charles Dubin; Teleplay: Irving Gaynor Neiman; Music: Robert Drasnin; Production: Metromedia Productions; Running Time: 74 minutes; Air Date: 10/29/71; Network: CBS

Night Slaves

In an effort to simplify his life, Clay Howard (James Franciscus) sells out to his business partner. On his way home that day, the brakes in his Jaguar fail, and he is involved in an accident that kills two people. Upon recovering from an operation to place a metal plate in his head, Howard and his wife Marjorie (Lee Grant) go on holiday, winding up in a small town to look for antiques. That night Howard awakens to find the residents of the town—including his wife—seemingly in a trance, climbing into trucks and leaving for parts unknown. Convinced at first it was just a dream, Howard later discovers clues that lead him to investigate the strange goings-on.

It is significant that Clay Howard wants to escape the slavery of materialism only to discover a people unknowingly enslaved to a much more devious master. It is also significant that he is immune from this slavery, explained by the metal plate in his head, but which could also be construed as his improved mindset. *Night Slaves* is a counter-culture riff on the science fiction film *It Came from Outer Space*. In that 1953 classic, the townspeople are individually inhabited by a benevolent alien force to affect spaceship repairs. In *Night Slaves*, the town as a whole is merely controlled for a few hours each night to accomplish the same.

Night Slaves, however, incorporates an inter-terrestrial love story when Howard meets and falls in love with "Naillil" (Tisha Sterling), the innocent and pretty alien assigned to watch him. This romance is made morally acceptable because the Howards' marriage is a shambles and, in fact, Marjorie is having an affair with Howard's partner Matt Russell (Scott Marlowe). Hence, Howard escapes yet another form of slavery: the shackles of marriage.

Ted Post takes the reins again, creating the mysterious atmosphere of the small town with ease. The romantic elements aren't handled as well, perhaps due to the rush the characters are in to fall in love and make life-changing decisions.

The (literally) sleepy town of Eldrid, California, where the Howards end up, claims to be "A Bit of the Old West," but this piece of information is used simply to explain the utilization of overlapping backlots at the Warner Bros. studio. The action is split between the dusty western town lot and the neighboring "residential" lot, neither of which is conventionally convincing, but the milieu does add to the unreal atmosphere.

The cast is rounded out by Leslie Nielsen, ever the cop in 60s and 70s television, as the local sheriff, and Andrew Prine in an overripe performance as the town halfwit. (The Internet Movie Database claims that Elisha Cook, Jr. acted in this film but he did not appear in the review copy.) Between the psychedelic opening credits, the strains of Bernardo Segall's "hip" soundtrack, and the hopeful yet naïve conclusion lies an enjoyable, lightweight science fiction fantasy.

Graduated magna cum laude from Yale, James Franciscus was a popular fixture on television with the series' *Naked City* in the 1950s, *Mr. Novak* in the 60s and *Longstreet* in the 70s. Although working steadily in television, Franciscus had his share of genre film work, including the Ray Harryhausen fantasy *The Valley of Gwangi*, *Marooned*, *Beneath the Planet of the Apes*, Dario Argento's *The Cat O'Nine Tails* and *Killer Fish*. He also formed a production company in the late 60s, focusing primarily on young people's fare, such as *Kidnapped* and *The Red Pony*. Franciscus was the voice of Jonathan Livingston Seagull, and made one other telefright, *One of My Wives Is Missing*. He died of emphysema in 1991.

Writer Jerry Sohl, whose novel formed the basis for *Night Slaves*, had plenty of genre experience writing for television's *Alfred Hitchcock Presents*, *The Twilight Zone*, *The Outer Limits*, *The Invaders* and the original *Star Trek*. His film credits include *Frankenstein Conquers the World*, *Die, Monster, Die!* and *Curse of the Crimson Altar*. Composer Bernardo Segall's credits include *Hallucination Generation*, *The Jesus Trip* and the telefright *Moon of the Wolf*.

CAST: James Franciscus, Lee Grant, Scott Marlowe, Andrew Prine, Tisha Sterling, Leslie Nielsen, Morris Buchanan, John Kellogg, Virginia Vincent, Cliff Carnell, Victor Izay, Raymond Mayo, Russell Thorson, and Nancy Valentine.

CREDITS: Director: Ted Post; Teleplay: Everett Chambers and Robert Specht, from the novel by Jerry Sohl; Music: Bernardo Segall; Production: Bing Crosby Productions; Vehicles Provided by The Ford Motor Corporation; Running Time: 71 minutes; Air Date: 9/29/70; Network: ABC

Darren McGavin battles *The Night Stalker* (1972).

The Night Stalker

Sometimes the stars align. Dan Curtis produced a little horror film for ABC that wasn't even heavily promoted at the time, and yet it became literally an overnight sensation, garnering the highest ratings ever for a television movie to date. *The Night Stalker* remains popular even today, an icon in the history of the telefilm. From the aging baby boomers who watched the film's debut in 1972, to new generations of fans who can appreciate its simple charms, it is, like the monster at its core, a thing seemingly immortal.

A killing in Las Vegas brings maverick newspaper reporter Carl Kolchak (Darren McGavin) back from vacation. The second and third killings exhibit the same method of operation: the blood has been drained from each of the victims, all women. After blood is stolen from a hospital and yet another victim is found, Kolchak is incensed when he's not allowed by the local authorities to report on the true nature of the crimes. Kolchak's girlfriend Gail (Carol Lynley) convinces him that a true vampire could be preying on the population, and after witnessing the superhuman strength of a man who was stealing more blood, Kolchak instructs the civic leaders in the ways of dealing with the vampire. Given exclusive rights to publish the story when the vampire is caught, Kolchak begins his vampire hunt.

The character of Carl Kolchak, the stubborn and difficult, yet nonetheless brilliant writer, is the ultimate outsider. Fired many times from newspapers across the country, Kolchak, who moans, "I'm becoming extinct in my own lifetime," is perfectly embodied by Darren McGavin. The crusty actor was a product of the Actor's Studio; his long career in television was capped in 1990 with an Emmy nomination for his support in *Murphy Brown*. His film career was unremarkable until his role as a smooth pusher in Otto Preminger's *The Man with the Golden Arm*. He landed the *Mike Hammer* series in the late 50s, and *The Outsider* in the late 60s, but Kolchak would remain his most enduring character. He would reprise the role in the telefright sequel *The Night Strangler*, and in the subsequent series *Kolchak: the Night Stalker*, where he battled the supernatural every week for one season. Late in his career, McGavin would guest star on the popular series *The X-Files* in a nod to his influential Kolchak character. McGavin, who appeared in one other telefright, *Something Evil*, passed away of natural causes in 2006.

The *Night Stalker* supporting cast is a who's who of gifted character actors. Simon Oakland plays Kolchak's long-suffering editor Tony Vincenzo. Oakland would accompany McGavin on the next Kolchak film and on the subsequent series. Ralph Meeker is FBI man Bernie Jenks, Kent Smith is the D.A., and the great Charles McGraw, the face of film noir, is the police chief. Elisha Cook, Jr. is Kolchak's buddy, Mickey Crawford, who tips him off to the vampire's lair, and Virginia Gregg, whom millions recognize but few would know her name, has a cameo as a victim's mother. Of the younger generation, Carol Lynley as Gail never looked more beautiful, and Larry Linville, playing Dr. Makurji, was on the brink of stardom as Maj. Frank Burns on *M*A*S*H*.

The monstrous vampire, identified as Janos Skorzeny, is played by veteran actor Barry Atwater, without a single line of dialogue. Fifty-three at the time, Atwater was forever a heavy or a cop in his long career (more than 100 film and television credits, stretching back to the mid-fifties). Atwater, who died of a stroke in 1978 without achieving conventional stardom, manages to convey a terrible power as the bestial bloodsucker.

The film's most horrific image comes as Kolchak is snooping around the old Victorian house found on the outskirts of Vegas (never mind the implausibility, the atmosphere is perfect). Kolchak creeps upstairs and discovers a kidnapped girl tied to the bed. The fiend has turned her into "his own private blood bank" by giving her stolen blood intravenously, so he can suck it out of her the old-fashioned way. The idea of that horrible fate no doubt gave nightmares to thousands of youngsters.

The decisions that worked in favor of the production seem like common sense now. First, the scope of the film is kept small, and the running time short. The exteriors, shot in Las Vegas in 1971, will tickle the fancy of those who know the city now or who just enjoy the markers of the time. The Kolchak narration not only cuts corners for the filmmakers, but provides a reassuring guide, and gives the viewer the sense of being complicit with Kolchak in the action. The practical approach taken to having a preternatural being in our everyday midst brings an immediacy perfect for the medium.

Director John Llewellyn Moxey puts his experience to work and doesn't waste a frame. The MGM DVD of the film, also includes *The Night Strangler* and a worthwhile interview with Dan Curtis. A classic of the genre and the medium, *The Night Stalker* is required viewing for fans of either.

CAST: Darren McGavin, Carol Lynley, Simon Oakland, Ralph Meeker, Claude Akins, Charles McGraw, Kent Smith, Barry Atwater, Larry Linville, Jordan Rhodes, Elisha Cook, Jr., and Stanley Adams. Also Virginia Gregg (uncredited).

CREDITS: Director: John Llewellyn Moxey; Teleplay: Richard Matheson, from an unpublished story by Jeff Rice; Music: Robert Cobert; Production: American Broadcasting Company; Vehicles Provided by Chrysler Corporation; Running Time: 75 minutes; Air Date: 1/11/72; Network: ABC

The Night Strangler

One year after defeating the modern-day vampire in *The Night Stalker*, intrepid reporter Carl Kolchak is back to take on a 100-year-old murderer. This time, Dan Curtis, the producer of the first film, assumes the directorial duties and the results, while entertaining, do not—and cannot—quite measure up to the original.

Carl Kolchak (Darren McGavin) finds himself in Seattle where, by chance, his editor from Las Vegas, Tony Vincenzo (Simon Oakland), has also landed. After promising to be good, Kolchak is hired by Vincenzo and assigned to cover the recent murder of an exotic dancer. A second and similar murder yields some startling facts: both women were not just strangled, but had their necks crushed by a killer with incredible strength, and both had a residue of rotting flesh present on their necks, as if they'd been throttled by a dead man. Digging deeper, Kolchak discovers an eerie pattern of murders occurring every 21 years, reaching back past the turn of the twentieth century. Despite the reticence of the local authorities, Kolchak forges ahead in his quest to catch this uncanny killer.

Seizing the elements of a successful formula isn't as simple as it may seem. Curtis and writer Richard Matheson attempt to recapture the magic that made a hit of *The Night Stalker* by making the same movie in a different city with a different monster. What made the first film unique was the freshness of character and approach, and the giddiness that shines through when the filmmakers are doing something for the fun of it. These are the things that cannot be knowingly recreated.

Certainly, revisiting the endearing characters of Kolchak and Vincenzo as another weird killer is on the loose was a good idea, and *The Night Strangler* is superior entertainment on its own merits. But something has been lost, and that is the sense of discovery.

The monster this time does not have the romantic appeal or repulsive fascination of the vampire. It is simply a man who, through the black arts, has managed to develop a flawed version of the elixir of life. Alchemy does have its compelling side but this is not the focus of the story. The viewer, who instantly grasps the concept of a vampire, is left slightly bewildered by the motivations and methods of Dr. Richard Malcolm (Richard Anderson). Half-hearted mumbo jumbo about the elixir requiring a component of human blood, and the vague timeframes of its practical application, just confuse the issue.

On the plus side, the milieu of the monster—a buried, semi-preserved nineteenth century world under Seattle—is what fascinates, and what is remembered by the viewer, not the monster himself. Curtis creates a mesmerizing, baroque setting for the villain with fog machines and colorful ambient lighting reminiscent of the gothic Italian horror films of the 1960s. These scenes were actually shot in the famous Bradbury Building in Los Angeles, a site used in many films and television shows, including *Blade Runner* and *The Outer Limits*.

Dan Curtis liked to people his movies with familiar, and sometimes forgotten, character actors from his youth, and *The Night Strangler* was no exception. The ubiquitous John Carradine plays Llewellyn Crossbinder, owner of the newspaper. It is he who utters the famous line, "This isn't fun town USA, this is Seattle." Wally Cox, in his last film role before succumbing to a heart attack one month after this movie aired, plays *Chronicle* archivist Titus Berry. The eccentric Al Lewis (Grandpa in *The Munsters*) has a great bit as a hypochondriac bum living in the Seattle underground. The Wicked Witch of the West, Margaret Hamilton, is Professor Crabwell of the University of Washington, who passes on some alchemy lore to Kolchak. Scott Brady, who always seemed to be stuck in Z-grade genre pictures in his latter years, has a juicy role here as a police captain.

The part of the monster is actually smaller here than the thin role of the vampire in *The Night Stalker*, but at least Dr. Malcolm is allowed a speech near the end of the film. The dependable Richard Anderson, an actor who can effortlessly switch between good guy and bad guy roles, does what he can with the limited screen time. (Anderson is known to TV fans as Oscar Goldman, the government agent to whom reported both *The Six Million Dollar Man* and *The Bionic Woman*.)

The Seattle of 1972 proves an interesting time capsule, and the city is even more of a character in this film than Vegas was in *The Night Stalker*. Kolchak has even more of a partner in this film too, the exotic dancer Louise Harper (Jo Ann Pflug). There isn't very much substance to the character however, aside from a couple of unfortunate costuming choices, and she's relegated to playing bait for the killer. Another exotic dancer is played by Nina Wayne, who is a dead ringer for her sister Carol. Her character is, surprisingly for the time, a lesbian associated with a decidedly butch partner (Virgina Peters).

The MGM DVD of the film also features *The Night Stalker* and a worthwhile interview with Dan Curtis. Not the classic the original Kolchak film was, *The Night Strangler* is still an excellent example of the genre.

CAST: Darren McGavin, Jo Ann Pflug, Simon Oakland, Scott Brady, Wally Cox, Margaret Hamilton, John Carradine, Nina Wayne, Al Lewis, Ivor Francis, Richard Anderson, Virginia Peters, Kate Murtagh, Diane Shalet, Anne Randall, Francoise Birnheim, and Regina Parton.

CREDITS: Director: Dan Curtis; Teleplay: Richard Matheson; Music: Robert Cobert; Production: ABC Circle Films; Vehicles provided by Chrysler Corporation; Running Time: 90 minutes; Air Date: 1/16/73; Network: ABC

Night Terror

Circumstances put scatterbrained housewife Carol Turner (Valerie Harper) on a late night road trip from Phoenix to Denver. Running low on gas, Turner spots a policeman who has pulled over a car for speeding. Before she can ask for directions to an open gas station, the cop is shot dead by The Killer (Richard Romanus). Turner flees, only to be relentlessly chased by The Killer in an all-night battle of wits.

The idea is simplicity itself: put a clumsy, inexperienced female into a cat-and-mouse game with a ruthless male killer, and watch as she gathers the resources to defeat her attacker. This lean little chase film turns out to be a gripping, tension-filled experience thanks to director E.W. Swackhamer, who rarely lets the pace slacken.

Significant to the success of *Night Terror* is the talented Valerie Harper as Carol. Although she began her acting career on stage, it was television that brought Valerie Harper fame and fortune. As Rhoda Morgenstern on *The Mary Tyler Moore Show*, she was nominated for four Emmys, winning three. Her popular character was then spun off for her own show, *Rhoda*, for which she was nominated for another four Emmys, winning once. Her work in film included *Freebie and the Bean*, *Chapter Two* and *Blame It on Rio*, before she embarked on the short-lived *Valerie* series. She continues to work in television and on the stage.

Early on, *Night Terror* goes to great lengths to depict Carol Turner as inept. She can't remember things from moment to moment, and seems practically incapable of handling the simplest familial responsibilities. This does come across as overkill, considering that it would be impressive for any person to come out on top in the nerve-racking situation in which Turner finds herself.

Turner proves to be not only resourceful but cunning. At one point, she encounters a car pulled over in a rainstorm. The flask-drinking owner (Nicholas Pryor) gets himself killed, and Turner takes the dead man's car instead of her own. But before leaving the scene, Turner has the wherewithal to back into The Killer's car, disabling it. Very few people would have taken the time to do this, let alone have had the idea in the first place. Moments like this put her character in the viewer's good graces.

Of course, it is necessary for Turner to somehow get off the main highway and onto a lesser-used road. That way, The Killer has a better chance to find her, and she has less chance of finding help. On a deserted road, Turner stumbles across a shut diner, and breaks in to use the phone. It is here that she's startled to discover a bum who is holing up inside the place. John Quade has a good cameo as the slightly dazed indigent, a decent but simple fellow more scared of her than she is of him. The recognizable character actor Quade has the rugged face of a bad guy, and the unexpectedly sweet personality Turner encounters is a pleasant surprise.

Richard Romanus manages to impart The Killer (no other name is given) with some depth, a task made especially difficult because he has very few lines. The Killer uses a voice synthesizer due, it is assumed, to some sort of injury that damaged his vocal chords. He has a scar on his neck that looks as if surgery were performed in the recent past. This mechanical voice is never put to menacing use in the film, and instead seems simply a source of frustration to an already unbalanced character.

A clever turn of events near the end of the film puts Turner and The Killer in the same vehicle—she unknowing of her danger—which sets up the final confrontation. We know that Turner will be victorious in the end, but *Night Terror* is a good example of a game well played.

CAST: Valerie Harper, Richard Romanus, Nicholas Pryor, John Quade, Michael Tolan, Beatrice Manley, Damon Raskin, Quinn Cummings, Madeline Taylor Holmes, John War Eagle, Jan Burrell, Gary Springer, Gary Barton, Frank Lugo, Charles Parks, and Edward Cross.

CREDITS: Director: E.W. Swackhamer; Teleplay: Carl Gabler and Richard DeNeut; Music: Fred Steiner; Production: Charles Fries Productions; Running Time: 90 minutes; Air Date: 2/7/77; Network: NBC

The Night They Took Miss Beautiful

Five finalists for the title of Miss Beautiful board a chartered plane in Miami headed for Nassau, for the announcement of the title's winner. Also aboard are two government agents, one of whom is transporting a lethal virus. Hijackers from the International Liberation Army take the plane to an old military base, and it becomes a waiting game to determine the fate of the hostages.

The Night They Took Miss Beautiful is yet another silly double jeopardy fright film (see *Fer de Lance*, *SST—Death Flight*, et al.). This time, a hostage situation is compounded by the danger of unleashing a virus capable of destroying life for miles around. The storyline provides writers Lou LaRose and George Lefferts the opportunity to form an indictment of beauty contests and shady government tactics, neither of which is particularly potent.

The contestants include Cindy Lou Barrett (Karen Lamm), Reba Bar Lev (Victoria Principal) and April Garland (Rosanne Katon). Principal, who was voted Miss Miami of 1969, was about to begin her most famous role in the long-running *Dallas* series. Here, she dons an "Israeli" accent and does a Groucho Marx impression. Katon would become *Playboy*'s Playmate of the Month for September 1978, and may be best known to genre fans for her roles in *The Swinging Cheerleaders* and *She Devils in Chains*.

Gary Collins plays the virus-carrying government agent Paul Fabiani, while Chuck Connors and Peter Haskell lock horns as airport security chief and government problem solver, respectively. Not given enough to do are Henry Gibson as the contest promoter and Stella Stevens as a former title holder. Phil Silvers plays the over-the-hill host of the pageant.

On the other side of the law are Sheree North, Gregory Sierra (*Barney Miller*) and Jonathan Banks (*Airplane!*) as the hijackers. North, who plays the strung-out junkie kidnapper Layla, was a professional dancer by the age of 10, married by 15 and a mother at 16. She modeled and made a few stag films before her first legitimate movie role in *Excuse My Dust*. Her big splash, however, first occurred on the stage where she created a wild dance number in the musical "Hazel Flagg." She was groomed by 20th Century–Fox as a blonde bombshell substitute for its troublesome star Marilyn Monroe, but by the end of the 50s her career was fizzling. After working primarily on television in the early 60s, North returned to the screen in *Destination Inner Space*, and would continue on in character roles in both media (*Madigan, Charley Varrick, The Shootist, Maniac Cop*) until her passing in 2005 from cancer. Her other telefrights include *Snatched* and *Maneater*.

The tedious scenario boils down to following the two threads, victims and rescuers, to determine which is the most hackneyed. With nothing but time on their hands, the hijackers put their prisoners through the expected paces, even forcing the unfortunate contestants to entertain their captors during the humiliation portion of the program. Things go from bad to worse when Cindy Lou's mom (Marcia Lewis) barters her daughter's sexual favors to one of the hijackers in an attempt to secure release. The filmmakers must have believed that bad taste would trump boredom as this predictable entry plays out to its inevitable end.

Of note among the talent that put this show together is rock promoter Don Kirshner, who executive produced and supervised the music. Director Robert Michael Lewis made the telefilm *The Invisible Man* starring David McCallum. Composer Walter Murphy is better known in the new millennium for working on the current batch of Warner Bros. cartoons.

CAST: (ao) Gary Collins, Chuck Connors, Henry Gibson, Peter Haskell, Karen Lamm, Sheree North, Victoria Principal, Gregory Sierra, Phil Silvers, and Stella Stevens. Also Rosanne Katon, Jonathan Banks, Lillian Muller, Burke Byrnes, Susette Carroll, Marcia Lewis, William Bassett, Phoebe Dorin, Santos Morales, Al Rossi, James Jeter, Paul Kent, Bill Overton, and Pat Corley.

CREDITS: Director: Robert Michael Lewis; Teleplay: George Lefferts, from a story suggested by Lou LaRose; Music: Walter Murphy; Production: Don Kirshner Productions; Running Time: 99 minutes; Air Date: 10/24/77; NBC

Nightmare in Badham County

AKA **Nightmare**

Note: This television movie was released to theaters overseas in a stronger version that included full-frontal nudity, profanity, lesbian sex and more extreme violence. This "continental" version was released in the U.S. on home video, and was used in the preparation of this review.

Cathy Philips (Deborah Raffin) and Diane Emery (Lynn Moodye), college students on a cross-country road trip, run afoul of Sheriff Danen (Chuck Connors) in a small southern town. After being accused of trumped-up charges, the girls are sent to the Badham County Farm, a prison work release facility, where they endure the hardships of incarceration. Their attempts to contact the outside world are repeatedly thwarted until a risky plan brings hope of escape.

Nightmare in Badham County is a very serious examination of the inherently corrupt prison farm system still in use today. The carefree gaiety of the big city girls is short-lived indeed, as they run up against the reality of bigotry and nepotism that sets their fortunes spinning quickly toward irredeemable doom.

Easily one of the most accomplished telefilms of the era, this is a difficult watch because of it. The exploitation elements common to the Women in Prison (WIP) movie were downplayed—at least in the televised version—in favor of a more realistic approach, focusing instead on what television does best: the character study. Certainly, the city-folk fear of being shanghaied into prison by vengeful southern rednecks is the main concern here, but the film is full of the frustration and pain of the "real" people who populate the hopeless environment.

The acting is of a much higher quality than would normally be found in the typical WIP film. Raffin and Moody are excellent as the indefatigable victims who think of very little other than finding a way of release. And they are concerned not only for themselves but also for the other tormented souls on the farm. Chuck Connors pulls out all the stops, and is very convincing as the evil sheriff who goes so far as to rape one of the girls. Della Reese is also terrific as an experienced and complacent prisoner. Robert Reed as the corrupt superintendent of the farm, and Tina Louise who runs the women's ward, play their less flashy roles with the required skill that makes their characters just as believable. Fans of the sexploitation cult film *The Cheerleaders* will note the cameo by Denise Dillaway, who undergoes a nude whipping.

Veteran director John Llewellyn Moxey shines by drawing superior performances from the actors, and by shying away from the shortcut of stereotypes as much as possible. Charles Bernstein contributes an inspired score that echoes the melancholy of the images with a simple folk song motif. Composer Bernstein began his career in exploitation cinema and remained a genre stalwart through the 1980s. A partial list of credits includes *The Man from O.R.G.Y.*, Marc Lawrence's *Daddy's Deadly Darling* aka *Pigs*, *Invasion of the Bee Girls*, *Love at First Bite*, *The Entity*, *Cujo*, *A Nightmare on Elm Street*, and *Deadly Friend*. His other telefrights include *Look What's Happened to Rosemary's Baby* and *Are You in the House Alone?*

At the end of the film, which was shot in Mississippi, it is claimed that "the farm system remains the subject of continuing public and judicial review." While there is a sense of timelessness in the subject matter, there is also a sense of opportunity for reform.

CAST: Deborah Raffin, Lynne Moody, (ao) Chuck Connors, Fionnuala Flanagan, Tina Louise, Robert Reed, Della Reese, and Lana Wood. Also Ralph Bellamy. (ao) Leslie Albers, Denise Dillaway, Simpson Hemphill, Annette Henley, Tom Keith, Mary Ann Kohler, John Malloy, Hal Thomas Phillips, John Clyde Rober, Jr., Essex Smith, Tommie Stewart, Rebecca Taylor, and Kim Wilson.

CREDITS: Director: John Llewellyn Moxey; Teleplay: Jo Heims; Music: Charles Bernstein; Production: ABC Circle Films; Running Time: 102 minutes; Air Date: 11/5/76; Network: ABC

The Norliss Tapes

David Norliss (Roy Thinnes), a writer specializing in books on the supernatural, is approached by Ellen Cort (Angie Dickinson), who swears she's seen her dead husband, James, come back to life. Norliss learns that James, a sculptor, had contracted a fatal disease, and had then seized on the legend of the Osiris scarab ring, an occult object that promised life after death. James was buried with the ring on his finger. Meanwhile, strange deaths are occurring where the victims are drained of blood. Norliss's investigation leads him to believe that the undead James is fulfilling a bargain to bring the demon Sargoth into our world. Norliss records his findings on a series of audio tapes.

The monster (Bob Schott) towers over Nick Dimitri in *The Norliss Tapes* (1972).

One of the lesser entries in the Dan Curtis canon, *The Norliss Tapes* suffers from an over-reliance on dialogue, shallow characterization, an unimpressive monster and too much shorthand logic. This unsold pilot is by Fred Mustard Stewart, who wrote the novel on which *The Mephisto Waltz* was based. The teleplay was adapted by William F. Nolan, whose credits include *Logan's Run* and Curtis's *Trilogy of Terror*.

Airing barely a month after Curtis's previous directorial effort, *The Night Strangler*, *The Norliss Tapes* seems a particularly slapdash project. Curtis hangs onto some of the elements that worked for the Kolchak films, such as telling the story in flashback and placing the protagonist against an unbelieving authority figure, etc., but these are simply formula touches, and leave the viewer cold and uninvolved. What made *The Night Stalker*—and to a lesser extent *The Night Strangler*—successful were the winning characters and interesting story, neither of which is present in *The Norliss Tapes*.

The most obvious comparison one can make is between Carl Kolchak of the *Night* films and David Norliss. Kolchak was a fighter, energetic and funny. Norliss is worn out, unable to write and generally unlikable. The only time Norliss shows some spark is at the end of the film in the short battle with the demon Sargoth, a monster that looks like the Incredible Hulk in a cape.

Angie Dickinson does what she can as the widow Cort but the other main characters are paper thin. Ellen's sister Marsha (Michele Carey) is around simply to be killed off. The same can be said for gallery owner Charles Langdon (Hurd Hatfield, criminally underused here), who lusts after the ring, and occult specialist Mme. Jeckiel (Vonetta McGee, *Blacula*), who pointed the way for James Cort. Sheriff Tom Hartley (Claude Akins, also a lawman in *The Night Stalker*) just wants to keep everything quiet.

There is plenty of atmosphere—the pouring rain around San Francisco hardly ever stops—but there is even more exposition, as the characters explain all the things we're not seeing. Fans of Thinnes, Dickinson and Curtis will find this an adequate time waster but all others will feel left out.

CAST: Roy Thinnes, Don Porter, Angie Dickinson, Claude Akins, Michele Carey, Vonetta McGee, Hurd Hatfield, Bryan O'Byrne, Robert Mandan, Edmund Gilbert, Jane Dulo, Stanley Adams, Bob Schott, George DiCenzo, Patrick Wright, and Nick Dimitri.

CREDITS: Director: Dan Curtis; Teleplay: William F. Nolan, based on a story by Fred Mustard Stewart; Music: Robert Cobert; Production: Metromedia Productions; Running Time: 72 minutes; Air Date: 2/21/73; Network: NBC

One of My Wives Is Missing

Wealthy automotive executive Daniel Corban (James Franciscus) and his new wife Elizabeth are honeymooning in the upstate New York resort of Skuylkill Village over the Labor Day weekend. Following an argument, Elizabeth disappears. Daniel calls the local police but Inspector Murray Levine (Jack Klugman) resists putting too much effort into the investigation. When a strange woman shows up claiming to be Elizabeth, Daniel sees his entire life, as he knows it, spinning out of control. Even Levine begins to believe Daniel is crazy.

One of My Wives Is Missing is a mystery where nothing—*nothing*—is as it seems. It is based on the play "Trap for a Single Man" by Robert Thomas (*8 Women*) and was made into the 1969 telefilm *Honeymoon with a Stranger* with Janet Leigh. It would subsequently be made for television again in 1986, as *Vanishing Act* with Mike Farrell.

The three leads are all terrific. Topbilled Jack Klugman, in his only telefright of the 1970s, is alternately lovable and questionable as the ex–Brooklyn cop. He keeps the audience guessing as to whether he believes Corban. James Franciscus gives a tour de force performance as the exasperated Corban, stymied at every turn, and Elizabeth Ashley, as the phony wife, makes for a delicious and ruthless villainess.

Florida native Elizabeth Ashley won a Tony Award for her very first Broadway performance in "Take Her She's Mine," and went on to further success in "Barefoot in the Park," in a part Neil Simon wrote specifically for her. After several roles in television she made her film debut in *The Carpetbaggers* in 1963. During a tempestuous marriage to her costar George Peppard, Ashley was largely absent from stage and screen. When the relationship collapsed, she made her way back in the early 70s with guest appearances on television's popular series, and was a smash as Maggie in a Broadway revival of "Cat on a Hot Tin Roof. "Although she focused her career thereafter largely in television, Ashley has dabbled in a few interesting films, such as *Rancho Deluxe, 92 in the Shade, The Great Scout & Cathouse Thursday, Coma, Vampire's Kiss* and *Happiness*. Her many years on the small screen were finally recognized in 1991 with an Emmy nomination for the series *Evening Shade*. Back in the 70s, Ashley gave typically fine performances in the telefrights *When Michael Calls* and *A Fire in the Sky*, and wrote a frank autobiography called *Actress: Postcards from the Road* in 1978.

The supporters here include Joel Fabiani (*All My Children*) as the priest, Father Kelleher, who brings home "Mrs. Corban." Familiar character actor Milton Selzer plays deli owner Sidney, and reliable Ruth McDevitt plays the fundraising lady who positively identifies Ashley as the real wife.

It would be impossible to further discuss the plot without ruining the experience for first-time viewers. There are many twists and turns, each holding a special pleasure in their execution. While definitely not played for laughs, *One of My Wives Is Missing* is leavened with humor. There is a running gag about a dumb deputy and some of the lines were well-worn long ago (Corban chooses a pastrami sandwich because he "loves Italian food"), but much of the humor is incisively funny. In one scene, Corban offers Father Kelleher a drink, saying, "It'll put hair on your shirt," and Levine says things were easier in New York because "all they had there was organized crime."

One of My Wives Is Missing was designed as the pilot for a series concerning the smalltown exploits of Inspector Levine. Filming at resorts in the San Bernardino National Forest, multiple Emmy Award–winning director Glenn Jordan does take the action outside a couple of times, but the bulk is confined to Corban's rented chalet. The *Wizard of Oz*–type ending confirms this is pure and preposterous fantasy, but it's also pure fun and occasionally even frightening.

CAST: Jack Klugman, Elizabeth Ashley, James Franciscus, Joel Fabiani, Milton Selzer, Ruth McDevitt, Byron Webster, Garry Walbero, and Tony Costello.

CREDITS: Director: Glenn Jordan; Teleplay: Pierre Marton; Music: Billy Goldenberg; Production: Spelling-Goldberg Productions; Automobiles furnished by Ford Motor Co.; Running Time: 94 minutes; Air Date: 3/5/76; Network: ABC

Ordeal

The very rich and very ornery Richard Damian (Arthur Hill) wants to see for himself a manganese mine in which he is considering investing. Damian, his wife Kay (Diana Muldaur) and a guide, Andy Folsom (James Stacy), head out on horseback across the desert for the four-hour ride to the mine. Along the way, Damian spooks his horse, and he falls off a ledge, breaking his leg. Kay and Andy leave him there to die, and arrange for the authorities to look for Damian in the other direction. After lying there for two days, Damian resolves to walk out of the desert for his revenge.

The spoiled, mean-spirited Richard Damian is not a sympathetic character, but neither is the conniving couple who leave him to die in the unforgiving desert in this little film noir. The story follows the two threads—Damian's ordeal and the couple's waiting game—for the month it takes for Damian to be found.

The noir elements here are less convincing than Damian's experiences in the wild. Kay is awfully quick to take advantage of the situation and Andy is quicker to take the bait. Granted, Kay Damian is an attractive woman, but there was no indication of any history between her and Andy that would support his jumping at the chance to be a murderer. What does work, however, is the disintegration of their relationship during the time they wait to hear that Damian is dead. By the time the giddy high of probably getting away with it wears off, the two are revealed to be completely and miserably incompatible. (Andy has a nice line when Kay begins to question his background: "Did you expect to get a bishop to help you knock off your husband?")

Arthur Hill must survive the hostile desert in *Ordeal* (1973).

Conversely (and much to the filmmakers' point), Damian's struggle to survive commands a new respect from the viewer. His character undergoes extreme duress, and through it learns a humbleness possible only for those who have been taught a life-changing lesson. We are told Damian never even had to light his own match so his accomplishment of staying alive in the worst of conditions is that much more astounding. Most urban or suburban dwellers would not survive but Damian is driven by revenge. By the end, Damian has grown to love the desert that nearly killed him, and the hate for his wife and her lover has become insignificant.

The smallest victory in the desert means another day of life. While the lovers luxuriate at the pool, Damian is straightening his broken leg and climbing down ledges with a makeshift rope. While they bicker about their next move, he is finding water in cacti and eating flowers and moths just to get enough nourishment to get through the day. What we discover along with Damian is how rich and alive the desert really is. He sees all manner of wildlife and learns survival tricks from them. If he can respect the cruel desert, it will reward him. There's a nice moment when Damian finally stumbles upon a watering hole after weeks of barely finding enough moisture to wet his tongue. Shortly thereafter it begins to rain and his laugh of "Now it rains!" is joyous indeed. By being made to seem small, Damian has grown in stature, and become part of the desert itself.

Ordeal is a remake of 1953's *Inferno*, which was shot in 3-D, and starred Robert Ryan, Rhonda Fleming and William Lundigan in the triangle roles. Director Lee H. Katzin (*Whatever Happened to Aunt Alice?*) has a genuine feel for the desert half of the story, which was filmed in Red Rock Canyon State Park in California. He made another desert survival telefilm called *Savages*, which adds the element of being tracked by a killer to the task of making it out of the desert alive. His other fright telefilms include *Terror Out of the Sky* and *The Stranger*, neither of which match the accomplishment here. Composer Pat Williams has been nominated 22 times for Emmys, winning four. His many diverse credits include music for the cult horror *SSSSSSS*, the Kurt Russell comedy *Used Cars*, John Waters' *Cry-Baby*, and the telefrights *Terror in the Sky* and *Short Walk to Daylight*.

Arthur Hill (*Owen Marshal, Counselor at Law*) gives a superb performance as the transformative Damian. Hill's capability for playing villains and fatherly authority figures serves him well in the role of a man who undergoes such a radical change. Diana Muldaur (*L.A. Law*) was expert at playing cold, calculating women, and she provides a trademark demonstration of that talent here.

James Stacy has led a particularly challenging life. Born in Los Angeles, the handsome actor made his debut in the Marlon Brando vehicle, *Sayonara*. He had a regular role on *The Adventures of Ozzie and Harriet*, made teen-oriented movies such as *A Swingin' Summer* and *Winter A-Go-Go*, and, in the late 60s, had a popular western series called *Lancer*. *Ordeal* would be his last film appearance before a drunk driver hit Stacy and his girlfriend as they motorcycled. The crash killed the girlfriend, and resulted in the loss of his left arm and left leg. Stacy returned to acting two years later but naturally his roles were limited. He received an Emmy nomination for playing a wounded Vietnam veteran in 1977's *Just a Little Inconvenience*. In 1996 Stacy was convicted of child molestation and sentenced to six years in prison. Before his trial, he attempted suicide by jumping off a cliff in Hawaii, but he survived. Back in the 70s he did make one other telefright, *Paper Man*.

CAST: Arthur Hill, Diana Muldaur, James Stacy, Macdonald Carey, Michael Ansara, Arch Whiting, Bill Catching, and Len Felber.

CREDITS: Director: Lee H. Katzin; Teleplay: Francis Cockrell and Leon Tokatyan, from a story by Cockrell; Music: Pat Williams; Production: 20th Century–Fox Television; Running Time: 91 minutes; Air Date: 10/30/73; Network: ABC

Panic on the 5:22

"What if tomorrow or the next day, the city, with all its violence and terror, invaded the train?"

The influence of the gritty, street-level crime thrillers of the early 1970s—such as *Dirty Harry*, *The French Connection* and particularly *The Taking of Pelham One Two Three*—was felt far enough afield to inspire this pale imitation. But where those films and others of their ilk sought to break cinematic molds, *Panic on the 5:22* struggles to fit an edgy idea into the contemporary television mold, a mold not about to bend let alone break. The result is what one would expect: a toothless and confused tiger in a box.

Three none-too-bright thugs decide to rob a private club car on an outbound commuter train from New York, peopled with the wealthy elite from the city. Instead of untold riches, the thugs discover that the rich don't carry money. This causes friction amongst the thieves, who find themselves trapped on a 45-minute train ride to nowhere.

Panic on the 5:22 was made by Quinn Martin Productions, a company famous for producing landmark television series including *The Fugitive*, *The F.B.I.*, *The Invaders*, *The Streets of San Francisco*, etc. The typical QM program had a narrator who introduced the evening's entertainment, and this film is no exception in that regard. It is an exception, however, in the florid, feeble quality of the narration spoken by the familiar but uncredited voice. The purple prose of the opening sequence, where the viewer is earnestly warned of impending doom, is nothing compared to the baroquely over-written finale wherein the fates of the thieves is learned. One of the thugs, we are told, turned out to be "an acolyte carrying holy cards to the electronic master"—in other words, a messenger in a computer room.

Subtitles advise us of the day of the week, as the wealthy passengers and low-life criminals are introduced before the fateful Friday they collide. Lynda Day George plays Mary Ellen, a sleep-around wife ("So long, what's-your-face"), and Laurence Luckinbill plays her cuckold husband, Lawrence, who's in advertising. Dana Elcar is Hal, the appropriately named head of a computer manufacturing firm, who has his pants ignominiously removed during the holdup. Ina Balin is the Countess, a perfume magnate who tells the art director for her latest advertising campaign, "You smell like an old Australian prostitute." Bernie Casey is Wendell Weaver, the basketball star whose autographs sell for 50 cents while Walt Frazier's sell for a dollar. Eduard Franz is Jerome, the financier who has his limousine stolen, and Andrew Duggan is Harlan, the ex–military officer in financial trouble.

The introductions of the fabulously rich passengers convey the hopelessly hip cynicism of writer Eugene Price, but he outdoes himself on the criminal element. The confession of Frankie (James Sloyan), in a church that he obviously spends too little time in, was trimmed before airing, presumably for its bad taste. Emil (Reni Santoni, *Dirty Harry*) is shown robbing an old Orthodox Jew because he must be carrying diamonds (he's not), and Eddie (Robert Walden, *Lou Grant*) is simply a rude jerk. However, the capper occurs as the three no-goodniks are on the way to heist the train, and Frankie decides on a lark to rob a liquor store as nonchalantly as if he were buying cigarettes.

Because the train robbery is quickly accomplished (since no one aboard has any cash), the 45-minute ride plays out in more or less real time. And since this is a message film, there is a lot of talk about hopelessness, the unfeeling rich, class distinctions, the merits of bravery and so on, all in the pseudo-hip language that television writers, ensconced in their ivory towers, figure everyone else uses. Finally, Mary Ellen, who had a nightgown and hotel key in her spilled purse, pulls the ultimate boner and convinces Emil, the slowest-witted thug, to remove his mask, thereby damning everyone to a certain death. Fortunately, the thugs fall out over this, and only one person dies and he's not rich.

Ultimately, it is only George the barman (Charles Lampkin) who gains the respect of the inept crew of thieves, because he's poor and he doesn't frighten easily. George is very philosophical, saying things such as "It is in the nature of trains to start and stop," and this is impressive to the thugs. Impressive is also the word to describe one passenger's luggage: a Stradivarius violin worth $165,000, which would be worth well over a half-million dollars today. However, "amusingly inferior" would be the words to describe this attempt at a social statement by out-of-touch filmmakers.

Director Harvey Hart made the cult horror films *Dark Intruder* with Leslie Nielsen and *The Pyx* with Karen Black.

CAST: (ao) Ina Balin, Bernie Casey, Linden Chiles, Andrew Duggan, Dana Elcar, Eduard Franz, Lynda Day George, Laurence Luckinbill, Reni Santoni, James Sloyan, and Robert Walden. Also Dennis Patrick, Robert Mandan, Charles Lampkin, Joseph Perry, Byron Morrow, Derick Stroud, George Kramer, Sam DeFazio, James Nolan, Mark Thomas, Bernie Kuby, Allen Joseph, and Arthur Adams.

CREDITS: Director: Harvey Hart; Teleplay: Eugene Price; Music: Richard Markowitz; Production: Quinn Martin Productions; Running Time: 73 minutes; Air Date: 11/20/74; Network: ABC

Paper Man

Note: *Paper Man* was also released briefly to theaters with an added 15 minutes. The longer version was released on home video and was used for this review.

College student Joel Fisher (Elliot Street) receives a credit card in the mail for someone named "Henry Norman." Instead of returning it, he and fellow students Karen

(Stefanie Powers), Jerry (James Stacy) and Lisa (Tina Chen) decide to commit a little harmless fraud. Although the students pay the bills, the bank becomes suspicious since Henry doesn't really exist. The group convinces computer nerd Avery Jensen (Dean Stockwell) to create an identity for Henry by inserting profile records into various company databases. When they get a bill for a gun that none of them bought, they realize that someone else is using the identity. Things turn deadly serious when the students start getting bumped off, and it looks as if the computer is the culprit.

Consider *Paper Man* a hi-tech murder mystery. Naturally, the technological advances since 1971 take the sheen off the mechanics, rendering many of the pieces of computer business quaint. But, surprisingly, much of the founding detail rings true. Many companies took advantage of the "time share" concept, and rather than spend fortunes on their own computers, rented time and space on the cutting edge processors usually found at universities. And it is certainly conceivable that talented and somewhat corrupt people could insert falsified records to create an identity. In fact, crimes of this nature were considerably easier in those pre–security measures days. Note as well that Lisa is working with the advanced technology of voice recognition, which has yet to permeate home computer systems even by the turn of the millennium.

On the other hand, the viewer must forgive the measures taken by the filmmakers to make computers dramatically and visually appealing. The giant wall of blinking lights used to give the computer something of a personality is simply window dressing. And, in the age before monitors had proliferated, it is artistic license to allow Karen to use a microfiche reader as if it were a computer screen.

The mystery element of the story is somewhat muddled: the details of just who is doing what to whom (and how) seem to be a bit much for the writers to keep straight. But being meticulous in this regard is not the point. What is now called "cyberphobia"—the fear of computers—is the real hook for the story. It is a fear as real then as it is now, and frankly, should be even more common given the pervasiveness of the technology in our daily lives. The faceless machine of our society (characters call it "Big Ugly"), which "keeps trying to stick numbers on people," was only beginning to get a foothold in the day-to-day lives of the population. Today it is practically impossible to be "off the grid," to be unknown in our civilization.

The cast of students in the film was rather long in the tooth even for secondary college. Elliot Street and Stefanie Powers were pushing 30, and James Stacy and Dean Stockwell were both 35 at the time.

Walter Grauman's directorial touch is present in some of the atmospherics. For instance, when Lisa is attempting to teach the computer to recognize the spoken word "breath," the response is "death" repeated over and over. This naturally scares her, and as she flees the room, running down the hall, the ceiling lights turn off one by one behind her, giving the impression that she's being chased by the computer. The trick is not unique in movies but it is used to great effect here.

The script has its unintentionally humorous moments as well. Lisa says, "No one will give students credit because they don't own anything," which is certainly not the case today. It is also interesting that most of the supporting cast members are given titles instead of proper names: Executive, Bureaucrat, Electronics Expert, etc. Keep a sharp eye out for a brief cameo by Marcy Lafferty (in her first film appearance) as a secretary. Lafferty would soon marry William Shatner, remaining his spouse until their 1994 divorce.

CAST: Dean Stockwell, Stefanie Powers, James Stacy, Tina Chen, Elliot Street, James Olson, Jason Wingreen, Dan Barton, Robert Patten, Sue Taylor, Johnny Scott Lee, Len Wayland, Dean Harens, Bob Golden, Marcy Lafferty, Craig Guenther, and Ross Elliott.

CREDITS: Director: Walter Grauman; Teleplay: James D. Buchanan & Ronald Austin, from a story by Anthony Wilson; Music: Duane Tatro; Production: 20 Century–Fox Television; Running Time: 90 minutes; Air Date: 11/12/71; Network: CBS

The Phantom of Hollywood

"I live in a world of castles, of palaces, of mansions, in dreams."—The Phantom

For the movie lover, this is one of the most potent, if only in irony, of television films: Hollywood—particularly MGM—capitalizes on its own destruction. In the early 1970s, the famous studio, bowing to financial pressures, was forced to sell off its famous back lots to developers. The locations for some of the most fondly remembered films of Hollywood's golden age were put up for sale, and many of the properties of the studio—costumes and the like—were auctioned off to collectors. Prior to the flattening of many of the standing sets, *The Phantom of Hollywood*, a modern take on *The Phantom of the Opera*, was filmed to take advantage not only of the lot but of the destruction itself. This can be viewed as heartless exploitation or nostalgic reverie, but either way the result is undeniably entertaining.

Worldwide Studios head Roger Cross (Peter Lawford) plans the sale of back lot #2 in order to generate cash flow for the venerable (but now struggling) movie company. After a couple of would-be vandals are found dead on the back lot, and two survey engineers disappear, rumors surface of the Phantom, a vengeful ghostly presence residing there. When Cross's daughter Randy (Skye Aubrey) is kidnapped and ransomed for ownership of the lot, press agent Ray Burns (Peter Haskell), studio detective O'Neal (Broderick Crawford) and cop Lt. Gifford (John Ireland) join forces to flush out the Phantom and rescue Randy.

The Phantom of Hollywood is a good old-fashioned B horror movie peopled with B-movie stars. There are supporting roles or cameos from Jackie Coogan, Kent Taylor and Regis Toomey. (The Internet Movie Database claims Elisha Cook, Jr. has a role in the film but he was not identifiable in the review copy.) The identity of the Phantom is revealed half an hour into the movie, so it won't spoil the experience of first-time viewers to learn that it is Karl Vonner (Jack Cassidy), an up-and-coming actor in the old days who had suffered severe burns during the shooting of one of his films. Cassidy also plays Karl's brother Otto, who worked for many years in the studio's still vault while hiding his scarred brother away on the back lot.

In a clever move, shots of the dilapidated back lot are interspersed with scenes from some of the old movies shot there. The film clips include appearances by stars such as Mickey Rooney, Robert Taylor and Vivien Leigh. When editor Jonathan (Coogan) puts together a nostalgia reel for the studio's farewell party to the lot, the clips used feature stars John Gilbert, Greta Garbo, Jean Harlow, Charles Laughton, Clark Gable, Katharine Hepburn and Cary Grant. The glamour of old Hollywood seems very far away indeed, and as Jonathan says in noting the studio's decision to raze its past, it is "yesterday down the drain."

Most of the action takes place on the back lot which adds considerable—and sometimes painful—production value. The lot consisted of "40 acres, a lake, river and exactly 117 trees," according to press agent Burns, and the rundown sets allow for some high-quality spooky night scenes. Watching crews bulldozing movie history—whether out of economic reality or manifest greed—will bring pangs to those sensitive to such things.

On the lighter side, the script does hold its amusements, intended or not. The vandals bent on destruction, who climb over the lot's fence, are of the television variety; they say things such as "Crazy place, huh? It turns me on!" Studio head Cross, claiming that the back lot is useless nowadays, says, "It might as well be a supermarket or apartment complex." Upon discovery of the dead body of a security guard, another victim of the

Jack Cassidy as *The Phantom of Hollywood* (1974).

Phantom, John Ireland says, "We're gonna run out of chalk." Ireland, in his only fright telefilm appearance, deserves special mention for striking just the right tone as the exasperated cop. In a nod to the standards of old, very little violence is actually shown in the film, only the moments leading up to the Phantom's strikes.

Trivia buffs will enjoy the inside joke that Skye Aubrey, who plays the studio head's daughter, was actually the daughter of one-time MGM president James Aubrey. For film fans, *The Phantom of Hollywood* is an irresistible double-edged sword. One can't halt progress or the passage of time, but at least this valentine to days gone by still exists.

CAST: (ao) Skye Aubrey, Jack Cassidy, Jackie Coogan, Broderick Crawford, Peter Haskell, John Ireland, and Peter Lawford. Also Gary Barton, Corinne Calvet, Billy Halop, John Lupton, Kent Taylor, Regis Toomey, Fredd Wayne, Bill Williams, Carl Byrd, Edward Cross, Damon Douglas, and Bill Stout.

CREDITS: Director: Gene Levitt; Teleplay: George Schenck, from a story by Robert Tom and George Schenck; Music: Leonard Rosenman; Production: MGM Television; Vehicles Provided by Chrysler Corporation and General Motors; Running Time: 71 minutes; Air Date: 2/12/74; Network: CBS

The Picture of Dorian Gray

"Sin is a thing that writes itself across a man's face, and cannot be concealed."

The second of the Curtis-produced films shot in England to air in America (see *Dracula*, *The Turn of the Screw*), *The Picture of Dorian Gray* was shown over two nights in the spring of 1973. The results, both in terms of the end product and in measure of success, were unspectacular.

London 1891. Dorian Gray (Shane Bryant), a sensitive and innocent young man, has his portrait painted by his friend Basil Hallward (Charles Aidman). Taken under the wing of the cad Lord Harry Wotton (Nigel Davenport), Gray embarks on a life of debauchery. Through a vague Faustian bargain, the portrait begins to take on the ugliness of every callous act, every unhealthy vice committed by Gray, while the man himself remains young-looking and beautiful. Eventually the piper is paid, and Gray's guilt-ridden attempt to destroy the painting results in his death.

Adapted and parodied in cinema many times before and since, this earnestly intended version is adequate in a *Masterpiece Theater* sense. Comparing favorably with Curtis's other two classical remakes mentioned above, this made-on-video production cannot hold the proverbial candle to the 1945 MGM film with Hurd Hatfield in the lead role. The comparison is unfair, no doubt, but another faithful, conservative telling of an oft-told tale sets itself up for such an assessment.

Shane Bryant has an "introducing" credit as Dorian on this, his third film. He is best remembered by fans for his parts in Hammer productions of the 70s, such as *Straight on Till Morning*, *Demons of the Mind* and *Frankenstein and the Monster from Hell*. Here, his handsome face puts him in good stead, but he lacks the gravitas required to portray the inner evilness of Dorian Gray.

Charles Aidman is convincing as the concerned artist Basil, but Nigel Davenport (Van Helsing in Curtis's *Dracula*), in the role of Lord Wotton, is no George Sanders, who assayed the role in the 1945 version. Smaller parts are played by Curtis favorite John Karlen and Fionnuala Flanagan, and there's an early role for *Escape to Witch Mountain*'s Kim Richards. Cult film fans will recognize Vanessa Howard as the doomed Sybil Vane. She was in the controversial films *Corruption* and *Mumsy, Nanny, Sonny and Girlie* before losing the acting bug. This was her final film appearance.

The grandest pleasure in any faithful version of Oscar Wilde's classic is in the man's brilliant, acerbic wit. Immortal lines such as "There is only one thing worse than being talked about and that is not being talked about," and "In love, we begin by deceiving ourselves and end by deceiving others," never seem to fade, pulling the viewer through the most dire productions.

Depicting the debauchery of Dorian Gray was never an option for a 1970s network television adaptation, nor was it for the 1945 classic. Here, director Glenn Jordan, who also took the reins of Curtis's *Frankenstein*, makes do with innuendo (note the single glance that suggests Gray's homosexual experimentations). Wilde's withering exposé of the sordid underbelly of polite Victorian (and Edwardian) society is here given a reverent but hardly classic treatment.

The portraits of Dorian Gray were produced by John Solie, whose movie poster art sometimes runs to exploitive and/or genre tastes. A sampling includes *Soylent Green*, *Big Bad Momma*, *Shaft in Africa* and *Candy Stripe Nurses*.

CAST: Shane Bryant, Nigel Davenport, Charles Aidman, Fionnuala Flanagan, Linda Kelsey, Vanessa Howard, John Karlen, Dixie Marquis, Brendan Dillon, William Beckley, Hedley Mattingly, Tom McCorry, Kim Richards, Patricia Tidy, Ben Wrigley, and Diana Wyatt.

CREDITS: Director: Glenn Jordan; Teleplay: John Tomerlin; Music: Robert Cobert; Production: Dan Curtis Productions; Running Time: 111 minutes; Air Date: 4/23–24/73; Network: ABC

The Possessed

The Helen Page School, a school for girls run by Louise Gelsen (Joan Hackett), is disrupted by a series of unexplained fires, one of which seriously injures a student. Kevin Leahy (James Farantino), an ex-minister who had lost the faith due to his drinking and adultery, shows up one day to combat the evil he is convinced is causing the mayhem. When the biology teacher, Paul Winjam (Harrison Ford), is burned alive, Gelsen, his former lover, becomes possessed of the evil spirit, and Leahy takes steps to free her.

'Tis *The Exorcist* to blame for the proliferation of movies like this (see also *Good Against Evil*). Some are worth watching, while others are pale imitations made merely to fleece the gullible. *The Possessed* falls into the latter category. Writer John Sacret Young (*China Beach*, *West Wing*) takes the flimsy framework of sexual shenanigans, and on it hangs a half-hearted tale of supernatural retribution.

The idea of spontaneous combustion is a scary one, and the execution of the fires in the film is handled quite well. But the logic behind their appearance is maddeningly vague. The film refuses to take a stand on the cause of the fires, spreading blame around as if to cover all the bases. The evil doesn't seem to be associated with one person, but instead is fed on the general sexual awakening occurring at the school, as if the idea of sex was enough to summon a demon to plague those with naughty thoughts. This is taking the leading undercurrent of *The Exorcist* to an irresponsible length.

Farentino, as the defrocked minister Leahy, sleepwalks through the role, but given the script's level of sophistication, one cannot blame him for wanting to get it over with. Early in the film Leahy has an automobile accident and almost dies. While stuck in the limbo between life and death, he experiences a vision where a voice literally tells him he's lost his faith, and that he should seek out and destroy evil. This is how his freelance exorcist job is born (the film was actually a pilot for a series concerning his priestly adventures).

Brooklyn-born Farentino was one of the last of the contract stars at Universal in the late 60s. He was ubiquitous on television from the early 60s through the 80s, including landing series work in *The Bold Ones: The Lawyers* and *Dynasty*. Although he was less visible on the big screen, he did make the genre entries *Psychomania* aka *Violent Midnight* and *Dead & Buried*, and one other telefright, *The Elevator*. Later in life, he had his personal problems, including being charged with stalking Frank Sinatra's daughter Tina, and being busted for cocaine in 1991, but he has since made a comeback, particularly on the stage.

Joan Hackett, on the other hand, refuses to be defeated by the mediocrity here and has fun with the pent-up character of Louise. In what amounts to a tour-de-force performance, Hackett runs circles around the rest of the cast, reveling in the variety of emotions allowed her. The possession of the title occurs late in the film when Gelsen turns greenish and starts spitting roofing nails, but the non-ending involving her salvation will frustrate even the most forgiving of viewers.

The film is noted for an early Harrison Ford role as Paul. Some of his winning personality shows through as the doomed biology teacher, but this isn't a showcase for his talent by any means. Claudette Nevins, who plays the assistant administrator Ellen Sumner, got her first break in the 3-D horror film *The Mask*. Amongst the student body are Diana Scarwid (*Psycho III*) and P.J. Soles (*Halloween*, *Rock 'n' Roll High School*). Eugene Roche plays a cop investigating the fire incidents.

The Possessed was filmed at Reed College in Portland, Oregon. The location adds some interest to the production, certainly, but it isn't exploited to the fullest and is mentioned merely as a novelty.

Before Jerry Thorpe committed completely to television as a director and producer, he made Robert Vaughn's anti–*The Man from U.N.C.L.E.* spy movie *The Venetian Affair*, and the highly regarded Glenn Ford vehicle *Day of the Evil Gun*.

CAST: James Farentino, Claudette Nevins, Eugene Roche, Harrison Ford, Ann Dusenberry, Diana Scarwid, Joan Hackett, Dinah Manoff, Carol Jones, P.J. Soles, Ethelinn Block, Susan Walden, Lawrence Bame, James R. Parkes, and Catherine Cunneff.

CREDITS: Director: Jerry Thorpe; Teleplay: John Sacret Young; Music: Leonard Rosenman; Production: Warner Bros. Television; Running Time: 74 minutes; Air Date: 5/1/77; Network: NBC

The President's Plane Is Missing

At a time of considerable international tensions, the president of the United States,

Jeremy Haines (Tod Andrews), leaves Washington on Air Force One for a holiday in Palm Springs. The Air Force loses contact with the plane over Arizona. The plane does indeed crash, and when the wreckage is discovered, the president's body is not found among the dead. The situation puts ill-prepared Vice-President Kermit Madigan (Buddy Ebsen) into the heart of a political power struggle that could mean nuclear war. Meanwhile, journalist Mark Jones (Peter Graves) investigates the president's disappearance.

While the pragmatic politics of yesteryear may seem a long time gone while viewing this thriller, there are remarkably prescient elements in the scenario that are still compelling today. We may no longer be fighting the Cold War, but the Hawk and Dove power struggle depicted in the film is one that continues—and will always continue. Director Daryl Duke keeps the tension taut and this, combined with fine performances and a literate script from Robert J. Serling's (Rod's brother) best-selling novel, make *The President's Plane Is Missing* superior entertainment.

Standouts among the large cast are Ebsen as the somewhat overwhelmed veep, Arthur Kennedy as press bureau chief Gunther Damon and Rip Torn as the calculating advisor George Oldenburg. Peter Graves is solid as the intrepid reporter who discovers the truth, and James Wainwright's approach as Gen. Dunbar is refreshingly low-key. Dabney Coleman's bad toupee distracts from his work as Senator Haines, the president's brother; watch for John Amos (*Good Times*) in an early role as a guard. Fans of the faux-hip musical *The Cool Ones* will want to keep a sharp eye out for its star, Gil Peterson, in a very small role as an airport tower controller.

Since the film is largely a mystery it would be unfair to divulge the outcome. But what is most fascinating today—besides the mechanics of the government and military emergency response teams—is the method used by influential persons in the White House to gain a power hold on the vice-president. The story turns on the willful manipulation of facts by an advisor (Oldenburg), to compel Vice-President Madigan to attack a foreign country without due cause. Oldenburg presents Madigan with satellite photos that "prove" a valid weapons of mass destruction threat in China, which requires—according to the Game Theory of nuclear determent developed at the Rand Corporation—a "Programmed Tactical Response"—in other words, a first strike. Any resemblance to real-life politics in the twenty-first century is purely coincidental.

CAST: (ao) Buddy Ebsen, Peter Graves, Arthur Kennedy, Raymond Massey, Mercedes McCambridge, and Rip Torn. Also Louise Sorel, James Wainwright, Dabney Coleman, Joseph Campanella, Richard Eastham, James B. Smith, Maida Severn, Ivan Bonar, Gary Haynes, Patty Bodeen, Robert Reiser, Byron Morrow, Bill Walker, Richard Bull, Vernon Weddle, Hoke Howell, Richard Stahl, Gil Peterson, Dale Tarter, James W. Gavin, Barry Cahill, Lillian Lehman, James Sikking, Barbara Leigh, Jerry Crews, Jeff Burton, John Rayner, George Barrows, Johnny Amos, John Ward, and Tod Andrews.

CREDITS: Director: Daryl Duke; Teleplay: Mark Carliner and Ernest Kinoy, based on the novel by Robert J. Serling; Music: Gil Melle; Production: ABC Circle Films; Vehicles Provided by Chrysler Corp. and General Motors Corp.; Running Time: 96 minutes; Air Date: 10/23/73; Network: ABC

Pursuit

AKA **Binary**

James Wright (E.G. Marshall), the leader of an extremist group called Americans for Better Nations, is under surveillance by federal authorities. Given the order to arrest Wright for conspiracy, agent Steven Graves (Ben Gazzara) delays in the hopes of gathering more conclusive evidence. While tailing him, Graves discovers that Wright had gained access to Graves' psychological profile. Wright is challenging Graves by piecing together a mysterious machine in a San Diego apartment just as the Republican National Convention is underway.

With the arrival of the president imminent, Graves learns that Wright has nerve gas in his possession and intends to release it remotely, potentially killing a million people, the President included.

Best-selling author Michael Crichton (*The Andromeda Strain*, *Jurassic Park*, etc.) directs a film based on his own novel for the first time here. This small-scope, cat-and-mouse thriller is a competent example of the genre told in *Dragnet* style. A digital countdown—started at 15 hours when the nerve gas is stolen in Utah—informs the viewer of the time remaining before it is set to be released. The idea of the personal challenge between terrorist madman and the cop bent on stopping him pays off best near the end of the film when a final puzzle must be solved.

All concerned do a professional, if low-key job. Ben Gazzara and E.G. Marshall are an interesting pair of actors to watch but this is a stretch for neither. Colorful William Windom as Graves' boss merely fills the space, as does Joseph Wiseman (*Dr. No*) as a consulting expert. Martin Sheen, who was a very busy actor in the 1970s, has a small part as a co-conspirator of Wright's.

As the alternative title *Binary* suggests, doubles are a theme of the film. The ZV nerve gas is actually two gases which are deadly only when combined. The theme extends to the two main characters who combine to initiate the action itself. Games are another theme—Graves is a puzzle solver, constantly working on a crossword, and Wright enjoys the game of toying with Graves, and building the complex mechanism with which to release the gas.

Jerry Goldsmith, one of the most famous composers for film and television, contributes a score that compliments the modest action. Crichton would go on to bigger and better things (*Westworld* came out the following year) but this proves not to be a bad start for his second career behind the camera.

It was never determined what the initials in E.G. Marshall's name stood for, exactly. He used to respond to the question with "Everybody's Guess." It *is* known that he was born in Owatonna, Minnesota, and far from being the strait-laced man he was often typecast as, he was actually quite the prankster. He began his acting career in film in the mid–40s, but soon moved into television where the bulk of his credits lie. He would then bounce effortlessly between the two media, playing authority figures and villains with equal ease, until his death (lung cancer) in 1998. He won two Emmys for his work in the series *The Defenders*, and will be remembered for another series, *The Bold Ones: The New Doctors* in the late 60s. He also worked as a narrator, as in the series *American Lifestyle* and *The Gangster Chronicles*. A few of his film credits include *The Caine Mutiny*, *12 Angry Men*, *Interiors*, *Superman II*, *Creepshow* and *Two Evil Eyes*. He also appears in the telefrights *Vampire* and *Disaster on the Coastliner*.

CAST: Ben Gazzara, E.G. Marshall, William Windom, Joseph Wiseman, Jim McMullan, Martin Sheen, Will Kuluva, Hank Brandt, Quinn Redeker, Conrad Bachmann, Joe Brooks, Robert Cleaves, Walt Davis, Dan Ferrone, Sid Grossfeld, Diki Lerner, and Len Wayland.

CREDITS: Director: Michael Crichton; Teleplay: Robert Dozier, based upon the novel by John Lange (Crichton); Music: Jerry Goldsmith; Production: ABC Circle Films; Vehicles Provided by Chrysler Corp.; Running Time: 74 minutes; Air Date: 12/12/72; Network: ABC

Red Alert

A water leak at a Minnesota nuclear plant sets off an erroneous alert chain in Proteus, the master computer in Colorado that controls the plant. Once Proteus seals off the containment building, trapping plant workers inside, by-the-book officer Henry Stone (Ralph Waite) will not override the computer and open the doors. Federal investigators Frank Brolen (William Devane) and Carl Wyche (Michael Brandon) discover that one of the workers had planted several bombs in the containment building, and that the accident had triggered one of the bombs

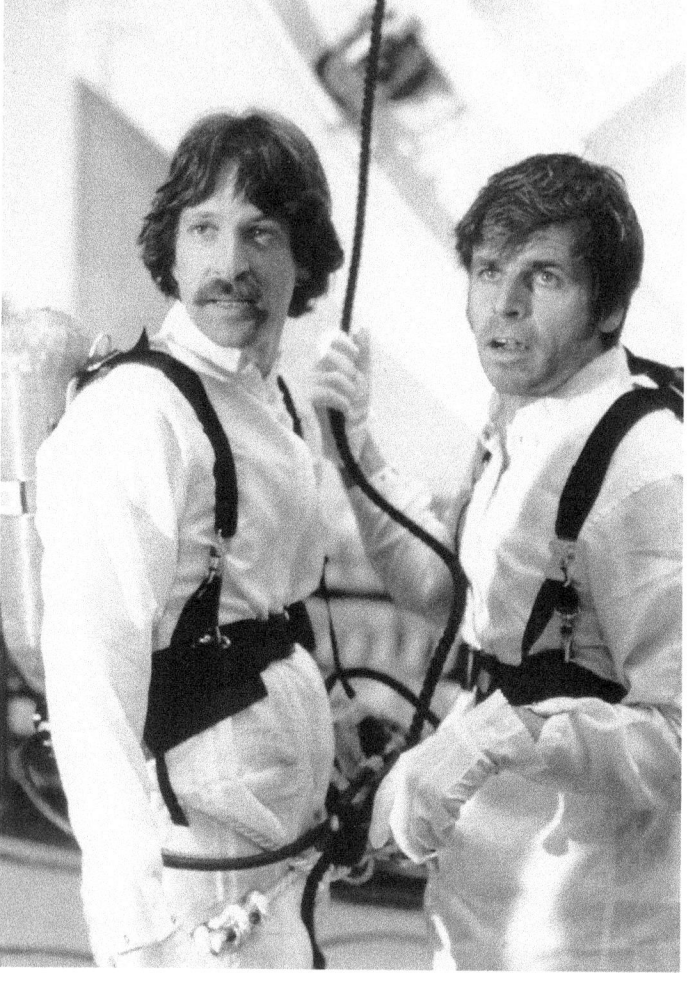

Michael Brandon (left) and William Devane attempt to avert nuclear disaster in *Red Alert* (1977).

are not the least bit believable.

Also remarkable is the number of subtitles that pop up alerting the viewer to the places, dates and times of events. No less than 17 of these appear over the course of the film's 96-minute running time—12 of them in the first half hour. Proteus, the master computer controlling 60 active nuclear plants around the country, relays messages such as "A nuclear excursion has occured (sic) situation critical," and "Alien presence in transfer tube." This same computer is relied upon, after it has proven error-prone, to figure the feasibility of sabotage.

Naturally, the situation has to be kept quiet, which entails arresting the local sheriff—this after Wyche has called his wife to get the kids out of town. Wyche's call on the sly to his wife snowballs into a mad rush at the airport because she called her mother who called a friend and so on, until a large percentage of the Minneapolis population is trying to get on flights out of the city.

early. Brolen breaches protocol by entering the sealed area in the hopes of locating the bombs before they blow up the plant.

Red Alert is a remarkable film for several reasons, none of which make it worth watching. Most obvious is the convoluted plot that relies on a highly improbable set of circumstances in its attempt to generate convincing tension. The major turning points in the story—a master computer going haywire and a human who won't second guess it, a worker sneaking bombs into a nuclear plant, an accident that happens the day sabotage is planned, a federal investigator who takes a wild chance that could kill millions—

It is William Devane who holds the film together. His solid and convincing presence make Frank Brolen the only credible character in the bunch. Devane would soon go on to major television stardom in the long-running *Knots Landing* series. He was born in Albany, New York, and began his career at the New York Shakespeare Festival and in a number of off-Broadway productions. Although no stranger to film, it was television that provided Devane with initial and greater stardom. Two of his performances in telefilms in the mid-70s—as JFK in *The Missiles of October*, and as John Henry Falk in *Fear on Trial*—led to one of television's most lucrative contracts, playing the lead in the *From Here to Eternity* mini-series. Devane's film roles include work in Robert Altman's *McCabe & Mrs. Miller*, Alfred Hitchcock's *Family Plot*, John Schlesinger's *Marathon Man*, *Rolling Thunder*, *The Dark*, *Space Cowboys* and *Hollow Man*. He is still acting circles around his co-stars on television today with series work on *West Wing*, *Stargate SG-1* and *24*.

Ralph Waite's (*The Waltons*) uptight Henry Stone—whose favorite phrase is "It's impossible!"—cracks under the pressure, never quite coming to grips with the fact that Proteus could be wrong. Michael Brandon's Carl Wyche is simply there to put a human face on the near-tragedy, and Adrienne Barbeau, as his wife Judy, has the thankless job of worrying.

Further down on the cast list is Jim Siedow as the despairing Howard Ives, who set the bombs in response to his daughter's death at the hands of the authorities. Siedow is best known for his role in the landmark horror film *The Texas Chain Saw Massacre*, and his heartfelt narration here is one of the few genuine moments in *Red Alert*. Another cult figure, M. Emmet Walsh, plays Sheriff Sweeney, the flummoxed local law man.

This Texas-filmed, pre–*China Syndrome* paranoid thriller can't decide if it is a disaster movie, a terrorist movie or a buddy movie, so it tries to be all three. The viewer would be well-advised to evacuate the area entirely.

CAST: William Devane, Michael Brandon, Adrienne Barbeau, Ralph Waite, David Hayward, M. Emmet Walsh, Don Wiseman, Don Rausch, Jim Danko, John Martin, Howard Finch, Dan Ammerman, Charles Krohn, Arnie Shayne, Charles J. Bailey, Dixie Taylor, Jim Siedow, Lois Fleck, Arnold Lipin, Malcolm Wittman, and Mike Scott.

CREDITS: Director: Billy Hale; Teleplay: Sandor Stern, based on the novel *Paradigm Red* by Harold King; Music: George Aliceson Tipton; Production: The Jozak Company; Running Time: 96 minutes; Air Date: 5/18/77; CBS

Reflections of Murder

Claire Elliott (Joan Hackett) owns and runs The Island School, a private school for boys, with her husband Michael (Sam Waterston), who wants to sell it to developers. Michael is physically and mentally abusive to Claire, and had once taken a teacher, Vicky (Tuesday Weld), for his lover. Michael's relationship with Vicky has since deteriorated as well. Vicky convinces Claire to kill Michael, and they drown him in the bathtub after drugging him. Then the pair throw his body in the unused pool and wait for it to surface.

Reflections of Murder is a remake of the 1955 suspense classic *Les Diaboliques*, by Henri-Georges Clouzot. It is also one of the finest telefilms—fright or otherwise—of the 1970s. The adaptation is by Carol Sobieski, who would go on to collect an Oscar nomination for her work on *Fried Green Tomatoes*. First-time viewers should be allowed to enjoy the mystery to the fullest so comments on the plot will be kept to a minimum.

Filmed in the Pacific Northwest (Seattle and Port Angeles, Washington, and Vancouver, British Columbia), this first-rate production—designed by Boris Leven (*West Side Story*, *The Sound of Music*)—takes full advantage of the fall scenery with gorgeous cinematography, a rarity for a telefilm. The scenes shot in the sleepy Seattle of the 70s look appropriately drab and uninviting compared to "the island" and its historical setting. The music by Billy Goldenberg, drawn from "The Well-Tempered Clavichord" by J.S. Bach, is a perfect compliment to the baroque, ethereal atmosphere.

The three leads are all excellent, although Waterston has a thankless role as the despicable Michael. Hackett (who coincidentally played the head of a girls' school in *The Possession*) is terrific as the fragile Claire, and the famous Tuesday Weld lends a centered gravity as the enabler Vicky. This would be the only fright telefilm appearance of the 70s for Waterston and Weld.

The supporters include Michael Lerner, the eccentric Lucille Benson, familiar character actor R.G. Armstrong, and Jesse Vint (*Macon County Line*) as the cop who stops to help the ladies with a flat tire. Chip, the young student who has a crush on Claire, is played by Lance Kerwin.

John Badham, who would soon make his breakthrough moneymaker *Saturday Night Fever*, pulls all the elements together for this highly recommended take on a classic story.

CAST: Tuesday Weld, Joan Hackett, Sam Waterston, Lucille Benson, Michael Lerner, Ed Bernard, R.G. Armstrong, Lance Kerwin, John Levin, Jesse Vint, William Turner, James A. Newcombe, Sam Henriot, Don Sparks, Sandra Coburn, and Rita Conde.

CREDITS: Director: John Badham; Teleplay: Carol Sobieski, based on the novel *Celle Qui N'Etait Plus* by Pierre Boileau and Thomas Narcejac; Music: Billy Goldenberg, adapted from J.S. Bach's "The Well-Tempered Clavichord"; Production: ABC Circle Films; Vehicles provided by Chrysler Corporation; Running Time: 98 minutes; Air Date: 11/24/74; Network: ABC

Revenge!

AKA There Once Was a Woman

Executive Frank Klaner (Bradford Dillman) discovers his briefcase has been switched. When given instructions to pick it up, he meets Amanda Hilton (Shelley Winters), who promptly knocks Frank out and chains him up in a cell below her basement. Hilton claims Frank impregnated her daughter, who, when rebuffed by Frank, committed suicide, and Hilton plans a deadly revenge. Meanwhile, when the police won't help, Frank's wife, Dianne (Carol Rossen), consults psychic Mark Hembric (Stuart Whitman) about Frank's disappearance. But she discovers that her own premonitions about the incident are stronger than the reluctant psychic's.

This superior, atmospheric thriller was adapted by Joseph Stefano from a novel by Elizabeth Davis. This was the only book of Davis's that made it to the screen, large or small, but she had a brief acting career that included roles in two films by cult director Herschell Gordon Lewis, *The Gruesome Twosome* and *How to Make a Doll*. Composer Dominic Frontiere contributes an impressive experimental electronic score that hums and howls, an eerie compliment to the gothic, unreal milieu.

The role of the psychic detective had been explored in telefilms before (*Sweet, Sweet Rachel*, *Ritual of Evil*), and would be later in Gene Roddenberry's tongue-in-cheek *Spectre*. *Revenge!* differs, however, in that psychic Mark Hembric is a con man who doesn't want to get involved in the mysterious disappearance of Frank Klaner. In fact, it is Dianne Klaner who possesses the intuition that solves the case. Hembric does accompany Dianne in her quest to find out what happened to her husband, but his talents as an escape artist are what come in handy when he is locked up with Frank in the basement cell.

Shelley Winters is perfectly cast as the decidedly odd Hilton. For the most part, she gives a composed performance as the misguided, determined kidnapper. Her eccentric ways and unsteady nature are indeed frightening, especially to the man held powerless in the dark. Bradford Dillman does his usual excellent work as the defensive but outmatched captive. Dillman remembered in his memoir *Are You Anybody?* that Winters would stop production during her more emotional scenes to play a recording of "Maria" from the *West Side Story* soundtrack, to get herself in the mood.

Whitman is also convincing as the fraudulent psychic whose tricks initially draw Dianne into believing he has the power of ESP. Wary of his racket being exposed, he nevertheless feels sorry for Dianne and, as mentioned, his contribution is more practical than supernatural. Rossen (*The Stepford Wives*), as the confused Dianne, manages to convey naiveté mixed with self-confidence as she follows her instinct through. She senses something wrong from the very beginning, and eventually begins to trust that she alone is the one with the capability of finding out the truth. As Frank says early in the film, "My wife gets all the premonitions in our family."

When Hilton takes Frank to her old Victorian mansion to retrieve the briefcase, she describes the aging relic as "one of the few survivors of the great earthquake. My husband's grandfather built it to keep his mad wife off the streets." The description sets the tone nicely as it is Hilton who is the mad one this time around. She claims Frank met her daughter at a data processing convention in Atlantic City, and took advantage of her. It never becomes absolutely clear whether this was the case or not, an ambiguity that rounds out the mystery, but Frank's remark to Hilton "Why couldn't she turn to you?" is particularly insightful. Meanwhile, Dianne has a dream (unfortunately, not depicted) that Frank is trying to catch a train which is coming towards him. Defying Hembric's claim that he possesses no ESP power at all, he tells Dianne, before knowing of the dream, to look for the parallel lines. Dianne interprets this as the railroad tracks in her dream, but it turns out to actually be the "pair of lions" outside the Hilton house.

There is ghoulish atmosphere to spare when a large trunk is delivered to Hilton, and she begins her preparations, which include lining the trunk with plastic. When she unwraps an axe and takes it downstairs where the drugged Frank lies, genuine chills begin to take hold. The bizarre scene where Hembric and Dianne barge in on Hilton is amusing at first, as Hembric uses his tricks to snowball the nervous woman, but she quickly turns the tables on the confidant huckster.

Leslie Charleson (*General Hospital*) is Dianne's sister who recommends Hembric, and Roger Perry (*The Thing with Two Heads*) plays a red herring colleague of Frank's, Pete Marsh. Director Jud Taylor would later work with Bradford Dillman again in *The Disappearance of Flight 412*.

CAST: Shelley Winters, Bradford Dillman, Carol Rossen, Stuart Whitman, Roger Perry, Leslie Charleson, Gary Clarke, Johnny Lee, George Burrafato, Pelly Sutton, and Jack Bradock.

CREDITS: Director: Jud Taylor; Teleplay: Joseph Stefano, based on the novel by Elizabeth Davis; Music: Dominic Frontiere; Production: Mark Carliner Productions; Running Time: 74 minutes; Air Date: 11/6/71; Network: ABC

Ritual of Evil

When one of his patients, Aline Wiley, commits suicide, psychiatrist David Sorell (Louis Jourdan) is drawn into the world of the "beautiful people"—the idle rich with more money than sense. Sorell unravels a mystery involving Satanic rituals, witchcraft and murder, and must foil a plot that puts Aline's sister Loey (Belinda Montgomery) in jeopardy.

Ritual of Evil was the second attempt to inspire a series about occult investigator David Sorell. The previous year's *Fear No Evil* introduced the character, but neither film would result in a series. Both films are superior television fare, however, featuring Louis Jourdan as Sorell and Wilfred Hyde-White as the occult expert Harry Snowden. Writer Robert Presnell, Jr. weaves the plot this time, but there is an acknowledgment credit at the beginning of the film noting that it is based on characters created by Richard Alan Simmons, who wrote the screenplay for *Fear No Evil*. There is no credit, however, for author Guy Endore (*The Werewolf of Paris*) who wrote the story for *Fear No Evil*.

Director Robert Day keeps the audience guessing right along with Sorell in this dream-like mystery that makes its way to an ambiguous ending like a meandering stream that finally just evaporates. *Ritual of Evil* drips with the atmosphere of stormy nights, Dutch-angled Black Mass rituals, and psychedelic dream sequences that titillate and misdirect the viewer. Clearly, this was Day's finest telefright of the decade.

The film rides on the effortless charm of Jourdan, as he puts together a puzzle whose pieces are too few and form an uncomfortable fit. Anne Baxter is fine as the drunkard aunt, Jolene Wiley, trying to disguise her guilt with drink and half-hearted attempts to woo family friend Edward Bolander (John McMartin) into marriage. Belinda Montgomery plays the young Loey as innocent and vulnerable, yet particularly perceptive. Georg Stanford Brown (*The Rookies*) is sub-par folk singer Larry Richmond, who rents a cottage on the grounds on the fabulous estate, and pays the price for his curiosity about the decadent family.

Sorell's major adversary here is Leila Barton (Diana Hyland), the source of the true occult strength that manipulates and ultimately destroys the Wiley clan. Barton is a photographer who has the power, invested by Satan, to control the thoughts and actions of other simply with the use of a photo of the intended victim. Barton, who claims "the world is ruled by Lucifer," exploits this power in a most interesting way when she calls Sorell's spirit to her, seducing him as he sleeps miles away.

Diana Hyland made a bit of a splash on Broadway in Tennessee Williams' *Sweet Bird of Youth*, before turning almost exclusively to television, with supporting roles in many of the popular series' in the 1960s and 70s, including a stint on *Peyton Place*. In 1976 she met John Travolta while making *The Boy in the Plastic Bubble*, and commenced a much-publicized affair with the younger actor. Just after winning the role of Dick Van Paten's wife on *Eight Is Enough*, the breast cancer that had earlier resulted in a double mastectomy took her life at the age of 41. Her Emmy for her support in *The Boy in the Plastic Bubble* was awarded posthumously, and was accepted on her behalf by Travolta.

There is much talk of gods and demons in *Ritual of Evil*, and a mention of Walpurgis Night, which is actually May Day Eve, a holiday similar to Halloween, when witches roam. When Barton seduces Sorell's spirit she invokes the names of the familiar gods of love and fertility, Ishtar, Isis and Aphrodite. More obscure (and misused) are the demons supposedly called upon to inflict harm. Mulsiber is simply another name for Vulcan, god of fire, Astaroth is a grand duke of Hell, who seduces by means of laziness and vanity, and Diabolis, called the god of lust, is really just a generic term meaning "divider." A minor annoyance to some viewers will be the overuse of hip terms such as "groovy" and "far-out" which wear thin

quickly and otherwise tend to date the production.

CAST: Louis Jourdan, Anne Baxter, Diana Hyland, John McMartin, Belinda Montgomery, Carla Borelli, Georg Stanford Brown, Rege Cordic, Dehl Berti, Richard Alan Knox, Johnny Williams, Jimmy Joyce, James LaSane, and Wilfred Hyde-White.

CREDITS: Director: Robert Day; Teleplay: Robert Presnell, Jr.; Music: William Goldenberg; Production: Universal TV; Running Time: 97 minutes; Air Date: 2/23/70; Network: NBC

Runaway!
AKA The Frozen Passage; The Runaway Train

A train carrying skiers down a mountain loses its brakes. All efforts to manually slow the train fail, until engineer Holly Gibson (Ben Johnson) suggests that another engine hook on from behind, and use its brakes to stop the runaway before it crashes into the station.

Academy Award winner Johnson is excellent as Gibson, the unruffled engineer of the brake-challenged ski train. Gibson is nostalgic as his retirement grows near, reminiscing about his youth and his 57-year love of trains, even as his train rolls on to near-certain disaster. His steady presence keeps this largely unexceptional but fairly lean thriller on track. This is yet another telefright from director David Lowell Rich, this time written by Gerald Di Pego, that joins the ranks of the era's other train-centered thrillers, *Disaster on the Coastliner* and *Panic on the 5:22*.

Filmed in Colorado, including the train station in Denver, *Runaway!* features snowy mountain scenery, and the usual stars with the usual issues to discuss, but the human drama takes a back seat to the various efforts to slow the train. When the main brakes fail, the emergency brakes burn out due to the speed of the train. The conductor enlists the help of the brakeman (Lou Frizzell), and

Theatrical release poster for *Runaway!* (1973).

passengers Nick Staffo (Ed Nelson) and John Shedd (Martin Milner), to try the manual brakes on each car. That doesn't work either. One other long shot, involving potentially closed brake lines, results in the brakeman's fall from the train.

In the human drama department, Staffo has decided to divorce his wife of many years, Ellen (Vera Miles), but they find togetherness in their fear. The situation also unites Shedd with his son Mark (Lee H. Montgomery), who disappointed his dad by not wanting to climb the mountain. At one point, Shedd plans to jump from the train with Mark but changes his mind, realizing he feels the same fear that his son did. Ben Murphy (just ending his run on the *Alias Smith and Jones* series) is Les Reever, a self-centered scammer who ends up helping Carol Lerner (Darleen Carr, *The Beguiled*) through her suicidal urge after her professor lover, Jack Dunn (Ray Danton), gives her the cold shoulder.

Danton is the unusual face here in his only 70s telefright. He was born in New York, and made his screen debut as a Native American in *Chief Crazy Horse*. Active in both film and television, Danton had his biggest mainstream acting success as the eponymous gangster in Budd Boetticher's *The Rise and Fall of Legs Diamond* (1960). In the mid–60s Danton went to Europe and starred as the East Indian pirate Sandokan in *Sandokan Fights Back* and *Throne of Vengeance*. He also made a dashing secret agent in the Eurospy offerings *Code Name: Jaguar*, *Secret Agent Super Dragon* and Jess Franco's *Lucky the Inscrutable*. Returning to the US, Danton made guest appearances in series and telefilms until the late 70s. He turned his talents to directing as well, with the features *Deathmaster*, *Crypt of the Living Dead* and *Psychic Killer*, and television series and specials. Danton passed away of kidney disease in 1992.

Fans of *Battlestar Galactica* will recognize Laurette Spang in a cameo, but it will take a shaper eye to spot her boyfriend, Kip Niven, who can be glimpsed sporting a moustache. These two also worked together as a romantic couple in *Maneater*.

The sequence where the other engine catches the runaway and slows it before disaster strikes is moderately exciting, but it also means there's no payoff for viewers expecting a crash.

CAST: Ben Johnson, Ben Murphy, Ed Nelson, Darleen Carr, Lee H. Montgomery, Martin Milner, Vera Miles, Ray Danton, Frank Marth, John McLiam, Lou Frizzell, Frank Maxwell, Bing Russell, Kip Niven, Laurette Spang, Ross Elliott, Kelley Miles, Judson Pratt, and Than Wyenn.

CREDITS: Director: David Lowell Rich; Teleplay: Gerald Di Pego; Music: Hal Mooney; Production: Universal TV; Running Time: 74 minutes; Air Date: 9/29/73; Network: ABC

Salem's Lot

AKA **Blood Thirst**

Salem's Lot is one of the triumvirate of most popular and well-known telefright films of the 1970s. Along with *Duel* and *The Night Strangler*, it is the film most remembered and championed by the millions that watched it. A product of the fertile imagination of the enormously popular novelist Stephen King, it garnered three Emmy nominations (graphic design, makeup and music), and was released in various incarnations to theaters all over the world. But unlike the lean surprises of the other two films, *Salem's Lot* implodes under the pressure of adapting a bloated bestseller.

Salem's Lot, Maine. Author Ben Mears (David Soul) returns to his boyhood home to write about the haunted Marsten House that frightened him as a child. Mears settles in and wastes no time expending his slender capital as a writer by taking up with a local teacher, Susan Norton (Bonnie Bedelia). He is startled to learn the abandoned house has been taken over by Richard K. Straker (James Mason) and the mysterious Kurt Barlow, who have opened an antique shop in town. The disappearance of a young boy and an outbreak of "pernicious anemia" amongst the town folk lead Mears to believe a vampire has infested Salem's Lot, and he takes action to eradicate the evil.

Brad Savage as a young vampire in *Salem's Lot* (1979).

King's novel is quite captivating and, at over 600 pages, very thorough in creating its milieu. The challenge given screenwriter Paul Monash (to fold the book into 180 minutes) must have been daunting indeed (for his efforts, Monash was nominated for an Edgar Allan Poe award). But the problem with the film isn't that the source was whittled down to just three hours viewing time, it's that it is longer than two hours. The best horror films cannot sustain mood or suspense for longer than a couple of hours, but the requirement to remain true to the tome that inspired it meant that *Salem's Lot* had less of a chance to be a successful horror film. It was triumphant by all the other measures of success, however.

In terms of set pieces, director Tobe Hooper (*The Texas Chain Saw Massacre*) pulls off several memorable moments. The sequence when Mike Ryerson (Geoffrey Lewis) and Ned Tebbets (Barney McFadden) pick up the cold wooden box containing the vampire, and transport it to the Marsten House, creates an unnerving atmosphere of building suspense. The fact that there is no payoff makes it even better.

When the vampirized Danny Glick (Brad Savage) floats outside his older brother Ralphie's (Ronnie Scribner) window, scraping to get in, the imagery is that of classic horror, and its power is due in part to the subtlety required of network television. The child victims in the film were a groundbreaking lot nonetheless. The depiction of children in peril on television was a long-standing censorial no-no, and here we have not only children attacked and prepared as food for a vampire, but there are children vampires attacking other children. However, nary a drop of blood is shown.

Ralphie dies from his brother's attacks, and as Mike Ryerson begins to fill his grave, the youngster compels Ryerson to free him from his coffin. This is another subtle sequence that retains some real power. The nagging question is how the subsequent vampire attack could happen in the daytime. Later in the film, Mears mentions talking with a friend "turned on to the occult," who tells him the vampires are dormant in daylight.

Someone always has to research vampire lore in these films, and in this case it is Jason Berk (Lew Ayres) who has books on monsters and the occult piled around him as he tries to figure out what is happening in his sleepy town. In contrast is the youngster Mark Petrie (Lance Kerwin) who loves monster movies, his room decorated with paraphernalia of the classic Wolf Man and Frankenstein films. When the undead Ralphie comes pawing at Mark's window, the lad's horror training serves him well as he deters the vampire with a cross from a monster model he was building.

The first time we get a good look at the vampire Barlow (Reggie Nalder, in wonderful makeup modeled after Max Schreck's from 1922's *Nosferatu*) is at the two-hour mark. Soon he is popping up all over town, most memorably in the Petrie kitchen. This scene is meant to contrast the mundane daily life with irredeemable and inescapable horror. Although it is handled with aplomb, the result is to reduce the vampire from a terrifying supernatural being to one who must rattle the dishes and knock over cereal boxes to make an impression.

Once inside the Marsten House, the film moves to another level. The set design is outstanding, and the creepy surroundings are used to full advantage in the scenes when Mark and Susan are prowling around unprepared for what lies in wait. Later as Ben and Mark are tracking down the vampire's resting place, the scene within the basement vault, where the lesser vampires lounge around the Barlow coffin, is eerie and foreboding.

Leading man David Soul, already a superstar from the *Starsky and Hutch* cop series, is lackluster at best as Ben Mears, and is one of the major detriments to the film. Hired as a popular hunk, Soul rarely rises to the occasion, and gives an uninspired performance. As love interest Susan Norton, Bonnie Bedelia should have been given more to do. Young Lance Kerwin comes across as the real hero of the film. James Mason, as Straker, is deliciously vague at all times, and exhibits a prissy confidence concerning his evil master and the doom that will befall the town.

The supporters carry the weight admirably. Kenneth McMillan (the pustule-covered Baron Harkonnen of *Dune*) does a solid, low-key turn as the sheriff who finally gives up and leaves town. The aforementioned Geoffrey Lewis does nice work as the victim Ryerson, and Fred Willard mines character gold as the adulterous realtor Larry

Crockett, who gets his comeuppance. The great Elisha Cook, Jr. once again plays the part of a crazy old man. Reggie Nalder, whom the fuss is all about, suffers the indignity of not even being billed.

Salem's Lot was Tobe Hooper's only excursion into television in the 70s, but he came back to the fold in the late 80s, working on the *Amazing Stories* and *Freddie's Nightmares* series, and he continues to dabble in television to this day.

CAST: David Soul, James Mason, Lance Kerwin, Bonnie Bedelia, Lew Ayres, Julie Cobb, Elisha Cook, Jr., George Dzundza, Ed Flanders, Clarissa Kaye, Geoffrey Lewis, Barney McFadden, Kenneth McMillan, Fred Willard, Marie Windsor, Barbara Babcock, Bonnie Bartlett, Joshua Bryant, James Gallery, Robert Lussier, Brad Savage, Ronnie Scribner, and Ned Wilson. Reggie Nalder (uncredited).

CREDITS: Director: Tobe Hooper; Teleplay: Paul Monash, based on the novel by Stephen King; Music: Harry Sukman; Production: Warner Bros. Television; Running Time: 183 minutes; Air Date: 11/17 & 24/79; Network: CBS

Satan's School for Girls

Student Martha Sayers flees the 300-year-old Salem Academy for Women in Massachusetts, and heads for her sister's house in LA. When her sister Elizabeth (Pamela Franklin) returns home, she finds Martha's body hanging in the living room. Not satisfied with the coroner's suicide verdict, Elizabeth enrolls incognito at the school to investigate, and discovers strange goings-on.

This intimate and fast-moving little film—most of the action takes place on the school grounds in the space of a couple of days—is part gothic mystery and part old-fashioned horror story. The images of Elizabeth in her nightgown carrying an oil lamp on a stormy night, as she delves into the hidden recesses of the old school, are straight out of the gothic thrillers of the nineteenth century. But rather than the sense that the filmmakers were falling back on clichés, the scenes evoke a comforting spookiness and an excitement of discovery.

Outside the school, the trappings of the 1970s are more jarring now than they were when the film was made. The shag rugs and macramé plant holders of the nearer past seem much more out of place than the older confines of the historic school. Of course, there are trickles of the modern that make their way into the hallowed halls, such as Joseph Clampett's (Roy Thinnes) white bucks and belt.

Clampett is the art teacher who says things such as "what we think we see is as real as what we actually see." He's the hunky instructor that all the girls have crushes on, so it goes without saying that he's trouble. Professor Delacroix (Lloyd Bochner), on the other hand, is the uptight science teacher whose experiments with rats creep out the student body. Bochner goes over the top playing the stressed-out Delacroix, delivering his lines as if about to burst. His classes take on an edgy absurdity as he stares down a student while spouting dramatic dialogue such as "the mind can be broken to any level by manipulation."

Pamela Franklin has somewhat of a cult following due to appearances in several genre films. Born in Yokohama, Japan, to British parents, she studied ballet before making her screen debut in the classic ghost story, *The Innocents*. She went on to genre roles in *The Nanny* with Bette Davis, Jack Clayton's *Our Mother's House*, Robert Fuest's *And Soon the Darkness*, Bert I. Gordon's *Necromancy* and *The Legend of Hell House*, as well as in many television shows and films before retiring in the early 80s.

Revealing just "what the devil's going on" at the school that could drive its young students to suicide or worse would be unfair to first-time viewers. Suffice it to say that everyone is not whom they seem to be, and trust is a thing too easily given. Among the girls Elizabeth trusts are the famous Kate Jackson, Jamie Smith Jackson (*Go Ask Alice*) and a young Cheryl Stoppelmoor, who was wisely advised to change her name to Ladd. Kate and Cheryl would, of course, work to-

Roy Thinnes is in charge of *Satan's School for Girls* (1973).

gether again as two of *Charlie's Angels* when Ladd replaced Farrah Fawcett in the lineup. Jo Van Fleet does an odd turn as the headmistress of the school, Jessica Williams, but other character support is surprisingly absent.

Satan really does appear in this production, albeit *sans* horns and hooves. Curiously, he is described as Malleus Maleficarum, the Hammer of Witches, which was a notorious book written in the Middle Ages and used by inquisitors to identify, prosecute and dispatch witches. In other words, Satan was the ultimate force behind the Inquisition.

CAST: Pamela Franklin, Kate Jackson, Lloyd Bochner, Jamie Smith Jackson, Roy Thinnes, Jo Van Fleet, Cheryl Stoppelmoor [Ladd], Frank Marth, Terry Lumley, Gwynne Gilford, Bill Quinn, Ann Noland, and Bing Russell.

CREDITS: Director: David Lowell Rich; Teleplay: Arthur A. Ross; Music: Laurence Rosenthal; Production: Spelling-Goldberg Productions; Vehicles furnished by Chrysler Corporation; Running Time: 74 minutes; Air Date: 9/19/73; Network: ABC

Satan's Triangle

A Coast Guard helicopter responds to a ship's mayday signal from inside the Bermuda Triangle. Upon finding the large sailboat, the pilots, Haig (Doug McClure) and Pagnolini (Michael Conrad), spot two dead bodies: one hanging from the mast, the other on the forward hatch. Haig boards the vessel and discovers another hanging body below decks. He also finds a lone survivor, Eva (Kim Novak), who tells the story of her strange experience.

The mysteries of the Bermuda Triangle have inspired other telefilms of the 1970s (see *The Bermuda Depths* and *Beyond the Bermuda Triangle*) but *Satan's Triangle* takes the cake. A narrator informs us at the beginning that "this is one explanation" for the baffling events that have occurred in that part of the ocean bordered by Miami, Puerto Rico and Bermuda. And indeed it is. It is also the most bizarre explanation: Satan did it.

The pair of would-be rescuers are diametric personalities: Pagnolini is religious and Haig is a glib ladies man. So it figures that, not only is Haig stuck overnight on the disabled ship with a female, she's a gorgeous female. When Haig and Eva were being airlifted to the helicopter, the cable broke, plunging them back into the sea. The high winds forced the copter to return to base, so the couple climbed back aboard the ship to spend the night waiting to be rescued. Haig says, "I believe in God, Santa Claus and the Easter Bunny. But the devil, I can't quite swallow." He will definitely revise his thinking come the morning.

Eva tells the story of how she was out fishing with Hal Bancroft (Jim Davis), a competitive jerk who had to land a marlin bigger than his brother-in-law's recent catch. Hal had offered the captain, Strickland (Ed Lauter), a $5000 bonus to help him pull it off. Just as Hal was about to reel in his prize, the crew spotted a man floating by on a piece of debris. The man turns out to a priest, Father Martin (Alejandro Rey), and as soon as he's brought aboard, the weather—and circumstances—take a turn for the worst. Most of the superstitious crew members abandon ship, and a wild storm engulfs the boat and results in the deaths of all aboard.

All but one. Eva relates that she was immediately attracted to the man of God. ("He was handsome, too handsome. It would have been easy to forget he was a priest.") She further confesses to Haig that she's a hooker, and had tried to seduce Father Martin ("Show me that you love me, Father!"). All this sleazy talk is too much for Haig, so he sleeps with her.

Before the two hit the sack, Haig goes through the effort to "prove" to Eva that the weird deaths of Hal, Strickland and Father Martin have logical—but exceedingly farfetched—explanations. But the joke will be on Haig, as the final outlandish twist reveals.

Writer William Reed Woodfield wrote the campy horror film *The Hypnotic Eye*, was instrumental in the *Mission Impossible* series, and penned the science fiction telefilm *Earth II*. However, he acquired even more fame as a photographer of movie stars for magazines such as *Life*, *Esquire* and *Playboy*. He was also a magician, and consulted in that capacity on *Mission Impossible*, as well.

Composer Johnny Pate was the music arranger on *Superfly*, and wrote the scores for the blaxploitation entries *Brother on the Run*, *Shaft in Africa* and *Bucktown*, and the horror films *So Evil, My Sister* and *Dr. Black, Mr. Hyde*.

Much of *Satan's Triangle* is shot through a gauzy filter that gives the action a surreal, dream-like look. Television veteran Sutton Roley had a penchant for visual flourishes, as his earlier telefright film *Sweet, Sweet Rachel* will attest. Roley also directed the superior but far more conventional *Snatched*. This startlingly peculiar Danny Thomas production will delight those with a taste for the odd, and those with a sense of humor.

CAST: Kim Novak, Doug McClure, Alejandro Rey, Ed Lauter, Jim Davis, Michael Conrad, Titos Vandis, Zitto Kazann, Peter Bourne, Hank Stohl, Tom Dever, and Trent Dolan.

CREDITS: Director: Sutton Roley; Teleplay: William Read Woodfield; Music: Johnny Pate; Production: Danny Thomas Productions; Running Time: 69 minutes; Air Date: 1/14/75; Network: ABC

The Savage Bees

On the Mississippi River, a large freighter collides with an abandoned boat from Brazil, unleashing a swarm of killer bees in the New Orleans area. Sheriff Donald McKew (Ben Johnson), whose dog was killed by the bees, teams up with assistant medical examiner Jeff DuRand (Michael Parks) and entomologist Jeannie Devereaux (Gretchen Corbett) to locate the swarm. Meanwhile, people are dying from bee attacks, and authorities from the National Bee Center summon Dr. Jorge Mueller (Horst Buchholz), who has a plan for neutralizing the threat.

The Savage Bees was television's first eco-horror film about killer bees from South America (*Killer Bees*, from 1974, featured vineyard bees supernaturally controlled by Gloria Swanson). This surprisingly languid, small-scope production does not have the usual star-studded cast or human drama dawdling associated with a disaster-oriented film, and the bee attacks are limited to only a couple of onscreen set pieces. It was directed by Bruce Geller, primarily a writer and producer, who created the popular *Mission Impossible* and *Mannix* series. This was the second of only two films he directed (the other was the theatrical release *Harry in Your Pocket*) before being killed, along with his wife, when the small plane he was piloting crashed in Buena Vista Canyon in 1978. It was written by Guerdon Trueblood, a specialist in the disaster subgenre of the telefright films in the 1970s.

The great Ben Johnson is top-billed as the determined sheriff of a small parish outside of New Orleans. Johnson, who passed away in 1996, was a gifted, natural actor who is equally convincing whether he's mourning his dead dog or intimidating the local politicians. Gretchen Corbett (*The Rockford Files*) gives an excellent performance as Devereaux, but Horst Buchholz is less than his normal charming self as the Brazilian doctor Mueller. Paul Hecht (*Kate & Allie*) runs the National Bee Center.

Sleepy-eyed Michael Parks is likable as the New Orleans doctor who immediately recognizes the problem threatening the city. The son of a truck driver, Parks spent a good deal of his youth in the 1950s wandering around doing odd jobs. In the 60s, he began to show up on television, usually as a disaffected youth, and was then cast as Adam in John Huston's *The Bible*. When NBC wanted an anti-establishment series molded after the theatrical hit *Easy Rider*, they cast Parks as the itinerant motorcycle rider in *Then Came Bronson*. What has followed since is a long career of guest star spots on television, including the curious telefright *The Werewolf of Woodstock*, and the occasional film role. In the 90s, he showed up in *Twin Peaks* and in the horror feature *From Dusk Till Dawn*. A favorite of Quentin Tarantino, Parks was cast in *Kill Bill Vol. 1* and *Vol. 2* in two different roles.

Mueller is the one who started the whole mess when the African bees he was experimenting with accidentally escaped in South America. The havoc they wreak near New Orleans, however, is relatively minor. On-screen deaths are limited to a farmer and a couple of partiers, who inadvertently cause the death of the good doctor Mueller. The farmer, Caziot, is played by the bee wrangler on the film, Dr. Norman Gary, who used hundreds of thousands of bees for the production. The scene where Caziot is attacked is quite effective because the bees kill him even though he dives in the water to avoid them.

The two doomed partiers mentioned stumble upon Mueller as he's attempting to swap the killer bees' queen with a queen of a less aggressive strain. When the bees attack the partiers, who are dressed as pirates, they begin flailing about, and one of their swords pierces Mueller's special protective suit. After killing Mueller, the bees swarm onto Devereaux's Volkswagen Beetle, trapping her inside. The solution is to slowly drive the "bug" through the streets of New Orleans to the Superdome, where the temperature can be lowered to 45 degrees, immobilizing the bees. As far-fetched as this may seem, Corbett does a good job communicating claustrophobic panic as the massive swarm engulfs the car.

Because Mardi Gras is going on, there are the requisite parade scenes, but these are mercifully kept to a minimum. James Best (*The Killer Shrews*) is the deputy mayor who gives DuRand and Devereaux the bureaucratic runaround. Co-producer Don Kirshner (the *Rock Concert* music show) was the music supervisor on the film. There is a short scene of voodoo paraphernalia, and a bee attack video is shown at the National Bee

Dual-language poster for Belgian release of *The Savage Bees!* (1976).

Center. *The Savage Bees* won an Emmy Award for Film Sound Mixing and inspired an inferior sequel, *Terror Out of the Sky.*

CAST: Ben Johnson, Michael Parks, Paul Hecht, Gretchen Corbett, Horst Buchholz, Bruce French, James Best, David L. Gray, Richard Charles Boyle, Elliot Keener, Boardman O'Connor, Danny Barker, Don Hood, Bill Holliday, Carol Sutton, Tiffany Gautier Chase, Shirl Cieutat, Judy Langford, Lyla Kay Owen, James Bowers, Sylvia "Kuumba" Williams, Tom Smith Alden, Christine Ellsworth, Kenneth Lorenzen, Wayne "V" Mack, Jack L. Morrison, Dr. Norman Gary, and Cary Wilmot Alden.

CREDITS: Director: Bruce Geller; Teleplay: Guerdon Trueblood; Music: Walter Murphy; Production: Alan Landsburg Productions, Don Kirshner Productions; Running Time: 90 minutes; Air Date: 11/22/76; Network: NBC

Savages

Big city lawyer Horton Maddock (Andy Griffith) recruits reluctant Ben Campbell (Sam Bottoms) as a guide in hunting bighorn sheep in the desert. The trigger-happy Maddock accidentally shoots an old prospector and tries to cover it up. When Ben won't agree to the plan, the crazed Maddock strips him of everything but his shorts and sends Ben across the desert to die.

Lee Katzin directed another desert survival picture, *Ordeal*, wherein Arthur Hill is left to die in the desert by his scheming wife and her lover. Hill survives, driven by revenge. In *Savages*, young Ben is pursued by the mad, scheming Maddock in a wicked cat-and-mouse game that Ben survives by outwitting his predator. Katzin shows an affinity for the subgenre: both films are competent, even compelling viewing. The minor weaknesses here—the plot mechanics that bookend the desert game—are not enough to spoil the overall experience.

Fans of *The Andy Griffith Show* will enjoy seeing their homespun hero playing the despicable character of Maddock. He shows up in his fancy safari outfit and proceeds to make life hell for Ben. Maddock's plan to chase Ben across the desert until he dies just to cover up an accident, is stretching credibility somewhat. But this is overlooked easily enough when it can be diplomatically assumed that Maddock is insane. When Ben calls him crazy, Maddock fires back with, "I've often been called that by those I've defeated."

It's easy not to like a lawyer, and Maddock is doubly infuriating as he shows up every time Ben seems to gain an advantage. It becomes maddening the way Maddock always seems to have the upper hand. Ben's ingenuity, however, eventually bests his tormentor, and the scene where Ben buries himself in the sand to lie in wait for Maddock is a thing of beauty. The mouse beats the cat at his own game.

The ending is an exercise in frustration as Maddock, with his superior lying abilities, twists the story to make it appear that Ben was the villain. Naturally, in the real world this would never hold up under any sort of scrutiny, but up to this point, *Savages* is an absorbing thriller worth the time.

Sam Bottoms debuted in Peter Bogdanovich's *The Last Picture Show*, but his turn as the tripped-out surfer Lance in *Apocalypse Now* is perhaps his finest role. Bottoms didn't make any other telefright films in the 70s. Griffith, however, can be seen in the low-key terrorist story *Strangers in 7A*, where he plays a victim for a change. And it's always good to see the underappreciated James Best (*The Dukes of Hazzard*), who plays the sheriff here.

Writer Robb White, whose novel *Death Watch* was the basis of *Savages*, partnered with showman William Castle on some of his best known films: *Macabre, House on Haunted Hill, The Tingler, 13 Ghosts* and *Homicidal.*

CAST: Andy Griffith, Sam Bottoms, Noah Beery, Jr., James Best, Randy Boone, Jim Antonio, and Jim Chandler.

CREDITS: Director: Lee H. Katzin; Teleplay: William Wood, based on the novel *Death Watch* by Robb White; Music: Murray McLeod and The Orphanage; Production: Spelling-Goldberg Productions; Vehicles furnished by Ford Motor Co.; Running Time: 75 minutes; Air Date: 9/11/74; Network: ABC

Scream of the Wolf

Dan Curtis teams up again with writer Richard Matheson, this time Matheson adapting the story "The Hunter" by David Case. While definitely a horror story, *Scream of the Wolf* is an unusual genre entry in the Curtis canon for several reasons—one of which, if discussed, would spoil the first-time viewer's experience, so that particular subject will be avoided.

After the horrific murder of a salesman along the California coast, adventure writer and former hunter John Wetherby (Peter Graves) is brought in to help the local police. The killer appeared at first to be a powerful animal, but Wetherby's investigation yields some disturbing facts: The animal seems to change from being four-legged to two-legged, and it has the ability to alter its scent, foiling efforts to track it. When another man is killed, Wetherby appeals to his old friend and fellow hunter, Byron Douglas (Clint Walker), for help in finding the killer. Douglas refuses. The mysterious killings continue, and Wetherby's girlfriend, Sandy Miller (Jo Ann Pflug), narrowly escapes death when she's attacked in her home. Can Wetherby finally convince Douglas to help, or is Douglas refusing because he is somehow connected to the killings?

Curtis and Matheson have fashioned a sharp, fast-moving thriller with *Scream of the Wolf*. The many fog-shrouded night scenes lend atmosphere galore, and the killings are not drawn-out stalking affairs but swift, exciting set pieces. The use of the camera from the killer's point of view—fast and low to the ground—is properly suggestive of an animal, and adds considerably to the action.

The choices for the two leads were inspired. Graves' usual persona as the confident hero takes on some unexpected depth here. His Wetherby is undeniably talented and knowledgeable, but he also knows when he's in over his head, and shows a little more vulnerability than usual. Graves, who started out as a band musician and radio announcer, is the brother of *Gunsmoke* star James Arness, and had his first critical nod for his supporting performance in *Stalag 17*. But it is Graves' science fiction output in the 50s that has garnered a lasting affection amongst genre fans. He can be seen fighting aliens and monsters in *Red Planet Mars*, *Killers from Space*, *It Conquered the World* and *Beginning of the End*. His first big hit on television was the Saturday morning adventure series *Fury*, but it would, of course, be the role of Jim Phelps in *Mission Impossible* that would catapult him to major stardom on the small screen. After the long run of that series, Graves appeared in the telefrights *The President's Plane Is Missing*, *Where Have All the People Gone?*, *SST—Death Flight* and *Death Car on the Freeway*. Graves scored another hit with his participation in *Airplane!* and *Airplane II: The Sequel*, where he parodied his serious persona to great effect. He continues to work in dramas and comedies today, including reprising Jim Phelps for two seasons in 1988 when *Mission Impossible* returned.

Clint Walker gives one of his finest performances in *Scream of the Wolf* as the eccentric and frightening Douglas. Rarely called upon to be more than a stoic hero, Walker seems to be enjoying the greater dimension given his character this time around.

Beyond these obvious points lies a more controversial topic: the relationship between Wetherby and Douglas. Charges of homoerotic subtext seem fully justified upon closer inspection. Wetherby is the Corvette-driving writer who seems to have given up the sport of hunting—and hanging around with Douglas—to embark on a lukewarm love affair with Sandy. It is clear the relationship between Wetherby and Sandy is strained, and Wetherby seems more than eager to seek out his old friend Douglas when difficulties arise. Douglas is playing hard to get, however.

The character of Douglas is decidedly odd (notice how Sandy is visibly repulsed by Douglas, and how she suffers a retaliatory attack after an uneasy meeting with him). Douglas is a twisted philosopher ("Only by risking our lives can we truly appreciate them"), and a very snappy dresser, and his home is decorated in a manner more akin to a fey art lover than a macho hunter. Douglas clearly dominates the relationship with

Clint Walker and friend in *Scream of the Wolf* (1974).

Wetherby, and Wetherby is acquiescent in his presence (the scene where Douglas convinces Wetherby to arm wrestle says much). Wetherby has tried to escape his past with Douglas, but Douglas literally confesses to wanting him back, and to taking actions to "arouse" him.

Far from detracting or distracting, this unexpected dimension of the main characters adds to the experience. It is refreshing, not only for a Curtis film, but for the genre and the medium itself at the time, that this type of conflict can play a major—albeit subtle—part in the story. And it is impressive to see these two actors more than happy to reach for something different from their average television roles. It is on these grounds that the film rises above the level of simplistic entertainment value, and it is recommended because of it.

Jo Ann Pflug previously worked with Curtis on *The Night Strangler*, but her role here is merely as a barrier between the two men. Other than being the victim of an attack, she is only peripherally involved. It could be that the casting of Don Megowan as Douglas's suspect valet is an in-joke because Megowan was in a minor cult item from 1956, *The Werewolf*. Curtis's court composer, Robert Cobert, contributes a score that is funkier than usual, a style that seems at odds with the visual intentions.

CAST: Peter Graves, Clint Walker, Jo Ann Pflug, Philip Carey, Don Megowan, Brian Richards, Lee Paul, James Storm, Dean Smith, Randy Kirby, Vernon Weddle, William Baldwin, Orville Sherman, Bonnie Van Dyke, Grant Owens, Douglas Bungert, Tom Dever, Chuck Hayward, and Kenneth Stimson.

CREDITS: Director: Dan Curtis; Teleplay: Richard Matheson, based on a story by David Case; Music: Robert Cobert; Production: Metromedia Productions; Running Time: 74 minutes; Air Date: 1/16/74; Network: ABC

Scream Pretty Peggy

Art student Peggy Johns (Sian Barbara Allen) takes a light housekeeping job at the home of sculptor Jeffrey Elliot (Ted Bessell) and his mother (Bette Davis). Mom's a drinker, and after she falls and hurts herself, Peggy moves in to take care of her. Peggy notices a sculpture that Elliot did of his sister who, he says, left for Europe three months ago. Elliot won't allow Peggy to clean a room above the garage, which piques Peggy's curiosity. After George Thornton (Charles Drake) comes around looking for his missing daughter, Peggy suspects there is more than meets the eye at the Elliot house.

This transparent psycho movie is from the mind of Jimmy Sangster, better known for his thrillers for Hammer Films in days gone by. Here, Sangster worked with Arthur Hoffe (in his only credit) to create a tired chiller whose surprise ending will be a surprise to no one.

Adding to the script's problems is the casting. Sian Barbara Allen (*You'll Like My Mother*) is simply annoying as the over-eager student Peggy, who ingratiates herself into this dysfunctional family. It seems her every other word is "Jeffrey," and by the end of the film there is a moment of sadness when she does not meet her well-earned demise. Ted Bessell is adequate as the artist Jeffrey, but can never quite shake the look of bewilderment from his face that was his stock in trade as Donald in *That Girl*. Poor Bette Davis must have been wondering what she was doing in this by-the-numbers gothic mystery, and she phones in her performance as the guilt-ridden mother.

There is very little of merit here besides some truly hideous sculpture ("I'm trying to portray the ultimate in evil"), and the presence of Charles Drake in a supporting role as the encyclopedia-salesman father who comes looking for his daughter. Drake's most famous role for genre fans is as the irritable sheriff in *It Came from Outer Space*. Although he never became a bona fide star, Drake appeared as support in many interesting films, including *The Maltese Falcon*, *Winchester '73*, *Harvey*, *Tobor the Great*, *All That Heaven Allows*, *The Swimmer*, and the telefright *The Screaming Woman*, before passing in 1994.

Trivia buffs should note the debut of multiple Tony nominee Tovah Feldshuh as the doomed Agnes Thornton, and Claude Rains' daughter Jessica as the woman in the job office. Gordon Hessler had the helm of *Scream Pretty Peggy*, and his work creates little suspense and even less believability.

Composer Robert (Bob) Prince provided the scores for Francis Ford Coppola's *You're a Big Boy Now*, the killer worm movie *Squirm*, the killer bear movie *Claws*, and the telefrights *Gargoyles*, *The Strange and Deadly Occurrence*, *Where Have All the People Gone?*, *The Dead Don't Die* and *Snowbeast*.

CAST: Ted Bessell, Sian Barbara Allen, Bette Davis, Charles Drake, Allan Arbus, Jessica

Bette Davis and Ted Bessell harbor a terrible secret in *Scream Pretty Peggy* **(1973).**

Rains, Christiane Schmidtmer, Johnnie Collins III, and Tovah Feldshuh.
CREDITS: Director: Gordon Hessler; Teleplay: Jimmy Sangster and Arthur Hoffe; Music: Bob Prince; Production: Universal TV; Running Time: 74 minutes; Air Date: 11/24/73; Network: ABC

The Screaming Woman

Wealthy Laura Wynant (Olivia de Havilland) is on the blunted edge of senility, and has recently returned home from a stint in a sanitarium. Out for a ride on her property, Laura stumbles across a dog digging in the dirt. When she investigates, she hears moans from beneath the earth, and concludes that a woman has been buried alive. When Laura alerts her son Howard (Charles Knox Robinson), they return to the spot but find nothing. Howard, whose bitchy, philandering wife Caroline (Laraine Stephens) wants to have Laura re-committed so they can control the estate, chalks the episode up to his mother's deteriorating mental faculties. Laura, however, is determined to prove that she is not senile, and sets out to somehow save the woman.

A fright film for the older set, *The Screaming Woman* is the only telefright of the decade based on a short story by the venerable science-fiction writer Ray Bradbury. The plot is simple, the conclusion foregone, and the result is adequate but far more frustrating than exciting or compelling. Getting from point A to point B puts the aging Laura through several humiliating episodes before her final vindication.

The cast is made up of famous movie stars of days gone by (de Havilland, Joseph Cotten as her lawyer, and Walter Pidgeon as her doctor), journeymen actors (Ed Nelson as the culprit, and Charles Drake as a neighbor), and relative newcomers (Robinson, making his debut, and Stephens).

Nelson, as Carl Nesbitt, is the standout as the fumbling would-be murderer who never really had a chance of getting away with the crime. Carl is having an affair, and when he tells the wife about it, they argue and he strikes her. Thinking her dead, he buries her on the Wynant property, but the dog immediately gives him away. One good scene is when Laura, searching for neighbors to help her dig, knocks on Nesbitt's door. The irony of Laura asking help from the criminal is not lost, and the two actors play it out in delicious fashion.

To be fair, there is one hauntingly frightful image in the film. It is of the wife, Helen Nesbitt (Jackie Russell), buried but still able to breathe. The camera delves under the ground and her face is visible, nearly covered in dirt, as she desperately tries to make enough noise to be heard. Interestingly, the characters at one point mention a real-life crime that had recently occurred in Florida, where a woman was buried alive by kidnappers. The event inspired a telefilm called *The Longest Night* which, curiously enough, was made by this film's director, Jack Smight, and would air a few months later on the same network.

This was de Havilland's only telefright film of the decade. Cotten would only make one more (*The Devil's Daughter*), as would Pidgeon (*Murder on Flight 502*) and Robinson (*Fer De Lance*). The music was by the famous John Williams (*Star Wars*), and the costume design was by none other than Edith Head. Lastly, those with a penchant for 1970s architecture will enjoy Laura's trek through the brand new housing development in her search for help.

Olivia de Havilland finds a woman buried alive in *The Screaming Woman* (1972).

CAST: Olivia de Havilland, Ed Nelson, Laraine Stephens, Joseph Cotten, Walter Pidgeon, Charles Knox Robinson, Alexandra Hay, Lonny Chapman, Charles Drake, Russell Wiggins, Gene Andrusco, Russell Thorson, Kay Stewart, Joyce Cunning, John Alderman, Ray Montgomery, Jan Arvan, Dee Carroll, Jackie Russell, Glen Vernon, and Shannon Terhune.

CREDITS: Director: Jack Smight; Teleplay: Merwin Gerard, based on the short story by Ray Bradbury; Music: John Williams; Production: Universal TV; Running Time: 73 minutes; Air Date: 1/29/72; Network: ABC

She Cried Murder

Model Sarah Cornell (Lynda Day George) sees a woman pushed in front of a subway car and gets a good look at the perpetrator. When she finally decides to talk to the police, she recognizes one of them, Joe Brody (Telly Savalas), as the man who committed the murder. Brody kidnaps Sarah's son to keep her quiet, but Sarah outwits Brody, resulting in his injury. Meanwhile, Brody's partner, Walter Stepanic (Mike Farrell), discovers that Brody was being blackmailed by the woman he killed. From here on in, it is a three-way chase between Brody, Sarah and Stepanic.

This weak thriller's only surprise is that it took two people to write the story. The actions of the main players, and the circumstances required to further the plot, are equally implausible. The pacing of these elements is so poor that the level of suspense is nonexistent, and the finale is ridiculously contrived.

Top-billed Telly Savalas was equally adept at playing heroes and villains, but his charisma is stifled here as the crooked cop, Brody. He practically phones in his performance, no doubt fully realizing the hopeless situation. The vacuous Lynda Day George looks frightened a lot as Sarah, but could engender no more sympathy than a mannequin. Mike Farrell plays good cop Stepanic at such a low key that he hardly seems interested in catching his long-time partner.

Savalas would soon take on his most famous role as the cop Kojak, and Farrell would be right behind him joining the cast of *M*A*S*H*. Neither would make another telefright film in the 70s.

Lynda Day George on the other hand was somewhat of a mainstay in the genre, showing up in *Panic on the 5:22*, *Mayday at 40,000 Feet*, *It Happened at Lakewood Manor* and *Cruise Into Terror*, but making very little of an impression in any of them. She made her debut in the Tony Curtis picture *The Outsider* in 1961, and met her future husband, Christopher George, when she worked on *The Gentle Rain*. The couple decided to make it official after they were both cast in *Chisum* in 1970. The pair worked together many times on television and in films (including *Day of the Animals*, *Mortuary*, and *Pieces*) before his death in 1983. She was nominated for an Emmy when she was part of the ensemble cast of *Mission Impossible*, and appeared as herself in a documentary about East Indian religion called *Aliens from Spaceship Earth*. She made another horror film, *Beyond Evil*, before retiring at the end of the 80s.

She Cried Murder was filmed in Toronto and directed by Herschel Daugherty, who made another weak woman-in-peril picture, called *The Victim*, with Elizabeth Montgomery. Neither of these films is better than mediocre, but the former makes the latter seem like quite an accomplishment.

Lynda Day George flees a crooked cop in *She Cried Murder* (1973).

CAST: Telly Savalas, Lynda Day George, Mike Farrell, Kate Reid, Len Birman, Jeff Toner, Murray Westgate, Robert Goodier, Richard Alden, Aileen Seaton, B. Hope Garber, and Stu Gillard.

CREDITS: Director: Herschel Daugherty; Teleplay: Merwin Gerard, based on a story by A. Roy Moore and Peter Jobin; Music: John Cacavas; Production: Universal TV; Running Time: 74 minutes; Air Date: 9/25/73; Network: CBS

She Waits

This forgotten gem is like comfort food to the telefright film fanatic. All the elements are present: a spooky old house, a ghostly presence, dire and unheeded warnings and a dark mystery revealed in the final moments. A fine cast and a first-rate visual and aural presentation ice the cake.

Mark Wilson (David McCallum) ignores his uneasy feelings and brings his new wife Laura (Patty Duke) home to meet his sick mother, Sarah (Dorothy McGuire). Mark's first wife, Elaine, died two years ago in the house under mysterious circumstances—though her death was ruled a suicide. Sarah implores Mark and Laura to leave the house immediately, but Mark will hear none of it. Laura begins to feel the presence of Elaine's ghost and manifests the signs of a nervous breakdown. Sarah confesses to Laura that she believes Mark killed Elaine, but there is more to the mystery, and Laura is poised to discover the terrible truth.

The foremost presence in *She Waits* is the haunting, melancholy waltz that serves as Elaine's theme. The superior score is by Morton Stevens, the prolific composer best known for writing the *Hawaii Five-O* theme. Stevens was the music supervisor for CBS in the 1960s, and his scores for 70s telefright films include *Strangers in 7A, Horror at 37,000 Feet, The Disappearance of Flight 412* and *The Strange Possession of Mrs. Oliver.*

Nearly all the action in *She Waits* takes place inside the rambling, 14-room mansion. There is almost no overhead lighting, and the moody photography makes for a palpable atmosphere of dread. Director Delbert Mann won an Oscar for *Marty* back in 1956, and his sure touch with the familiar elements keeps things moving towards the revelatory conclusion. Mann, unfortunately, didn't lend his talents to any other telefright films in the 70s.

The same can be said for the lovely Dorothy McGuire, who was also seen in another gothic chiller, the 1946 classic, *The Spiral Staircase*. McGuire's Sarah seems a bit

David McCallum deals with a family ghost in *She Waits* (1972).

overwrought, but once it is revealed that for two years she has harbored the perception that her son was a murderer, her character takes on a most sympathetic tone. One of her best lines in this production comes as she's trying to convince Laura to leave: "As you move closer to death, the dead move closer to you."

The dependable Lew Ayres lends support (and tranquilizers) as the family doctor. He barely has a chance to leave the house with all the excitement going on. The Wilson housekeeper, Mrs. M, is played by another recognizable veteran of film and television, Beulah Bondi. Hers is a calming, rational presence typified by her remarks about LA: "What self-respecting ghost would want to live in a place like this?" David McCallum does a fine turn here as the husband Mark, only half-heartedly trying to avoid the inescapable truth.

The star of the show, Patty Duke, is fine as the severely shaken Laura. She has the run of emotions here as the conduit for the vengeful ghost Elaine to reach back to the land of the living, but Duke's well-known histrionics are kept in check. Fans of the actress can find her in several telefright films of the era, including a particularly rich part in *Curse of the Black Widow*.

The validity of Laura's ghostly possession by Elaine is up to interpretation. It could truly be the dead wife speaking through her, or merely Laura's suggestible personality playing tricks. One hint could be that when Laura hears Elaine's voice, it happens to be Duke's own. Another can be found in the frenzied finale, which turns on the idea that the death of a drunken person leaves a confused ghost. One could argue that an otherworldly being would not be susceptible to the effects of alcohol. Either way, *She Waits* is an entertaining slice of hokum that will be appreciated by the faithful.

CAST: Patty Duke, David McCallum, Lew Ayres, Dorothy McGuire, Beulah Bondi, James Callahan, and Nelson Olmstead.

CREDITS: Director: Delbert Mann; Teleplay: Art Wallace; Music: Morton Stevens; Production: Metromedia Productions; Running Time: 74 minutes; Air Date: 1/28/72; Network: CBS

She's Dressed to Kill

AKA Someone's Killing the World's Greatest Models

Toward the end of the telefright film's golden age, production values such as lighting and photography improved, while script and star quality declined considerably. Witness *She's Dressed to Kill*, a dreary body count movie set in the world of high fashion, a film as empty-headed as the models on display.

Has-been, alcoholic high-fashion designer Regine Danton (Eleanor Parker) is determined to make a comeback, and schedules a private showing of her latest designs. Before the big day, one of Regine's favorite models from Irene Barton's (Jessica Walter) modeling agency is killed by poisoned lipstick, and replaced by newcomer Alix Goldman (Connie Sellecca). During the fashion show at Regine's isolated mansion—accessible only by cable car—another model is killed by hairspray that had been replaced by nerve gas. When a storm rises and the power goes out, the entire company is stranded, and the deaths continue at an alarming rate.

Amongst those clamoring for work are Academy Award–nominated actress Eleanor Parker, who hams it up as the drunken Regine, and the well-respected Clive Revill, as the flaming columnist, Victor De Salle. Shakespearean actor Revill was born in New Zealand, and has been twice-nominated for Broadway's Tony Award for his work in *Irma La Douce* and as Fagin in *Oliver!* Although he has largely played foppish, pompous characters, his film roles have run the gamut. He was in *The Headless Ghost*, several Eurospy entries (*Modesty Blaise*, *The Double Man*, *Italian Secret Service*, *Nobody Runs Forever*), the Raquel Welch vehicle *Fathom*, *The Assassination Bureau*, *The Private Life of Sherlock Holmes*, *The Legend of Hell House*, and *Zorro, the Gay Blade*, and was the voice of Alfred in several of the animated *Batman* episodes.

Jessica Walter, as modeling agency head Irene, is a standout here, but she's rewarded for her superior work by being killed off in one of those scenes where the victim says, "Oh, it's you," and lets their guard down. Top-billed John Rubinstein is the shallow photographer Alan Lenz, who finds true love with a plain Jane, Laura Gooch (Gretchen Corbett). Connie Sellecca shows off her judo skills as the novice model Alix, and gets romantic with the sheriff (Jim McMullen) who comes to the rescue.

Regine's fall from grace has resulted in her being surrounded by ex-cons and other questionable characters, such as thug Jonathan Banks and Peter Horton, who would soon make a ripple in shows such as *St. Elsewhere* and *thirtysomething*. Horton plays Tony Smith, who is the actual creator of Regine's comeback designs—none of which sell. He has a screaming match with

Regine in a scene that may drive the faint-hearted from the room.

No less than seven bodies pile up during the course of the film. As if that wasn't enough, the filmmakers toss in references to homosexuality (both male and female) and prostitution to spice things up. Nasty remarks ("Ugly women should be destroyed at puberty"), a less-than-stellar fashion show (gowns furnished by Travilla), a killer who shows up in transparent disguise, and a few moments of stunt work on the cable car do little to redeem this lifeless, predictable film by Gus Trikonis.

Blade Runner fans will note the presence of Joanna Cassidy as one of the victim models, and some may recognize the Palm Springs Aerial Tramway that doubles as Regine's private cable car.

CAST: John Rubinstein, Jessica Walter, Connie Sellecca, Jim McMullan, Clive Revill, Gretchen Corbett, Barbara Cason, Cathee Shirriff, Corinne Calvet, Eleanor Parker, Peter Horton, Jonathan Banks, Marianne McAndrew, Louise Caire Clark, Seamon Glass, Walter Mathews, Eugene Peterson, Russ Marin, Joanna Cassidy, Noah Keen, Grayce Spence, Lister Shaw, Casey Brown, Gail Joy, Marlena Amey, and Cassandra Gaviola.

CREDITS: Director: Gus Trikonis; Teleplay: George Lefferts; Music: George Romanis; Production: Barry Weitz Productions; Running Time: 98 minutes; Air Date: 12/10/79; Network: NBC

Short Walk to Daylight

AKA **The Night the Earth Shook**

An early morning earthquake traps eight people in a New York subway. Policeman Tom Phelan (James Brolin) tries to keep the ragtag group together as they fight their way through the collapsed tunnels to freedom.

This focused, realistic disaster movie eschews the human drama (although each person has their moment to vent) in favor of detailing the defeats and triumphs of the group as they make their way above ground. Director Barry Shear (*Wild in the Streets*, *Across 110th Street*) keeps the film moving, just barely allowing the audience time to breathe. Racial tensions are the primary source of conflict between the characters, but the common ground of survival is the great equalizer here.

James Brolin plays Phelan, complete with New York accent. Brolin won an Emmy for his support as Dr. Steven Kiley in the long-running *Marcus Welby, M.D.* series, and has been nominated four times since, including one for the 2003 telefilm *The Reagans*, wherein he played Ronald. His film credits include the genre entries *Westworld*, *The Car*, *The Amityville Horror* and *Night of the Juggler*. He spoofed his leading man persona, as himself, in Tim Burton's *Pee-wee's Big Adventure*. His series work includes stints in *Hotel*, *Pensacola: Wings of Gold* and *West Wing*, and he still shows up in high-profile films today, such as Steven Soderbergh's *Traffic* and Steven Spielberg's *Catch Me If You Can*. Brolin has been known as "Mr. Streisand" since his marriage to Barbra in 1998.

Refreshingly, Tom Phelan doesn't know all the answers, appealing, at one point, to everyone to cooperate because he's trying his best. Phelan relies on conductor Ed Mullins (James McEachin) to help make the decisions of which direction the group should head. Turned back by an impassable collapse at the next station, the two de facto leaders agree to follow the tunnel under the river to reach Brooklyn. With the river pouring into a breach in the tunnel, the film's most suspenseful scenes occur as the group crosses the raging water.

Second-billed Don Mitchell, who spent a few years pushing Raymond Burr's wheelchair around as Mark Sanger in the *Ironside* series, plays Alvin, who has a problem with white cop Phelan. Joanne, from Iowa (Brooke Bundy, *A Nightmare on Elm Street 3 & 4*), and Sylvia (Suzanne Charny) are two young ladies who decided to take the subway after seeing a play, in order to save money. Abbey Lincoln plays waitress Dorella, who just wants to get home to her kids. Lazaro

Perez plays junkie musician Jax, and Laurette Spang, in her film debut, plays his girlfriend Sandy. Jax goes crazy without his fix, and commits suicide by grabbing the electrified third rail.

The idea of an earthquake in New York may be stretching credibility (even the characters remark on the unusual event); in fact, there is an alternate version of the film that adds a subplot about the bombs of a radical group triggering the disaster. The special effects are not the show here and consist mainly of debris-laden tunnels, rushing water and an explosion, and all are seen only from the perspective of the survivors.

The city itself is never shown in the film. When the group finally sees daylight, the movie simply ends without a peek topside. Efficient, self-contained, with believable characters and credible action, *Short Walk to Daylight* is a fine example of the disaster genre.

CAST: James Brolin, Don Mitchell, James McEachin, Abbey Lincoln, Brooke Bundy, Lazaro Perez, Suzanne Charny, Laurette Spang, and Franklin Cover.

CREDITS: Director: Barry Shear; Teleplay: Philip H. Reisman, Jr. and Gerald Di Pego, story by Edward J. Montagne; Music: Patrick Williams; Production: Universal TV; Running Time: 68 minutes; Air Date: 10/24/72; Network: ABC

Ski Lift to Death

AKA Snowblind

Friday morning. Lee Larson (Deborah Raffin) comes back home to Silver City, Colorado, after winning the World Freestyle Cup skiing competition in Vermont. She is accompanied by Marv Gillman (Clu Gulager), an agent who wants her to sign a lucrative endorsement contract. But longtime boyfriend, and former ski champion, Dick Elston (Charles Frank) wants Larson to settle down with him instead. Meanwhile, mobster-front businessman Ben Forbes (Howard Duff) is taking a ski holiday while deciding whether to testify in front of a grand jury, and an assassin is there to make sure he doesn't. When a vicious wind comes up, several of these players become stranded in two ski lifts that break down high above the slopes.

A disaster film only by a stretch of the imagination, this ski-centered drama is typical of the disposable fare offered by the networks as the golden age of the television movie wound down. It takes an hour for the so-called disaster to strike, and the time until then is filled with human drama, a freestyle ski competition and a disco dancing contest. More a soap opera on skis, the ski lift peril of *Ski Lift to Death* seems an afterthought designed to allow the ski patrol to show off by rescuing the trapped celebrities.

Deborah Raffin (*God Told Me To*) and Charles Frank (*All My Children*) make attractive leads, but the conflict revolving around capitalizing on one's talent is minor indeed. The agent Gillman isn't much of a bogeyman, and unlike real life, compromises are made to appease everyone. Howard Duff is fine as the corrupt businessman Forbes, but he's not asked to do much accept discuss his decision with his lover Vicki Gordon (Gail Strickland, *Dark Shadows*), who has a conflict of her own. The assassin, Clevenger (Pierre Jalbert), who attends the local church, proves to be decidedly inept at his job.

Duff's hard-boiled voice is what first brought the actor fame. He was born in Bremerton, Washington, and struck gold on the radio as detective Sam Spade. After WWII, Duff went into the movies, debuting in the film noir *Brute Force*. What followed were primarily supporting parts (*While the City Sleeps*) or leads in B pictures (*Spaceways*), and many appearances in television, most memorably in *Felony Squad* in the late 1960s. Later, he had recurring roles in the nighttime soaps *Flamingo Road* and *Knots Landing*. Duff married Ida Lupino in 1951, and they subsequently appeared together in several films and television shows, including their own series *Mr. Adams and Eve*.

The smaller side stories in *Ski Lift to*

Death are of even less interest. Local reporter Andrea Mason is played by Veronica Hamel, who would make her mark in the series *Hill Street Blues*. She embarks on an affair with network executive Ron Corley, played by stalwart Don Galloway, fondly remembered as Sgt. Ed Brown on the *Ironside* series.

Hot dog skier Mike Sloan (a pre–*Miami Vice* Don Johnson) falls for underage waitress Wendy Bryant (Lisa Reeves) after she knocks 'em dead at the big T-shirt dance contest, a senseless and pandering event where Mike was a judge.

This three-day ski holiday (subtitles inform the viewer of the weekend day on which the action takes place) was filmed at Banff National Park in Alberta, Canada. Director William Wiard didn't make any other telefright films in the 70s, but he would go on to make the deliciously absurd *This House Possessed* in 1981. Composer Barry De Vorzon was nominated for an Oscar a few years earlier for the song "Cotton's Dream" in *Bless the Beasts and the Children*. The song is better remembered as "Nadia's Theme," after Olympic gymnast Nadia Comaneci adopted it for her routines, and as the theme for the daytime drama *The Young and the Restless*.

CAST: Deborah Raffin, Charles Frank, Don Galloway, Gail Strickland, Don Johnson, Veronica Hamel, Howard Duff, Clu Gulager, Lisa Reeves, Pierre Jalbert, Suzy Chaffee, Walter Marsh, Jim Roberts, Graham McPherson, Donald Mackay, Bruce Macleod, Steve Orchin, Murray Ord, Darlene Bradley, Trevor Hayden, Glenn Beck, Tony White, Jim Love, Jack Olsen, Leni Pear, Kathy Wetherell, Jackie Verner, Kendall Hunter, Rick Wood, Jay Lerew, Byron Tarchuck, Rick Bowie, Darryl Bowie, Ed Lincoln, and Joan Teorey Lincoln.

CREDITS: Director: William Wiard; Teleplay: Laurence Heath; Music: Barry De Vorzon; Production: The Jozak Company; Running Time: 94 minutes; Air Date: 3/3/78; Network: CBS

Skyway to Death

Several people become stranded thousands of feet above the desert in a Palm Springs Aerial Tramway car because disgruntled ex-employee Walter Benson (Billy Green Bush) sabotaged the power room at the base. With the Santa Ana winds picking up, an attempted helicopter rescue not only fails, but damages the car's braking system in the process. It's up to car operator Barney Taylor (Bobby Sherman) and engineer passenger Bob Parsons (Joseph Campanella) to manually apply the brake before the car crashes into the building below.

The Palm Springs Aerial Tramway cars have been in many films, including the telefrights *Hanging by a Thread* and *She's Dressed to Kill*. Here most of the action takes place on the stranded car as the passengers bond before the heroic efforts of Taylor and Parsons save them. Gordon Hessler directs with efficiency, and thanks to a decent cast, the results are not as painful as they could have been.

Our cast of unfortunates this time include Stefanie Powers as Nancy Sorenson, who, with her persistent lover Parsons, brought her "aunt" Louise (Ruth McDevitt) out of the old folks home for a day trip. Parsons never lets up from his proposals of marriage to divorcee Sorenson, remarking, "What I hear is a woman who's been burned once and is afraid to go back to the stove again." Journeyman Campanella was a familiar face on television since the mid-50s. He made the telefright rounds in the 70s with work in *Murder Once Removed*, *You'll Never See Me Again*, *The President's Plane Is Missing* and *Terror on the 40th Floor*.

Also stuck in the car are Martin Leonard (Ross Martin) and his wife Ann (Nancy Malone, *Fright*). Leonard has been cheating on her for years but, as is the custom in these films, they air their dirty laundry in public and work it out. Severn Darden, a leading force in the Second City comedy troupe, plays Steve Kramer, a pickpocket who steals Leonard's wallet at the summit. After the Leonards' spat, Kramer feels compelled to return the wallet in one of the few amusing scenes.

Cult favorite John Astin plays Andrew Tustin, an acrophobic who took the tram as part of an attempt to conquer his fear of heights. Although *The Addams Family* only ran for a couple of years, Astin's portrayal of Gomez Addams has been indelibly etched on the pop culture. Astin was first noticed for a small role in *West Side Story*, but he had already played many bits in television, and landed his first series, *I'm Dickens, He's Fenster* in 1962. Since *Addams Family* run ended in 1966, Astin has been in demand, doing guest spots on series (including as the Riddler on *Batman*), telefilms (the hilarious *Evil Roy Slade*) and movies (*Candy*, *Freaky Friday*, the *Killer Tomato* films). He has also made a second career of directing, primarily for television, including several *Night Gallery* episodes. Astin was nominated for an Oscar for his 1968 short subject, *Prelude*. His decade-long marriage to Patty Duke produced two sons, Sean and Mackenzie, both actors.

Lastly is Bobby Sherman as the car operator Taylor. Pop star Sherman got his first big break in television as the stuttering Jeremy Bolt in *Here Come the Brides*, and he continued in lightweight roles into the 70s and 80s. Taylor's cohorts on the ground include Tige Andrews (*The Mod Squad*) as boss Sam Nichols and character actor David Sheiner. Cult actor Billy Green Bush, as Benson, the fellow who started this whole mess, had one of his early roles in *Five Easy Pieces*, and played cops and sheriffs in films as far-reaching as *Electra Glide in Blue*, *Tom Horn* and *Jason Goes to Hell*.

Some impressive stuntwork, and lines such as "Put the actuator into the receptacle," keep this routine thriller from falling completely to earth. Fans planning a pilgrimage should note that the Tramway is closed for two weeks every October for maintenance.

Composer Lee Holdridge, who was born in Haiti, was just beginning a career that has so far seen him nominated for ten Emmys, winning two for his work on the *Beauty and the Beast* series in the 80s. His name is also on *Jonathan Livingston Seagull*, *American Pop*, cult favorite *The Beastmaster*, *Mr. Mom* and *Splash*.

CAST: Ross Martin, Stefanie Powers, Bobby Sherman, Tige Andrews, Nancy Malone, David Sheiner, John Astin, Joseph Campanella, Ruth McDevitt, Severn Darden, Billy Green Bush, and Lissa Morrow.

CREDITS: Director: Gordon Hessler; Teleplay: David Spector; Music: Lee Holdridge; Production: Universal TV; Running Time: 74 minutes; Air Date: 1/19/74; Network: ABC

Smash-up on Interstate 5

"39 vehicles will be involved, 62 people will be injured, 14 will die."

The Fourth of July weekend sets the stage for a massive accident on a Southern California freeway. The human drama of those involved is explored before the event, putting faces on the statistics.

The film begins with the pile-up, and then backs up 43 hours to introduce many of those who will be unknowing participants. Subtitles throughout, such as "Saturday Morning ... 23 Hours Before Smash-Up," mark the countdown before the production wrecks a lot of cars.

Highway patrolman Sam Marcum (Robert Conrad) introduces the film with the quote above. Sam is a macho kind of guy who is sweet on nurse Laureen (Donna Mills), but she resists his advances because of the danger inherent in his work. Her sister, Barbara (Sian Barbara Allen), is pregnant with the baby of another highway patrolman, Officer Hutton (an early role for Tommy Lee Jones).

Hutton has a minor run-in with a group of bikers whose members include none other than Sue Lyon (*Lolita*). Later, these bikers threaten divorcee Erica (Vera Miles) when she runs out of gas, and even rip open her shirt in a bold moment for network television. Fortunately, Erica is saved by free-spirited trucker Dale (David Groh). Erica and Dale hit it off so well they sleep together that night. Groh was Valerie Harper's boyfriend in the *Rhoda* series.

The previous evening Erica visited a disco in one of the film's more amusing sequences. She comes under the scrutiny of the painfully hip Danny (Herb Edelman), who says things such as "You've got great flesh," and smokes dope on the dance floor. Erica had gone there to meet her friend Trudy, who is played by Terry Moore. Moore was in *Mighty Joe Young*, and got an Oscar nomination for *Come Back, Little Sheba*. Around the time of filming, Moore was claiming that she was once the secret wife of Howard Hughes.

Officer Hutton also has a confrontation with car thief Lee Bassett (Scott Jacoby). Bassett gets shanghaied for a ride by Pete (George O'Hanlon) and Penny (Bonnie Ebsen), who had just robbed a grocery store.

Bonnie Ebsen happens to be Buddy Ebsen's daughter. Buddy plays Al Pearson, who is married to June (Harriet Nelson of *Ozzie and Harriet* fame). June has heart trouble and the two are struggling with her terminal condition. At one point, June attempts suicide by walking into the ocean, but Al saves her. Nelson's son David is in the film too, playing one of the highway patrolmen.

Most of these people will collide in the smash-up. Some will live through the experience and some will not. The accident itself was filmed on Interstate 210 at La Crescenta, California, and while it is not that spectacular, it does feature many cool cars. Another good car movie from the era is Hal Needham's *Death Car on the Freeway*.

The music is by prolific composer Bill Conti, whose 150 credits reach back only to 1969. Writer Elleston Trevor (actually Trevor Dudley Smith), whose novel *Expressway* inspired the film, wrote *The Quiller Memorandum*, which was filmed under that name in 1966 with George Segal and generated the series *Quiller* in 1975.

CAST: Robert Conrad, Sian Barbara Allen, Buddy Ebsen, Herb Edelman, David Groh, Scott Jacoby, Joe Kapp, Sue Lyon, Vera Miles, Donna Mills, Harriet Nelson, George O'Hanlon, Jr., Terry Moore, Bonnie Ebsen, Tommy Lee Jones, David Nelson, Joel Parks, Barry Hamilton, Don Carrara, Cindy Daly, Lisa Daniels, John Dewey-Carter, and Roger Hampton.

CREDITS: Director: John Llewellyn Moxey; Teleplay: Eugene Price and Robert Presnell, Jr., based on the novel *Expressway* by Elleston Trevor; Music: Bill Conti; Production: Filmways Pictures; Running Time: 91 minutes; Air Date: 12/3/76; Network: ABC

Snatched

The wives of three wealthy businessmen are kidnapped and held in a remote lighthouse for a $3 million ransom. The men have 36 hours to come up with the money, and, against instructions, call in the police. There are two complicating factors, however: one wife is a diabetic without her insulin, and one husband refuses to pay.

Snatched is an excellent, twisty thriller from Sutton Roley. The visual flourishes the director used in his other telefright films, *Sweet, Sweet Rachel* and *Satan's Triangle*, are less prevalent here, but visual interest is maintained with inventive camerawork. The lighthouse location, the strangely rococo hotel room where the husbands wait, and the finale, filmed in an industrial surrounding, are all shot with a compelling eye. The tension builds nicely throughout to the final scenes that feature a hectic footrace from phone booth to phone booth for the drop instructions, *a la Dirty Harry*.

The cast is also first-rate and somewhat unusual. The three wives, Kim Sutter, Barbara Maxvill and Robin Wood, are played by Sheree North, Barbara Parkins and Tisha Sterling, respectively. Parkins came into prominence with her role in *Peyton Place*. She stayed with the series for its entire run, and was nominated for an Emmy in the process. She carried her fame into film, landing a role in the iconic *Valley of the Dolls*, and has been working sporadically in both media since. Her films include Rene Clement's *The Deadly Trap* and the horror anthology *Asylum*. Parkins has appeared in *Playboy* several times, and she can be seen fully clothed in the telefright *A Taste of Evil*.

The husbands are Bill Sutter (Leslie Nielsen), Paul Maxvill (John Saxon) and Duncan Wood (Howard Duff). Nielsen and

(Left to right) Howard Duff, Robert Reed, and John Saxon are involved in a kidnapping scheme in *Snatched* (1973).

Duff are, of course, familiar to telefright fans, but John Saxon makes a rare appearance here. Saxon was a male model before he made his screen debut in the mid–1950s. He was popular with the teen set for a while and worked in westerns as well. On television, he scored in *The Bold Ones: The New Doctors* in the late 60s, and is remembered for the double shot of science fiction telefilms that failed to gain a series: *Planet Earth* and *Strange New World*. For fans of genre movies though, "The Sax" is revered for his many roles in horror, action and exploitation films. From Mario Bava's *The Girl Who Knew Too Much*, *Blood Beast from Outer Space* and *Queen of Blood* in the 60s, to *Enter the Dragon* with Bruce Lee, *Black Christmas*, *Blazing Magnums*, *Violent Protection* with Maurizio Merli, and the low-rent *The Bees* in the 70s, to *Cannibal Apocalypse*, Dario Argento's *Tenebre* and *A Nightmare on Elm Street* in the 80s, Saxon has been, and continues to be, there for his fans.

The bad guys in *Snatched* are an interesting trio as well. Ringleader Boone is played by the fine character actor Anthony Zerbe, in his only telefright film. Zerbe has been playing mostly villains in film and television since the mid–60s. His film roles include *Cool Hand Luke*, *The Omega Man*, *The Parallax View*, the telefilm *KISS Meets the Phantom of the Park*, *The Dead Zone*, *Licence to Kill*, two of the *Matrix* movies, and many more. Interestingly, he won his Emmy for playing a good guy, Lt. K.C. Trench, in the David Janssen series *Harry O*.

Boone's cohorts are Whit (Richard Davalos) and Cheech (Frank McRae). McRae was a former football player turned to acting, and Davalos—trivia fans will note—has the distinction of being on the cover of alternative rock band The Smiths' album entitled "Strangeways, Here We Come."

As mentioned, the husbands call in the cops, one of whom, Detective Frank McCloy (Robert Reed), is a personal friend of the men. His steadiness is much needed when one of the husbands refuses to pay the ransom because his wife cheats on him constantly. As one can imagine, this causes quite a bit of consternation until he changes his mind. But late in the game, a final card is played when one of the wives reveals that she was in on the kidnapping plot from the beginning; she and her lover had planned the entire operation.

When the final curtain falls, there is nothing left but deep irony or tragedy for all three couples. This film, from one of the more interesting directors in the genre, comes recommended.

CAST: (ao) Howard Duff, Leslie Nielsen, Sheree North, Barbara Parkins, Robert Reed, John Saxon, Tisha Sterling, and Anthony Zerbe. Also Richard Davalos, Frank McRae, Bart LaRue, Howard Platt, and John Gilgreen.

CREDITS: Director: Sutton Roley; Teleplay: Rick Husky, from a story by Sandra Bruzzese; Music: Randy Edelman; Production: ABC Circle Films; Running Time: 75 minutes; Air Date: 1/31/73; Network: ABC

Snowbeast

The Winter Carnival at Rill Lodge in Colorado is about to get underway when medal-winning skier Gar Seberg (Bo Svenson) and his wife Ellen (Yvette Mimieux) arrive. Seberg is looking for work, and his old friend Tony Rill (Robert Logan), whose family owns and runs the lodge, hires him. When a skier disappears and then a member of the ski patrol is killed, it looks as if a Bigfoot-type monster is on the rampage. Rill and the Sebergs join forces with Sheriff Paraday (Clint Walker) to track and kill the beast.

Snowbeast is another ski-centered telefright (see *Ski Lift to Death*), this time written by the esteemed Joseph Stefano. The least of Stefano's telefright output of the 1970s, it is a dull and plodding non-thriller. Director Herb Wallerstein has no affinity for the genre; this was the only horror film of his career.

Lead Svenson seems completely uninvolved with what little action is going on around him, as does Walker as the sheriff. Logan is even worse. If casting director Sam Christiansen was responsible for putting Svenson, Walker and Logan in the same film, it is fitting that *Snowbeast* was his one and only credit.

Even Mimieux doesn't offer much respite from the doldrums of the production. Ellen and Tony were apparently a hot item years ago, but this old flame angle is extinguished without igniting any fire. The character of Ellen professes equality, and carries a gun when the four go out on the monster hunt, but she is also there to make dinner for the boys.

Filmed at Crested Butte Ski Resort in Colorado, *Snowbeast* features long sequences of people on skis or snowmobiles, a guaranteed way of riveting the viewer to the television set. One scene of local color is the preparations for crowning the "Snow Queen" in the gymnasium. This is where the monster breaks a window in another unprovoked attack, and causes a panic amongst the youngsters inside. During all the running around on the basketball floor, it appears as if Sylvia Sydney, who plays the owner of the lodge, sustained a real injury when a boy knocked the 67-year-old actress down.

The filmmakers try to make a Bigfoot connection to their "snowbeast" by mentioning the then-trendy monster, but the parallels are just empty comparisons to fill the time. The beast is played by Michael J. London in a hairy suit, glimpses of which are fleeting at best, even in the ridiculous death-by-ski-pole finale.

CAST: Bo Svenson, Yvette Mimieux, Robert Logan, Clint Walker, Sylvia Sidney, (ao) Thomas W. Babson, Jacquie Botts, Kathy Christopher, Jamie Jamison, Richard Jamison, Liz Jury, Ric Jury, Rob McClung, Anne McEncroe, Victor Raider-Wexler, Prentiss Rowe, and Michael J. London.

CREDITS: Director: Herb Wallerstein; Teleplay: Joseph Stefano; Music: Robert Prince; Production: Douglas Cramer Productions; Running Time: 86 minutes; Air Date: 4/28/77; Network: NBC

Sole Survivor

Note: A legitimate discussion of *Sole Survivor* requires that the plot, in its entirety, be revealed. First-time viewers may wish to bypass the following review of this highly recommended film.

The ghosts of the flight crew of a B-25 that crashed in the Libyan desert have awaited the plane's discovery for 17 years. When the wreckage is spotted by an oil exploration flight, an Air Force investigation team is sent in to determine its provenance. Included in the team are Lt. Col. Gronke (William Shatner), Maj. Devlin (Vince Edwards) and Gen. Hamner (Richard Basehart), the only survivor of the B-25 crew, that was thought lost over the Mediterranean. While Gronke just wants to wrap up the routine investigation, Devlin senses that Hamner's story concerning the flight is an attempt to cover his cowardice. In the days that follow, Hamner is haunted by the ghosts of his dead friends until he comes to terms with his actions.

Another touchstone of the telefilm, *Sole Survivor* is a haunting tale that left its mark on a generation. Its power lies in a strong cast and excellent writing, but mostly in the plight of the ghosts who haunt the vast desert. They have waited many long years for their bodies to be discovered and returned home, passing the time by playing endless games of baseball. Throughout the film they stand watch, unable to make themselves known to their modern counterparts, maddeningly impotent in the face of injustice. At last the weight of his guilt breaks Hamner, and a gesture he makes in a drunken rage ironically reveals where the bodies of his compatriots lie. Each ghost in turn disappears as their remains are gathered in flag-draped body bags until there is but one left, one body undiscovered, one man's ghost left alone in the desert for eternity. It is in this shattering moment—a primal

Vince Edwards (left) and Richard Basehart in *Sole Survivor* (1970).

fear realized—that *Sole Survivor* achieves the status of a classic.

The three leads are matched perfectly to the roles they play: Basehart as the defiant and finally broken Gen. Hamner, Shatner as the acquiescent Lt. Col. Gronke and Edwards as the determined Maj. Devlin. Basehart brings a potent confidence to the general who is in denial over his decision to abandon his crewmates. In the midst of the investigation, Maj. Devlin remarks, "I'm not your enemy, general." Basehart's retort, "Then don't make me yours," is wickedly delivered. When the truth comes out, Basehart manages to shape the general with some pathos. We can only pity the man.

Shatner, the edgy, self-serving actor, molds beautifully into Gronke, who is more concerned with preserving his pension by not offending the general. Gronke has some of the best lines in the picture, such as "The Libyan desert is no place to make waves," and, in a desperate moment, "Don't ask me, I'm only the man in charge."

The gravity that Edwards brings to Devlin is evident from the beginning. At first it seems the major is driven to bring down Hamner. But in one of the best scenes, Devlin and Hamner confront each other, and Devlin reveals that he too had his moment of panic, and that it cost the lives of innocent children. Devlin has his own ghosts to deal with, his own torment to bear.

The ghostly crew consists of lesser-known actors: Lou Antonio, Lawrence P. Casey, Dennis Cooney, Brad David and Patrick Wayne. Most familiar are Antonio, who made the rounds of popular drama television—in fact, he was in a *Star Trek* episode—before devoting all of his time to directing, and John Wayne's son Patrick, an actor not known for range, who does fine as the men's commanding officer.

Sole Survivor was undoubtedly inspired by the true story of an intact B-24 bomber discovered in the Libyan desert in 1959. The "Lady Be Good" was lost in 1943 after a bombing mission in Italy. The bodies of eight of her nine crew members were recovered. The same story inspired a 1960 episode of *The Twilight Zone* entitled "King Nine Will Not Return." In it, Robert Cummings sees a newspaper headline about the plane's discovery, and goes into a reverie about being stranded with the wreck in the desert. It turns out that it was indeed his plane and, having missed that doomed mission, he lived with the guilt for years.

The plane used in *Sole Survivor* was an Air National Guard B-25J dumped in El Mirage Dry Lake, San Bernardino County, where filming took place. Director Paul Stanley made no other telefrights in the 1970s.

CAST: Richard Basehart, Vince Edwards, William Shatner, Lou Antonio, Lawrence Casey, Dennis Cooney, Brad David, Patrick Wayne, Alan Caillou, Timur Bashtu, Ian Abercrombie, David Cannon, John Winston, and Noah Keen.

CREDITS: Director: Paul Stanley; Teleplay: Guerdon Trueblood; Music: Paul Glass; Production: Cinema Center 100 Films; Running Time: 94 minutes; Air Date: 1/9/70; Network: CBS

Someone's Watching Me

AKA High Rise

Escaping a failed love affair, Leigh Michaels (Lauren Hutton) starts life over by moving to LA. She gets a job as a director of live television for a local station, and moves into a high rise apartment. Almost immediately she begins receiving strange phone calls, and gifts arrive from a mysterious travel company. Her new boyfriend, Paul Winkless (David Birney), and a co-worker, Sophie (Adrienne Barbeau), try to help Leigh catch the stalker when the police are less than effective. After Sophie is killed by the increasingly desperate psycho, Leigh and Paul step up their investigation and draw the killer into the open.

Someone's Watching Me was John Carpenter's first film for television. Carpenter had already directed *Dark Star* and *Assault on Precinct 13*, and his breakthrough film, *Halloween*, had opened in theaters only a month before the initial airing of this thriller (although *Halloween* was actually filmed later than *Someone's Watching Me*). The rest, as they say, is history. Some of the Carpenter touch is evident here—the prowling camera, the inside jokes and the strong woman in peril—but Carpenter's obvious intent is to pay his respects to Alfred Hitchcock.

Mentions of *Rear Window* are apt. Spying with telescopes and witnessing a murder from afar come to the fore as direct homage. But Carpenter twists these elements and throws the influences of the Italian thriller—the giallo—into the mix as well. *Someone's Watching Me* is a stylish, elegant thriller that builds its suspense with efficiency, but it is also cold and remote, with unlikable or underdeveloped characters, and a payoff that lacks punch.

Key to the success—or lack thereof—is the heroine, Leigh Michaels. Screenwriter Carpenter's attempts to define Michaels as endearingly goofy are wide of the mark. Her little jokes and conversations with herself paint the character as weak, immature and even unbalanced, not exactly the type of person the audience can identify with. The beautiful Lauren Hutton is just that, all face. The camera may love her but her charisma is nil, and there is little weight to the performance. Hutton was a cover girl extraordinaire and a shill for Revlon cosmetics before breaking into acting. This role is relatively early in her second career and it shows.

The other two main characters don't fare much better as written. Paul is a cute but bland philosophy teacher with no personality whatsoever. He pulls some strings and gets a cop friend to look into the incidents that are terrorizing Leigh but, as expected, this is an impotent attempt to control the situation. David Birney, who broke through with the *Bridget Loves Bernie* sitcom, is normally a likable enough leading man, but his presence adds nothing to the underwritten Paul. Sophie is a matter-of-fact lesbian, which is refreshing in itself, but one wonders why it is she who is doomed to be the killer's victim. Adrienne Barbeau, who met Carpenter on this production and married him soon thereafter, does what she can with Sophie, but again the character is only sketched, and simply around to fill a particular purpose.

Why Carpenter was nominated for an Edgar Allan Poe Award for best television feature is a mystery in itself. Picking apart a film is not valid criticism but there are nagging questions that must be asked. Why does Leigh leave her drapes open day and night? Doesn't she realize she's on display to the apartment building directly across from her? It's an hour into the film before she picks up on the fact she's being spied upon through those very windows. As mentioned, the stalker sends gifts to Leigh, one of which is a telescope, and he calls her to ask if she's enjoying the view. It would seem that Leigh, this director of live television, is not sharp enough to know that she's being handed the entire plot on a platter.

Far more successful are the visuals and set pieces. Carpenter may require his characters to be dumb just to further the plot, but watching them be dumb is a treat. The camera is constantly on the move or presenting us with interesting points of view, and lighting is keyed to accentuate the psychological state of our heroine. These technical details have always been Carpenter's strong point, and he doesn't disappoint here.

There are two sequences that stand out. At one point, Leigh, who has figured out which apartment holds the stalker, enters the building opposite to investigate. Sophie remains behind and watches Leigh through the telescope. When Leigh looks back at Sophie through the stalker's telescope, she sees Sophie being attacked in a nifty twist on Hitchcock. It is probably the most emotionally successful scene in the film.

The other scene betrays the influence of the giallo, a type of adult mystery filled with images of women in peril, that came into its own with Italian films of the 60s and 70s. Leigh has been drawn down to the laundry room in the bowels of her apartment building on the pretext of meeting the stalker. She brings a knife which she immediately drops through a grating in the floor and into the duct below. She must remove the grate and climb into the duct to retrieve the knife.

When she hears noises, she replaces the grate on top of her, and holds tight in the duct while a suspicious character stands directly above her. The typical giallo is not known for its logic and the same can be said here, but the circumstance is pure nightmare.

Carpenter likes to throw in knowing nods to genre cinema or its culture to keep aficionados amused. Two of these in this film are the name of the apartment house, Arkham Tower (from H.P. Lovecraft), and the flash of an old movie when Leigh plugs in her tiny television set. The film looks to be *House of Wax* or perhaps *Nightmare in Wax*, but it is anyone's guess since the snippet runs for only a couple of seconds.

The identity of the stalker is not revealed until the very end, but *Someone's Watching Me* is not a mystery. Rather, Carpenter taps into a genuine vein of fear, the fear of knowing you're being watched but are powerless to prevent it. In the film, Sophie calls the surveillance a rape; it is a violation of privacy, certainly, but more a violation of the expectation of privacy. Carpenter's point, intended or not, is that our expectations in that regard may be too high to be fulfilled.

CAST: Lauren Hutton, David Birney, Adrienne Barbeau, Charles Cyphers, Grainger Hines, Len Lesser, John Mahon, James Murtaugh, J. Jay Saunders, Michael Laurence, George Skaff, Robert Phalen, Robert Snively, Jean Le Bouvier, James McAlpine, Edgar Justice, and John Fox. CREDITS: Writer-Director: John Carpenter; Music: Harry Sukman; Production: Warner Bros. Television; Running Time: 97 minutes; Air Date: 11/29/78; Network: NBC

Something Evil

Steven Spielberg's most famous telefilm is, of course, *Duel*. Whereas *Duel* is an action picture, *Something Evil* is a mood piece, slowly building an atmosphere of dread and inescapable malevolence. *Duel* was slick and simple, drawing on clearly defined fears, but *Something Evil* is complex and somewhat vague, dependent upon interpretations from the viewer. Comparing the two films, as is inevitable given the high profile of the director, is apples to oranges in all but one respect: the result. Frankly, *Something Evil* is a frustrating failure as a horror film.

At her insistence, Marjorie Worden (Sandy Dennis) and her husband, Paul (Darren McGavin), buy a rundown Pennsylvania farmhouse hours away from Paul's work in New York. After the family moves in, strange and indefinable things begin to happen: Marjorie hears the cries of a child in the barn; she discovers jars holding indescribable things in the shed; she becomes tense and easily irritated; and her relationship with her son and husband becomes strained. At the urging of her neighbor, Harry Lincoln (Ralph Bellamy), Marjorie studies magic circles and incantations to ward off evil. Finally, fearful that she is becoming possessed of something that lives in the house, Marjorie locks the children in their room and throws away the key. She is about to discover that the evil is taking a different form, and it will take a different approach to repel.

At the center of the film is Marjorie, as played by Sandy Dennis. Dennis, who passed away in 1992, came to prominence in films such as *Who's Afraid of Virginia Woolf* (for which she won an Oscar), *Up the Down Staircase* and *The Out-of-Towners*. Her appeal, however, was an acquired taste, and she never found lasting fame after her early, impressive roles. Here, as the sensitive artistic Marjorie, Dennis comes across as manipulating and unpleasant, hardly the heroine that audiences will take to their hearts. She is intolerant to the ways of the people who live in the area, yet grasping when she realizes there is something wrong. She is frustrated that her husband isn't around to help, but it was her idea of moving to the country that results in their physical separation.

Darren McGavin is the often-absent Paul, who works for an advertising firm. Paul is forever acquiescing to his wife's wishes, taking her frantic phone calls, and dropping everything to return to her. His aggravation at her mood swings and demands reaches a climax when she insists that they leave the house after they'd only been there a short while. He mentions to her that he's seen her like this before, an unsubtle hint of her instability.

It is the son Stevie (Johnny Whitaker, *Family Affair*) who eventually takes the brunt of his mother's temper. He seems amazingly well-adjusted given her volatile behavior, and we fear more for his well-being than the tortured Marjorie. Ralph Bellamy has an excellent part as Harry Lincoln, the wise neighbor who pays the price for wanting to educate and assist Marjorie, and John Rubenstein has a strange and ill-defined role as Lincoln's nephew Ernest.

Much is made of pentacles and incantations but neither shows much value when it comes down to defeating the Evil, which is part of the point of the story. This "something" that inhabits the house is manifested in unexplained and ultimately ineffective ways. From a prologue, we know that the previous landowner was somehow made to fall from the hay loft to his death, but we don't learn if the problem with the house has a deeper history. Marjorie hears the cries from the barn but this symptom never crystallizes further. The mysterious glowing jar in the shed, which later shows up in the house, is a red blob that drives Marjorie batty, but it certainly doesn't go far in chilling the viewer.

The conclusion that love is stronger than symbols when dealing with demonic forces is less than satisfying, and seems more like a quaint sentiment out of step with the times. Spielberg's visual sense, however, is as intact as ever via the use of fisheye lenses and sweet touches, such as the distortion of Marjorie's face in a mirror. But overall, *Something Evil* comes across as an impressionistic horror by a painter in a hurry to move on to Something Else.

Spielberg is credited in the cast of the film (he has one line as a studio engineer), as is cult actor Bruno VeSota though his cameo was not readily apparent. The Oscar-nominated Robert Clouse, who wrote the film, is better known as a director (his nominations were for two shorts he made in the early 60s). He helmed the Travis McGee story *Darker Than Amber* with Rod Taylor but his main claim to fame was the Bruce Lee breakthrough film *Enter the Dragon*. After Lee's death, Clouse was assigned the task of piecing together scenes from several of Lee's previous films to generate the notorious rip-off known as *Game of Death*. Clouse, who passed away in 1997, was completely deaf, relying on assistant directors to verify that the actors had spoken their lines correctly.

CAST: Sandy Dennis, Darren McGavin, Jeff Corey, Johnny Whitaker, John Rubinstein, Ralph Bellamy, David Knapp, Laurie Hagan, Herb Armstrong, Margaret Avery, Norman Bartold, Lois Battle, Bella Bruck, Lynn Cartwright, John J. Fox, Alan Frost, Carl Gottlieb, John Hudkins, Crane Jackson, Michael Macready, Paul Micale, Margaret Muse, John Nolan, Connie Hunter Ragaway, Elizabeth Rogers, Steven Spielberg, Bruno VeSota, Debbie Lempert and Sandy Lempert.

CREDITS: Director: Steven Spielberg; Teleplay: Robert Clouse; Music: Wladimir Selinsky; Production: Belford Productions; Vehicles furnished by Ford Marketing Corporation; Running Time: 73 minutes; Air Date: 1/31/72; Network: NBC

Spectre

Eminent criminologist William Sebastian (Robert Culp) receives a call for help from Anitra Cyon (Ann Bell), who believes her elder brother, Sir Geoffrey (James Villiers), is possessed by the demon Asmodeus. Sebastian summons his old friend, Dr. Hamilton (Gig Young), and the two depart for London to investigate. Three years earlier, the Cyon clan undertook a remodel of their home, an old abbey, and unknowingly released the imprisoned demon from beneath a druid circle on their land. Since that time, the Cyons have led an increasingly decadent lifestyle, amassing wealth and power at an astounding rate. Sebastian and

Hamilton seek to return the demon to the depths, but all is not as they had originally believed.

Spectre was produced as a pilot for a supernatural series at Elstree Studios in England for 20th Century–Fox, and aired in the US on NBC. Written by Gene Roddenberry from his original story and directed by Clive Donner (*Old Dracula*), it is certainly one of the wildest and most challenging—for American audiences, anyway—telefilms of the golden age. *Spectre* is a rollercoaster ride through a fantasy land of demons and spells, and is wickedly fun from beginning to end.

The credits unfold over the famous and disturbing painting "The Garden of Earthly Delights" by Hieronymus Bosch, while a jaunty harpsichord tune cues the viewer to the tongue-in-cheek attitude of the production. The arrival of the good doctor at Sebastian's ultra-modern pad kicks off the adventure of another investigator into the occult (see *Revenge!*, *Ritual of Evil*, et al.).

Culp plays Sebastian with deadly seriousness, which helps the viewer accept the strange and almost nonstop bizarre happenings. Dr. Hamilton is played for a bit more humor by Oscar winner Gig Young, in his next-to-last film. The following year, Young shot his new bride and then committed suicide at the age of 64.

No sooner has Hamilton come through the door when the arrival of Anitra Cyon is announced by Sebastian's valet, Lilith (Majel Barrett, wife of Roddenberry—Nurse Chapel on the original *Star Trek*). Sebastian is suspicious of Anitra because the girl is supposedly in London at the moment. When she tries to seduce him, he rightly proclaims her a succubus, and uses the Apocryphal Book of Tobit to destroy her. Tobit is the third book of the "apocrypha," the non-canonical Old Testament books of the Catholic Bible, and was written about 200 BC. The tale of Tobit is about an Israelite who was carried as a captive to Nineveh, and may correlate to Sebastian's imminent journey to London. Tobit, being the third book, may also, or only coincidentally, relate to the demon Asmodeus, who represents the third deadly sin of lust, and who has supposedly been unleashed.

The Cyon clan consists of the aforementioned Ann Bell (as Anitra), who was in *Dr. Terror's House of Horrors* and *The Witches*, John Hurt (*Alien*) as Mitri, and James Villiers (*Blood from the Mummy's Tomb*, *Asylum*), who plays Sir Geoffrey to the wicked hilt. Others of the Cyon household may be recognizable to genre fans including Sydna, the chauffeur (Jenny Runacre, *The Creeping Flesh*), the female butler (Angela Grant, *Tales from the Crypt*) and the maids, Penny Irving (*House of Whipcord*) and Vicki Michelle (*Virgin Witch*). Gordon Jackson (*The Creeping Unknown*), playing Inspector Cabell, will be a familiar face to Anglophiles as well.

As Sebastian and Hamilton navigate the supernatural labyrinth on their quest to defeat the mighty demon, they encounter a veritable funhouse of monsters and spooky goings-on. These include lots and lots of fire, witches, hairy beasts, dwarves and even a giant lizard being. Several of the scenes are adult-oriented, including implied sexual shenanigans (one featuring an array of S&M accoutrement) and near-incest. The version of the film playing on American cable television includes several flashes of bare breasts that were certainly not present in the original network airing.

CAST: Robert Culp, John Hurt, Gordon Jackson, Ann Bell, James Villiers, Gig Young, Majel Barrett, Jenny Runacre, Angela Grant, Penny Irving, Vicki Michelle, Michael Latimer, Lindy Benson, and Sally Farmiloe.

CREDITS: Director: Clive Donner; Teleplay: Gene Roddenberry and Samuel A. Peeples, based on an original story by Gene Roddenberry; Music: John Cameron; Production: Norway Productions; Running Time: 98 minutes; Air Date: 5/21/77; Network: NBC

The Spell

Plain and overweight, Rita Matchett (Susan Myers) is tormented by her high school classmates, and having a difficult time with her affluent family at home. A series of strange "accidents" begin to happen to Rita's antagonists that point to a supernatural cause. Rita's mother (Lee Grant) discovers that her daughter is experimenting with witchcraft, and must find the means to fight it.

Naturally, *The Spell* is compared to *Carrie*—a tormented youngster takes a supernatural revenge—but where Carrie had an unexplained power within her, Rita employs witchcraft and, granted, some talent of her own to exact retribution. And where *Carrie* was clearly an exploitation piece, *The Spell* takes a more low-key, realistic approach to the problems and unorthodox solutions of the outsider teenager.

Rita is played by first-timer Susan Myers, who gives a very convincing performance as the put-upon but intelligent and dangerous outcast. It would seem her career never blossomed since there are only a modest number of credits to her name. Oscar-winner Lee Grant gives another good performance as the beleaguered parent who tries to understand her increasingly troubled child. The relationship between these two is especially well-written, and keeps the entire show grounded in reality.

The feisty, multi-talented Grant has been in show business since age four. She won a Critic's Circle Award for her first role on Broadway in *Detective Story*, and followed that with an Oscar nomination (and won Best Actress at Cannes) when she reprised the role in the film version. No sooner had good fortune smiled on her than she was blacklisted for a decade because her then-husband was accused of being a leftist during the Red Scare. When she returned to acting she won an Emmy for her work in *Peyton Place* and another for the 1971 telefilm *The Neon Ceiling*. She would go on to three more Oscar nominations, winning one for *Shampoo*. She is also a director, winning a Directors Guild Award for the telefilm *Nobody's Child* in 1986. Grant has lent her talents to the occasional genre film including the telefright *Night Slaves* and the features *Damien: Omen II*, *The Swarm*, *The Mafu Cage* and *Visiting Hours*.

James Olson takes on another thankless role as the father who has reached his limit with his troublesome eldest daughter. His response is punishment until he can send her away forever. Rita's younger sister, Kristina, is an early role for the 14-year-old Helen Hunt who would go on to a stellar career in film and television.

The "accidents" that occur throughout the film are, for the most part, modest in nature. The first is a fall during a rope climb in gym class for a girl who is particularly nasty to Rita. Apparently Rita had predicted the event to others in her class, which quickly silenced those her teased her. Next is a close-call hit-and-run for her father by a family friend who had been hexed by Rita, and then a near-drowning for her sister as a warning. The most horrific, however, is the blood-boiling death of a woman who had spied on Rita's witchcraft activity. It is the most disturbing image of the film.

Rita learns of her powers and explores the occult with her gym teacher-counselor, Jo Standish. Standish has psychic talents of her own she would like to use to build a community of "sensitives." Rita, however, would like to remain special, which results in their falling out. Standish is played by Lelia Goldoni, familiar to genre fans for her roles in *Hysteria* and *Theater of Death*. She also shows up as a nun in the telefright *Good Against Evil*.

The Spell was expanded for release on video by about ten minutes. Most likely, the scenes with the parapsychologist Dale Boyce (Jack Colvin) have been embellished because they are practically nonsensical to the rest of the plot. Most viewers who give this unfairly maligned film a chance will be surprised by the final twist.

Director Lee Philips, a one-time actor (*Peyton Place*, *Violent Midnight*) who migrated over to directing in the early 1960s, also made the alien horror telefright *The Stranger Within*. Writer Brian Taggert went on to pen *Visiting Hours*, the giant rat movie *Of Unknown Origin* and *Poltergeist III*.

CAST: Lee Grant, Susan Myers, Lelia Goldoni, Helen Hunt, Jack Colvin, James Olson,

James Greene, Wright King, Barbara Bostock, Doney Oatman, Richard Carlyle, Kathleen Hughes, Robert Gibbons, and Arthur Peterson.

CREDITS: Director: Lee Philips; Teleplay: Brian Taggert; Music: Gerald Fried; Production: Stonehenge Productions; Running Time: 87 minutes; Air Date: 2/20/77; Network: NBC

SST—Death Flight

AKA Death Flight; Flight of the Maiden; SST: Disaster in the Sky

America's first SST airplane, appropriately named "Maiden One," is making a promotional flight from New York to Paris with a star-studded passenger list. Unfortunately, a disgruntled mechanic (George Maharis) has added detergent to the hydraulic fluid, which corrodes the seals and makes the plane lose maneuverability. An attempt to reroute electrical power to fix the problem results in an explosion that unleashes a deadly strain of Senegal flu, which was headed for the Pasteur Institute.

One disaster wasn't enough for this film, so the combination of mechanical and medical problems land *SST—Death Flight* in the category of double jeopardy (see *Fer de Lance, Mayday at 40,000 Feet*). Doubling the problems, however, does not double the entertainment value of this tired thriller. Adding insult to injury are the not-so-special effects, which are amongst the cheapest and most unconvincing of the era. In this case, director David Lowell Rich's familiarity with airborne frights breeds boredom.

The rundown of stars this time includes pilot Robert Reed, flight attendants Tina Louise and Billy Crystal (in his only telefright of the 70s), Martin Milner as an ex-footballer turned passenger cheerleader, his wife Susan Strasberg, Barbara Anderson as a reporter, Burgess Meredith as the plane's designer, Lorne Greene as the owner, Season Hubley who won the trip, her fiancé John De Lancie, Peter Graves as Season's old flame and Doug McClure as an ex-pilot who helps old adversary Reed when the going gets tough.

Lesser lights are press agent Bert Convy and his girl, "Miss SST," Misty Rowe. Brock Peters plays the doctor who brought the flu aboard, Regis Philbin plays a reporter on the ground, and Richard Derr (*When Worlds Collide*) plays the governor who has one line.

At least *SST–Death Flight* has some unintentionally funny dialogue in its favor. Witness Season Hubley deliver this line when defending her romance with the older Peter Graves: "Don't equate age and virility, it doesn't track!" Or Pete's response to getting smacked by Season's new boyfriend: "Five years ago I'd have seen that punch coming. Maybe six." Martin Milner takes the unofficial role of humorous support for the frightened passengers by saying things such as "'An in-flight problem' just means the pilot has dropped his glass eye into his martini." But Bert Convy has the topper with a word he *can't* say—abortion—when arguing with his pregnant girlfriend Misty Rowe: "I won't say the word, but having a baby's going to ruin your figure."

When the contaminated plane is refused a landing in Paris, London comes to the rescue, but doctor Brock reminds Reed that landing there will spread the flu across the city, potentially killing thousands. In a bizarre turn, Milner convinces the passengers to take Brock's advice and fly to Senegal, where the flu has already done its damage. One last problem, a lack of fuel, forces the plane to make a crash landing in the middle of nowhere. If there had been more money and time, the film could have turned into a desert survival adventure but, mercifully the doomed flight, and film, ends there.

Despite the fact the cast includes the stars of *Route 66*, George Maharis and Martin Milner, the two do not have a scene together. Apparently, a scene involving a dash of nudity by Misty Rowe (one-time Miss Radiant Radish) was shot to attract foreign distribution.

CAST: (ao) Barbara Anderson, Bert Convy, Peter Graves, Lorne Greene, Season Hubley,

Tina Louise, Doug McClure, George Maharis, Burgess Meredith, Martin Milner, Brock Peters, Robert Reed, and Susan Strasberg. Also Misty Rowe, Billy Crystal, John De Lancie, Regis Philbin, Robert Ito, Tom Stewart, Sherwood Price, Paul Napier, Tim Pelt, Alain Patrick, Richard Derr, Ric Carrott, Shawn Randall, Walter Mastow, and Chrystie Jenner.

CREDITS: Director: David Lowell Rich; Teleplay: Robert L. Joseph and Meyer Dolinsky, based on a story by Guerdon Trueblood; Music: John Cacavas; Production: ABC Circle Films; Running Time: 94 minutes; Air Date: 2/25/77; Network: ABC

The Strange and Deadly Occurrence

Michael and Christine Rhodes (Robert Stack and Vera Miles) and their daughter Melissa (Margaret Willock) move to the country outside of LA, and strange things begin happening. The house has a morbid history: it was built on the ruins of a Spanish mission where a man, despondent over the death of his wife, had killed the resident priest, and committed suicide by setting fire to the place. And its previous owner had mysteriously drowned in the pool. At first, there are minor disturbances such as power outages, spooked horses, and a thermostat with a mind of its own. But soon, a presence is felt in the house, and a creepy man is hanging around offering to buy the property. When pleas to the police prove fruitless, the family vows to get to the bottom of the mysterious events.

The Strange and Deadly Occurrence is an excellent thriller directed with a sure hand by the prolific John Llewellyn Moxey, an expert with the telefright film. For a change, the plot unfolds in a logical manner, and the strength of the terrorized family is believable. Also refreshing is the father's attitude towards his wife and daughter: he actually believes what they say instead of second guessing their experiences. The film was written by Sandor Stern, whose telefilm track record is not that impressive, but who pulls out a clear winner here.

The leading cast is first-rate. Robert Stack and Vera Miles, two very popular and capable actors, make a terrific, loving couple whose smarts match their looks. Their daughter Melissa is played with a casual flair by Margaret Willock (*The Creature Wasn't Nice*), in only her second film. The Rhodes family is a close-knit unit, respectful of each other and never condescending, a family you can root for without a second thought.

Stack's film career was launched back in 1939, with publicity announcing him as "the first boy to kiss Deanna Durbin," in *First Love*. After his service in WWII, he was noticed for his work in *The High and the Mighty* and received an Oscar nomination for *Written in the Wind*. But television became the medium that would bring Stack lasting fame after his career-defining—and Emmy-winning—role as Eliot Ness in *The Untouchables*. He scored a solid hit with the series *The Name of the Game* in the late 60s, and hosted the *Unsolved Mysteries* series, thereafter concentrating on guest star spots and telefilms. His theatrical releases include the first Hollywood 3-D film, *Bwana Devil*, Sam Fuller's *House of Bamboo*, the terrific adventure *The Corrupt Ones*, the telefright *Murder on Flight 502*, Steven Spielberg's *1941*, and his image-spoofing turn in *Airplane!* The dependable, much-beloved actor wrote an entertaining autobiography entitled *Straight Shooting* in 1980, and he passed away in 2003 of a heart attack.

Supporting the family trio are friends Felix (Herb Edelman) and Audrey (Dena Dietrich), who don't have an abundance of screen time, but also don't have ulterior motives. The sheriff who has a hard time believing that anything is wrong at the Rhodes place is played by the great character actor L.Q. Jones, whose credits reach back to the mid–50s. He hit it big in westerns such as *The Hunting Party*, *The Wild Bunch*, and many others. Jones also produced and acted in the cult items *The Brotherhood of Satan* and *A Boy and His Dog*.

The creepy fellow who wants to buy the Rhodes' house, Dr. Gilgreen, is played by Ted Gehring, best known as Ebenezer

Sprague in the long-running *Little House on the Prairie* series. But the really bad guy, who hasn't been mentioned yet, is played by cult figure Bill McKinney, one of the great screen villains. His movie debut was in the genre film *She Freak*, but he's best remembered as one of the hillbillies who assaults Ned Beatty in *Deliverance*. McKinney became one of Clint Eastwood's stock players, making eight films with him, and has had a long career of scaring people.

In addition to the disturbances mentioned in the plot synopsis above, many other annoying things put the Rhodeses through the paces, including gophers in the kitchen cabinets, a tub that runs over, Christine getting locked in the sauna (the astute viewer will notice the patch Miles wears to cover her breasts in this scene where she is supposedly nude), loud pounding sounds, wild screams and a dead man in the pool. The scene which usually strikes a chord with viewers is when Melissa's headless sewing dummy trundles toward her in the dark of her bedroom. A fun finale wraps everything up nicely in this, one of the most enjoyable telefrights of the era.

CAST: Robert Stack, Vera Miles, L.Q. Jones, Herb Edelman, Dena Dietrich, Ted Gehring, Margaret Willock, James McCallion, Aldine King, John Gruber, Phil Chambers, E.A. Sirianni, Gene Massey, Jr., and Bill McKinney. CREDITS: Director: John Llewellyn Moxey; Teleplay: Sandor Stern, based on a story by Sandor Stern & Lane Slate; Music: Robert Prince; Production: Alpine Productions; Vehicles Provided by Chevrolet; Running Time: 74 minutes; Air Date: 9/24/74; Network: NBC

(Left to right) Margaret Willock, Vera Miles and Robert Stack are menaced in *The Strange and Deadly Occurrence* (1974).

The Strange Possession of Mrs. Oliver

The prim and proper Miriam Oliver (Karen Black) is in a stifling marriage to her dominating, insensitive lawyer husband, Greg (George Hamilton). One day while shopping, Miriam is drawn to a sexy red sweater and blonde wig she thinks will spice up her dull life. Greg, however, is taken aback by her new look. Miriam, feeling increasingly marginalized, rents a beach cottage and, donning her wig and sweater, enters a nearby bar where she's recognized as a woman called Sandy. Miriam's visions of a burning house, and strange dreams of her own funeral, fuel a desire to get to the bottom of her mysterious transformation.

Famed author Richard Matheson wrote the original screenplay for this psychological mystery, and telefright regular Gordon Hessler directed. The team strives for an eerie, dream-like atmosphere, kicking things off with Miriam's recurring nightmare of a fog-shrouded graveyard, where she sees herself in a coffin. The entire production has a claustrophobic and unreal sense. Miriam passes the time in a haze, haunted by disturbing images, and oppressed by the demands of her conservative husband. The overall result, however, is a somnambulistic and rather dreary film, with a final revelation best described as too little, too late.

Karen Black's Miriam/Sandy is much like her dual role in the "Millicent and Theresa" segment of *Trilogy of Terror*—one prudish and the other a free spirit. The filmmakers drive home this dichotomy without mercy. When at the store buying the sweater and wig, the salesperson says, "It'll make a new woman of you." Husband Greg claims, "You're becoming a different person," and so on. George Hamilton has the thankless role as Greg, who is so uptight that he complains the gardener is trimming trees the wrong day of the week. Greg doesn't understand what's happening to his wife, naturally, but she reassures him with the frightening line, "I'm still the girl you always approved of."

Offbeat actress Black has somewhat of a cult following, originating, no doubt, from her standing in the counterculture of the 1960s. He first major role was in Francis Ford Coppola's *You're a Big Boy Now*, but audiences really took note of her turn as a prostitute in the 1969 mega-hit *Easy Rider*. The next year she received an Oscar nomination for *Five Easy Pieces*, and Black has ever since been following a winding path of mainstream features, independent oddities and television appearances. Her films include *The Pyx*, *The Great Gatsby*, *Airport 1975*, a pair of Robert Altman films (*Nashville* and *Come Back to the Five and Dime, Jimmy Dean*), Hitchcock's *Family Plot*, Dan Curtis's *Burnt Offerings*, *Killer Fish*, Ruggero Deodato's *Cut and Run*, *Invaders from Mars*, the Crispin Glover comedy *Rubin and Ed*, *House of 1000 Corpses*, and many more.

The supporting cast offers a few bright spots. Robert F. Lyons as Mark, the fellow who recognizes Miriam as Sandy, will be familiar from other telefrights of the era, and so will the ever-welcome Lucille Benson, as a housekeeper. Keep an eye out for the "Old Man" whom Miriam approaches for directions: it's none other than William Kerwin, who was in many of the 60s exploitation epics of the notorious Herschell Gordon Lewis.

Some viewers may appreciate the 70s shopping mall experience in the film, for nostalgia's sake, but most will be sincerely depressed by the daytime disco scene of the seedy bar Miriam enters by the beach. Fire is at the heart of the mystery in the film, the motif echoed in fireplaces, bonfires, even a food warmer, but unfortunately it never spread to this damp and lifeless production.

CAST: Karen Black, George Hamilton, Robert F. Lyons, Lucille Benson, Jean Allison, Burke Byrnes, Gloria LeRoy, Asher Brauner, Charles Cooper, Danna Hansen, William Irwin, Nancy Hahn Leonard, Macon McCalman, Bob Palmer, Delos V. Smith, and Sunny Woods.

CREDITS: Director: Gordon Hessler; Teleplay: Richard Matheson; Music: Morton Stevens; Production: The Shpetner Company; Running Time: 71 minutes; Air Date: 2/28/77; Network: NBC

The Stranger

AKA **Stranded in Space**

Some entertainments rise above their hackneyed plots, simplistic structures, and threadbare special effects to become something worth treasuring in spite of their shortcomings. Or because of them. Count *The Stranger* as one such entertainment that succeeds, whether due to its familiar, comfortable cast, or simply because of a nostalgic sense of ambience. It is an ultimately viewable slice of hokum that will appeal, if not to a majority, then to those of a certain age, who will be swayed by its modest pleasures.

Problems during a space flight cause astronaut Neil Stryker (Glenn Corbett) to black out. When he revives, he is confined to a hospital room long enough to become suspicious of his surroundings. Several subtle ploys by Stryker prove to him that he's not back in America after all. Stryker is actually undergoing interrogation while drugged each night; during one of these sessions, he manages to escape. Once outside, the three moons in the night sky betray the fact that Stryker has landed on another planet—one very much like Earth, but one very different as well. The planet is called Terra, and it is run by the Perfect Order, which has created a hive-like dystopian society where the citizens are rewarded for betraying one another for thinking or acting against the common good. Stryker convinces a reluctant doctor, the beautiful Bettina Cooke (Sharon Acker), to help him, and she takes him to Dylan MacAuley (Lew Ayres), a rebellious space scientist, who may be able to get Stryker off the planet and headed for home.

The Stranger is not serious or challenging science fiction. It is, instead, a 12-year-old boy's fantasy, a game that poses no threat, but as such it is a surprisingly pleasant pastime. The Perfect Order, which has been in place for 35 years, comes complete with patriotic march music, and daily platitudes the populace is expected to repeat and remember. On this day the Wake Thought is "To work for the Perfect Order is to live in harmony and peace with one's self"—none too challenging to be sure. In this harmonious society, citizens are kept under "protective surveillance" by the Department of Protection, are given national ID numbers and are, curiously, all left-handed. To be made an Honor Citizen, one gains points by betraying free-thinkers who are taken to Ward E for reorientation. And the televisions can see as well as be seen.

The B-movie cast is a recognizable ensemble down to the cameos. Glenn Corbett (*Homicidal*), in his only 70s telefright, had an easygoing, James Bond type of competency about him that works well here. His Stryker gets all the lucky breaks of course, but Corbett makes it look challenging to survive. His nemesis is Benedict, played by the great Cameron Mitchell, who looks swell in his tailored suit and black turtleneck. Mitchell is very convincing as a man so uncomfortable with Stryker that he would take extreme measures to put an end to this free thinker. The love interest, Bettina, is played by the lovely Sharon Acker (*Point Blank*), who never became a superstar but instead lent her talents far and wide in smaller roles. The scofflaw scientist, MacAuley, who enjoys outwitting the Perfect Order, and who lives in an fairy-tale, idyllic setting, is played by Lew Ayres, in his wizened way.

The faces, if not the names, of the supporters will undoubtedly be recognizable to most. Tim O'Connor is Dr. Revere, who is sent to Ward E for taking Stryker's side. Steve Franken is Benedict's right hand man, and George Coulouris runs the bookshop that proves a short-lived haven for Stryker. Dean Jagger as Webster, Benedict's superior, does what he does best: understated villainy. There's even a cameo by Virginia Gregg, as the nurse who overdoes the reorientation on the good doctor Revere.

As described by Benedict, Stryker is "cursed with an absolute freedom of thought, cursed with an inquisitive nature, an uncontrollable spirit," all attributes we consider assets, not faults. It is no wonder that Stryker runs. The film manages one good chase scene that features some impressive helicopter flying, but all the other special effects are hopelessly low rent. Notice the weapons chosen for the Perfect Order guards all look to be of German WWII origin, strengthening a Nazi parallel. The ambience, however, is strictly 70s futurist: a mix of orange carpeting, wood paneling and sterile surfaces that will delight aficionados.

The Stranger is not exactly a remake of the 1969 British film, *Doppelganger* aka *Journey to the Far Side of the Sun*, which starred

Roy Thinnes, but more a riff on the same idea. Left open-ended for a series that never materialized, *The Stranger* concludes with an excellent freeze-frame of Stryker, haunted by the triple-moon sky behind him.

CAST: Glenn Corbett, Cameron Mitchell, Sharon Acker, Lew Ayres, George Coulouris, Steve Franken, Dean Jagger, Tim O'Connor, Jerry Douglas, Arch Whiting, H.M. Wynant, William Bryant, Virginia Gregg, Steven Marlo, Ben Wright, and Buck Young.

CREDITS: Director: Lee H. Katzin; Teleplay: Gerald Sanford; Music: Richard Markowitz; Production: Bing Crosby Productions; Automobiles Furnished by Chrysler Corp.; Running Time: 95 minutes; Air Date: 2/26/73; Network: NBC

Stranger in Our House

AKA Summer of Fear

Neither Wes Craven nor Linda Blair needs an introduction to genre fans nowadays. Where Blair was already a star at the time *Stranger in Our House* was made, director Craven was still only a cult figure, having made the drive-in hits *The Last House on the Left* and *The Hills Have Eyes*. This film was Craven's introduction to the big time, and the result is an above average entry in the teen witch genre (see *The Spell*).

When Rachel Bryant's (Linda Blair) aunt and uncle are killed in a car wreck, her cousin Julia (Lee Purcell) moves in with Rachel's family. Rachel senses something odd about Julia; when Rachel's horse attacks the girl, Rachel becomes even more suspicious that something is amiss with her cousin. Meanwhile, Julia has ingratiated herself with the rest of the family, ostracizing Rachel. When Rachel discovers a wax effigy of her horse among Julia's things, she consults Prof. Jarvis (Mcdonald Carey), a family friend and expert on the occult, who loans her some books on witchcraft. By now Julia has stolen away Rachel's boyfriend Mike (Jeff McCracken), and even her father is falling under Julia's spell. After Prof. Jarvis has a stroke, Rachel becomes determined to unmask Julia as a witch.

Airing on Halloween, 1978, on NBC, against *Devil Dog the Hound of Hell* on CBS, *Stranger in Our House* proved to be every bit as good as its competition. The simple story, based on the young people's bestseller *Summer of Fear* by Lois Duncan, is told with competence and efficiency, and instead of being a star-studded event, features a cast of largely unknowns at the time.

Linda Blair, complete with unattractive perm, comes across once too often as a whiner, but gives a fine performance overall. One particular scene stands out: after her horse goes wild at a competition and breaks a leg, it must be put down. Rachel is naturally distraught, and Blair pulls out all the stops in a very convincing emotional outburst. At other times, such as when wearing a cowboy hat or sporting giant red blotches on her face (the hives she is hexed with to keep her from a school dance), the actress's appearance is just this side of ludicrous.

Rachel's father, Tom, is played by Jeremy Slate, and her mother, Leslie, by the elegant and beautiful Carol Lawrence. Neither made any other 70s telefrights, but Slate was in the sleeper cult item *The Centerfold Girls*. Rachel's brother, Peter, is played by Jeff East, soon to assay the role of the young Clark Kent in *Superman* (East had his voice dubbed by Christopher Reeve in that production). East was also in the cult film *The Hazing*, and worked with Craven again in *Deadly Blessing*.

Lee Purcell was already an experienced actress by the time she took the role of the witch Julia. Purcell is excellent as the despicable stranger with supernatural powers. Julia goes through a transformation from hesitant outsider into a sexy manipulator, and Purcell pulls it off with charm and just the right touch of nastiness. The popular Mcdonald Carey is around long enough to remind us that "the magic of yesterday is today's technology."

Some may be surprised by the witch lore invented for the film. While the wax effigy of Rachel's horse smacks of authentic voodoo ritual, the "fact" that witches are only vulnerable when they're asleep, or that they

Turkish theatrical release poster for *Stranger in Our House* (1978).

don't photograph, may be considered news. Julia was also able to invoke hives by drawing red blotches on a picture of Rachel. Neither the burned moth on a map nor the long tooth Rachel finds in Julia's suitcase are explained, nor need they be. Just finding teeth is creepy enough. We never witness any of Julia's rituals, which actually works in the film's favor, making Rachel's discoveries that much more mysterious.

The now-famous Fran Drescher (*The Nanny*) has a small part in her only 70s telefright as Rachel's friend, and some will notice that the veterinarian who puts down Rachel's horse is John Steadman, who worked with Craven in *The Hills Have Eyes*. The fiery car wreck at the beginning of the film was stock footage also used in Steven Spielberg's *Something Evil* years earlier. The old movie Rachel's younger brother (James Jarnagin) is watching may be Carl Dreyer's classic *Vampyr*. The car battle near the end of the film features a Dodge Charger and a Ford Thunderbird, and the trashing of those fine vehicles may bring tears to the eyes of motorheads.

Stranger in Our House is a 70s telefright rarity in that it has been given a fancy DVD release from Artisan, of the international version, which includes a commentary with Craven (who was working on *Cursed* at the time) and co-writer–executive producer Max Keller. The following are a few tidbits from that commentary.

- Since Blair was a horse person, the disturbed dog in the book was changed to a horse.
- The film was shot in a Hidden Hills, California house that was vacated by the owner during the filming.
- The film was the first 35mm production for Craven.
- The scene where Rachel finds the tooth was stolen from Roman Polanski's *The Tenant*.
- The film was so popular that NBC showed it twice within six months. which completed the contract with the producers. They immediately sold it to CBS, who again showed it twice in six months.
- The scenes between Julia and Rachel's father were considered controversial at the time because of the younger woman's seduction of an older man. In fact, the filmmakers had to fight NBC to keep them in the film.
- Craven felt bad about destroying those cool cars, too.

CAST: Linda Blair, Lee Purcell, Jeremy Slate, Jeff McCracken, Jeff East, Carol Lawrence, Mcdonald Carey, Fran Drescher, James Jarnagin, Sierra Pecheur, Billy Beck, Patricia Wilson, Gwil Richards, Frederick Rule, Helena Makela, Nicole Keller, John Steadman, Kerry Arquette, Kim Wells, and Beatrice Manley.

CREDITS: Director: Wes Craven; Teleplay: Glenn M. Benest, Max A. Keller, based on the novel *Summer of Fear* by Lois Duncan; Music: Michael Lloyd, John D'Andrea; Production: Finnegan Associates; Running Time: 99 minutes; Air Date: 10/31/78; Network: NBC

The Stranger Within

Artist Ann Collins (Barbara Eden) has a surprise for her husband, David (George Grizzard): she's pregnant. The only problem is that due to Ann's difficulties in attempting to have a child three years earlier, David had had a vasectomy. Despite Ann's protests to the contrary, everyone around her naturally suspects her of having taken a lover. Ann's behavior becomes increasingly erratic, nearly tearing the couple apart. In a bizarre twist, the pregnancy is accelerating and Ann's body is undergoing a radical physical change. Finally, under hypnosis, Ann reveals that she is bearing an extraterrestrial child.

Few 70s telefrights seem as inspired by a *National Enquirer* headline as *The Stranger Within*. Its one-joke alien baby plot feels as if it was dashed off on a cocktail napkin, and its near-hysterical central performance could be the product of parody. The name Richard Matheson, whose short story inspired the film, was made of gold at the time, and one can almost picture the esteemed writer laughing all the way to the bank.

Barbara Eden is pregnant with an alien baby in *The Stranger Within* **(1974).**

As Ann, Barbara Eden is put through every emotional pace possible, and she responds with a deeply off-center performance, very little of which is conventionally convincing. She begins by over-salting her food, keeping the house chilled, and staring off into the sky instead of doing her housekeeping chores. The house quickly turns into a pigsty because David can't be bothered to wash a dish. Ann takes to speedreading textbooks, drinking masses of scalding hot coffee, and bitching about the stereo being too loud. Soon she's graduated to speaking in tongues and eating strange raw meats.

The manifestations of Ann's physical changes are even more startling, or amusing, depending on one's point of view. Not only is Ann ready to give birth to a fully formed child in three months, but she seems to have the power to miraculously self-heal wounds inflicted in her many long walks in the nearby fields. One minute she's covered in deep scratches and near death, and the next, she's radiant with calm and beauty. Her doctor, Edward Klein (Nehemiah Persoff), is flummoxed. When Ann's blood type begins changing, Klein checks around with a few colleagues, but comes up empty. This is especially surprising given that at the end of the film we discover that Ann is not alone. In fact, she's joined by dozens of women who have undergone the same experience, all at the same time. One has to wonder how the news of these bizarre pregnancies escaped Klein's attention. Persoff's performance is that of a turtle trying to tuck inside its shell, so embarrassed is he of his only 70s telefright appearance.

The rest of the very small cast is dwarfed by the antics of the star. George Grizzard plays the long-suffering David, whose first words to Ann when she announces her predicament are "We'll take care of it." The subject of abortion is one of the major conflicts of the story, of course

(Eden actually says the word once), and the operation is planned three times before Ann finally puts the kibosh on the idea. Usually what happens is that Ann experiences extreme pain and discomfort on the way to have the baby "taken," and the operation is postponed.

David Doyle (of *Charlie's Angels* fame) and Joyce Van Patten play the Collins' friends, Bob and Phyllis. Bob is the party entertainment hypnotist who manages, on the second try, to reach into the troubled psyche of Ann, and glean the alien plot. Under hypnosis, Ann describes herself thusly: "Now I am alien, forgotten, lost," and the alien's home planet is evoked in this middle school phrasing: "To walk the shores of orange seas, cool. To shed the crimson, darkling plains, cool. To raft the silent waters, cool. Drink the wind, gray silent wind, so cool."

Clocks (as in biological) and time (as in accelerated pregnancy) are the strained motifs here. While this symbolism is evident in its meaning, there is one curious behavior by David that is less clear. He is forever backing his Chevrolet out the very long driveway to their house, while Ann manages to always drive her car out head first. Does this mean David is in constant retreat, or reversing his position, trying to escape the inevitable? Or is it that he's a bad planner? We may never know. Director Lee Philips made the much more conventional *The Spell*, a middling teen witch film that looks quite good compared to this farce.

CAST: Barbara Eden, George Grizzard, Joyce Van Patten, David Doyle, and Nehemiah Persoff.

CREDITS: Director: Lee Philips, Teleplay: Richard Matheson, based on his short story; Music: Charles Fox; Production: Lorimar Productions; Automobiles furnished by Chevrolet Motor Division; Running Time: 75 minutes; Air Date: 10/1/74; Network: ABC

The Strangers in 7A

Artie Sawyer (Andy Griffith) is the superintendent of a New York City apartment building. He decides to take advantage of his wife Iris's absence over the Fourth of July weekend to visit his local watering hole. At the bar, Artie is seduced by the lovely Claudine (Susanne Hilder), who says she needs a place to stay for the night. Artie lets her into the apartment of a vacationing tenant, but instead of being rewarded with sex, he is surprised when her three friends show up. It turns out the seduction was a plot to secure an apartment in a building next to the bank the gang intends to rob. When the elaborately planned heist goes sour, and one of the gang is killed, the others plant a bomb in the apartment building to insure their escape. It's up to hostage Artie to foil their plans.

Prolific telefright director Paul Wendkos takes a stab at the urban thriller, a subgenre not particularly popular on television at the time outside of the usual police stories (see *Panic on the 5:22*). Shot in New York City, this heist-gone-wrong tale turns into a minor terrorist-hostage situation in the closing reel, putting the hapless Artie in the role of hero. Primarily a morality tale, *The Strangers in 7A* warns of the price of infidelity (even if not consummated), and follows the standard "crime does not pay" ethic of countless other films. Writer Eric Roth, working from Fielden Farrington's novel, went on to bigger and better things, namely high-profile films such as *Forrest Gump*, *The Horse Whisperer* and Steven Spielberg's *Munich*.

Andy Griffith handles the role of disenchanted Artie with ease. Stuck in a job beneath his abilities, he seeks to improve his lot by taking an unspecified correspondence course. His relationship with his wife Iris has degenerated to the point of boredom, and her positive attitude only reminds Artie of how far he's fallen. It is natural he would so easily fall for the sensual Claudine, who tantalizes him with her young body, which promises to revitalize his virility. The legendary Ida Lupino invests Iris (who returns home unexpectedly and becomes involved in the mess) with a strength of character that puts Artie to shame, but he is redeemed by saving the day in the end.

The criminal element is led by Billy (Michael Brandon, *Four Flies on Gray Velvet*), a brash hothead who is Claudine's boyfriend. It was Billy who planned the heist, but he is not respected by his cohorts, Riff (James A. Watson, Jr.) and Virgil (Tim McIntire), who put up with his superiority act only for the money. The point is made that the three met in Vietnam, and are gleefully using the skills taught by the military for their criminal activities. Watson was in *Killdozer*, and McIntire, who passed away at an early age of heart failure, was the son of character actors John McIntire and Jeanette Nolan. He was the voice of Blood, the dog in *A Boy and His Dog*.

There is little else remarkable about this middle-of-the-road production, other than a bit part for Victoria Carroll as the bank employee who opens a safe deposit box for Billy and Claudine. Carroll, who had a recurring role on the sitcom *Alice*, later made a second career as a voice artist on animated productions such as *The Smurfs*, and the Scooby-Doo movies, etc.

CAST: Andy Griffith, Ida Lupino, Michael Brandon, James A. Watson, Jr., Tim McIntire, Susanne Hildur, Connie Sawyer, Victoria Carroll, Joe Mell, Squire Fridell, Virginia Vincent, and Marc Hannibal.

CREDITS: Director: Paul Wendkos; Teleplay: Eric Roth, based on the novel by Fielden Farrington; Music: Morton Stevens; Production: Mark Carliner Productions; Running Time: 74 minutes; Air Date: 11/14/72; Network: CBS

Sweet, Sweet Rachel

"If I had my life to live over, I should devote myself to psychic research rather than psychoanalysis."—Sigmund Freud

Wealthy Rachel Stanton (Stefanie Powers) witnesses her husband's strange death when he jumps out a window while calling her name. When she starts hearing voices blaming her for what happened, Rachel consults Lucas Tanner (Alex Dreier), a psychic detective. Hypnotizing Rachel to discover what happened that night, Tanner experiences the same vision her husband did on the night he died. Rachel's aunt Lillian (Louise Latham) and uncle Arthur (Pat Hingle) move in with her, and when Rachel's mental health deteriorates, Tanner becomes convinced she is being psychically manipulated. After Rachel's aunt dies mysteriously, Tanner determines to get to the bottom of this complicated case.

The plot synopsis above does not begin to describe the labyrinthine twists and turns of this challenging, baroque entry in the psychic detective subgenre (see *Spectre*, *Revenge*, et al.). *Sweet, Sweet Rachel* is unconventional storytelling in the extreme, and has a daring visual style to match. Director Sutton Roley pulls out all the stops for this occult mystery, using a variety of wide-angle lenses and employing a camera that tends to obscure all but the most vital information being presented. The result is a film that is interesting from a technical standpoint, but emotionally remote. The bottom line is, the visual flourishes cannot disguise the shortcomings of the far-fetched, half-baked script.

Interest in occult matters was at its peak in the early 1970s, fallout from the experimental social phenomena of the late 60s. Here, a windfall of psychic elements spreads the focus too thin, and the conjecture required to validate them takes on an esoteric air. Tanner seems dangerously susceptible to suggestion, but this lends credence to his theories of psychic terrorism. He believes that someone is using telepathic hypnosis—the ability to brainwash from a distance—to reach Rachel's mind and therefore her money. To combat this diabolical plot, Tanner conceives of the idea of hypnotizing his psychic assistant, and, while he's under, having the assistant telepathically hypnotize another psychic, presumably the villain. Logically, the plot has reached a brick wall in the maze of its own making.

The role of the victim, Rachel, is a relatively minor but emotionally strenuous one, and Stefanie Powers does a fine job with it. Tanner (who keeps an office bottle handy) is played by former news commentator Alex Dreier, an actor with an effective everyman presence. *Sweet, Sweet Rachel* was a pilot which was picked up as *The Sixth Sense*, but when it came time to choose the lead, Gary Collins was deemed to have more potential than Dreier, especially in romantic situations. The dull, short-lived series was soon absorbed into *Night Gallery* by having its hour-long episodes edited to 30 minutes.

Dreier's blind, psychic assistant Carey is played by Chris Robinson, a soap opera regular. He had once played a monster in *Beast From Haunted Cave*.

The potential villains number three in the film: Rachel's manipulating Aunt Lillian, her uncouth swine of an uncle, Arthur, and their bitter, vindictive daughter, Nora (Brenda Scott, *Simon, King of the Witches*). At least two of these people are psychic, and at least two of them have bad intentions toward Rachel. And all three wear round eyeglasses. Sorting out the various roles is not entirely possible until the final seconds of the movie, unless the viewer is psychic as well.

Among the many arresting images the film has to offer are the talking, bleeding bust of Rachel's husband, and the decidedly creepy ghost of Aunt Lillian. Although the film is bursting with well-intentioned creativity, the experience of watching *Sweet, Sweet Rachel* is to enter a funhouse of ideas, whose foremost reward is coming out the other end intact.

CAST: Alex Dreier, Pat Hingle, Louise Latham, Steve Ihnat, Brenda Scott, Chris Robinson, Stefanie Powers, Richard Bull, Mark Tapscott, John Hillerman, William Bryant, John Alvin, and Rod McCarey.

CREDITS: Director: Sutton Roley; Teleplay: Anthony Lawrence; Music: Laurence Rosenthal; Production: American Broadcasting Company; Vehicles provided by Chrysler Corporation; Running Time: 71 minutes; Air Date: 10/2/71; Network: ABC

Tarantulas: The Deadly Cargo

A plane carrying coffee beans—and, unbeknownst to the pilots, tarantulas—from Ecuador crash lands in a field outside of Finleyville, "The Home of the Tree-Ripened Oranges." The deadly spiders naturally make for the town's fruit warehouse, killing people along the way. Rather than damaging the valuable crop by spraying pesticides, the locals pipe in the sound of wasps, which immobilizes the spiders, and a team goes in to pick them up. However, an accident knocks out the power, stopping the wasp noise, which revives the spiders and traps the people inside.

A tedious and silly disaster film with a third-tier cast, this telefright competes with *Terror Out of the Sky* (the dreadful sequel to the interesting *The Savage Bees*) as the least effective bug horror film made for television. For reasons best known to industry insiders, *Tarantulas* was nominated for Emmys in the Film Sound Editing and Film Sound Mixing categories. It didn't win.

And it won't win many fans either, even in the so-bad-it's-good category. Contrived from beginning to end, *Tarantulas* features no standout performances (or hammy has-been stars chewing the scenery), no suspenseful moments, and no exciting death-by-spider scenes. It was shot without benefit of an interesting location, and its pacing is best described as lackadaisical.

Despite these drawbacks, the film is, surprisingly, not a total loss. The opening scenes are the highlight, as two hot dog pilots, Buddy (Tom Atkins) and Fred (Howard Hesseman), are preparing to fly 9,300 ill-gotten pounds of coffee (conveniently, already roasted) to San Francisco. In order to pay one last "export fee," the hard-drinking buddies smuggle three paying Ecuadorians aboard the doomed plane. Thanks mostly to Hesseman's amusing charisma, the film actually takes off as scheduled. But when the plane crashes in Finleyville, it takes the movie with it. Hesseman is a cult figure even as a success on mainstream television. He started out as a member of the improvisational comedy troupe "The Committee," but got his first big break in the film *Billy Jack*. However, he will always have a place in the hearts of a generation of television watchers

Theatrical release poster for *Tarantulas: The Deadly Cargo* (1977).

A Taste of Evil

as the DJ, Dr. Johnny Fever, on the hit series *WKRP in Cincinnati*.

The two biggest names in the rest of the cast are Claude Akins as the fire chief and Pat Hingle as the retired doctor. The younger set is represented by soap opera star Charles Frank and Deborah Winters, who had a short career that included the cult film *Blue Sunshine* and the unexceptional horror flick, *The Outing*.

The viewer will notice that the mayor, who doubles as production manager at the warehouse, uses a cane for walking. The actor's name is Bert Remsen, and he uses a cane because back in 1964, he broke his back and nearly died on the set of the *No Time for Sergeants* television series, when a crane fell on him. The accident put him out of acting for many years, but he worked as a casting director after recuperating. Later, director Robert Altman gave him a role in *Brewster McCloud*, and he continued to work for the director on many of his films.

The scientific spider details mentioned in the film are not too far from accurate. The deadly cargo are identified as "Phoneutria nigriventer," a genuine, poisonous South American spider commonly known as the "wandering spider." The expert in the film claims they are the most aggressive and venomous spiders in the world. Actually that honor (if any spider can truly be described thusly) goes to its close cousin, "Phoneutria fera," but this is a fine point indeed. He also says they are called banana spiders, which is not true. Of course, there are many types of spiders used in the film, including many of the manufactured variety to beef up the numbers.

This was the final film in the short career of director Stuart Hagmann (*The Strawberry Statement*). The music is by Mundell Lowe, a jazz musician known for his scores for better films such as *Billy Jack* and *Everything You Always Wanted to Know About Sex But Were Afraid to Ask*.

CAST: Claude Akins, Charles Frank, Deborah Winters, Bert Remsen, Sandy McPeak, Pat Hingle, Tom Atkins, Howard Hesseman, John Harkins, Charles Siebert, Penelope Windust, Edwin Owens, Alex Colon, Lanny Horn, Jerome Guardino, Jorge Cervera, Jr., Noelle North, Bill Striglos, Steve Bonino, Mary-Nancy Burnett, Bill Erwin, Anita Keith, Iris Korn, Matthew Laborteaux, John Medici, Ruben Moreno, Joseph Reale, and Laird Williamson.

CREDITS: Director: Stuart Hagmann; Teleplay: John Groves and Guerdon Trueblood; Music: Mundell Lowe; Production: Alan Landsburg Productions; Running Time: 96 minutes; Air Date: 12/28/77; Network: CBS

A Taste of Evil

Young Susan Wilcox (Barbara Parkins) returns home from treatment in Switzerland, seven years after being raped in her playhouse as a child. After her father died, Susan's mother Miriam (Barbara Stanwyck) married family friend, Harold Jennings (William Windom), who has a reputation for drinking. Susan doesn't remember her attacker but she suspects it was Harold. In the next few days, Susan has several frightening experiences, but no one, not even her doctor, the concerned Michael Lomas (Roddy McDowall), believes her. One day, Susan finds a body in the underbrush. When the supposed corpse grabs her leg, Susan flees to the playhouse, grabbing a shotgun left by the handyman. When Harold, who has just returned from a business trip, comes to look for her, Susan shoots and kills him. But this is not the end of the deepening mystery surrounding the tormented Susan.

From the pen of Hammer Films' Jimmy Sangster comes this twisting gothic mystery, directed by the dependable John Llewellyn Moxey. Viewers familiar with psychological terrors will smell a plot against the vulnerable Susan almost immediately. But the enjoyment here is in the telling, and in the performances of a fine cast. With a good half-hour left in the show, a major twist reveals Susan's attacker, which leaves the final reels for a sweet comeuppance. If one ignores the little logic holes and forgives the minor manipulations, this is a rewarding, enjoyable suspense film.

Barbara Parkins is fine as the beleaguered Susan, her façade of strength giving way quickly under the weight of returning horrors. But this is just as much Barbara Stanwyck's show, as the mother who has grown distant from her child. Familiar character actor Arthur O'Connell, as the handyman John, shines in a sympathetic performance, and Roddy McDowall suspiciously skirts the periphery as Dr. Lomas.

The great William Windom as Harold is, unfortunately, not given enough to do here. The ever-disheveled Windom has never lacked for work, appearing in seemingly every television show on the air since the mid–50s. His first series was *The Farmer's Daughter* in the early 60s, with the ill-fated Ingrid Stevens, but many more remember the James Thurber–inspired *My World and Welcome to It*, a brilliant comedy, too sophisticated for network executives, for which he won an Emmy. Windom also had a long run from the mid–80s to the mid–90s as Dr. Hazlitt in *Murder She Wrote*. His film roles include the prosecutor in *To Kill a Mockingbird*, the Frank Sinatra oddity *The Detective*, Robert Altman's *Brewster McCloud*, *Escape from the Planet of the Apes*, and an uncredited role in *Planes, Trains & Automobiles*. Windom's guest shot as Commodore Matt Decker on the original *Star Trek* is still appreciated by fans of the show, and one of his finest hours is the *Night Gallery* episode "They're Tearing Down Tim Riley's Bar," a Rod Serling–scripted nostalgia piece considered the series' best.

Thick with gothic atmosphere in the second half, *A Taste of Evil* is reminiscent of many of the psychological thrillers that Sangster wrote in the early 1960s. Neither a classic nor simply derivative, it is a comfortable, competent example.

CAST: Barbara Stanwyck, Barbara Parkins, Roddy McDowall, William Windom, Arthur O'Connell, Bing Russell, and Dawn Frame. CREDITS: Director: John Llewellyn Moxey; Teleplay: Jimmy Sangster; Music: Robert Drasnin; Production: Aaron Spelling Productions; Automobiles furnished by General Motors Corp.; Running Time: 71 minutes; Air Date: 5/13/72; Network: ABC

Terror in the Sky

Anyone who's seen *Airplane!* knows the plot of *Terror in the Sky*—it was obviously the primary inspiration for the popular comedy. But while *Terror in the Sky* is ripe for parody, with much unintentional humor in situation and dialogue, it is also fast-moving, well-acted and exciting.

Ex-Vietnam helicopter pilot George Spencer (Doug McClure) barely makes a chartered flight from Minneapolis to Seattle. When a "violent, deadly form" of food poisoning incapacitates the pilots and many of the passengers, it is up to the reluctant Spencer to bring the plane down in Seattle, with a little help from ground control.

Rather than the bloated, star-studded air disaster film one would expect, *Terror in the Sky* has only a few choice roles filled with second-tier actors, and manages to wrap things up in a sprightly 75 minutes. Compared to many of its top-heavy brethren, there is only a sprinkling of human drama, and the action focuses instead on the formidable mechanics of landing the T400 aircraft. *Terror in the Sky* is actually a remake of the 1957 film *Zero Hour*, which was itself a big screen version of the television drama "Flight into Danger."

Food on commercial flights is going the way of the dodo, so it may come as a shock when flight attendant Janet Turner (Lois Nettleton) takes dinner orders for either lamb chops or chicken pot pie. However, when she mentions the airline has never used this caterer before, modern flyers will count the decreasing amenities as a blessing. Nettleton is terrific as the optimistic stewardess corralled into helping Spencer in the cockpit. (Pointing at the co-pilot's seat, Spencer says to Turner, "Put it there, you've just been made assistant hero.")

Since there's no first class section on the small plane, Dr. Ralph Baird (Roddy McDowall) is stuck with hard-partying football fans (Keenan Wynn is the main troublemaker here). When folks start getting sick, Baird volunteers to assist in whatever way he can. After pilot Wilson (Ken Tobey, *The*

Thing from Another World) and co-pilot Stewart (Sam Melville, *The Rookies*) succumb to the food poisoning, Baird muses on the chances that one of the passengers can help: "All we have to hope for is that one of them knows how to fly a plane, and hasn't had chicken for dinner." Even more comical is the off-hand way Baird chooses to make the announcement so as not to alarm the passengers: "Oh, there's one more thing … is there anyone on board with any flying experience at all?"

But this is Doug McClure's show all the way. His Spencer is scared clear down to his shoes when he realizes he can't possibly back out of the practically impossible job of bringing the plane down. Sitting in the pilot's chair, Spencer—and the viewer—is overwhelmed with the vast number of gauges, buttons and lights that must be contended with in a very short time. In one of the intended moments of humor, Spencer looks at Turner and says, "I don't want to stunt your growing confidence in me but where is the radio?" Later, weary of the unimaginable stress, Spencer describes the flight as "a wagonload of corpses" in one of the film's more descriptive metaphors. In what could be his best performance ever, McClure puts the viewer in the pilot's seat, convincing us it is the scariest seat on the plane. Six years later in *SST—Death Flight*, McClure would again play the washed-up pilot pressed back into service.

The baby-faced McClure made a career of playing young sidekicks, even into his 40s. He started playing in westerns, as most everyone did in 1950s television; this culminated in his role of Trampas for the entire run of *The Virginian*. None of his other series (*Search*, *The Barbary Coast*, etc.) matched the length or popularity of that one, but McClure worked steadily as a guest star on other series and in telefilms until his death of lung cancer in 1995. His film roles include *Gidget*, *Shenandoah*, the telefright *Satan's Triangle*, *The Land That Time Forgot*, *At the Earth's Core*, *The People That Time Forgot*, *Warlords of Atlantis*, *Humanoids from the Deep*, *The House Where Evil Dwells* and *Tapeheads*.

Leif Erickson is experienced pilot Marty Treleaven, who talks Spencer down. Erickson is confidence personified here, a rock solid presence as he calmly explains the instruments and delivers instructions. Jack Ging really gets into his role as the no-nonsense controller who thinks of everything. His rapid-fire *Dragnet*-style of barking orders is priceless.

At the darkest moment, Keenan Wynn sums up the situation for the rest of the wondering passengers: "The two pilots are sick and the boy in the blue jeans is flying the airplane." Viewers should have no fear, however, to join this surprisingly effective and enjoyable flight.

CAST: (ao) Leif Erickson, Doug McClure, Roddy McDowall, Lois Nettleton, and Keenan Wynn. Also Jack Ging, Sam Melville, Leonard Stone, Sidney Clute, Christopher Dark, Loretta Leversee, Patricia Mattick, Victor Izay, Kenneth Tobey, Ed McCready, Kit Woodhouse, Sue Casey, Marvin Dean Stewart, Renny Roker, David Frank, Robert Dowdell, and Lee Stanley.

CREDITS: Director: Bernard L. Kowalski; Teleplay: Stephen & Elinor Karpf and Dick Nelson, from a story by Arthur Hailey; Music: Pat Williams; Production: Paramount Television; Vehicles furnished by Chrysler Corporation; Running Time: 75 minutes; Air Date: 9/17/71; Network: CBS

Terror on the Beach

Neil Glynn (Dennis Weaver) takes his family—wife Arlene (Estelle Parsons), son Steve (Kristopher Tabori) and daughter DeeDee (Susan Dey)—on a camping holiday. On the way, the family is run off the road by some hippies in an old fire truck and a dune buggy, but Neil declines to involve the police. Once at their beach destination, the Glynns settle in, but are soon involved in an escalating campaign of terror by the same group of kids. After their van is sabotaged, the family is determined to survive the ordeal by turning the tables on their tormentors.

The horror subgenre that focuses on

Susan Dey is threatened by two masked thugs in *Terror on the Beach* (1973).

terrorized families trapped in remote locations is an acquired taste, to be sure. The most famous example is, of course, Wes Craven's *The Hills Have Eyes*, but there have been any number of films made before and since that revel in roughly the same aspect. *Terror on the Beach* is a fairly benign example that seems to want to warn Americans not to venture outside the safety of the suburbs, or they'll be fair game for hooligans with nothing better to do than menace the traditional family unit.

The familial tensions on display in the early going have a comic book depth at best. Son Steve doesn't want to go back to college, which ruffles the feathers of his father, Neil. Daughter DeeDee chides her mother, Arlene, about women's lib and subservience. Tired of the general discord, Arlene urges her clan to "start behaving like a civilized family," which apparently means singing songs around the campfire.

The uncivilized "family" of television hippies is led by the charismatic Jerry (Scott Hylands), a Manson-like (but cleaner) anarchist with no greater agenda on his mind but to raise a little hell. Surprisingly, this occasionally takes the form of moderately sophisticated psychological warfare. The scene where Neil is fooled by a swimmer's distress calls—which turn out to be a mannequin dressed in his daughter's clothes—has a sense of the surreal about it. The scene where the hippies start playing a record of jungle sounds late at night, and then feed the family's reaction back through the speakers (the hippies bugged the Glynns' van), takes on an interesting flavor of the bizarre despite the lack of believability.

The family's beach terror survival routine includes rigging up trip wires with cans and bottles to warn of the hippies' encroachment, and setting up lights to blind the intruders, followed by throwing sharp objects at them. Eventually, Neil backs off his pacifist stance and solves the problem with his fists, by duking it out with Jerry. In the meantime however, there is much chasing of the women with the dune buggies, until one hippie falls from his vehicle and is captured by the family. In a small victory for civilization, DeeDee cleans the man's wounds instead of making an example of him.

Weaver recaps his everyman-under-pressure role, and Parsons doesn't have to stretch much either as the long-suffering mom. Tabori has a little more to work with as the son with growing pains, but the only highlight with the DeeDee character is a shot of Susan Dey in a bikini.

The captured hippie is played by Henry Olek, who debuted in the outrageous exploitation entry *The Pink Angels*, about transvestite bikers. One of the female troupe is Roberta Collins, who worked the exploitation market almost exclusively in the 1970s with roles in *The Big Doll House*, *Eaten Alive*, *Women in Cages*, *Death Race 2000*, *Caged Heat*, and many more. Billy Goldenberg overdoes it with his spooky soundtrack for this Paul Wendkos film, which turns out to be more irritating than illuminating.

CAST: Dennis Weaver, Estelle Parsons, Kristoffer Tabori, Scott Hylands, Susan Dey, Michael Christian, Henry Olek, Roberta Collins, Jackie Giroux, Betsy Slade, Carol Ita White, David Knapp, and Walter Beakel.

CREDITS: Director: Paul Wendkos; Teleplay: Bill Svanoe; Music: Billy Goldenberg; Production: Bedford Pictures, Inc.; Running Time: 74 minutes; Air Date: 9/18/73; Network: CBS

Terror on the 40th Floor

It's Christmas Eve in Los Angeles, and the hard liquor is flowing freely at an office party in a skyscraper. After the party, seven people remain behind to extend the celebration. When a drunken maintenance man starts a fire, the seven are trapped on the top floor while firefighters, who don't realize there are still people in the building, try unsuccessfully to get the blaze under control.

A blatant swipe of *The Towering Inferno*, *Terror on the 40th Floor* lacks all the positive attributes of the blockbuster disaster film. Aside from a few impressive pyrotechnics, this is simply a routine smoke opera.

The couplings begin with executive vice-president Dan Overland (John Forsythe) and calculating seductress Darlene Foster (Anjanette Comer). Via flashback we learn that Overland is struggling through a difficult time with his wife, Thelma (Pippa Scott), since the death of their son.

Howard Foster (Joseph Campanella) is bucking for promotion, so he entices Ginger Macklin (Laurie Heineman, *As the World Turns*) to open her personnel files for him. Foster's flashback reveals that he's a shallow, grasping man, so after he discovers in the files that he's not getting his promotion, he attempts to rectify the situation, and volunteers to go down the elevator shaft to try to get into the floor below. He falls to his death.

Salesman Kelly Freeman (Don Meredith, with loud sport jacket) puts the moves on star-struck Betty Carson (Kelly Jean Peters). Kelly's a coward, so he doesn't get a flashback. Loner Lee Parker (Lynn Carlin) does get one, however. We learn that she's pregnant, and her boyfriend isn't happy about it. Carlin was Oscar-nominated for her debut in John Cassavetes' *Faces*, and she was in the cult shocker *Deathdream*.

The home video release of *Terror on the 40th Floor* is missing a reel early in the action, which explains why the film runs 85 minutes instead of the approximately 95 minutes it should. It would appear that a tense confrontation between Overland and Foster about Foster's promotion was in that missing reel, as well as some explanation of why the telephones don't work, etc. Not that it makes much difference, frankly. This tired effort from director Jerry Jameson would be of little interest even at its original length.

Fans of Mel Brooks' *Young Frankenstein* will appreciate the cameo by Danny Goldman, who was the student chiding Gene Wilder in the classroom about the pronunciation of "Frahnkensteen."

CAST: John Forsythe, Joseph Campanella, Lynn Carlin, Anjanette Comer, Laurie Heineman, Don Meredith, Kelly Jean Peters, Pippa Scott, Louis Guss, Hank Brandt, John Finnegan,

(Left to right) Joseph Campanella, Anjanette Comer and Lynn Carlin hope to survive a skyscraper fire in *Terror on the 40th Floor* (1974).

Danny Goldman, Mark Tapscott, Bob Hastings, Tracie Savage, Kevin Nudis, Dean Santoro, Tracy Brooks Swope, Tim Herbert, Art Lewis and Norman Alden.

CREDITS: Director: Jerry Jameson; Teleplay: Jack Turley, based on a story by Edward J. Montagne and Jack Turley; Music: Vic Mizzy; Production: Montagne Productions; Running Time: 85 minutes; Air Date: 9/17/74; Network: NBC

Terror Out of the Sky

AKA The Revenge of the Savage Bees

Jeannie Devereaux (Tovah Feldshuh), now working at the National Bee Center, is still haunted by her experience in *The Savage Bees*. When one of the employees is killed by swarming bees, Devereaux and her boss, David Martin (Efrem Zimbalist, Jr.), discover the deadly strain of South American bee has somehow infiltrated the Center's hives. The hives are destroyed, but three queens have already been shipped out. Devereaux and Martin enlist the help of her pilot boyfriend, Nick Willis (Dan Haggerty), to use his plane to track down the shipments. The trio is successful twice, but the third queen has already created a swarm of killers headed directly toward a small California community.

Instead of New Orleans during Mardi Gras, the killer bees threaten a middle-of-nowhere dirt league baseball game in this impoverished and unnecessary sequel to *The Savage Bees*. Writer Guerdon Trueblood returns to lower the ante (but undoubtedly raise his salary) with a dreary, shameless film completely lacking in suspense and star power. Director Lee H. Katzin does what he can with the material but *Terror Out of the Sky* is hopeless.

Scenes from *The Savage Bees* kick off the film, as the new Jeannie Devereaux has nightmares about driving that bee-laiden Volkswagen Beetle into the Superdome. Unfortunately for her (and the viewer), her worst fear will come true again in the open fields around Merced, California, only this time she will drive a school bus covered in bees, and will have a troupe of Boy Scouts along for the ride. Devereaux's boss, David Martin, is played by Efrem Zimbalist, Jr. (*The F.B.I.*), who certainly brings conviction to the role. One scene has an unprotected Zimbalist carrying a loaded hive up a hill with bees swarming all over him, a level of dedication well beyond the call of duty. Martin is in love with Devereaux, but she is torn between him and her current beau, Nick, played by the burly Dan Haggerty, in order to form a pointless love triangle. Haggerty was still riding the fame of his series *The Life and Times of Grizzly Adams* here, before being busted for possession of cocaine in 1984.

Dr. Gary Norman is back as the bee wrangler for the film, and again plays a role, this time as an ill-fated beekeeper. The finale has Martin trying to convince the local yahoos to put off their baseball game because the bees are headed their way. The bees hate colors and noise, so naturally the brightly colored marching band starts up, attracting the bees. Devereaux draws the bees away by honking the horn of a school bus, and then driving the bee-covered vehicle to a dilapidated missile silo. Once there, Martin, trouper that he is, attracts the bees to himself with pheromone, and takes them into the silo's vent tunnels and kills the bees with insecticide. Rather than take a chance that some bees could escape, Martin, who was injured inside the tunnel, opts to stay trapped in the poisoned atmosphere, so Nick gets the girl by default.

Steve Franken, who plays a scientist, had an eco-horror experience with ants in the previous year's *It Happened at Lakewood Manor*. Lonny Chapman is a beekeeper who doesn't want to give up his killer queens, and Ike Eisenmann is one of the Boy Scouts who unwisely joins Devereaux in the bus. This movie is recommended only for very patient bug fans.

Composer William Goldstein, whose scores include the series *Fame*, the Chuck Norris actions pictures *An Eye for an Eye* and *Forced Vengeance*, and Wes Craven's *Shocker*, has achieved some success in the area of electronic music, including music for the first video game with a full-blown score, "King's Quest IV."

CAST: Efrem Zimbalist, Jr., Dan Haggerty, Tovah Feldshuh, Lonny Chapman, Ike Eisenmann, Joe E. Tata, Richard Herd, Charles Hallahan, Bruce French, Steve Franken, Ellen Blake, Gwen Van Dam, Norman Gary, Philip Baker Hall, Poindexter (Yothers), Steve Tannen, Tony La Torre, and Melinda Peterson.

CREDITS: Director: Lee H. Katzin; Teleplay: Guerdon Trueblood and Doris Silverton; Music: William Goldstein; Production: Alan Landsburg Productions, Don Kirshner Productions; Running Time: 94 minutes; Air Date: 12/26/78; Network: CBS

Trapped

AKA **Doberman Patrol**

Robbed, beaten unconscious and left in the men's room of Noonan's Department Store, Chuck Brenner (James Brolin) awakes to find himself locked in, with vicious guard dogs on every floor. Unable to make a phone call, the injured Brenner struggles to outwit the animals in his quest to reach the ground floor. Meanwhile, Brenner's ex-wife Elaine (Susan Clark) and her new husband David Moore (Earl Holliman) search for Brenner when he doesn't show up at the airport to say goodbye to his daughter.

Brolin's other telefright, *Short Walk to Daylight*, was a realistic survivor tale, but *Trapped* is a contrived, exploitive piece, with little to offer in the way of convincing cinema. Frank De Felitta wrote and directed this film that modern viewers will find even harder to believe than did the contemporary audience. De Felitta is best known for writing the novels and screenplays for *The Entity* and *Audrey Rose*, neither being tales dependent on realism.

Right off the bat, the viewer is expected to believe that store employees would not check the men's rooms as part of the closing routine—especially since dogs so vicious that their handlers have to dress like hockey goalies, will be unleashed. Brenner makes it into an office, but the phone only goes to the store's switchboard, a forgivable happenstance given the time period. But when he doesn't have change to use the pay phone, credibility goes out the window, because even in 1973, emergency calls to the operator didn't require a coin.

The escalators are blocked off and a dog is left on each floor; most are Dobermans and one is a white German Shepherd. Brenner manages to lock two of the dogs up (one of them leapt the escalator barrier to join the other) but not before suffering a bite to his leg. Losing blood rapidly, Brenner searches the store for weapons, then sets a mop afire to force another dog into a lockable room. When Brenner finally realizes he should have set off the sprinkler system with the fire, he drops his last match, setting up a scene where he knocks an armoire over on one of the dogs. De Felitta nicely juxtaposes Brenner's scramble to the top of the armoire with a dog's scramble to breach the escalator barrier, but this is one of the few thoughtful cinematic moments of the production.

The finale has Brenner reaching the first floor mezzanine and snagging a bow and arrow set with a fishing pole. Luckily, he had lashed himself to the railing before trying this because he passes out before he can shoot the dog guarding the floor. The dog manages to climb to the mezzanine; with the snarling animal inches away from Brenner's face, the cavalry arrives in the form of the cops and the dog wranglers.

The least probable aspect of the story has to do with Brenner's ex-wife Elaine and her husband David. Elaine and David are leaving for Mexico City with Elaine and Brenner's daughter, Carrie. Brenner was supposed to show up at the airport with a doll for Carrie but he never arrived. David seems to have a sixth sense about Brenner's predicament, and convinces Elaine to skip the international flight and go looking in bars for Brenner (who has a history of drunken disappearing acts). The whole point of this is, of course, to have someone to rescue Brenner, but it hardly qualifies as believable.

This may be considered a cheap shot, but for the bulk of the film Susan Clark sports a noticeable canker sore on her lip that the filmmakers try to disguise in various ways. She hides her face behind a food menu even while delivering her lines, covers up her lip with a drinking glass at one point, and with a phone at another. Director De Felitta obliges by shooting her from the other side, or keeping her mouth in shadow. It almost becomes amusing except for the embarrassment this must have caused Clark.

The department store clerk, Miss Havemayer, is played by Ivy Jones, who just happens to be De Felitta's daughter. The bartender queried by Elaine and David will be recognized by most viewers. He is Bob Hastings, an ubiquitous character actor of the time, who shows up in the telefrights *Terror on the 40th Floor* and *Conspiracy of Terror*. Hastings is also the voice of Commissioner Gordon on the animated *Batman* series.

Credited as animal supervisor is Lou Schumacher, who provided similar services in the genre films *Night of the Lepus* and *Kingdom of the Spiders*, among others. He also owned the dog used in *A Boy and His Dog*. "Animal Action" is credited to Karl Miller, trainer for many films, including (in the 70s) *The Doberman Gang*, *They Only Kill Their Masters*, *Dracula's Dog*, and another James Brolin film, *The Amityville Horror*.

CAST: James Brolin, Susan Clark, Earl Holliman, Robert Hooks, Ivy Jones, Bob Hastings, Tammy Harrington, Marco Lopez, Erica Hagen, Mary Robinson, and Elliot Lindsey.

CREDITS: Writer-Director: Frank De Felitta; Music: Gil Melle; Production: Universal TV; Running Time: 74 minutes; Air Date: 11/14/73; Network: ABC

Trilogy of Terror

AKA **Tales of Terror; Terror of the Doll**

Trilogy of Terror arrived midway through the 1970s, Dan Curtis's decade of glory. The anthology proved quite popular, riding primarily on the third story, and Curtis would repeat the format, if not the success, two years later with *Dead of Night*. Each of the three stories stars Karen Black and comes with the required twist ending—which will not be revealed here. The one exception is the second story, "Millicent and Therese," since the twist will surprise no one, and that fact is a point of discussion.

In "Julie," plain–Jane literature teacher Julie (Black) catches the eye of student Chad (Robert Burton), who convinces her to join him at the drive-in movies. Chad slips Julie a mickey, and takes her to a motel where he photographs her in compromising positions, having his way with her as well. Chad uses the photos to blackmail Julie into debauchery, but Chad will soon get the surprise of his life.

The second-best story of the bunch, "Julie" has a clever twist that may surprise more than a few. This little tale of manipulation is hampered only by the network broadcast standards, which wouldn't allow a more detailed depiction of the time that Julie spends under Chad's corrupt imagination. That aside, Black is convincing as the beleaguered Julie, and soap opera regular Burton is fine as the devious Chad. Curtis used Burton again in *The Curse of the Black Widow*.

Chad takes Julie to "an old vampire movie, all in French with English subtitles … a classic." The film turns out to be Curtis's own *The Night Stalker*, shown in black and white. (Whether the few snippets of French heard correspond correctly to the film clip is anyone's guess.) The shot of the drive-in screen showing the film is accomplished with simple camera trickery. The other in-joke is played when Chad registers as "Mr. and Mrs. Jonathan Harker" at the motel. Chad, like Harker, is an unknowing victim.

Chad's buddy, Eddie, is played by *Dark Shadows* alumni Jim Storm, and the young man showing up for tutoring at the end of the story is Gregory Harrison, in his first credited role. Harrison would go on to play Logan in the *Logan's Run* series and Gonzo Gates in *Trapper John, MD*.

In "Millicent and Therese," spinster Millicent lives with her Satanic sister, blonde bombshell Therese (both played by Black), who corrupts the souls of her suitors. Millicent's only respite from the torment of the evil Therese is to detour the girl's lovers before it is too late for them. Finally, Millicent hits on the idea of using Therese's own methods against her, fashioning a voodoo doll in one last desperate attempt to end Therese's escapades.

The twist in this story of dual personalities cannot possibly fool anyone. The fact that Black plays both sisters is obvious since very little effort is expended to disguise the actress in either role. The viewer, already gleaning this, may expect the twist to reveal that the two sisters are indeed different actresses. But no. So it should be fair to wonder about the point of all this. Perhaps the audience is expected simply to marvel at Black's acting skills. It would be impossible for Curtis to think he was pulling the wool over anyone's eyes, so it may be best to call it a bad job and move on.

Again, the subject of sexual deviancy is prevalent, with mentions of incest and sado-masochistic cavorting. These are somehow tied to Satanism, another misstep of the filmmakers. When Millicent confronts Therese's current conquest, Thomas, with his and her sister's wickedness, he says to Millicent, "I'm afraid you're the one that really needs help." He doesn't realize how true that is since he is unknowingly addressing both women. Thomas is played by Curtis

Karen Black in one of her four roles in *Trilogy of Terror* **(1975).**

regular John Karlen, and the little girl whose doll is broken by Therese is even closer to the director: she's his daughter.

In "Amelia," Amelia (Black) buys a Zuni fetish doll for her new beau on his birthday. Planning to give the gift to him that night, Amelia must first cancel her standing date with her oppressive mother. After the difficult phone call to her mom, Amelia thinks twice and cancels her evening with her boyfriend. In the meantime, the chain that prevents the doll from coming to life—according to the scroll that came with it—falls off, and Amelia is suddenly under attack by the little monster known as He Who Kills.

This is the story everyone remembers, and it is the strongest of the three by far. Richard Matheson based his screenplay on his own short story, "Prey." (The other two stories were Matheson's as well but were adapted for the small screen by William F. Nolan.) The relentless pursuit of Amelia by He Who Kills is supremely frightening, and deftly handled by Curtis. But Matheson brings elements to the story which are often overlooked. Amelia's deeply troubled relationship with her mother, which bleeds over to her mishandling of the new boyfriend, suggests that Amelia is unstable at best, but more than likely psychotic. It would not be too far-fetched to propose that the attack and the aftermath are products of her diseased mind, not supernatural forces. Amelia's remark while looking at the doll—"Even your mother wouldn't love you"—implies that she is identifying a bit too closely with the repulsive thing, and that she is shortly to succumb to an internal demon.

Psychology aside, the majority of the segment is good, clean macabre fun. The way the Zuni carries the knife in its toothy little mouth as it climbs up her bedspread, or the cringe-inducing moment when Amelia tries to grab the knife blade as the beast is sawing through the suitcase, or when the little beggar gets her by the neck, are just some of the premium shocks. This short masterwork carries the entire film into classic status.

CAST: Karen Black, Robert Burton, John Karlen, George Gaynes, James Storm, Kathryn Reynolds, Orin Cannon, Gregory Harrison, and Tracy Curtis.

CREDITS: Director: Dan Curtis; Teleplay: "Julie" and "Millicent and Therese" by William F. Nolan, based on stories by Richard Matheson, "Amelia" by Richard Matheson, based on his short story "Prey"; Music: Robert Cobert; Production: Dan Curtis Productions; Running Time: 73 minutes; Air Date: 3/4/75; Network: ABC

The Turn of the Screw

Miss Jane Cubberly (Lynn Redgrave) accepts a position as governess to two orphan children, Miles and Flora, at Bligh

House, a remote and rambling house in the country. A growing unease compels Jane to unravel the recent, sordid history of the household. The previous governess, Miss Jessel (Kathryn Scott), and the master's valet, Peter Quint (James Laurenson), were an evil pair, who, before their untimely but well-deserved deaths, were an unhealthy influence on the children. The specters of Quint and Jessel appear to Jane, and the children's increasingly abhorrent behavior leads her to believe the ghosts have returned for Miles and Flora.

The Turn of the Screw was the last of Dan Curtis's interpretations of the classics to air (see *Dracula*, *The Picture of Dorian Gray*). Like the others, it was shot in England on videotape, giving it a flat soap opera look, but his time an authentic period location enhances the sense of realism. Henry James' nineteenth-century story has been adapted many times on film, most famously as 1961's *The Innocents*. Curtis's two-hour version was shown over two nights in the spring of 1974.

Curtis may have been satisfying a personal desire to remake these classic tales, but his talent as a director seemed better suited to the contemporary thriller. *The Turn of the Screw* is slow, talky and hardly as compelling as it should have been. The proper mood never takes hold due, in part, to the lighting requirements of shooting on videotape that make it difficult to create a spooky gothic atmosphere.

Megs Jenkins, reprising her role in *The Innocents* as housekeeper Mrs. Grose, is the most believable of the bunch. As the children, little Eva Griffith plays precocious Flora and, in his debut, Jasper Jacob is the frog-blinding, ant-drowning Miles. Jacob was a last-minute replacement for Mark Lester who wasn't up to the part, and Curtis's decision to cast him is the stuff of great debate. Jacob is older than the Miles described by Henry James which, in this author's opinion, lessens the impact of Miles' amorous advances to Jane, one of the key themes in the story. To make matters worse, Jacob gives an annoying, self-conscious performance, which serves to undermine the efforts of those around him.

New Zealander James Laurenson played Pink's father in *Pink Floyd the Wall*, and Kathryn (Leigh) Scott is another *Dark Shadows* alumnus. A one-time Bunny in the New York Playboy Club, Scott wrote a book, *The Bunny Years*, about her experiences, which was the basis for a documentary film made in 1999. The DVD release of *The Turn of the Screw* includes interviews with Curtis and Redgrave.

CAST: Lynn Redgrave, Megs Jenkins, John Baron, Anthony Lagdon, Kathryn Scott, James Laurenson, Benedict Taylor, Jasper Jacob, and Eva Griffith.

CREDITS: Director: Dan Curtis; Teleplay: William F. Nolan based on the novel by Henry James; Music: Robert Cobert; Production: Dan Curtis Productions; Running Time: 118 minutes; Air Date: 4/15–16/74; Network: ABC

The UFO Incident

AKA **Interrupted Journey**

On September 19, 1961, Barney and Betty Hill (James Earl Jones and Estelle Parsons) returned home to Portsmouth, New Hampshire from their vacation in Montreal. When they arrived, the couple realized they'd lost two hours over the course of their drive. Over the coming months the couple's anxieties increased: Barney's ulcers reached the point where he was advised to take a leave of absence from his work, and Betty had recurring nightmares about being taken aboard a spacecraft. The couple tried to come to grips with the phenomenon by repeatedly driving around the area where they suspected something happened, but their flashes of recollection bring them no peace. Finally, in 1963, Barney and Betty consulted Dr. Benjamin Simon (Barnard Hughes), and underwent separate hypnosis sessions to clear up the couple's amnesia. These sessions revealed a shared experience of abduction by extraterrestrial beings, and medical examinations aboard a UFO.

Based largely on the hypnosis sessions conducted by Dr. Simon (as documented in John G. Fuller's book, *The Interrupted Jour-*

James Earl Jones and two aliens in *The UFO Incident* (1975).

ney), *The UFO Incident* is a fascinating look at one of the most famous cases of alien abduction. Director Richard A. Colla (*Fuzz*) intersperses the sessions with the home life of the Hills, and recreations of the experience. The film takes its time, building the real-life characters beautifully, weaving a tale at once frightening, compelling and hauntingly convincing. Not exploitive in the least, this is not a film for those seeking alien thrills or special effects, but it is undeniably powerful for those with an interest in the subject.

James Earl Jones is excellent as the troubled Barney. The difficulties of an interracial couple in the early sixties weigh heavily on Barney, who is constantly on guard for any perceived bigotry in a country which was just beginning to face the realities of racial strife. The real Barney Hill died of a stroke in 1969 at the age of 46.

Betty is played with a naïve and practical strength by Estelle Parsons, in one of her finest roles. She brings a genuine curiousness to Betty about the experience, and the love and understanding she shows Barney make her character a true heroine. Parsons is best remembered for her Oscar-winning role in 1967's *Bonnie and Clyde* (she was also nominated the next year for *Rachel, Rachel*). She had originally studied to be a lawyer, and that background led her to become the first network political news reporter, on *The Today Show* in the early 50s. Parsons has divided her time between film (Warren Beatty's *Dick Tracy*) and television (*Terror on the Beach*, *Roseanne*) since the 70s.

Barnard Hughes matches the leads with a thoughtful performance as the confused Dr. Simon. Naturally skeptical, Simon is as eventually convinced of the reality of the Hills' story over the course of the therapy.

The most famous artifact of the Hills' experience is the star map drawn by Betty while under hypnosis. At the time of Betty's recall, three stars in the constellation she described were not known to astronomers, nor was the necessary computer power available to accomplish the vast numbers of calculations needed in pinpointing the stars' location. The map remained a mystery for years until technological advances made it possible to identify, with little doubt, just what the map represented: It shows the southern constellation of Reticulum, specifically the Zeta 1 and Zeta 2 Reticuli, 37 light years away, and not visible from the northern hemisphere.

Vic Perrin, who was the Control Voice in the *Outer Limits* series, introduces and closes the film. *The UFO Incident* is a fine example of the power of television to convince in human terms and, without the use of special effects, to describe events visually.

CAST: James Earl Jones, Estelle Parsons, Barnard Hughes, Dick O'Neill, Beeson Carroll, Terrence O'Connor, Jeanne Joe, and Lou Wagner.

CREDITS: Director: Richard A. Colla; Teleplay: Hesper Anderson and Jake Justiz, based on the book *The Interrupted Journey* by John G. Fuller; Music: Billy Goldenberg; Production: Universal TV; Running Time: 92 minutes; Air Date: 10/20/75; Network: NBC

A Vacation in Hell

Four women on a tropical island holiday decide to accompany fellow tourist and ladies man Alan (Michael Brandon) on a day trip of boating. After the inflatable boat is damaged when the troupe later come ashore, they vote to hike their way through the jungle back to the hotel. Soon lost and with darkness approaching, they make camp on the jungle floor. In the middle of the night, when a native boy stumbles upon the group, Alan, thinking they were under attack, kills him. The boy's father discovers the body, and tracks the group through the jungle.

This unrealistic survival story seems to exist for two reasons: one, to articulate the failings of men, fostering a sense of camaraderie and strength amongst the women. The other is to leer at the female body.

Each of the four women has had her difficulties with men. Denise (Priscilla Barnes, *Three's Company*) is the pampered beauty who's skating through life on her looks, and avoiding any meaningful relationship. Barbara (Andrea Marcovicci, *The Hand*) suffered abuse as a child from her father, and wants to take it out on every man she meets. Evelyn (Barbara Feldon, *Get Smart*) is working her way through a troubled divorce. Her nubile daughter, Margret (Maureen McCormick, *The Brady Bunch*) is confused by her mother's negativity towards men. (Interestingly, director David Greene [*The Shuttered Room*] had his own travails with the opposite sex. He was married seven times.)

The male contingent is represented by ineptitude and savagery. Wolf and liar Alan got the women into the mess by bribing the club's boatman so he could take Denise out without having to return the boat. Hence, when disaster strikes, the group could not depend on the club sending help. Alan is the one who deepens the group's trouble by killing the boy, who was entranced by Denise's mirror. When the boy's father shows up, Alan shoots himself in the foot with the rifle the boy was carrying. The Hunter (Ed Ka'ahea), as his character is called, had left his son alone in the jungle with the gun, in some sort of manhood ritual that involved the boy killing a wild boar.

The unnamed tropical paradise of the film looks suspiciously like an Hawaiian island, and the hotel is called Club Horizon (an obvious nod to the popular Club Med), whose isolated slices of civilization protect the tourists from the "real" islands on which they're built. If there's any moral to the story, it must be to never leave the safety of people like yourselves because it's a jungle out there.

Quotable dialogue is one of the few highlights of the film. When the distrustful Barbara tells Denise that she doesn't need a man to feel good about herself, Denise replies, "Then what are you doing here?" As Evelyn muses about her divorce, she tells Denise that her husband left her for another woman who "looked a bit like you." Again Denise delivers the zinger: "Oh yes, they often do." Near the end, with the native man approaching, Barbara vows to kill him because he's sure to kill them; "He's a man, isn't he?" Indeed, two people don't make it back to the club but neither was intended to die by the hands of the "savage."

The camera tends to leer at the female flesh of Barnes and McCormick, sometimes embarrassingly so. McCormick as the sexy, 16-year-old Margret (McCormick was actually 23) has the strangest scene in the movie. She gets a little tipsy on some rum that Denise brought along in a flask, and dances around the jungle in slow motion, stripping down but growing up into a woman. Another strange moment occurs when the women stumble upon a ruin and enter it to escape the torrential rain. When they make a fire, Margret declares them the four elements, and the women bond as they sing "London's Burning." The non-ending will frustrate those who expected some sort of payoff, but the wisest of viewers won't have bothered in the first place.

CAST: (ao) Priscilla Barnes, Barbara Feldon, Maureen McCormick and Andrea Marcovicci. Also Michael Brandon and Ed Ka'ahea.

CREDITS: Director: David Greene; Teleplay: Shelley Katz and D.B. Ledrov; Music: Gil Melle; Production: David Greene Productions; Running Time: 97 minutes; Air Date: 5/21/79; Network: NBC

Vampire

Husband and wife architects John and Leslie Rawlins (Jason Miller and Kathryn Harrold) have just completed the design of a new church. Just as the groundbreaking was to begin, the mysterious Anton Voytek (Richard Lynch), who claims to own the land, hires the Rawlins to excavate the site to look for millions of dollars worth of lost artworks buried there decades before. When word of the value of the art reaches authorities, Voytek is arrested. Voytek vows revenge on the Rawlins for breaking his trust, and soon Leslie is found dead in a manner suggestive of a vampire. Meanwhile, the remains of a priest, a long-lost friend of retired cop Harry Kilcoyne (E.G. Marshall), are found at the site. Rawlins and Kilcoyne team up to track the vampire in the hopes of destroying him.

Overshadowed by the bloated *Salem's Lot*, which aired the following month, the lean and moody *Vampire* is an uptown take on the fabled monster. It was written by the team responsible for the popular series *Hill Street Blues*, Steven Bochco and Michael Kozoll, and was stylishly directed by veteran E.W. Swackhamer. The director makes the best of the San Francisco–area locations, which lend a seasonal look to this unsold series pilot.

As in any vampire tale, credibility lies with the monster, and *Vampire* strikes gold in that department with the casting of Richard Lynch as the charismatic Anton Voytek. The face of the fair-haired Lynch has a curious combination of attraction and repulsion supremely suited to the sophisticated bloodsucker.

The role of Voytek is Lynch's favorite to date. The Brooklyn-born actor spent many years on the New York stage before his film debut in the critically acclaimed *Scarecrow* (1973). Since that time, he has had many roles, usually as a villain, in television and in exploitation and action pictures. Among these are the gritty cop thriller *The Seven-Ups*, the odd horror film *The Premonition*, Larry Cohen's *God Told Me To*, the telefright *Good Against Evil*, *The Sword and the Sorcerer* and Ruggero Deodato's *Cut and Run*. The scarring that is occasionally noticeable on Lynch's face and neck were a result of setting himself on fire while under the influence of LSD in 1967. Somewhat of a renaissance man, Lynch can play several musical instruments and speak multiple languages.

In a curious and welcome disregard of the youth market, Voytek's sworn enemies are played by mature stars, Jason Miller and E.G. Marshall. Miller will forever be known for his first film role, as Father Karras in *The Exorcist*. Here, he brings a palpable weight of despair to the role of Rawlins, who loses his wife to the vampire. If it weren't for his determination to destroy Voytek, Rawlins would most assuredly have destroyed himself. Marshall is splendid as the practical Kilcoyne, who focuses Rawlins on their common goal. Marshall gave seemingly effortless performances, whether his character was on the side of good or evil.

Humorless and gothic, *Vampire* has more than its share of striking images: the shadow of the unveiled cross that marks the site of the new church scorching the earth beneath it, Voytek's classic and powerful emergence from that spot of ground, Voytek running down the empty streets at dawn, his clothing smoking as tries to beat the sun back to his coffin, John discovering the body of his wife, the spooky lairs of the vampire, etc. Of course, this being 1979, there must be a disco scene (and a mention of cocaine), but for the most part, *Vampire* has a timeless quality about it.

The supporting cast includes Barrie Youngfellow (who was in the horror fandom film *Nightmare in Blood*) as Kilcoyne's neighbor, and Adam Farrar (Leonardo DiCaprio's stepbrother) as her son. Jessica Walter doesn't have enough to do as Voytek's lawyer, nor does Kathryn Harrold (*Nightwing*) as Leslie Rawlins. Aficionados will note the surprising cameo by cult actor Joe Spinell (*Maniac*) as Captain Desher.

Composer Fred Karlin was nominated for Oscars four times, winning once for the song "For All We Know" that was heard in *Lovers and Other Strangers*. His other scores include *Up the Down Staircase*, *Westworld* and its sequel *Futureworld*, and the telefright *Bad Ronald*.

CAST: Jason Miller, Richard Lynch, E.G. Marshall, Kathryn Harrold, Barrie Youngfellow, Michael Tucker, Jonelle Allen, Jessica Walter, David Hooks, Wendy Cutler, Joe Spinell, Stu Klitsner, Scott Paulin, Byron Webster, Brendon Dillon, Herb Braha, Adam Starr, Tony Perez, Nicholas Gunn, and Ray K. Goman.

CREDITS: Director: E.W. Swackhamer; Teleplay: Steven Bocho and Michael Kozoll; Music: Fred Karlin; Production: MTM Enterprises; Running Time: 90 minutes; Air Date: 10/7/79; Network: ABC

The Victim

AKA **Out of Contention**

Concerned for her sister Susan, who's having marital problems, Kate Wainwright (Elizabeth Montgomery) drives down in a rainstorm from San Francisco to Monterey to see her. When Kate arrives, Susan is nowhere to be found, so Kate makes herself at home thinking her sister will show up soon. What Kate doesn't know is that Susan has been killed, and her body is in the basement. Kate slowly realizes that something is wrong, and that she may very well be in danger herself.

This blatant and poorly executed Hitchcockian exercise has only one thing going for it: the lovely and talented Elizabeth Montgomery. Without her, *The Victim* would be just another forgotten, inept thriller. Director Herschel Daugherty has no feel for suspense (see *She Cried Murder* for further evidence), but Montgomery tries to pick up the slack as best she can, in her first film after the long-running *Bewitched* series.

The initial tip-off that the film is treading a well-worn path comes early, just after Susan (Jess Walton, *You'll Never See Me Again*) gets off the phone with Kate. Susan turns to the camera and says, "What're you doing here?" with a frightened look on her face. The suspects have just been narrowed down considerably.

The pacing in the film is miserable. When Kate stops for gas in the pouring rain, she gets out of her car and runs over to use the pay phone, not once but twice, and for no good reason. But the worst example is the number of times Daugherty sends Kate down into the basement where the body is hidden. The first time, the audience is shown Susan's body shoved into a trunk. The second time, the routine is repeated exactly. The third time, a point-of-view shot implies someone is down there. The fourth time, we see the body is gone. The fifth time, it doesn't matter anyway: the situation has become laughable.

Oscar and Emmy winner Eileen Heckart plays Mrs. Hawkes, the housekeeper. She's cranky and perhaps a bit off her rocker, so she's prime suspect material. Heckart brings much more to her role than she needs to, which adds a little color to the predictable proceedings. Susan's friend, Edith (Sue Ane Langdon), calls twice while Kate is there. She serves only the purpose of exposition.

Over the course of the evening, Kate discovers that her sister's car is still there (another trip out into the rain to check it), as well as her keys and purse. When she calls Susan's husband Ben (George Maharis) at his office, she is told he hasn't worked there in a month, but he never told Susan that. The phone line is cut and the power is shut off from, where else, the basement. By this time, the viewer has lost all faith in Kate's ability to recognize danger signals. When she finally decides to leave, her car won't start, but we could have predicted that.

When Ben, who was supposed to be on a business trip, shows up, Kate tries to catch him in lies, but the character is so transparent anyway it's surprising he doesn't have "killer" written across his forehead. Maharis is capable of better work, so the blame must fall on Daugherty once again. Montgomery's voice is very scratchy in these scenes with Maharis. One can surmise that either her many trips into the rain took its toll on her, or these scenes were shot after the ending, which features Kate screaming her head off.

Strictly out of left field is the scene where a tree comes through the upstairs window. There's no suspense in this, but it's an excuse to send the cops into the basement to get materials to fix it up.

As in *SST—Death Flight*, Richard Derr has a walk-on, this time as a highway patrolman. And keep an eye out for a cameo by a six-toed cat. Another fleeting moment, this one for fans of *Bewitched*, is that little look Montgomery gives when she lies to the telephone operator about her call being an emergency. It was second nature for Montgomery to excel, but only her fans will find much here to enjoy.

CAST: Elizabeth Montgomery, Eileen Heckart, Sue Ane Langdon, George Maharis, Jess Walton, Richard Derr, Ross Elliott, John Furlong, George Jue, and Michael Keller.

CREDITS: Director: Herschel Daugherty; Teleplay: Merwin Gerard, based on a short story by McKnight Malmar; Music: Gil Melle; Production: Universal TV; Running Time: 74 minutes; Air Date: 11/14/72; Network: ABC

The Werewolf of Woodstock

Woodstock, New York, 1969. One night shortly after the famous rock festival, blue-collar drunkard Bert Anderson (Tige Andrews) heads out to beat up any hippies he can find still hanging around. He takes to the abandoned stage where the bands had played and proceeds to tear it apart until he is struck by a power line. Surviving the electrocution, Bert turns into a werewolf at night and prowls the countryside. He kills a cop the first night, and eventually kidnaps a hippie girl who came there with her band to record a demo record. LA cops, Kendy (Meredith MacRae) and Moody (Michael Parks), who were visiting Woodstock to get tips on handling rock show crowds, team up with local cop Lt. Martino (Harold J. Stone) to corral the monster.

The *Werewolf of Woodstock* can only be described as a live-action cartoon aimed primarily at children. The characters in this low-budget Dick Clark production are broadly drawn, and the simplistic action features very little in the way of disturbing horror images. Director John Moffitt worked primarily on television specials, including the Emmy and the American Music award shows. The writers were Bill Lee and Hank Saroyan: Lee was the writer and producer of *American Bandstand's 25th Anniversary* (the Dick Clark connection), and Saroyan, a sometime voice artist for cartoons, directed all of the *Muppet Babies* series episodes.

Most surprising about the production is

the relatively high-profile cast. Tige Andrews (*The Mod Squad*) plays the werewolf, but his face is seen only at the beginning before turning into the monster, and at the end in the requisite scene where the dead monster resumes his prior form. The rest of the time he is wrapped in bandages or in werewolf makeup; it is highly doubtful that Andrews did his own stunt work. The werewolf makeup is limited but not terrible, distinguished in that it is obviously designed to resemble the long-haired, hippie-type personages that Anderson hates so much. The makeup is by Joe Blasco, who worked on David Cronenberg's *Shivers*, *Rabid* and two of the notorious Ilsa films, among other genre pictures.

Kendy is the one who comes up with the scientific explanation for Anderson's conversion to a werewolf. It has something to do with "severe electrical shock altering tissues and organs," but science is tossed out the window for a supernatural solution when Kendy shows up at the end with a silver bullet. The werewolf is indeed shot with that bullet, but he also falls from a great height, so which killed him is anyone's guess. MacRae (*Petticoat Junction*) shows some enthusiasm in her smallish role, but Parks, wearing a silly knit cap, seems simply to be marking time. Stone (whose Lt. Martino cooks in his office when he's under stress) gives his performance all the gusto one would expect from an old pro.

The hippie rock band on site to record a demo song drives a psychedelic VW bus, and features two recognizable actors in Belinda Balaski as Becky and Andrew Stevens as Dave. Balaski would show up in *Piranha*, *The Howling* and *Gremlins*, and Stevens in *Massacre at Central High* and *The Fury*, among others. Becky, the free-spirited hippie who changes her dog's name every week to another astrological sign, is kidnapped by the werewolf. Frightened at first, Becky reasons with the beast, and even comes to feel sorry for it. In a nod to nearly every monster movie ever made, the werewolf lugs her around until it is killed.

The band participates in one attempt to capture the werewolf by playing loud music to attract it, then switching to "white noise" in order to confuse the beast; the difference between the two types of playing will be difficult for viewers to notice. This tack doesn't work anyway, and the werewolf escapes, picks up his girl, Becky, and steals a dune buggy, fleeing to a nearby power station for the finale.

The Werewolf of Woodstock was shot on video with Southern California doubling poorly as upstate New York; it may have played on *The ABC Afternoon Playbreak*, but this has not been confirmed. Credited as production consultant is Bud Cardos, who acted in cult shockers such as *Hell's Angels on Wheels*, *Nightmare in Wax*, *Satan's Sadists*, *Five Bloody Graves*, etc., and directed *Kingdom of the Spiders*, *The Dark*, and other genre offerings. The rock music score is attributed (in a spoken credit) to Jerry Cole and Al Bruno, on whom no other cinematic information was available.

CAST: Michael Parks, Harold J. Stone, Meredith MacRae, Ann Doran, Richard Webb, Belinda Balaski, Tige Andrews, Robert Weaver, Andrew Stevens, Danny Michael Mann, Dean Webber, John O'Connell, Bobby Clark, Bob Dix, Floyd Carver, and Gary Johnson.

CREDITS: Director: John Moffitt; Teleplay: Bill Lee, Hank Saroyan; Music: Jerry Cole and Al Bruno; Production: Dick Clark Teleshows; Running Time: 67 minutes; Air Date: 1/24/75; Network: ABC

When Michael Calls

AKA **Shattered Silence**

On an impulse, lawyer Doremus Connelly (Ben Gazzara) decides to visit his ex-wife Helen (Elisabeth Ashley) and their little daughter. Coincidentally, Helen has been receiving mysterious phone calls from someone claiming to be Michael, her nephew who has been dead for 15 years. Helen had taken in Michael and his brother Craig (Michael Douglas) years ago when their mother, her sister, went insane, and committed suicide in the asylum. Michael ran away and died in a blizzard when he was still a child, but he had blamed Helen for his mother's death.

The phone calls persist, and when Helen's close friend, the doctor who signed her sister's commitment papers, is murdered, Doremus fears for Helen, and determines to unravel the mystery.

Not exactly a body count movie (only two people die), *When Michael Calls* is instead a mystery that concerns itself with the machinations of the insane, specifically, the psychotic. Director Philip Leacock keeps the action focused in this small-town, small-circle mystery, and the irony of the ending, which won't be revealed here, exposes the fine line between sanity and madness. The film's writer was nominated for an Edgar Allan Poe award for Best Television Feature, but the enormously popular *The Night Stalker* prevailed.

The film, shot in Toronto, benefits from the unusual winter setting and a fine, largely unknown cast. The biggest names are Ben Gazzara and Elizabeth Ashley, both of whom give solid, low-key performances. Doremus arrives unannounced in the hopes of reuniting his family, and is given the unique opportunity to protect those whom he loves when they are threatened by the voice from the past. Though not the catalyst of events, it is interesting that the calls begin just when Doremus shows up. It is either very bad timing on the part of the killer, or very good timing for Helen, the primary object of the killer's revenge. Regardless, the tragedy that tore apart a family years ago serves to pull another family together.

Michael Douglas plays Helen's nephew Craig, the psychologist at the Greenleaf School for Boys. It's an early role for the actor who would very soon gain lasting stardom in the long-running *The Streets of San Francisco* series. Here, Douglas does good work as the doctor who can offer insight into how fragile and unforgiving the mind can be for those in the throes of mental illness. Craig seems to be driven to this work because of the tragic way his mother, and consequently his brother, suffered.

The phone calls to Helen are particularly creepy. The child's voice on the other end of the line calls her by her nickname "Aunty-my-Helen," and howls about being lost in the snow. His cries of "I'm dead, aren't I?" are chilling, and hint at a supernatural element reminiscent of *The Twilight Zone*.

As mentioned, the first to die is the retired Dr. Britton (Larry Reynolds, *My Bloody Valentine*), who signed the commitment papers for Helen's sister. He is a beekeeper foiled when the chloroform he uses to sedate his bees is switched with bee venom, which causes the bees to swarm. He is pulled from the bee room by his wife, Elsa, played by Marian Waldman, whose short career included the notorious horror films *Deranged* and *Black Christmas*.

The second to die is the too-curious Sheriff Washbrook played by Albert S. Waxman, who would go on to steady work in the *Cagney & Lacey* series. Waxman was also the voice of Rudnick in the animated cult film *Heavy Metal*.* The music is by Oscar winner (for *Hello Dolly!*) Lionel Newman.

CAST: Ben Gazzara, Elizabeth Ashley, Michael Douglas, Albert S. Waxman, Karen Pearson, Larry Reynolds, Marian Waldman, Christopher Pellett, Alan McRae, Steve Weston, Robert Warner, Michelle Chicoine, and John Bethune.

CREDITS: Director: Philip Leacock; Teleplay: James Bridges, based on a novel by John Farris; Music: Lionel Newman; Production: Palomar Pictures Corporation; Running Time: 88 minutes; Air Date: 2/5/72; Network: ABC

Where Have All the People Gone?

One August Sunday, Steven Anders (Peter Graves) and his children, David and Deborah (George O'Hanlon, Jr. and Karen Quinlan), are fossil hunting in the High Sierras with their friend and guide, Jim (Noble Willingham). The family is in a cave

---

*The Internet Movie Database claims that Gerald McRaney (*Major Dad*) is in the film but he wasn't spotted in the home video copy, which expands the film somewhat from its original version.

when a flash of light and an earthquake hit. Jim tells them about the light, and they discover the radio is dead and no one can be reached on the shortwave. Soon, Jim gets sick and dies. Fearing a nuclear disaster, the family walks down the mountain. When they reach the small town where Jim lived, the place is empty, and David can't reach an operator on the pay phone. They find a Geiger counter at Jim's house and there's no radiation, which means the food is safe to eat. The car generators are knocked out but, finding a fresh battery, the family gets a car running and heads for home. No one is on the roads.

Where Have All the People Gone? is a serious end-of-the-world story, where the audience knows only as much as the intrepid Anders clan. Luckily for them, and us, David is a science buff who makes guesses based on the various clues as they make their way home. After Jim dies, his body turns to dust which throws a wrench into the nuclear disaster theory, as does the lack of radiation. The mystery of what happened is as compelling as the family's struggle to get home—perhaps *more* compelling.

Peter Graves is a steady presence as the father, Steven. He relies on his son's knowledge, and doesn't make rash judgments about the situation or the few people they meet on the long journey home. George O'Hanlon, Jr. and Kathleen Quinlan both turn in convincing performances (the two would soon work together again, not as siblings but as a romantic pair in *The Missing Are Deadly*). Familiar character actor Noble Willingham's role as Jim amounts to little more than a cameo.

The first person the Anders find is a silent woman we eventually discover is called Jenny (Verna Bloom, *High Plains Drifter*). The Anders take her along with them and slowly her reason returns, and we learn of the terrible trauma that affected her so strongly.

The growing band of travelers next encounters a man (Dan Barrows) whose car has broken down—and uses his gun to steal theirs. Barrows was an original member of the improvisational comedy troupe The Committee, whose most famous member is Howard Hesseman. Barrows' film debut was in *Billy Jack*, and his milquetoast persona served him well in both counterculture and mainstream offerings since.

The next person to join the Anders is a boy, Michael (Michael-James Wixted), whose parents were killed by passing ruffians. The Anders take a horse and buggy for the next leg of their journey, Steven remarking, "Two weeks ago I was manufacturing plastic cups and now I'm harnessing horses."

Surviving attacks by wild dogs, the clan finally makes it to an empty LA in an eerie sequence very similar to ones in *The Omega Man*. The final scenes shed some light on the disaster, but, in the final message of hope, the clan must move on where it can begin again by living off the newly cleansed Earth. This logical and non-exploitive disaster film is recommended for those without a need for a special effects extravaganza.

CAST: Peter Graves, George O'Hanlon, Jr., Kathleen Quinlan, Verna Bloom, Michael-James Wixted, Noble Willingham, Jay W. MacIntosh, Doug Chapin, Ken Sansom, and Dan Barrows.

CREDITS: Director: John Llewellyn Moxey; Teleplay: Lewis John Carlino and Sandor Stern, based on a story by Lewis John Carlino; Music: Robert Prince; Production: Jozak Company; Running Time: 74 minutes; Air Date: 10/8/74; Network: NBC

The Woman Hunter

Bermuda. Paul Carter (Stuart Whitman) is present at a party where the hostess is murdered, and her jewelry is stolen. Three years later, Carter is in Acapulco stalking fabulously wealthy Dina Hunter (Barbara Eden), who has just left the hospital after a car accident in which she killed a man. Carter arranges to meet the vulnerable Dina, wooing her away from her distracted husband Jerry (Robert Vaughn). One night, Dina sneaks over to Carter's place and discovers evidence that he has been following her and is after her jewels. Dina panics and involves the police but they don't believe her due to her fragile mental state. However,

Dina will soon find out the truth behind Carter's actions.

This silly little thriller, a Mexican vacation for all involved, focuses on the difficulties of the idle rich, who must contend with annoying jewel thieves and Machiavellian intrigue within their ranks. *The Woman Hunter* is brightly colored fluff with an appealing cast, but is hardly challenging in the mystery department. It should be enjoyed like a piece of candy, or one of those cocktails that includes a paper umbrella, perfect while reading on the beach. The title is a curious play on words given that the main character is named Dina Hunter: is it *woman* hunter or woman *hunter*? This quandary is the most puzzling aspect of the film.

Barbara Eden parades around in a series of fashionable outfits, behavior similar to her role in *A Howling in the Woods*, her previous telefright. Frankly, it is difficult to take her seriously, although playing someone fabulously wealthy was probably not much of a stretch. Dina has her share of marital discord—it is her money, not his—and it's no wonder since husband Jerry is a cold fish. Robert Vaughn gets the thankless role while Stuart Whitman gets to be the sexy suspected jewel thief, skin diver (in only his skin) and top-notch artist, Paul Carter.

Carter ingratiates himself—a little too easily—with the Hunters by offering to paint her portrait (she had her previous portrait taken down because she didn't "want to look at strangers"). When her behavior turns flighty, he tells her to wear the earrings she has on when she poses because "they're perfect for you: elegant, beautiful and ice cold." After discovering that Carter's only after her jewels, Dina baits him by wearing them to a fancy reception. This is where Dina goes a bit off the deep end and does a sexy solo dance on the dance floor, much to the cha-

Barbara Eden in a publicity still for *The Woman Hunter* **(1972).**

grin of Jerry who's trying to coerce some of the guests into investing in a real estate deal he's cooked up.

The not-so-gripping finale involves a car chase between Dina in a big Chrysler and Carter in a funky Volkswagen Thing. The outcome will not surprise many viewers, but the journey to reach it is an enjoyably tacky if empty exercise. Larry Storch (*F Troop*) will be recognized as the joke-telling drunk at the party in Bermuda that kicks off the adventure, but some may miss the fact that the hostess is played by his wife, Norma.

CAST: Barbara Eden, Robert Vaughn, Stuart Whitman, Sydney Chaplin, Enrique Lucero, Larry Storch, Norma Storch, Aurora Munoz, and Victor Hugo Jauregui.

CREDITS: Director: Bernard L. Kowalski; Teleplay: Brian Clemens and Tony Williamson, based on a story by Brian Clemens; Music:

George Duning; Production: Bing Crosby Productions; Automobiles furnished by Chrysler Corporation; Running Time: 70 minutes; Air Date: 9/19/72; Network: CBS

Women in Chains

Crusading parole officer Sandra Parker (Lois Nettleton) arranges to be sent to prison under the name Sally Porter, to get evidence against brutal cellblock matron Claire Tyson (Ida Lupino). Once inside, the only person who knows Sandra's true identity, her colleague, Helen, is killed, leaving Sandra to fend for herself. Tyson discovers the ruse and plans for Sandra to have an "accident."

This by-the-numbers WIP shocker uses the tired "undercover" routine to no great effect. Sandra fakes the required paperwork and changes her look (including phony needle marks), only to discover the usual prison shenanigans—television style.

Among the clichéd characters are the framed newcomer, Melinda (Belinda Montgomery), whom Sandra takes under her wing; the tough cookie, Dee Dee (Jessica Walter), who panders to Tyson; the harmonica-playing junkie, Althea (Hazel Medina); the mentally disturbed Alice (Katherine Cannon, *Private Duty Nurses*); and the fatalistic old-timer, Billie (Lucille Benson). The expected action takes the form of a catfight in the dining hall, some implied lesbianism and the lockdown that drives everybody crazy. Tyson is played by the great Ida Lupino, but she is not given much of an opportunity to shine.

The other performances are uniformly adequate, and veteran director Bernard L.

Ida Lupino plays an evil prison matron in *Women in Chains* (1972).

Kowalski does little to present any visual interest or evoke an emotional response. When Helen (Penny Fuller), Sandra's only link to the outside world, is killed, the viewer will no doubt roll his eyes in recognition of the oft-used plot twist. Naturally, Sandra tries to get a letter out (which Tyson rips up) and make a call (she gets put on hold until caught), but the audience is well ahead by this time.

At one point, Sandra is put into solitary—with Melinda. The reason for this is so that Melinda can spill the beans about the plot to have Sandra killed. Sandra slips out too easily at dinner time, and has the required knock-down-drag-out with Tyson. When the warden arrives, he believes Sandra, for some reason, and the film closes with her tearful farewell to her cellmates. The end.

Familiar character actor John Larch has a couple of small scenes as Sandra's boss, and the beautiful BarBara Luna is another one of her cellmates. Joyce Jameson (*Tales of Terror*, *The Comedy of Terrors*) is listed in the credits but she was not spotted. For a much more credible look at female prison life, even for television, see *Nightmare in Badham County*.

CAST: (ao) Ida Lupino, Belinda Montgomery, Lois Nettleton, and Jessica Walter. Also John Larch, Penny Fuller, BarBara Luna, Hazel Medina, Neile Adams, Kathy Cannon, Lucille Benson, Alice Backes, Barbara Baldavin, William Bryant, Hollie Hayes, Judy Strangis, Joyce Jameson, Noah Keen, Tracee Ann Lyles, Kathleen O'Malley, and June Whitley Taylor.

CREDITS: Director: Bernard L. Kowalski; Teleplay: Rita Lakin; Music: Charles Fox; Production: Paramount Television; Running Time: 71 minutes; Air Date: 1/25/72; Network: ABC

You'll Never See Me Again

Only once were the works of author Cornell Woolrich aka William Irish adapted for a 1970s telefright film. His dark stories were more suited to the film noir style that flourished in the 40s and 50s, resulting in many suspense classics, such as *Phantom Lady*, *The Window*, *Black Angel* and, most famously, *Rear Window*. Woolrich's output fell off in the late fifties, just as the film noir gave way to the more realistic style of crime film that would dominate the movies for decades. The "neo-noir" cycle that took hold in the 90s—and which should be considered a bona fide crime subgenre in the twenty-first century—inspired the television series *Fallen Angels*, which adapted several of his stories, but Woolrich had been dead for nearly thirty years by that time. Woolrich passed away in obscurity in 1968, his funeral unattended.

Architect Ned Bliss (David Hartman) has an argument with his wife, Vicki (Jess Walton), and she leaves, presumably for her mother's house. The next day he calls his in-laws but Vicki is not there. After checking around and coming up empty, Ned informs the police. Ned drives to his in-laws' home in the hopes of gaining a clue to her disappearance, but only succeeds in upsetting her parents. While there, Ned notices that the parents' living room is off-center, but he thinks nothing of it. Upon his return home, the cops, tipped off to find Vicki's bloody shirt in Ned's car, threaten Ned with arrest for murder. Ned flees, hoping to clear his name and find out what happened to Vicki before the cops catch up to him.

You'll Never See Me Again is a moderately entertaining but formulaic paranoid thriller—until the mystery is revealed in the far-fetched ending, the clue to which is the conspicuously off-center room in Vicki's parents' house. While the answer to the mystery will probably not be guessed by the viewer, this is not because it is clever but rather because is it outlandish.

Although David Hartman is likable enough, he isn't much of an actor, and it was obviously asking too much of him to carry this film. The subtleties required to play the tormented Ned are beyond the reach of the inexperienced actor. Hartman was offered contracts with two professional baseball teams (Boston Braves and Philadelphia Phillies) when he graduated high school, but he decided to go to college instead. After a stint in the Air Force, he worked in Broadway musicals, and then signed with Universal, landing a recurring role on *The Virginian*. He had just come off *The Bold Ones: The New Doctors* prior to this film, and would soon score a short-lived series called *Lucas Tanner*, but he was much better suited for his many years as host of *Good Morning America*.

Suspicion as to Vicki's whereabouts is thrown towards a tight-lipped gas station attendant (Bo Svenson) but a savvy audience will not fall for it, realizing instead that the solution lies a bit further down the road. The cops, in the person of Lt. Stillman (Joseph Campanella), are too quick to take the easy way out and blame Ned, forcing him on the run to solve the mystery himself. In one amusing scene, Ned suspects his colleague Bob (Colby Chester, *The Young and the Restless*) of harboring Vicki, and he busts into Bob's apartment only to find him and their boss's wife in a compromising position.

Ned is also taken to a hospital to see a girl with amnesia, but this scene doesn't generate much suspense given that it occurs too early in the film to resolve the mystery. The film picks up steam once the fugitive Ned returns to the parents' house, but this quickly dissipates when the mystery is revealed, and the remainder turns into a predictable chase.

Vicki's parents are played by veterans Ralph Meeker and Jane Wyatt. Meeker isn't given much of a chance to show his capabilities, but Wyatt gives a good performance in the final scenes. The Internet Movie Database claims Ben Gazzara is in the cast but he was not spotted in the film.

CAST: David Hartman, Jane Wyatt, Ralph Meeker, Jess Walton, Joseph Campanella, Colby Chester, George Murdock, Bill Vint, Brett Parker, Larry Watson, Ned Wertimer, Jewell Lain, and Jessica Jones.

CREDITS: Director: Jeannot Szwarc; Teleplay: William Wood and Gerald Di Pego, based on the short story by Cornell Woolrich; Music: Richard Clements; Production: Universal TV; Running Time: 70 minutes; Air Date: 2/28/73; Network: ABC

Appendix: Telefright Chronology

Title	Date	Network
Sole Survivor	1/9/70	CBS
Ritual of Evil	2/23/70	NBC
The Brotherhood of the Bell	9/17/70	CBS
How Awful About Allan	9/22/70	ABC
Night Slaves	9/29/70	ABC
The House That Would Not Die	10/27/70	ABC
Crowhaven Farm	11/24/70	ABC
Dr. Cook's Garden	1/19/71	ABC
Terror in the Sky	9/17/71	CBS
Deadly Dream	9/25/71	ABC
Five Desperate Women	9/28/71	ABC
Sweet, Sweet Rachel	10/2/71	ABC
Murder Once Removed	10/29/71	CBS
Howling in the Woods	11/5/71	NBC
Revenge!	11/6/71	ABC
Paper Man	11/12/71	CBS
Duel	11/13/71	ABC
Black Noon	11/15/71	CBS
The Devil and Miss Sarah	12/4/71	ABC
The Night Stalker	1/11/72	ABC
Women in Chains	1/25/72	ABC
She Waits	1/28/72	CBS
The Screaming Woman	1/29/72	ABC
Something Evil	1/31/72	CBS
When Michael Calls	2/5/72	ABC
The Eyes of Charles Sand	2/29/72	ABC
Taste of Evil	5/13/72	ABC
The Woman Hunter	9/19/72	CBS
Haunts of the Very Rich	9/20/72	ABC
Moon of the Wolf	9/26/72	ABC
Short Walk to Daylight	10/24/72	ABC
Family Flight	10/25/72	ABC
The Victim	11/14/72	ABC
The Strangers in 7A	11/14/72	CBS
Gargoyles	11/21/72	CBS
Home for the Holidays	11/28/72	ABC
Pursuit	12/12/72	ABC
The Devil's Daughter	1/9/73	ABC
Frankenstein	1/16/73	ABC
The Night Strangler	1/16/73	ABC
A Cold Night's Death	1/30/73	ABC
Snatched	1/31/73	ABC
Horror at 37,000 Feet	2/13/73	CBS
The Norliss Tapes	2/21/73	NBC
The Stranger	2/26/73	NBC
You'll Never See Me Again	2/28/73	ABC
The Picture of Dorian Gray	4/23/73	ABC
Dying Room Only	9/18/73	ABC
Terror on the Beach	9/18/73	CBS
Satan's School for Girls	9/19/73	ABC
She Cried Murder	9/25/73	CBS
Runaway!	9/29/73	ABC
Isn't It Shocking?	10/2/73	ABC
Don't Be Afraid of the Dark	10/10/73	ABC
The President's Plane is Missing	10/23/73	ABC
Ordeal	10/30/73	ABC
Trapped	11/14/73	ABC
Scream Pretty Peggy	11/24/73	ABC
Frankenstein: The True Story	11/30/73	NBC
Maneater	12/8/73	ABC
The Cat Creature	12/11/73	ABC
Scream of the Wolf	1/16/74	ABC
Skyway to Death	1/19/74	ABC
Killdozer	2/2/74	ABC
Cry Panic	2/6/74	ABC
Dracula	2/8/74	CBS
The Elevator	2/9/74	ABC
The Phantom of Hollywood	2/12/74	CBS
Killer Bees	2/26/74	ABC

Appendix

Title	Date	Network
The Invasion of Carol Enders	3/8/74	ABC
The Turn of the Screw	4/15/74	ABC
Last Bride of Salem	5/8/74	ABC
Hurricane	9/10/74	ABC
Savages	9/11/74	ABC
Terror on the 40th Floor	9/17/74	NBC
The Strange and Deadly Occurrence	9/24/74	NBC
The Stranger Within	10/1/74	ABC
The Disappearance of Flight 412	10/1/74	NBC
Death Sentence	10/2/74	ABC
Where Have All the People Gone	10/8/74	NBC
Fer de Lance	10/18/74	CBS
Bad Ronald	10/23/74	ABC
Death Cruise	10/30/74	ABC
All the Kind Strangers	11/12/74	ABC
Panic on the 5:22	11/20/74	ABC
Reflections of Murder	11/24/74	ABC
Betrayal	12/3/74	ABC
The Missing Are Deadly	1/8/75	ABC
Satan's Triangle	1/14/75	ABC
The Dead Don't Die	1/14/75	NBC
Death Stalk	1/21/75	NBC
The Werewolf of Woodstock	1/24/75	ABC
The Legend of Lizzie Borden	2/10/75	ABC
Trilogy of Terror	3/4/75	ABC
Conspiracy of Terror	4/10/75	NBC
The UFO Incident	10/20/75	NBC
Beyond the Bermuda Triangle	11/6/75	NBC
Murder on Flight 502	11/21/75	ABC
One of My Wives Is Missing	3/5/76	ABC
Death at Love House	9/30/76	ABC
Look What's Happened to Rosemary's Baby	10/29/76	ABC
Nightmare in Badham County	11/5/76	ABC
Mayday at 40,000 Feet	11/12/76	CBS
The Savage Bees	11/22/76	NBC
Flood!	11/24/76	NBC
Smash-Up on Interstate 5	12/3/76	ABC
Night Terror	2/7/77	NBC
The Spell	2/20/77	NBC
SST–Death Flight	2/25/77	ABC
The Strange Possession of Mrs. Oliver	2/28/77	NBC
Dead of Night	3/29/77	NBC
Snowbeast	4/28/77	NBC
The Possessed	5/1/77	NBC
Fire!	5/8/77	NBC
Red Alert	5/18/77	CBS
Spectre	5/21/77	NBC
Good Against Evil	5/22/77	ABC
Curse of the Black Widow	9/16/77	ABC
Killer on Board	10/10/77	NBC
The Night They Took Miss Beautiful	10/24/77	NBC
It Happened at Lakewood Manor	12/2/77	ABC
Count Dracula	12/22/77	PBS
Tarantulas: The Deadly Cargo	12/28/77	CBS
The Dark Secret of Harvest Home	1/23/78	NBC
The Bermuda Depths	1/27/78	ABC
Cruise Into Terror	2/3/78	ABC
The Initiation of Sarah	2/6/78	ABC
The Ghost of Flight 401	2/18/78	NBC
Ski Lift to Death	3/3/78	CBS
Death Moon	5/31/78	CBS
Are You in the House Alone?	9/20/78	CBS
Devil Dog: The Hound of Hell	10/31/78	CBS
Stranger in Our House	10/31/78	NBC
A Fire in the Sky	11/26/78	NBC
Someone's Watching Me	11/29/78	NBC
Terror Out of the Sky	12/26/78	CBS
Express to Terror	2/7/79	NBC
The Darker Side of Terror	4/3/79	CBS
Hanging by a Thread	5/8/79	NBC
A Vacation in Hell	5/21/79	NBC
Death Car on the Freeway	9/25/79	CBS
Vampire	10/7/79	ABC
The Death of Ocean View Park	10/19/79	ABC
Disaster on the Coastliner	10/29/79	ABC
Salem's Lot	11/17/79	CBS
She's Dressed to Kill	12/10/79	NBC

Note: The air date of *Force of Evil* is unknown but is assumed to be sometime in 1977.

Bibliography

Ashley, Elizabeth. *Actress*. New York: M. Evans, 1978.

Brooks, Tim. *The Complete Directory of Prime Time TV Stars*. New York: Ballantine, 1987.

Brown, Julien, ed. *The Chronicle of the Movies*. New York: Random House, 1991.

Dillman, Bradford. *Are You Anybody?* Santa Barbara, CA: Fithian, 1997.

Katz, Ephraim. *The Film Encyclopedia*. New York: Putnam, 1979.

Lentz, Harris M., III. *Science Fiction, Horror & Fantasy Film and Television Credits*. Jefferson, NC: McFarland, 1983.

Marill, Alvin H. *Movies Made for Television*. New York: Da Capo, 1980.

Sherman, Fraser A. *Cyborgs, Santa Claus and Satan*. Jefferson, NC: McFarland, 2000.

Shipman, David. *The Great Movie Stars*. New York: St. Martin's, 1972.

Stack, Robert. *Straight Shooting*. New York: Berkley, 1980.

Stanley, John. *The Creature Features Movie Guide*. New York: Warner, 1984.

Terrace, Vincent. *Television 1970–1980*. La Jolla, CA: A.S. Barnes, 1981.

Weldon, Michael. *The Psychotronic Encyclopedia of Film*. New York: Ballantine, 1983.

INDEX

Aames, Willie 71
Abbott, John 18
Abercrombie, Ian 161
Acker, Sharon 172
Ackroyd, David 29
Adams, Arthur 122
Adams, Brooke 107
Adams, Dallas 73
Adams, Lillian 76
Adams, Neile 201
Adams, Stanley 112, 118
Aidman, Charles 88, 126
Airhart, Teddy, Jr. 106
Akins, Claude 96, 112, 118, 180
Albers, Leslie 116
Albert, Edward 37, 94
Albertson, Mabel 82
Alda, Alan 90
Alda, Robert 58
Alden, Carrie Wilmot 144
Alden, Norman 26, 185
Alden, Richard 150
Alden, Tom Smith 144
Alderman, John 149
Alexander, Phoebe 29
Alfosa, Joe 104
Allan, Jacquelyn 90
Allan, Jed 20
Allen, Cecilia 66
Allen, Jonelle 194
Allen, Sian Barbara 147, 157
Allison, Jean 58, 170
Allyson, June 27
Alvarez, Abraham 104
Alvin, John 99, 178
Alzamora, Armand 104
Alzola, Mickey 74
Ambrose, David 49
Amey, Marlena 153
Ammerman, Dan 131
Amos, Johnny 128
Anderson, Barbara 52, 167
Anderson, Hesper 192
Anderson, John 69

Anderson, Michael, Jr. 82
Anderson, Richard 113
Anderson, Veronica 81
Anderson, William C. 87
Andre, E.J. 32
Andrews, Edward 58
Andrews, Norman J. 96
Andrews, Tige 156, 196
Andrews, Tod 128
Andrusco, Gene 149
Ansara, Michael 121
Antonio, Jim, Jr. 86, 144
Antonio, Lou 161
Applegate, Roy 26
Appleton, V.X. 81
Arbus, Alan 147
Areno, Lois 8
Armendariz, Pedro, Jr. 52
Armstrong, Herb 164
Armstrong, Mark 40
Armstrong, R.G. 45, 132
Arquette, Kerry 174
Arquette, Rosanna 29
Arvan, Jan 149
Ashley, Elizabeth 66, 119, 197
Ashton, Peter 81
Asner, Edward 79
Astin, John 156
Astin, Patty Duke *see* Duke, Patty
Atkins, Tom 180
Attaway, Ruth 11
Atwater, Barry 112
Auberjonois, Rene 29
Aubrey, Skye 125
Austin, Ron (Ronald) 81, 123
Automobiles furnished by Chevrolet Motor Div. 56, 169, 176
Automobiles furnished by Chrysler Corp. 22, 26, 52, 80, 82, 83, 90, 112, 113, 125, 128, 129, 132, 140, 172, 178, 182, 200
Automobiles furnished by Ford

Motor Co. 16, 35, 41, 69, 105, 110, 119, 144, 164
Automobiles furnished by General Motors Corp. 50, 80, 125, 128, 181
Avalos, Luis 75
Avery, Brian 71
Avery, Carol 39
Avery, Margaret 164
Ayres, Jerry 49, 69
Ayres, Lew 139, 152, 172

Babcock, Barbara 139
Babson, Thomas W. 159
Bach, J.S. 132
Bachardy, Don 73
Bachelor, Dino 66
Bachmann, Conrad 129
Backes, Alice 201
Badham, John 3, 90, 132
Badiyi, Reza S. 60
Baer, Parley 58
Baggetta, Vincent 107
Bailey, Charles J. 131
Bain, Barbara 109
Baker, Tom 73
Balaski, Belinda 196
Baldavin, Barbara 201
Baldwin, William 147
Balhatchet, Bill 29
Balin, Ina 122
Balsam, Talia 88
Balzer, Robert L. 94
Bame, Lawrence 127
Banks, Jonathan 115, 153
Barbeau, Adrienne 30, 131, 163
Barbour, Thomas 50
Barker, Danny 144
Barnes, Julian 73
Barnes, Priscilla 193
Barnes, Richard 21
Barnett, Jim 35
Baron, John 190
Barr, Sharon 46
Barrett, Majel 165

Index

Barrett, Stan 15
Barrows, Dan 198
Barrows, George 128
Barry, Donald 60
Barry, Gene 44
Bartlett, Bonnie 96, 99, 139
Bartold, Norman 164
Barton, Dan 123
Barton, Gary 114, 125
Basch, Harry 26
Basehart, Richard 68, 102, 161
Bashtu, Timur 161
Basinger, Kim 75
Bassett, William 115
Bast, William 97
Battle, Lois 164
Baumes, Wilfred Lloyd 18
Baxter, Anne 134
Baxter, Meredith 18, 88
Beackel, Walter 184
Beal, John 99
Beatty, Ned 56
Beck, Billy 174
Beck, Glenn 155
Beckley, William 126
Bedelia, Bonnie 139
Beery, Noah, Jr. 144
Begley, Ed, Jr. 32, 61
Bell, Ann 165
Bellamy, Earl 64, 68
Bellamy, Ralph 107, 116, 164
Beller, Kathleen 8
Bellin, Thomas 30
Bendixsen, Mia 81
Benedict, Dirk 24
Benest, Glenn M. 174
Benet, Brenda 81
Bennett, Joan 60
Benson, Deborah 58
Benson, Jay 39
Benson, Lindy 165
Benson, Lucille 12, 46, 54, 132, 170, 201
Benson, Norland 102
Benson, Robby 6
Beredino, John 106
Bergen, Polly 37, 107
Berger, Senta 1
Berley, Kandy 96
Bernard, Ed 132
Bernard, Joseph 35
Bernstein, Charles 8, 101, 116
Berry, Patricia 22
Berti, Dehl 134
Bessel, Ted 147
Best, James 144
Beswick, Martine 45
Bethune, John 197
Betrayal 3
Betz, Carl 34, 93
Bick, Joni 97
Biehn, Michael 66

Bikel, Theodore 107
Bill, Tony 8, 79, 87
Birman, Len 96, 150
Birney, David 163
Birnheim, Francoise 113
Bissell, Whit 68
Black, Karen 170, 189
Black, Walter 67
Blair, Linda 174
Blake, Amanda 12
Blake, Ellen 186
Blake, Elta 66
Blankfort, Michael 66
Blasco, Joe 196
Blees, Robert 27
Bloch, John W. 42
Bloch, Robert 18, 31
Block, Ethelinn 127
Blondell, Joan 31, 35
Bloom, Verna 198
Blye, Maggie 102
Bochner, Lloyd 22, 66, 140
Bocho, Steven 194
Bodeen, Patty 128
Bogert, William 66
Boileau, Pierre 132
Bolin, Nick 46
Bonaduce, Danny 107
Bonar, Ivan 128
Bond, Michael 8
Bond, Rene 12
Bondi, Beulah 152
Bonino, Steve 180
Bonner, Frank 62
Bonney, Gail 46
Bono, Sonny 107
Boone, Brendon 77
Boone, Randy 144
Borelli, Carla 134
Borgnine, Ernest 64, 75
Bosch, Hieronymous 165
Bosley, Tom 37
Bostain, Heather Ann 94
Bostock, Barbara 167
Bottoms, Sam 144
Botts, Jacquie 159
Bourne, Peter 141
Bourneuf, Philip 71
Bowers, James 144
Bowie, Darryl 155
Bowie, Rick 155
Bowker, Judi 21
Bowles, Billy 83
Boyer, Philip 101
Boyle, Richard Charles 144
Bracken, Kathleen 102
Bradbury, Ray 149
Bradley, Darlene 155
Bradock, Jack 133
Brady, Scott 113
Braha, Herb 194
Brand, Neville 42, 64, 93

Brandon, Michael 131, 177, 193
Brandon, Peter 76
Brandt, Hank 36, 129, 184
Brauner, Asher 170
Braverman, Michael 24
Bremers, Beverly 20
Brennan, Claire 102
Brennan, Walter 79
Bress, Herbert 49
Bridges, James 197
Bridges, Lloyd 34, 49, 69, 79
Brill, Charlie 58
Brinkerhoff, Burt 89
Brittany, Morgan 36, 87
Brolin, James 154, 187
Bronson, Lillian 46
Brooks, Joe 129
Brooks, Linda 40
Brotherson, Eric 12
Brown, Casey 153
Brown, Georg Stanford 134
Brown, Lew 41
Brown, Murray 52
Brown, Pamela 52
Brown, Roger Aaron 9, 36
Brown, T.K. 79
Brownell, Barbara 92
Bruck, Bella 164
Bruno, Al 196
Bruzzese, Sandra 159
Bryant, Jennifer 15
Bryant, Joshua 15, 96, 139
Bryant, Shane 126
Bryant, William 15, 102, 172, 178, 201
Bryer, Paul 20
Buchanan, Jim (James D.) 81, 123
Buchanan, Morris 48, 110
Buchholz, Horst 32, 144
Buckman, Tara 36
Bulifant, Joyce 77
Bull, Richard 128, 178
Bundy, Brooke 154
Bungert, Douglas 147
Burger, Neal R. 48
Burke, Paul 22
Burnett, Mary-Nancy 180
Burns, Mark 21
Burns, Tim 74
Burr, Fritzi 96
Burr, Raymond 49
Burr, Robert 62
Burrafato, George 133
Burrell, Fred 50
Burrell, Jan 114
Burton, Jeff 128
Burton, Normann 20
Burton, Robert 27, 189
Burton, Wendell 109
Busch, Robert S. 96
Bush, Billy Green 156

Index

Bush, Owen 60
Butler, Robert 104
Butterfield, Sean 40
Byrd, Carl 125
Byrnes, Burke 115, 170

Cacavas, John 58, 150, 168
Caesar, Harry 49
Caesar, Sid 27
Caffey, Michael 44
Cahill, Barry 128
Caillou, Alan 161
Callahan, James 152
Callardo, Edward 96
Calvet, Corinne 125, 153
Calvin, John 29
Cameron, John 165
Campanella, Joseph 109, 128, 156, 184, 202
Campbell, Brent 6
Campos, Rafael 96
Candy, John 97
Cannon, David 161
Cannon, Kathy 201
Cannon, Orin 32, 58, 189
Canova, Diana 40
Cardos, Bud 196
Carey, Mcdonald 121, 174
Carey, Michele 118
Carey, Philip 147
Carlin, Lynn 184
Carliner, Mark 128
Carlino, Lewis John 198
Carlo, East 13
Carlyle, Richard 167
Carnell, Cliff 110
Carol, Jack 45
Carpenter, John 3, 163
Carpenter, Thelma 46
Carr, Darlene 81, 136
Carradine, John 18, 22, 35, 113
Carrara, Don 157
Carroll, Beeson 192
Carroll, Dee 149
Carroll, Susette 115
Carroll, Victoria 177
Carrott, Ric 86, 168
Cartwright, Lynn 164
Carver, Floyd 196
Case, David 147
Casey, Bernie 74, 92, 122
Casey, Lawrence 161
Casey, Sue 182
Cason, Barbara 153
Cass, Dave 15
Cassidy, Jack 125
Cassidy, Joanna 153
Catching, Bill 62, 102, 121
Cattrall, Kim 76
Cervera, Jorge, Jr. 180
Chaffee, Suzy 155
Challenger, Rudy 96

Challis, John 52
Chambers, Everett 110
Chambers, Phil 169
Chambliss, Woody 74
Chandler, Jim 102, 144
Chandler, John 106
Chapin, Doug 198
Chaplin, Sydney 199
Chapman, Lonny 77, 86, 149, 186
Charleson, Leslie 133
Charny, Suzanne 154
Chase, Tiffany Gautier 144
Chastain, Thomas 42
Chen, Tina 75, 123
Chester, Colby 202
Chicago Deadline 2
Chicoine, Michelle 197
Chihara, Paul 29, 30, 39, 66
Chiles, Linden 122
Chomsky, Marvin 61
Christi, Frank R. 58
Christian, Michael 184
Christian, Natt 96
Christopher, Kathy 159
Cieutat, Shirl 144
Clancy, Tom 75
Clark, Bobby 196
Clark, Dane 107
Clark, Louise Carie 153
Clark, Oliver 77
Clark, Susan 187
Clarke, Angela 75
Clarke, Gary 60, 133
Clarke, Robert 16
Clay, Stanley 48
Cleaves, Robert 41, 52, 129
Clemens, Brian 199
Clements, Calvin 44
Clements, Richard 202
Clouse, Robert 164
Clute, Sidney 182
Cobb, Julie 139
Cobb, Vincent 92
Cobert, Bob (Robert) 27, 33, 52, 58, 71, 89, 112, 113, 118, 126, 147, 189, 190
Coburn, Sandra 132
Cockrell, Francis 121
Coit, Stephen 69
Cole, Jerry 196
Coleman, Dabney 9, 16, 56, 128
Colla, Richard A. 192
Collins, Gary 115
Collins, Jack 36, 41, 68
Collins, Johnnie, III 148
Collins, Patrick 58
Collins, Roberta 184
Colomby, Scott 8
Colon, Alex 180
Colton, Jacque Lynn 49
Colvin, Jack 86, 166

Comer, Anjanette 32, 42, 67, 184
Conde, Rita 132
Conlon, Bud 66
Connell, Gordon 75
Connell, Jim 74
Connell, John 6
Connelly, Christopher 88
Connors, Chuck 81, 115, 116
Connors, Mike 40
Conrad, Michael 141
Conrad, Robert 67, 157
Conrad, Sid 58
Conrad, William 16
Constantine, Michael 20, 37
Conti, Bill 157
Converse, Frank 24, 50, 96
Convy, Bert 77, 167
Conway, Bert 58
Coogan, Jackie 125
Cook, Elisha (Jr.) 32, 112, 139
Cooney, Dennis 161
Cooper, Charles 20, 170
Corbett, Glenn 172
Corbett, Gretchen 144, 153
Cord, Alex 64
Cordic, Rege 134
Corey, Jeff 27, 164
Corley, Pat 115
Cornthwaite, Robert 46
Corrington, John William 94
Corrington, Joyce 94
Corsaut, Aneta 9
Costello, Mariclare 20
Costello, Tony 119
Coster, Nicolas 66
Cotsworth, Staats 50
Cotton, Joseph 46, 149
Coulouris, George 172
Count Dracula 3
Cover, Franklin 154
Cox, Wally 113
Craig, Helen 99
Cramer, Douglas S. 18
Craven, Wes 3, 174
Crawford, Broderick 100, 102, 125
Crenna, Richard 45, 66
Crews, Jerry 128
Crichton, Michael (John Lange) 3, 129
Cristal, Linda 31
Crockett, Dick 106
Crosby, Bing 50
Crosby, Joan 97
Crosby, Kathryn 87
Cross, Dennis 22
Cross, Edward 114, 125
Crowley, Pat 69
Crystal, Billy 168
Cullen, Kerrie 75
Cullen, William Kirby 69

Index

Culliton, Patrick 64
Culp, Robert 2, 19, 68, 165
Cummings, Quinn 114
Cunneff, Catherine 127
Cunning, Joyce 149
Curtis, Dan 3, 27, 33, 52, 58, 71, 113, 118, 147, 189, 190
Curtis, Howard 96
Curtis, Tracy 27, 189
Cutler, Wendy 194
Cyphers, Charles 163

Daheim, John 29
Daly, Cindy 157
Daly, Tyne 85
D'Andrea, John 174
Daniels, Lisa 157
Daniels, William 96
Danko, Jim 131
Danner, Blythe 8, 50
Dano, Royal 106
Danova, Cesare 37
Danton, Ray 136
Darby, Kim 52
Darden, Severn 156
Dark, Christopher 182
Daugherty, Herschel 150, 195
Daughter of the Mind 2
Davalos, Elyssa 76
Davalos, Richard 159
Davenport, Nigel 52, 126
David, Brad 161
Davis, Bette 29, 147
Davis, Brent 48
Davis, Elizabeth 133
Davis, Jim 141
Davis, Roger 94
Davis, Walt 129
Day, Loraine 107
Day, Robert 42, 88, 134
Dayton, June 22
De Angeles, Richard 40
Death Once Removed 3
DeBenning, Burr 77
Decker, Will 40
Deemer, Ed 58
DeFazio, Sam 122
De Felitta, Frank 188
DeLain, Marguerite 36
De Lancie, John 168
DeLano, Michael 27, 58
Delevanti, Cyril 22
Delman, David 20
Demarest, William 52
Demian, Marcus 102
DeNeut, Richard 114
Denise, Gita 52
Dennehy, Brian 92
Dennis, Sandy 164
De Roy, Richard 85
Derr, Richard 168, 195
Desmond, Trudy 96

DeTreaux, Monica 52
Devane, William 131
Dever, Tom 141, 147
DeVille, Paul R. 106
De Vorzon, Barry 155
De Vries, Mark 37
Dewey-Carter, John 96, 157
Dey, susan 184
Diamond, Arnold 73
DiCenzo, George 88, 118
Dickinson, Angie 118
Dietrich, Dena 169
Dillaway, Denise 116
Diller, Barry 2
Dillman, Bradford 48, 60, 67, 97, 106, 133
Dillon, Brendon 31, 126, 194
Dimitri, Nick 118
Dimster, Dago 49
Di Pego, Gerald 136, 154, 202
Di Santi, John 13
Disney, Doris Miles 12
Dix, Bob 196
Dixon, Ivan 62
Dodd, Molly 83
Dolan, Trent 83, 141
Dolinsky, Meyer 168
Donat, Peter 77
Donnelly, Tom 40
Donner, Clive 165
Donner, Robert 81
Donovan, Tom 97
Doran, Ann 32, 68, 196
Dorin, Phoebe 115
Douglas, Damon 125
Douglas, Diana 66
Douglas, James 97
Douglas, Jerry 31, 172
Douglas, Michael 197
Douglas, Sarah 52
Douglass, Amy 54
Dowdell, Robert 182
Doyle, David 176
Dozier, Robert 129
Drake, Charles 147, 149
Drake, Tom 102
Drasnin, Robert (Jackson) 22, 50, 109, 181
Dreier, Alex 178
Drescher, Fran 174
Drier, Moose 92
Drury, James 44
DuBarry, Denise 30
Dubin, Charles 109
Duff, Howard 155, 159
Duffy, Patrick 86
Duggan, Andrew 66, 122
Duke, Daryl 128
Duke Astin, Patty 27, 64, 77, 96, 100, 152
Dukes, David 66
Dulo, Jane 118

Duncan, Lois 174
Duning, George 15, 200
Dunn, Liam 90, 94
Durock, Dick 29
Durrell, Michael 29
Durren, John 96
Dusay, Marj 66
Dusenberry, Ann 127
Duvall, Susan 88
Dynarski, Gene 54
Dzundza, George 139

Eagle, John War 114
East, Jeff 174
Eastham, Richard 128
Easy Rider 2
Ebsen, Bonnie 157
Ebsen, Buddy 81, 128, 157
Eccles, Ted 9
Edelman, Herb 157, 169
Edelman, Randy 159
Eden, Barbara 85, 176, 199
Edgerton, Justin 97
Edwards, Sam 86
Edwards, Vince 42, 102, 161
Egan, Richard 82
Eggar, Samantha 6
Ego, Sandra 62
Eilbacher, Bobby 15
Eilbacher, Cindy (Cynthia) 9, 22, 66, 69
Eilbacher, Lisa 9
Eisenman, Ike 45, 186
Elcar, Dana 56, 122
Elliot, Tom 30
Elliott, Ross 22, 123, 136, 195
Ellsworth, Christine 144
Emrys-Roberts, Kenyon 21
Endore, Guy 133
Englund, Dinah 41
Englund, Morgan 41
Enriquez, Rene 92
Erickson, Leif 34, 182
Erwin, William (Bill) 83, 180
Estrada, Erik 64
Evans, Gene 64
Evans, Maurice 16
Evers, Jason 62
Express to Terror 3

Fabiani, Joel 119
Fairchild, Morgan 87
Fame Is the Name of the Game 2
Farber, Arlene 6
Farentino, James 58, 127
Farmer, Buddy H. 36
Farmilo, Sally 165
Farrell, Henry 60, 82, 83
Farrell, Mike 150
Farrell, Sharon 60
Farrington, Fielding 177
Farris, John 197

Index

Farrow, Tisa 88
Fawcett-Majors, Farrah 107
Fear No Evil 2
Felber, Len 121
Feldon, Barbara 193
Feldshuh, Tovah 148, 186
Fell, Norman 42
Fenady, Andrew J. 15, 104
Fenady, Georg 77
Fenwick, Moya 97
Ferguson, Austin 104
Ferragher, Lou 102
Ferrer, Jose 104
Ferrone, Dan 129
Fiedler, John 9
Field, Logan 16
Field, Sally 79
Fienberg, Ron 56
Finch, Howard 131
Fink, John 79
Finlay, Frank 21
Finnegan, John 20, 184
Finney, Jack 33
Firestone, Eddie 26, 54
Fisher, Cindy 9
Fitzpatrick, Jerry 102
Fix, Paul 77
Flanagan, Fionnuala 99, 116, 126
Flanders, Ed 99, 139
Fleck, Lois 131
Flory, Med 79
Flynn, Gertrude 45
Fogel, Jerry 45
Fontane, Char 58
Ford, Glenn 16, 48
Ford, Harrison 127
Forest, Irene 27
Forster, Robert 30
Forsyth, Rosemary 16
Forsythe, John 1, 24, 26, 109, 184
Foster, Alan 102
Foster, Buddy 15
Foster, Susan 79
Fox, Charles 56, 176, 201
Fox, John (J.) 163, 164
Foxworth, Robert 39, 46, 71, 92
Frame, Dawn 181
Franciosa, Tony 2, 27
Francis, Anne 26, 79
Francis, Ivor 60, 113
Francis, Missy 75
Franciscus, James 110, 119
Frangipane, Ronald 6
Frank, Charles 155, 180
Frank, David 182
Franken, Steve 92, 107, 172, 186
Franklin, Carl Mikal 86
Franklin, Frederick 45
Franklin, Pamela 140
Franz, Eduard 16, 122

Freedman, Jerrold 19
Freeman, Joan 39
Frees, Paul 58, 75
French, Bruce 27, 92, 144, 186
Frick, Elise 11
Frid, Jonathan 46
Fridell, Squire 105, 177
Fried, Gerald 24, 49, 167
Fries, Debbie 88
Frizzel, Lou 45, 54, 136
Frontiere, Dominic 62, 79, 133
Frost, Alan 164
Frye, Virgil 18
Fudge, Alan 8
Fuller, John G. 75, 192
Fuller, Penny 201
Fuller, Robert 49
Furia, John 40
Furlong, John 195

Gabler, Carl 114
Gail, Max 27
Gainter, Roy 66
Galardo, Yolanda 107
Gale, West 37
Galico, Paul 66
Gallery, James 139
Galloway, Don 155
Garber, B. Hope 150
Gargoyles 3
Garrett, Leif 15, 68
Gary, Dr. Norman 144, 186
Gavin, James W. 64, 77, 128
Gaviola, Cassandra 153
Gay, Jennifer 88
Gayle, Rozelle, Jr. 46
Gaynes, George 189
Gazzara, Ben 102, 129, 197
Geer, Will 16, 86, 90
Gehring, Ted 8, 12, 77, 169
Geller, Bruce 144
Gentry, Donald 94
Gentry, Robert 71
George, Christopher 24, 102
George, Lynda Day 24, 92, 102, 122, 150
Gerard, Merwin 89, 149, 150, 195
Gerritsen, Lisa 85
Getz, John 94
Gfeller, Kennette 88
Gibbons, Robert 35, 167
Gibbs, Marla 104
Gibbs, Norman Alexander 49
Gibson, Henry 115
Gielgud, John 73
Gilbert, Edmond 118
Giles, Sandra 8
Gilford, Gwynne 140
Gilgreen, John 159
Gill, Beverly 79
Gillard, Stu 150

Gillen, Jeff 13
Gillette, Anita 92
Ging, Jack 48, 182
Giroux, Jackie 184
Glass, Paul 67, 161
Glass, Seamon 153
Glenn, Scott 74
Gold, Ernest 12
Gold, Tracey 29
Goldberg, Leonard 2
Golden, Bob 123
Goldenberg, Billy (William) 52, 54, 99, 119, 132, 134, 184, 192
Goldman, Danny 185
Goldoni, Lelia 76, 166
Goldsmith, Jerry 16, 129
Goldstein, Herb 13
Goldstein, William 186
Goldstone, James 26
Golonka, Arlene 58
Goman, Ray K. 194
Goodier, Robert 150
Gordon, Carl 49
Gordon, Gerald 92
Gordon, Larry 67
Gordon, Margie 75
Gordon, Ruth 90, 100
Gorman, Mari 27
Gorshin, Frank 36
Gortner, Marjoe 102
Gottlieb, Carl 164
Gough, Gerald 40
Graham, Scott 16
Graham, William A. 13
Grahame, Gloria 15
Grant, Angela 165
Grant, Grayce 29
Grant, Lee 110, 166
Grauman, Walter 8, 22, 123
Graves, Peter 36, 128, 147, 167, 198
Gray, David L. 144
Gray, Randy 77
Greenberg, Leon 40
Greene, David 193
Greene, James 167
Greene, Lorne 167
Gregg, Virgina 22, 112, 172
Gregory, Nigel 52
Grey, Elizabeth 27
Grieves, Russ 31
Griffin, Jack 58
Griffith, Andy 144, 177
Griffith, Eva 190
Griffith, James 68
Grimes, Tammy 81
Grizzard, George 176
Groh, David 157
Groom, Sam 12, 13, 77
Gross, Dennis 12
Grossfeld, Sid 129

Index

Groves, John 180
Gruber, John 74, 169
Grusin, Dave 34, 85
Guardino, Jerome 180
Guenther, Craig 123
Gulager, Clu 155
Gunn, Moses 79
Gunn, Nicholas 194
Guss, Jack 29
Guss, Louis 184
Gustafson, Steve 29
Guthrie, Richard 62
Gwynne, Michael C. 19

Hack, Shelley 36
Hackett, Joan 32, 67, 83, 127, 132
Hackman, Bob 107
Hagan, Earl 96
Hagan, Laurie 164
Hagen, Erica 188
Haggerty, Dan 186
Haggerty, H.B. 27
Hagman, Larry 85, 86
Hagmann, Stuart 180
Hagon, Rex 97
Haid, Charles 39
Haig, Sid 36
Hailey, Arthur 182
Halahan, Charles 186
Hale, Billy 131
Hall, Grayson 74
Hall, Philip Baker 102, 186
Hall, Sam 71
Halop, Billy 125
Hamel, Veronica 155
Hamilton, Barry 157
Hamilton, George 31, 36, 58, 96, 170
Hamilton, Margaret 113
Hamilton, Murray 96
Hamilton, Patricia 97
Hampton, Roger 157
The Hanged Man 2
Hanmer, Don 107
Hannibal, Marc 177
Hansen, Al 35
Hansen, Danna 170
Hansen, William 71
Hardester, Crofton 27, 35
Hardin, Jerry 86
Hardin, Ty 64
Harding, Paul 97
Harens, Dean 123
Harkins, John 76, 180
Harlow, Bill 77, 102
Harmon, David P. 107
Harmon, Deborah K. 75
Harout, Magda 8
Harper, Valerie 114
Harrington, Curtis 3, 18, 31, 45, 83, 94

Harrington, Tammy 188
Harris, Albert 39
Harris, Jo Ann 24
Harris, Johnny 88
Harris, Julie 79, 83
Harris, Robert H. 83
Harrison, Gregory 189
Harrold, Kathryn 194
Hart, Christine 32
Hart, Harvey 122
Hartley, Ted 75
Hartman, David 202
Harvard, Elvenn 62
Haskell, Peter 60, 115, 125
Hastings, Bob 20, 185, 187
Hatfield, Hurd 118
Haufman, Glorie 107
Havilland, Olivia de 149
Hawkins, Robert 97
Haworth, Jill 79
Hay, Alexandra 149
Hayden, Trevor 155
Hayes, Holly 201
Haymes, Dick 12
Haynes, Gary 128
Haynes, Lloyd 100
Hays, Robert 88
Hayward, Chuck 147
Hayward, Cynthia 48
Hayward, David 131
Head, Edith 149
Heath, Laurence 155
Hecht, Paul 144
Heckart, Eileen 195
Hedison, David 18
Heflin, Nora 88
Hefti, Neil 20
Heims, Jo 116
Heineman, Laurie 184
Helmond, Katherine 99
Helton, Edna 68
Hemingway, Carole 49
Hemphill, Simpson 116
Hendrick, Hank 66
Henley, Annette 116
Henreid, Monica 52
Henriot, Sam 132
Herbert, Pitt 22, 26
Herbert, Tim 54, 185
Herd, Richard 186
Hershey, Barbara 68
Hesseman, Howard 75, 180
Hessler, Gordon 12, 148, 156, 170
Hewitt, Alan 99
Heywood, Bill 66
Hickford, Susie 21
Higgins, Colin 46
Hildur, Susanne 177
Hill, Arthur 121
Hill, Mariana 35
Hill, Phyllis 79

Hillerman, John 178
Hincks, C.J. 41
Hindy, Patricia 89
Hines, Grainger 163
Hingle, Pat 49, 178, 180
Hinton, David 96
Hobbs, Heather 30
Hobbs, Peter 41
Hock, Johnny 30
Hoffe, Arthur 148
Hoffman, Angela 9
Hogan, Bosco 21
Holdridge, Lee 156
Holliday, Bill 144
Hollier, Emory 106
Holliman, Earl 26, 187
Holm, Celeste 37
Holmes, Madeline Taylor 114
Honig, Howard 27, 58
Hood, Don 144
Hooks, David 194
Hooks, Robert 187
Hooper, Tobe 3, 139
Horn, Lanny 180
Horner, Penelope 52
Horton, Peter 153
Hoshi, Shizuko 62
Howard, Susan 96
Howard, Vanessa 126
Howe, Jeannette 83
Howell, Hoke 128
Howland, Kathleen 29
Hubley, Season 167
Hudkins, John 164
Huffman, David 100
Hughes, Barnard 50, 192
Hughes, Kathleen 167
Hunt, Helen 166
Hunter, Kendall 155
Hunter, Kim 9
Hurley, Karen 32
Hurt, John 165
Husky, Rick 159
Hutchins, Will 81
Hutton, Jim 52
Hutton, Lauren 163
Hyde, Jacquelyn 77
Hyde-White, Wilfred 134
Hyland, Diana 134
Hylands, Scott 184

Ihnat, Steve 178
Ingalls, Don 68, 88
Ingham, Jonathan 11
Ingham, Nicholas 11
Instone, John 11
The Invasion of Carol Enders 3
Ireland, John 125
The Iron Horse 2
Irving, Penny 165
Irwin, William 170
Isherwood, Christopher 73

Index

Israel, Charles E. 29
Itkin, Steve 69
Ito, Robert 62, 168
Ives, Burl 11
Izay, Victor 110, 182

Jackson, Crane 164
Jackson, Gordon 165
Jackson, Jamie Smith 140
Jackson, Jon 40
Jackson, Kate 35, 37, 94, 140
Jacob, Jasper 190
Jacoby, Scott 9, 157
Jaeckel, Richard 34
Jagger, Dean 16, 172
Jalbert, Pierre 155
James, Henry 190
Jameson, Jerry 58, 66, 87, 185
Jameson, Joyce 201
Jamison, Jami 159
Jamison, Richard 159
Janssen, David 62, 102, 106
Jarnagin, James 174
Jarrett, Renne 18
Jason, Peter 49
Jauregui, Victor Hugo 199
Jenkins, Megs 190
Jenner, Chrystie 168
Jerro, Steve 49
Jeter, James 86, 115
Jobin, Peter 150
Joe, Jeanne 192
Johnson, Ben 136, 144
Johnson, Don 155
Johnson, Gary 196
Johnson, Ken 97
Johnson, Russell 75, 81
Johnston, Velda 85
Jones, Carol 127
Jones, Ivy 187
Jones, James Earl 192
Jones, Jessica 202
Jones, L.Q. 169
Jones, Tommy Lee 157
Jordan, Glenn 71, 119, 126
Jory, Victor 45
Joseph, Allen 122
Joseph, Robert L. 168
Jourdan, Louis 2, 21, 134
Joy, Gail 153
Joyce, Jimmy 134
Joyce, Stephen 29
Jue, George 195
Jury, Liz 159
Jury, Ric 159
Justice, Edgar 163
Justiz, Jake 192

Ka'ahea, Ed 193
Kai, Carole 39
Kandel, Stephen 42
Kane, Artie 45
Kapp, Joe 157
Karlen, John 58, 71, 88, 126, 189
Karlin, Fred 9, 194
Karnes, Robert 58
Karp, David 16
Karpf, Elinor 45, 74, 182
Karpf, Stephen 45, 74, 182
Katkov, Norman 64
Katon, Rosanne 115
Katz, Shelley 193
Katzin, Lee H. 121, 144, 172, 186
Kayahara, Lydia Lei 39
Kaye, Celia 52
Kaye, Clarissa 73, 139
Kazann, Zitto 141
Keach, Stacy 6
Keach, Stacy, Sr. 92
Kearney, Gene Raser 89
Keen, Noah 153, 161, 201
Keener, Elliot 144
Keith, Anita 180
Keith, Tom 116
Keller, Max A. 174
Keller, Michael 195
Keller, Nicole 174
Kellogg, John 110
Kelly, Roz 27
Kelsey, Linda 126
Kemp, Sally 89
Kennedy, Arthur 128
Kennedy, Burt 6
Kent, Paul 61, 115
Kercheval, Ken 45, 48
Kerwin, Lance 132, 139
Kessler, Bruce 24, 39
Ketchum, David 58
Keyes, Earl 29
Kiley, Richard 109
The Killers 1
Kimbro, Art 8
King, Aldine 169
King, Harold 131
King, Kathryn 40
King, Stephen 139
King, Wright 167
Kinoy, Ernest 128
Kirby, Bruce 20
Kirby, Randy 147
Kiser, Virginia 49
Kjellin, Alf 34
Klein, Sonny 106
Klitsner, Stu 194
Klugman, Jack 119
Knapp, David 164, 184
Knopf, Christopher 19
Knox, Richard Alan 134
Kobe, Gail 99
Kohler, Mary Ann 116
Korn, Iris 180
Kotani, Tom 11

Kowalski, Bernard L. 15, 182, 199, 201
Kozoll, Michael 194
Kramer, George 122
Krohn, Charles 131
Kuby, Bernie 122
Kulik, Buzz 9
Kuluva, Will 129

Laborteaux, Matthew 180
Ladd, Alan 2
Ladd, Cheryl (Stoppelmoor) 140
Ladd, Diane 46
Lafferty, Marcy 123
Lagdon, Anthony 190
Lain, Jewel 202
Lakin, Rita 97, 201
Lamas, Fernando 107
Lamm, Karen 92, 115
Lamour, Dorothy 35
Lampkin, Charles 86, 122
Landau, Martin 40
Landers, Alan 86
Landford, Wallace W. 96
Lang, Doreen 41, 82
Lang, Jennings 1
Lang, Perry 40
Lang, Richard 69
Langdon, Sue Ane 195
Lange, Hope 22, 62
Lange, John *see* Crichton, Michael
Langford, Judy 144
Larch, John 9, 66, 201
LaRose, Lou 115
LaRue, Bart 159
LaSalle, Richard 64, 68, 77
LaSane, James 134
Lasser, Louise 90
Latham, Louise 56, 178
Latimer, Michael 165
La Torre, Tony 186
Lau, Wesley 26
Lauber, Ken 26
Laurence, Michael 163
Laurenson, James 190
Lauter, Ed 141
Lawford, Peter 125
Lawrence, Anthony 178
Lawrence, Carol 174
Lawrence, J.H. 52
Lawrence, Kenneth 83
Lawrence, Steve 58
Lawrence, Vicki 58
Laws, Maury 11
Leach, Britt 12
Leachman, Cloris 41, 56, 79
Leacock, Philip 56, 96, 197
Learned, Michael 86
Leatherbury, Jill 40
Le Bouvier, Jean 163

Index

Ledger, Jason 26
Ledrov, D.B. 193
Lee, Bill 196
Lee, Jennifer 105
Lee, Johnny Scott 123, 133
Lee, Ruta 85
Lefferts, George 115, 153
The Legend of Lizzie Borden 3
Lehman, Lillian 128
Lehne, John 30
Leigh, Barbara 128
Leigh, Janet 34
Leighton, Margaret 73
Lembeck, Michael 79
Lempert, Debbie 164
Lempert, Sandy 164
Lenard, Grace 46
Lenz, Kay 87
Leon, David 8
Leonard, Nancy Hahn 170
Leopold, Thomas 86
Le Pore, Richard 62
Lerew, Jay 155
Lerner, Diki 129
Lerner, Fred 96
Lerner, Michael 96, 132
LeRoy, Gloria 170
Leslie, Bethel 50
Lesser, Len 163
Leversee, Loretta 182
Levin, Ira 50, 101
Levin, John 132
Levine, Larry 60
Levitt, Gene 125
LeVouvier, John 32
Lewis, Abby 50
Lewis, Al 113
Lewis, Art 185
Lewis, Fiona 52
Lewis, Geoffrey 106, 139
Lewis, Marcia 115
Lewis, Robert Michael 115
Lincoln, Abbey 154
Lincoln, Ed 155
Lincoln, Joan Teorey 155
Lindley, Barbara 52
Lindsey, Elliot 188
Linville, Larry 112
Lipin, Arnold 131
Lippe, Jonathan 48
Livingston, Barry 58, 86
Livingston, Jock 46
Llewelyn, Doug 77
Lloyd, Michael 174
Lloyd, Norman 29
Lockamy, Jay 40
Locke, Rosanna 27
Lockhart, June 27
Lockwood, Alexander 54
Lockwood, Gary 75
Lofton, Carrie 54
Logan, Frank 13

Logan, Robert 159
London, Jerry 93
London, Michael J. 159
Long, Richard 37
Lopez, Marco 188
Lord, Marjorie 104
Lorenzen, Kenneth 144
Loring, Lynn 15, 81
Lormer, Jon 20, 71, 99
Lorre, Peter, Jr. 18
Louise, Tina 100, 116, 168
Love, Jim 155
Lovecraft, H.P. 163
Lowe, Mundell 180
Loy, Myrna 58, 92
Lucero, Enrique 199
Luckinbill, Laurence 41, 122
Lugo, Frank 114
Luke, Keye 18
Lumley, Terry 140
Luna, BarBara 201
Lund, Deanna 77
Lupino, Ida 177, 201
Lupton, John 125
Lussier, Robert 139
Lye, Reg 52
Lyles, Tracee Ann 201
Lynas, Jeff 96
Lynch, Richard 76, 194
Lynley, Carol 42, 58, 68, 112
Lyon, Sue 157
Lyons, Robert F. 36, 48, 75, 170

MacIntosh, Jay W. 198
Mack, Wayne "V" 144
Mackay, Donald 155
MacKillop, Ed 93
MacLean, Peter 49
Macleod, Bruce 155
MacLeod, Murray 20, 41
MacMahon, Pat 66
MacMurray, Fred 13
Macnee, Patrick 32
MacOwen, Michael 21
MacRae, Meredith 196
Macready, Michael 164
Macy, Bill 35
Maharis, George 100, 107, 168, 195
Mahon, John 163
Makela, Helena 174
Malet, Arthur 49
Mallon, Don 52
Malloy, John 116
Malmar, McKnight 195
Malone, Nancy 156
Maloney, Patty 52
Malooly, Maggie 86
Malpas, George 21
Mancini, Henry 60
Mandan, Robert 118, 122

Manley, Beatrice 67, 114, 174
Mann, Danny Michael 196
Mann, Delbert 152
Mannix, Julie 49
Manoff, Dinah 127
Mansour, Phillip 102
Marcovicci, Andrea 193
Margolin, Janet 61
Marin, Andrew Peter 9
Marin, Russ 153
Markowitz, Richard 36, 104, 122, 172
Marlo, Steven 77, 102, 172
Marlowe, Scott 110
Marquis, Dixie 126
Marsh, Linda 29
Marsh, Nicole 11
Marsh, Walter 155
Marshall, E.G. 49, 129, 194
Marshall, Edward 12
Martell, Arlene 20
Marth, Frank 136, 140
Martin, Jayne Lyn 8
Martin, John 131
Martin, Pepper 107
Martin, Ross 56, 156
Martin, Todd 79
Marton, Pierre 119
Masak, Ron 58
Mason, James 73, 139
Massey, Gene 96
Massey, Gene, Jr. 169
Massey, Raymond 128
Mastow, Walter 168
Matheson, Richard 33, 52, 54, 56, 112, 113, 147, 170, 176, 189
Mathews, Janina 40
Mathews, Walter 153
Mathias, Anna 75
Matranga, Tony 49
Mattick, Patricia 182
Mattingly, Hedley 126
Mattson, Robin 8
Maxwell, Frank 136
Mayberry, Russell 62
Mayo, Raymond 110
McAlpine, James 163
McAndrew, Marianne 153
McCall, Jack 13
McCallion, James 169
McCallum, David 73, 152
McCalman, Macon 170
McCambridge, Mercedes 128
McCarey, Rod 178
McCay, Peggy 76
McCloskey, Leigh 11
McClung, Rob 159
McClure, Doug 141, 168, 182
McCorey, Tom 126
McCormick, Maureen 193
McCowan, George 107
McCracken, Jeff 174

McCready, Charles 15
McCready, Ed 182
McDaniel, Charles A. 13
McDevitt, Ruth 119, 156
McDougall, Don 105
McDowall, Roddy 58, 68, 181, 182
McEachin, James 16, 31, 154
McEnroe, Anne 159
McFadden, Barney 139
McFadden, Tom 105
McGarvin, Dick 32
McGavin, Darren 112, 113, 164
McGee, Vonetta 118
McGovern, Don 94
McGraw, Charles 44, 112
McGraw, Marty 40
McGreevey, John 22
McGuire, Dorothy 152
McHattie, Stephen 100
McIntyre, Tim 177
McKeand, Nigel 52
McKinley, J. Edward 99
McKinney, Bill 169
McLarty, Gary 102
McLeod, Murray 144
McLiam, John 136
McMartin, John 134
McMillan, Kenneth 139
McMullan, Jim 129, 153
McNamara, Ed 97
McNamara, Patrick 96
McNeil, Claudia 26, 106
McPeak, Sandy 49, 180
McPherson, Graham 155
McRae, Alan 197
McRae, Frank 159
McWilliams, Caroline 40
Medici, John 180
Medina, Hazel 201
Meeker, Ralph 26, 31, 112, 202
Megowan, Don 147
Mell, Joe 177
Melle, Gil 19, 73, 93, 105, 128, 188, 193, 195
Melville, Sam 182
Menard, Ken 86
Menard, Tina 45
Meredith, Burgess 168
Meredith, Don 58, 102, 184
Meriwether, Lee 24
Merrill, Dina 61
Merrow, Jane 81
Meuldijk, Belinda 21
Micale, Paul 164
Michaelian, Katharyn 105
Michaelian, Michael 105
Michaels, Barbara 82
Michaels, Drew 104
Michelle, Vicki 165
Milavic, Jack 13
Miles, Joanna 29, 66

Miles, Kelly 136
Miles, Vera 2, 64, 85, 136, 157, 169
Milford, John 104
Milland, Ray 2, 15, 24, 30, 31, 100, 102
Miller, Allan 75
Miller, James 12
Miller, Jason 194
Miller, Karl 187
Mills, Donna 13, 27, 64, 77, 79, 100, 157
Milner, Martin 68, 86, 136, 168
Mimieux, Yvette 15, 45, 49, 159
Mims, William 62
Mitchell, Cameron 68, 77, 172
Mitchell, Chuck 58
Mitchell, Dallas 20
Mitchell, Don 154
Mitchell, Mitch 39
Mizzy, Vic 87, 185
Moffat, Donald 44
Moffitt, John 196
Molinare, Richard 8
Molinaro, Al 102
Monash, Paul 139
Montagne, Edward J. 154, 185
Montgomery, Belinda J. 46, 134, 201
Montgomery, Elizabeth 99, 195
Montgomery, Lee H. 32, 136
Montgomery, Phillip 62
Montgomery, Ray 149
Moody, Lynne 116
Mooney, Hal 136
Moore, A. Roy 150
Moore, Terry 157
Moorehead, Agnes 73
Morales, Santos 115
Moreno, Ruben 24, 180
Morgan, Gary 104
Morgan, Judson 99
Morgan, Read 86
Morley, Carol 50
Morrison, Jack L. 144
Morrison, Shelley 20
Morrow, Byron 75, 107, 122, 128
Morrow, Lissa 156
Morrow, Vic 27, 42
Mosley, Roger E. 24
Moss, Stewart 20
Moxey, John Llewellyn 3, 20, 79, 82, 112, 116, 157, 169, 181, 198
Muldaur, Diana 121
Mullavey, Greg 48
Muller, Lillian 115
Munoz, Aurora 199
Murdock, George 85, 202
Murphy, Ben 136
Murphy, Joan 13

Murphy, Walter 115, 144
Murtagh, Kate 113
Murtaugh, James 163
Muse, Margaret 164
Myers, Susan 166

Nadder, Robert 27
Nalder, Reggie 31, 139
The Name of the Game 2
Napier, Paul 168
Narcejac, Thomas 132
Navarro, Bob 45
Needham, Hal 36
Negele, Jim 36
Neiman, Irving Gaynor 107
Nelson, Cris 89
Nelson, David 157
Nelson, Dick 104, 182
Nelson, Ed 104, 136, 149
Nelson, Gene 61
Nelson, Harriet 36, 157
Nelson, Herbert 34
Nemec, Dennis 66
Nettleton, Lois 97, 182, 201
Neufeld, John 41
Nevins, Claudette 127
Newcombe, James A. 132
Newland, John 52
Newman, Lionel 197
Nicholas, Denise 66
Nielsen, Leslie 110, 159
Night Gallery 2
Nimoy, Leonard 104
Niven, Kip 66, 102, 136
Nolan, Jim (James) 30, 122
Nolan, John 164
Nolan, Lloyd 64, 90
Nolan, William F. 118, 189, 190
Noland, Ann 140
Nolte, Nick 40
Norman, Marc 67
Norris, Chistopher 102
North, Noelle 180
North, Sheree 102, 115, 159
Norton, B.W.L. (Bill) 74
Novak, Kim 141
Nuckols, William 58
Nudis, Kevin 185
Nuyen, France 39, 81

Oakland, Simon 112, 113
Oatman, Doney 167
O'Brian, Hugh 24, 107
O'Brien, Edmond 90
O'Byrne, Bryan 27, 118
O'Connell, Arthur 181
O'Connell, John 196
O'Connell, William 31
O'Connor, Boardman 144
O'Connor, Terrence 192
O'Connor, Tim 172
O'Feldman, Rick 13

Index

O'Hanlon, George, Jr. 104, 157, 198
O'Hara, Jenny 66, 76
O'Hara, Shirley 54
O'Herlihy, Dan 76
O'Keefe, Michael 29
Olek, Henry 184
Oliver, Louis James 104
Olmstead, Nelson 152
Olsen, Jack 155
Olsen, Merlin 66
Olson, Eric 20, 68
Olson, James 123, 166
O'Malley, Kathleen 201
O'Neil, Tricia 8
O'Neill, Dick 192
Opatoshu, David 20
Oppenheimer, Alan 40, 75
Orchin, Steve 155
Ord, Murray 155
Orgill, Paul S. 29
Oringer, Annie 40
Oringer, Barry 34, 40
The Orphanage 144
O'Steen, Sam 101
O.T. 21
Overgard, William 11
Overton, Bill 115
Owen, Lyla Kay 144
Owens, Albert 88
Owens, Edwin 180
Owens, Grant 147

Page, Harrison 58
Pagett, Nicola 73
Palance, Jack 52
Palmer, Anthony 58
Palmer, Bob 170
Pan, George 62
Parfrey, Woodrow 22
Parker, Brett 202
Parker, Eleanor 79, 153
Parker, Judith 8
Parkes, James R. 127
Parkins, Barbara 159, 181
Parkinson, Patti 6
Parkinson, Tim 6
Parks, Charles 114
Parks, Joel 157
Parks, Michael 144, 196
Parsons, Estelle 184, 192
Parsons, Milton 31
Parton, Regina 113
Pataki, Michael 49
Pate, Johnny 141
Patrick, Alain 37, 62, 168
Patrick, Dennis 122
Patten, Robert 123
Patterson, Pat 41
Paul, Lee 147
Paulin, Scott 194
Paulo, Rene 96

Pear, Leni 155
Pearson, Karen 197
Pecheur, Sierra 174
Peck, Richard 8
Peeples, Samual A. 165
Pellerin, Tony 40
Pellet, Christopher 197
Pelt, Tim 168
Peluce, Meeno 75
Penhaligon, Susan 21
Penn, Leo 29
Pennington, John 52
Penny, Joe 39
Perez, Lazaro 154
Perez, Tony 194
Perkins, Anthony 83
Perkins, Jack 94
Perrin, Vic 73, 192
Perry, Joseph 122
Perry, Roger 20, 77, 133
Persoff, Nehemiah 176
Peters, Brock 168
Peters, Gerald Saunderson 81
Peters, Kelly Jean 184
Peters, Virginia 113
Peterson, Arthur 167
Peterson, Eugene 153
Peterson, Gil 128
Peterson, Melinda 186
Petrie, Daniel 85, 106
Petrie, George 66, 107
Petty, Kevin 11
Pflug, Jo Ann 113, 147
Phalen, Robert 163
Philbin, Phil 13
Philbin, Regis 168
Philips, Lee 167, 176
Phillips, Hal Thomas 116
Phillips, Robert 106
Piazza, Ben 62
Pickard, John 102
Pickins, Slim 44
Picon, Molly 107
Pidgeon, Walter 107, 149
Pine, Phillip (Phil) 34, 89
Pine, Robert 16
Plato, Dana 13
Platt, Howard 159
Pleasence, Donald 29
Plumb, Eve 69
Pomes, Don 39
Poppick, Eric 49
Porter, Don 99, 118
Post, Ted 50, 67, 110
Powell, Jane 102
Powell, Michael 90
Powell, Ricky 20
Powers, Stefanie 66, 123, 156, 178
Prange, Laurie 29
Pratt, Judson 136
Pravda, George 52

Pravda, Hanna Maria 52
Presnell, Robert, Jr. 134, 157
Price, Eugene 122, 157
Price, Sherwood 168
Priest, Dan 106
Priest, Robert 52
Prince, Robert (Bob) 31, 74, 148, 159, 169, 198
Prince, Ron 49
Principal, Victoria 115
Prine, Andrew 110
Pryor, Nicholas 114
Purcell, Lee 174
Purcil, Karen 9

Quade, John 75, 114
Quaid, Dennis 8
Queensbury, Ann 21
Quillan, Eddie 30
Quinlan, Kathleen 104, 198
Quinn, Bill 140
Quinn, Pat 90

Raffill, Stewart 102
Raffin, Deborah 116, 155
Ragaway, Connie Hunter 164
Ragin, John S. 94
Raider-Wexler, Victor 159
Raines, Jessica 86
Rainey, Ford 85
Rains, Jessica 147
Raistrick, George 21
Raksin, David 75
Rambo, Dack 76
Ramrus, Al 30
Ramsey, Logan 20, 44
Randall, Anne 113
Randall, Shawn 168
Rankin, Arthur, Jr. 11
Raskin, Damon 114
Rasulala, Thalmus 96
Rausch, Don 131
Raymond, Lina 29
Rayner, John 128
Read, Martin 52
Reale, Joseph 180
Redeker, Quinn 129
Redgrave, Lynn 190
Reed, Jordan 50
Reed, Robert 79, 116, 159, 168
Reed, Suzanne 13
Reese, Della 116
Reeves, Lisa 155
Rego, Patricia 11
Reid, Kate 150
Reiser, Robert 128
Reisman, Philip H., Jr. 154
Remsen, Bert 180
Revill, Clive 153
Rey, Alejandro 141
Reynolds, James 45
Reynolds, Kathryn 189

Index

Reynolds, Larry 197
Rhind, Burke 66
Rhoades, Barbara 20
Rhodes, Hari 102
Rhodes, Jordan 112
Rhodes, Richard 40
Rice, Jeff 112
Rice, Milt 74
Rich, David Lowell 81, 136, 140, 168
Richards, Brian 100, 147
Richards, George 11
Richards, Gwil 174
Richards, Kim 45, 126
Richardson, Ralph 73
Richmond, Branscombe 39
Richmond, Ken 92
Riley, Doris 11
Roat, Richard 61
Rober, John Clyde, Jr. 116
Roberts, Jim 155
Robertson, Dale 2
Robinson, Charles Knox 62, 149
Robinson, Chris 178
Robinson, Mary 188
Roche, Eugene 75, 127
Roddenberry, Gene 165
Rodman, Howard 20
Rogers, Elizabeth 68, 77, 164
Rogers, Stephen 86
Roker, Renny 182
Roley, Sutton 141, 159, 178
Roman, Eric 41
Romanis, George 102, 153
Romanus, Richard 114
Ronard, Jason 49
Rooney, Mickey, Jr. 13
Roper, John 96
Rorke, Hayden 99
Rose, Calvin 101
Rose, David 44
Rosenman, Leonard 18, 125, 127
Rosenthal, Laurence 35, 41, 46, 82, 83, 107, 140, 178
Ross, Arthur A. 140
Rossen, Carol 75, 133
Rossi, Al 115
Roth, Eric 177
Rowe, Gerry 40
Rowe, Misty 168
Rowe, Prentiss 159
Rubenstein, John 85, 153, 164
Rubes, Susan 97
Rugolo, Pete 37, 42
Rule, Frederick 174
Rule, Janice 44
Runacre, Jenny 165
Rush, Barbara 36, 60, 106
Russel, Tony 89
Russell, Bing 41, 136, 140, 181

Russell, Jackie 149
Russo, Eddie 105
Russo, Lo 105
Ruymen, Ayn 86
Ryan, Deborah 88
Ryan, Natasha 76

Sadler, Tracy Anne 11
St. Clair, Elizabeth 52
St. John, Jill 2
Salem's Lot 3
Salt, Jennifer 74
Sammeth, Barbara 46
Sande, Serena 106
Sanders, Beverly 100
Sanders, Richard 76
Sanford, Gerald 172
Sangster, Jimmy 76, 148, 181
Sansom, Ken 20, 198
Santoni, Reni 122
Santoro, Dean 185
Sapinsley, Alvin 106
Saraceno, Carol 88
Sarafian, Richard 49
Saroyan, Hank 196
Sarrazin, Michael 73
Saunders, J. Jay 163
Savage, Brad 139
Savage, John 6
Savage, Tracy 86, 99, 185
Savalas, Telly 150
Saville, Philip 21
Savory, Gerald 21
Sawaya, George 106
Sawyer, Connie 67, 177
Saxon, John 159
Scalplock 2
Scarwid, Diana 127
Schallert, William 41
Scheerer, Robert 92
Schenck, George 39, 125
Schifrin, Lalo 76
Schmidtmer, Christiane 148
Schott, Bob 118
Schuller, Frank 13
Schumacher, Lou 187
Scott, Brenda 178
Scott, Debralee 39
Scott, Jacqueline 54
Scott, Kathryn 190
Scott, Martha 46
Scott, Mike 131
Scott, Pippa 9, 184
Scott, Simon 48
Scribner, Ronnie 139
Seaton, Aileen 150
See How They Run 1
Seel, Charles 54
Segall, Bernardo 106, 110
Selinsky, Wladimir 164
Sellecca, Connie 11, 153
Selzer, Milton 22, 119

Senensky, Ralph 37
Serling, Robert J. 128
Severn, Maida 128
Seymour, Jane 73, 96
Shakar, Martin 29
Shalet, Diane 113
Shaner, John (Herman) 30
Shaner, Madeleine 30
Shannon, Russell 30
Sharp, Sandra 8
Sharrett, Michael 77
Shatner, William 49, 81, 161
Shaw, Lister 153
Shaw, Reta 109
Shayne, Arnie 131
Shear, Barry 154
Sheen, Martin 129
Sheffield, Ray 30
Sheiner, David 30, 156
Shelley, Dave 107
Shelley, Mary 71, 73
Shelly, Bruce 58
Shepherd, Jack 21
Shepherd, Suzan 15
Sherbanee, Maurice 37
Sherman, Bobby 156
Sherman, Orville 147
Shire, David 69, 90, 94
Shirriff, Cathee 153
Shore, Dinah 36
Sidney, Sylvia 35, 159
Siebert, Charles 180
Siedow, Jim 131
Siegel, Don 1
Sierra, Gregory 115
Sikking, James 61, 128
Silla, Felix 52
Silva, Henry 15
Silvers, Phil 115
Silverton, Doris 186
Simmons, Richard Alan 133
Simms, William 18
Simpson, George 48
Sirianni, E.A. 169
Skaff, George 163
Slade, Betsy 184
Slate, Jeremy 174
Slate, Lane 90, 169
Sloyan, James 122
Smight, Jack 73, 149
Smillie, Bill 31, 104
Smith, Dean 147
Smith, Delos V. 170
Smith, Donald R. 96
Smith, Essex 116
Smith, James B. 128
Smith, Kent 18, 48, 83, 112
Smith, Lane 49
Smith, Paul (L.) 20, 49
Smith, William 22
Smithers, William 16
Snively, Robert 163

Index

Snyder, Lorrie 40
Sobiesky, Carol 132
Sohl, Jerry 110
Soles, P.J. 127
Solow, Herbert F. 93
Somers, Suzanne 92
Sommars, Julie 66
Sondergaard, Gail 18
Sorel, Louise 128
Sorensen, Paul 58, 104
Soul, David 48, 139
Soule, Olan 97
Sowards, Jack B. 26, 37
Spang, Laurette 102, 136, 154
Sparks, Don 132
Specht, Robert 110
Spector, David 156
Spelling, Aaron 2
Spence, Grayce 153
Spencer, Roy 52
Spielberg, Steven 3, 54, 164
Spies, Adrian 77
Spinell, Joe 194
Springer, Gary 114
Spurlock, Shelley 9
Stack, Elizabeth 88, 107
Stack, Robert 107, 169
Stack, Rosemary 107
Stacy, James 121, 123
Stacy, Michelle 64
Stahl, Richard 76, 128
Stanley, Lee 182
Stanley, Paul 161
Stanwyck, Barbara 82, 181
Starr, Adam 194
Steadman, John 174
Stefano, Joseph 79, 133, 159
Stein, Judie 20
Steiner, Fred 61, 114
Stenborg, Helen 50
Stephens, James 40
Stephens, Laraine 149
Stephens, Nancy 36
Sterling, Tisha 12, 110, 159
Sterlino, Philip 107
Stern, Sandor 96, 131, 169, 198
Stern, Steven Hilliard 75
Stetson, Lee F. 96
Stevens, Andrew 196
Stevens, Craig 58, 94
Stevens, Leslie 62
Stevens, Morton 48, 81, 152, 170, 177
Stevens, Stella 24, 58, 115
Stevens, William 74
Stewart, Fred Mustard 118
Stewart, Kay 149
Stewart, Marvin Dean 182
Stewart, Mel 40
Stewart, Tom 168
Stewart, Tommie 116

Stimson, Kenneth 147
Stockwell, Dean 123
Stockwell, Guy 48
Stohl, Hank 141
Stoker, Bram 21, 52
Stokes, Ron 20
Stone, Andy 101
Stone, Fred 52
Stone, Harold J. 196
Stone, Leonard 182
Stoppelmoor, Cheryl *see* Ladd, Cheryl
Storch, Larry 199
Storch, Norma 199
Storm, James (Jim) 48, 92, 96, 147, 189
Stout, Bill 125
Straight, Beatrice 96
Strangis, Judy 201
Strasberg, Susan 71, 168
Street, Elliot 123
Street, Lori 29
Strickland, Amzie 37, 99
Strickland, Gail 155
Striglos, Bill 180
Stroock, Gloria 36
Stroud, Derick 122
Stroud, Don 34, 58
Stuart, Gloria 68, 99
Stuart, Norman 99
Stumpf, Randy 8
Sturgeon, Theodore 93
Sukman, Harry 13, 139, 163
Sullivan, Barry 86
Sullivan, D.J. 101
Summers, Hope 41
Sutton, Carol 144
Sutton, Frank 86
Sutton, Pelly 133
Svanoe, Bill 184
Svenson, Bo 71, 159
Swackhamer, E.W. 3, 35, 40, 41, 114, 194
Swait, Jim 13
Swanson, Gloria 94
Swanson, Sterling 52
Swanson, Ted 52
Sweet, Dolph 39
Swenson, Karl 85
Swope, Tracy Brooks 185
Sylvester, William 52
Symonds, Robert 99
Szwarc, Jeannot 46, 202

Tabori, Kristoffer 61, 184
Taggert, Brian 167
Takada, Terry 39
Talbot, Nita 58
Talbott, Michael 88
Tannen, Steve 186
Tapscott, Mark 178, 185
Tarchuck, Byron 155

Tarkington, Rockne 49
Tarter, Dale 128
Tata, Joe E. 186
Tatro, Duane 124
Taylor, Benedict 190
Taylor, Dane A. 96
Taylor, Dixie 131
Taylor, Jud 48, 133
Taylor, June Whitley 201
Taylor, Kent 125
Taylor, Mark L. 75
Taylor, Rebecca 116
Taylor, Rod 61
Taylor, Sue 123
Tedrow, Irene 104
Telezynska, Izabella 21
Terhune, Shannon 149
Thinnes, Roy 15, 81, 118, 140
Thomas, Clarence 13
Thomas, Mark 46, 122
Thomas, Robert 118
Thompson, Hilary 24
Thompson, Marshall 24
Thorpe, Jerry 127
Thorson, Russell 110, 149
Tidy, Patricia 126
Tipton, George (Aliceson) 79, 131
Tobey, Kenneth 182
Todd, Beverly 75
Tokatyan, Leon 121
Tolan, Michael 114
Tom, Robert 125
Tomasino, Jeana 40
Tomayko, Paul 40
Tomerlin, John 126
Toner, Jeff 150
Toomey, Regis 125
Torn, Rip 128
Travolta, Ellen 8
Trentham, Barbara 39
Trevor, Elleston 157
Trikonis, Gus 30, 153
Tristan, Dorothy 90
Troy, Louise 22
Trueblood, Guerdon 61, 92, 144, 161, 168, 180, 186
Tryon, Thomas 29
Tucker, Michael 194
Tully, Paul 86
Turich, Felipe 62
Turley, Jack 87, 185
Turner, Arnold 61
Turner, William 132
Tyburn, Gene 26

The UFO Incident 3
Urich, Robert 93
Ursone, Lois 45

Valentine, Nancy 110
Vance, John Holbrook 9

Index

Van Dam, Gwen 186
Vanders, Warren 102
Vandis, Tito 141
Van Dyke, Barry 92
Van Dyke, Bonnie 147
Vane, Sutton 78
Van Fleet, Jo 140
Vanner, Sue 21
Van Patten, Joyce 176
Van Sickel, Dale 54
Varela, Jay 96
Vaughn, Heidi 71
Vaughn, Robert 199
Venture, Richard 29
Verner, Jackie 155
Vernon, Glen 149
VeSota, Bruno 164
Vickers, Yvette 31
Vida, Joseph W. 96
Vigoda, Abe 36, 46
Villiers, James 165
Vincent, Virginia 110, 177
Vint, Bill 85, 202
Vint, Jesse 48, 132
Voland, Herb 41

Wagner, Lou 192
Wagner, Robert 35
Wainwright, James 93, 128
Waite, Ralph 131
Walbero, Gary 119
Walden, Lois 104
Walden, Robert 122
Walden, Susan 127
Waldman, Marian 197
Walker, Bill 128
Walker, Clint 93, 147, 159
Walker, Greg 74
Walker, Johnnie, Jr. 96
Walker, Keith 104
Walker, Rock 74
Wallace, Art 50, 152
Wallace, Earl (W.) 27, 58
Wallach, Eli 19
Wallerstein, Herb 159
Wallis, Shani 102
Walsh, M. Emmet 131
Walter, Jessica 79, 86, 153, 194, 201
Walton, Jess 195, 202
Ward, John 128
Ward, Simon 52
Ware, Clyde 6
Warner, Robert 197
Wasserman, Lou 1
Waterston, Sam 132
Watkins, Linda 9
Watson, James A., Jr. 93, 177
Watson, Larry 202
Watson, William 69
Waxman, Albert S. 197
Wayland, Len 123, 129

Wayne, Fredd 125
Wayne, Nina 113
Wayne, Patrick 161
Weathers, Carl 11
Weaver, Dennis 54, 184
Weaver, Fritz 99
Weaver, Robert 196
Webb, Richard 196
Webber, Dean 196
Webber, Robert 42
Webster, Byron 119, 194
Weddle, Vernon 12, 41, 128, 147
Weinberger, Sybil 97
Weiss, Arthur 64
Weld, Tuesday 132
Wellman, Maggie 66
Wells, Aarika 40, 58
Wells, Kim 174
Wendkos, Paul 16, 76, 79, 99, 177, 184
Werner, Fred 40
Wertimer, Ned 202
West, Adam 60
Westgate, Murray 97, 150
Westlake, Donald E. 58
Weston, Steve 197
Wetherall, Virginia 52
Wetherell, Kathy 155
Whitaker, Johnny 164
White, Al 66
White, Carol Ita 184
White, Dan 13
White, Donna 39
White, Robb 144
White, Tony 155
White, Will J. 58
Whiting, Arch 121, 172
Whiting, Leonard 73
Whitman, Stuart 18, 133, 199
Whitmore, Stanford 60
Whitten, Leslie H. 106
Whittington, Dick 54
Wiard, William 155
Wiggins, Red 40
Wiggins, Russell 149
Wightman, Bruce 21
Wilcox, Larry 42
Wilde, Cornel 74
Wilde, Oscar 126
Wilder, Yvonne 41
Wilding, Michael 73
Willard, Fred 139
Williams, Allen 58
Williams, Bert 102
Williams, Bill 66, 125
Williams, John 149
Williams, Johnny 134
Williams, Pat (Patrick) 121, 154, 182
Williams, Sylvia "Kuumba" 144

Williamson, Fred 58
Williamson, Laird 180
Williamson, Tony 199
Willingham, Noble 198
Willock, Margaret 169
Wilson, Anthony 101, 124
Wilson, Kim 116
Wilson, Ned 139
Wilson, Patricia 99, 174
Windom, William 129, 181
Windsor, Marie 139
Windust, Penelope 180
Winfield, Paul 81
Wingreen, Jason 26, 58, 123
Winn, Katherine 82
Winningham, Mare 40
Winslow, Dick 40
Winston, John 161
Winston, Stan 74
Winter, Edward 48
Winters, Deborah 180
Winters, Shelley 46, 88, 133
Wise, Alfie 36
Wiseman, Don 131
Wiseman, Joseph 129
Witthans, Robert 39
Wittman, Malcolm 131
Wixted, Michael-James 198
Wolfe, Ian 46
Wolfington, Iggie 99
Wood, Lana 116
Wood, Lynn 75, 99
Wood, Rick 155
Wood, William 36, 79, 144, 202
Woodbury, Woody 13
Woodfield, William Read 141
Woodhouse, Kit 182
Woods, Lesley 9, 52
Woods, Sunny 170
Woodson, Julie 11
Woodworth, Daniel 94
Woolrich, Cornell 202
Wordon, Hank 15
Words, Sylvester 58
Wright, Ben 172
Wright, Patrick 118
Wright, Teresa 58, 68
Wrigley, Ben 126
Wyatt, Diana 126
Wyatt, Jane 202
Wyenn, Than 136
Wyllie, Meg 41
Wynant, H.M. 58, 81, 172
Wynn, Keenan 58, 182

Yohn, Erica 76
York, Francine 68
Yothers, Poindexter 186
Young, Buck 100, 102, 172
Young, Cameron 58
Young, Gig 165

Index

Young, John Sacret 127
Young, Robert Malcolm 69, 75
Youngfellow, Barrie 194

Zaremba, John 99
Zee, John A. 35
Zerbe, Anthony 159

Zimbalist, Efrem, Jr. 186
Zinn, Brad 66
Zuckert, Bill 45, 61

www.ingramcontent.com/pod-product-compliance
Ingram Content Group UK Ltd.
Pitfield, Milton Keynes, MK11 3LW, UK
UKHW050530150426
5217IPUK00026B/1873